Month-By-Month
GARDENING
IN
TEXAS

Dale Groom & Dan Gill

COOL
SPRINGS
PRESS

Nashville, Tennessee

A Division of Thomas Nelson, Inc.
www.ThomasNelson.com

Groom, Dale.
        Month-by-month gardening in Texas / Dale Groom and Dan Gill
        p. cm.
        Includes bibliographical references (p.   ).
        ISBN 1-888608-21-8
        1. Gardening -- Texas I. Gill, Dan, 1954- II. Title.

SB453.2.T4 G76 2000
635'.09764--dc21

                                                              00-031561

Published by Cool Springs Press, a Division of Thomas Nelson, Inc.,
P.O. Box 141000, Nashville, Tennessee 37214.

First printing 2000

Printed in the United States of America
10 9 8

Horticultural Nomenclature Editor: Joe Walker White, Ph.D., Extension Horticulturist,
        Louisiana State University Agricultural Center

Dale Groom, The Plant Groom™ may be contacted at **plantgrm@cleaf.com** or P.O. Box 365,
        Eustace, TX 75124

Visit the Thomas Nelson website at: www.ThomasNelson.com

Dedication

To the memory of Flora Mae Miller-Groom, Lillie Victoria Pearce-Miller and Blair (Doc) Miller of
Indian Creek and Brownwood, Texas: the mother, grandmother, and grandfather
who taught me grass-roots-level gardening in Texas.
—Dale Groom

Acknowledgements

I wish to acknowledge my wife of thirty-one years, Judy, for understanding the time involved
in putting accurate gardening information into book form; Sam Cotner, Ph.D., Department Head,
Horticulture, Texas A & M, for encouraging words and information; Brian Cummins, Van Zandt
County Extension Agent, and Rick Hirsch, Henderson County Extension Agent, for information; and
the readers of my Ask The Plant Groom™ column and listeners to my live call-in The Plant Groom™
radio program on KTBB for letting me assist them in their various needs. As for the attendees
of my various talks, clinics, seminars, and other "in person" presentations throughout Texas: I
acknowledge your questions and comments assisting me in providing accurate, reliable, and useful
gardening information to fellow Texans statewide. Thank you and . . . *Great Gardening!*
—Dale Groom, The Plant Groom™

Dedication

To the memory of my grandmothers, Opal Oden and Hazel Gill, who nurtured my love
of gardening, and to the Texas Master Gardeners for their outstanding efforts to
educate gardeners around the state.
—Dan Gill

Acknowledgements

Books do not get written without a great deal of support. I would especially like to thank Dr. Joe White,
Extension Horticulturist, who spent many hours carefully reviewing the manuscript of this book;
Rosemary Sims for her knowledge of old garden roses; Peggy Cox for information on perennials and herbs;
Uncle Burt Brumley, a great Texas gardener; Lori Howard, who faces the challenge of gardening in the Panhandle;
and my editor, Billie Brownell, whose cheerful attitude and guidance helped make writing this book possible.
—Dan Gill

Contents

Contents

Benefits of a Gardening Schedule

Gardeners are usually drawn to checklists when we read articles or magazines about gardening. We appreciate seeing what should be done and when in a concise, neat form. ***Think of this book as a large, expanded checklist.*** It's full of timely information that relates specifically to the unique growing conditions of Texas. It will help you know what to do when, and allow you to develop a schedule for your landscape based on the types of plants you like to grow.

Schedules are appropriate in gardening because seasons are cyclic. The same type of weather generally occurs at about the same time from year to year. The seasons and the weather that they typically bring dictate what should or should not be done in the garden. Plants grow, bloom, die, or are dormant according to the changing seasons, and the same gardening activities are done about the same time from year to year. Understanding this concept will allow us to better understand how to garden more effectively and efficiently.

But seasons are not the same from one geographical location to another, especially in Texas, and gardeners need schedules that are accurate for where they garden. New gardeners do not have the experience to know the rhythm of the seasons, and more knowledgeable gardeners often wish for a clear explanation of what to do at a particular time. This book will help you avoid mistakes by providing a gardening schedule for Texas that will help you be a better gardener.

Gardening Checklist

- Planning
- Planting and Transplanting
- Care and Maintenance
- Watering
- Fertilizing
- Pest Control
- Pruning
- Mowing

Gardening in Texas

Climatic Conditions

The climate of Texas is relatively mild. The United States Department of Agriculture divides the state into four hardiness zones based on the average minimum temperatures experienced during the winter. One-half of our state is in zones 8 and 9, with average winter lows of 10 to 20 degrees Fahrenheit in zone 8. Coastal areas around Houston, Corpus Christi, and Padre Island are in zone 9 and experience average winter lows of 20 to 30 degrees. Our relatively mild climate allows a year-round growing season for flower and vegetable gardens, particularly in the southern two-thirds of the state. Zone 7 may reach lows of 10 to 0 degrees and zone 6 in our Panhandle may reach 0 to -10 degrees. Texas is, overall, considered to have a relatively mild winter climate.

Average Freeze Dates

Last freeze dates and first freeze dates are of great importance to many garden activities, but it is important to understand that no one knows when the last or first freeze will actually occur during a particular year. Average dates can be helpful, but freezes can and do occur before the average first freeze date and after the average last freeze date. You must use experience and information from knowledgeable local individuals (friends, professional horticulturists, local nurseries, and your County Agent with the Texas Agricultural Extension Service) when making planting decisions.

The first frosts usually occur in northwest Texas in early November, in areas around Dallas/Forth Worth in mid- to late November, and along the Gulf Coast in early to mid-December. Experience shows that first freezes are more likely to occur later rather than earlier than these average dates.

Average last freeze dates are particularly important to gardeners who want to set out tender vegetables and bedding plants in the spring. North Texas freezes generally end in late March, freezes in areas south of Austin usually end in early to mid-March, and freezes along the Gulf Coast generally end in mid- to late February. Late freezes will occasionally occur after these dates. The conservative gardener should probably consider the frost-free date—when the chance of freezing temperatures is very unlikely—to be about four weeks after the average-last-freeze date.

Average Annual Rainfall Amounts

Average annual rainfall is abundant in some areas. Amounts range from near 60 inches in southeast Texas to 9 inches in El Paso. Unfortunately, the rain does not appear regularly. Some areas of the state may receive 5 to 10 inches of rain or more in a single rainfall and then go for weeks or months without significant precipitation. Well-drained beds are needed to handle periods of high rainfall, and proper irrigation is important during dry periods, especially during hot weather.

Texas's Gardening Seasons

According to the calendar, spring, summer, fall, and winter begin and end at the same time everywhere in the United States. Common sense tells us, though, that the dates for spring gardening activities must be very different between Maine and Texas.

Gardening in Texas

Spring begins in early February in south Texas when deciduous trees like **magnolias** and **redbud** trees begin to bloom and grow. When the calendar tells us that spring has officially begun, we in Texas can say, "It's past in south Texas and arriving in north Texas," while at the same time in Maine it could be snowing. All Texas gardeners need to divide the year in a way that makes sense for us.

The terms spring, summer, fall, and winter carry strong associations with certain types of weather, and that can be a problem for Texas gardeners. Winter, for instance, brings to mind a picture of snow-covered dormant gardens with little or no activity. What we actually experience in our state is episodes of cold weather interspersed with periods of mild temperatures. Planting and harvesting vegetables, planting hardy annuals, perennials, trees, and shrubs, and controlling weeds and insects continues throughout the season.

To get around those preconceived notions, we can divide the gardening year into seasons that more accurately reflect the weather we have at that time. We can divide the gardening year into a first warm season (spring), a hot season (summer), a second warm/cool season (fall), and a cool/cold season (winter), depending on the zone you live in. There are no sharp boundaries between these seasons, and gardeners should always be aware that unusually high or low temperatures may occur at any time, especially during season transitions.

The first warm season of the year runs from late March through mid-May. This warm season is characterized by mild to warm daytime highs generally in the 70s and 80s Fahrenheit, cool nights in the 50s and 60s, and limited danger of nighttime freezes. It is a lovely time of the year that is appreciated by gardeners and non-gardeners alike.

The first warm season is an excellent time to plant tender annuals and perennials in the landscape. Trees, shrubs, and ground covers can be fertilized as well as lawns to encourage the vigorous growth that takes place in this season. Tender vegetables such as **tomatoes, peppers, squash,** and **snap beans** can be planted now after all danger of frost/freeze has passed. New plantings of trees and shrubs in the landscape should be completed as soon as possible since hot weather is right around the corner. The first warm season also includes the peak blooming of the spring bulbs and cool-season bedding plants that were planted several months before, such as **pansies, dianthus, petunias, snapdragons,** and **sweet peas.** For new bed planting, focus on warm-season plants such as **marigolds, periwinkles, lantanas,** and **zinnias** that will bloom for a long time, rather than cool-season plants that will play out as temperatures heat up in May.

May offers a transition into the hot season, which is characterized by brutally hot days in the upper 80s and 90s and warm nights in the mid- to upper 70s. The hot season is our longest season, and it can last through September. High humidity, rainy periods, drought conditions, insects, and diseases combine with heat to make this a stressful time of year for many plants. Numerous trees, shrubs, and perennials that are grown successfully up North cannot be grown here because they will not tolerate the hot season. Tropical perennials such as **hibiscus, gingers, blue daze, banana,** and **pentas** really shine during the hot season, and many gardeners plant them every year even though they are prone to freeze injury or death.

Gardening in Texas

If there is a down time in our gardens, the hot season is it. In July and August, and often September, it is so hot that many gardeners retreat to the air-conditioned indoors and spend less time in the garden than at any other season. But in spite of the heat, the hot season is a time of lush growth and abundant flowers from those plants that can deal with it.

There are a variety of things to do during the hot season. Controlling pests such as weeds, diseases, and insects is an important part of gardening at this time of year. Trees and shrubs grown in containers can be planted in the landscape but will require more care, and their survival is often not as sure as those planted during the cool season. Pruning is important to control the growth of a variety of plants, but avoid heavy pruning on spring-flowering trees and shrubs after June. Provide irrigation to the landscape during hot, dry periods.

Late September and early October offer a transition into the second warm season, which may last until late November. The weather at this time of year is similar to that of the first warm season, generally mild and pleasant. This is not the end of the gardening year as it is in the colder climates that have cold, harsh winters. For us, this time of year celebrates the flowers that are still lingering and looks toward a mild cool season. As the heat diminishes,

garden activities become more pleasurable . . . and there is lots to do. Many cool-season vegetables like **broccoli, lettuce, cabbage,** and **turnips** may be planted now. Flower gardeners can usually plant cool-season bedding plants like **pansies, snapdragons,** and **dianthus.** Deciduous trees, shrubs, and perennials begin to lose their leaves in November and finally enter dormancy, but we use so many broadleaf evergreen plants in our landscapes that they rarely look barren.

Late November to early December sees the arrival of the cool/cold season and the possibility of freezing temperatures. Although snow and severe freezes in the teens can occur, harsh weather rarely lasts long. Much of the time, the weather is mild with lows above freezing and highs in the 50s, 60s, and even 70s, particularly in the southern half of

the state. Tropical plants can be covered or brought in for protection on those occasional freezing nights. Along the Coast, the planting of cool-season vegetables and bedding plants can continue. This season is by far the best time to plant hardy trees, shrubs, ground covers, and herbaceous perennials. In March and April, the cool season makes a transition into the first warm season, bringing us full circle.

Soil Conditions in Texas

The condition and type of soil in which you garden have a profound effect on the health and growth of your plants. One of the most common mistakes novice gardeners make is putting too little effort into learning about their soil and what is needed for proper bed preparation.

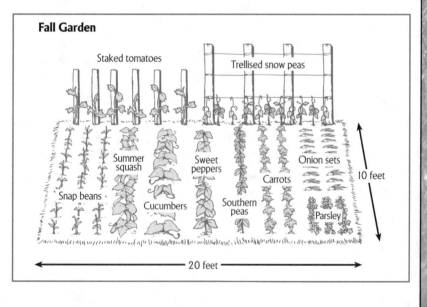

Fall Garden

Staked tomatoes

Trellised snow peas

Summer squash

Sweet peppers

Onion sets

Snap beans

Cucumbers

Southern peas

Carrots

Parsley

10 feet

20 feet

Gardening in Texas

Soil is the primary source of water and nutrients for the plant and must also provide sufficient air (oxygen) to the root system. Ideally, a soil should be about 25 percent water, 25 percent air, 45 percent minerals (sand, silt, and clay), and 5 percent organic matter.

There are many different kinds of soils in Texas, from light sands to loams to heavy clays. A thorough knowledge of the characteristics of the soil in which you garden is necessary for making decisions about vegetable gardening, ornamental beds, and landscaping. If you need to modify the soil, this knowledge is vital to soil improvement, planting, watering, and fertilizing.

Learning about your soil is a matter of experience, talking to individuals who are knowledgeable about the soils in your area, and educating yourself. A great place to start is your local office of the Texas Agricultural Extension Service. Your County Agent will be able to familiarize you with the characteristics of the soil in your area. In addition, you can have your soil tested by the soil-testing laboratory in College Station for a modest fee. Kits to submit soil samples for analysis are available at your local Extension office. The soil laboratory at Stephen F. Austin University will also test your soil. Contact them at (409) 468-4500.

A soil sample from each unique area of your landscape or special garden should be submitted, especially if you suspect that the soils may be different due to past treatment or location. For example, one sample may be submitted from your front lawn area and another from a rose bed in the front yard, as the soils would have been treated differently over the years. A sample from the back lawn area is probably very similar to the front lawn and does not usually need to be tested.

Take soil from several spots in the area you wish to be tested according to the instructions on the soil test kit. Along with the soil you will submit a form that includes pertinent information such as the plants you are growing or intend to grow in the area.

The test results will tell you the texture of your soil and the relative proportion of sand, silt, and clay. You will also learn the pH of the soil, which reveals how acidic or alkaline it is. A pH of 7 is neutral, lower numbers indicate an acid soil condition, and higher numbers mean the soil is alkaline. A pH between 5.5 to 7.5 is generally acceptable for most plants. The pH can be made higher if necessary with the addition of lime, or lowered with the addition of sulfur and iron to the soil.

The fertility of the soil is indicated by the levels of phosphorus, potassium, calcium, and magnesium, which should all be medium to high. The fertilizer recommendations you will receive from the laboratory are based on these levels and the types of plants you will grow where the soil sample was taken. The amount of sodium in the soil is also reported. Excessive amounts of sodium are detrimental to plants, so the level should be low or very low. This knowledge can be especially important to gardeners along the Gulf Coast or those using irrigation water high in sodium.

A test which many horticulturists say is optional, but which you should really have done, is made to determine the percentage of organic matter. Ask your county extension service for help. Adequate amounts of organic matter are very important for plant growth. Levels of 2 percent are considered adequate, 5 percent ideal.

Gardening in Texas

Planning the Garden

Many gardeners may become confused when it comes to designing their home landscapes. Landscaping efforts can be disappointing even when you have spent a substantial amount of money. The important thing to know is that developing an attractive, properly functioning landscape is a process.

The first step of the process is to determine the style your garden will have. Look at other plantings and gardens to determine the style you are most comfortable with. Gardening and landscaping books and magazines have photographs that can inspire and help you with decisions. The style you choose should be a matter of taste. The style you select will guide the aesthetic elements of the landscape design. For specific information on landscape plant dimensions, colors, and culture, review the book *Dale Groom's Texas Gardening Guide* (Cool Springs Press, 1997).

There are two major styles you might want to consider first. The *formal style* is characterized by bilateral symmetry, clipped plantings, geometrically shaped plants and beds, orderly rows of plants regularly spaced, traditional garden accents (classical statues for example), a central decorative feature such as a fountain, and "crisp" building materials (smooth painted wood, cut stone, brick). Everything is kept neatly manicured. This style can be very effective, but it can also appear stiff, lifeless, and boring. It is a relatively high-maintenance style.

The second general style is *informal* and the one we prefer. Plants are allowed to develop their natural forms (pruned but not regularly sheared), and they are arranged irregularly in a way that reflects nature. The lines in the landscape and the shape of the beds tend to be curved and flowing. There are few straight edges and no geometric shapes. Building materials are more relaxed and may even be rustic. This style of landscape design is generally less demanding when it comes to maintenance.

As an alternative, or in addition, you may want to use elements of one of the distinct design styles that have developed through many centuries of landscape design. If you have sufficient design skill, you may even be able to combine the features of one style with those of another. Some of the popular *ethnic styles* are Japanese, Chinese, Spanish, French formal, and country cottage. There are also *ecological styles* such as desert-like, tropical, and native. Get a feel for what suits your taste and the style of your home.

Now you go through the process to develop a landscape design. The following steps will help you organize your thoughts and efforts so that what you end up with is what you want and need.

1 *List your needs.* Think about yourself and your family, and decide what your landscape should include to provide for their needs. Write the list on paper. It might include such features as privacy, outdoor living area (patio, deck, courtyard, etc.), shade, flower beds, vegetable garden, swimming pool, greenhouse, children's play

area, and storage. Write down all the things you want from your landscape. Be thorough.

2 *Study your site.* Become familiar with the grounds. Notice the compass directions. Which areas are shady or sunny, wet or dry, level or sloping? Note existing features such as trees, buildings, beds, fences, wires, and walks. Make a simple sketch of the property showing the relevant features. Better yet, create a scale drawing. A scale drawing is much more effective when you actually start to do the design. Any inexpensive book on landscaping will have directions for doing a scale drawing. A good scale for home designers to work with is $1/4$ inch = 1 foot.

Once the drawing is done, make copies of it to mark up. You will be playing with various ideas and need copies for trying out those ideas. You may also use tracing paper. Never draw on the original.

3 *Diagram your space needs.* In this step you decide how much space different activities and areas will need and their location in the landscape. At this time you will see how many things in your list you will actually be able to fit into the landscape. Draw circles or ovals on your scale drawing copy to indicate the size and location of areas: the vegetable garden, the play area, the patio, and so forth. Try several arrangements until the best one is found.

4 *Shape the spaces.* Now determine the shapes of the areas. You may have indicated a flower bed with an oval to show where and how big it will be; now you decide how it will actually be shaped. Although you don't select the plants at this stage, you decide on the characteristics that the plants should have (size, flowering, color, evergreen, etc.). This is a creative stage that will be guided by the previous steps as well as by the style you have determined for your garden. If you have a working knowledge of plants you like, now is a good time to create designs with them in mind.

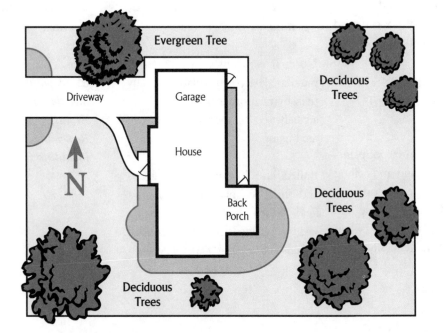

5 *Select the materials.* Now you select the materials that will be chosen to create the landscape. If you listed "privacy" in Step 1, Step 2 determined which view needed to be blocked, Step 3 determined the location of a privacy screen, Step 4 determined the size of the screen (how tall, how wide), and Step 5 will determine what the screen will be made of. You may choose a holly hedge, a lattice fence, or a brick wall. Let your plan guide you when selecting your plants and surfacing materials. Cost will be a factor in these decisions, of course.

Planting

Woody plant materials such as trees and shrubs are sold in one of three forms: bare root, balled and burlapped, or container grown. Trees are generally planted into individual planting holes, while shrubs are usually planted in well-prepared beds.

Bare root: Because bare-root plants are perishable, shipping and selling bare root is the least common method. You should purchase and plant bare-root plants only when they are dormant, generally from December through February. Roses are still sold bare root, and mail-ordered plants are also sometimes shipped bare root. Never allow the roots to dry out. Plant bare-root plants immediately or as soon as possible after you get them, and be sure they are planted at the same level they were growing previously. This can sometimes be difficult to determine, but look at the stem carefully and you can often detect the original soil line. Stem tissue is usually a lighter color below the ground.

It is better to plant a little too shallow than too deep. Make a mound of soil in the bottom of the hole where the plant will be planted, spread the roots over the mound, and fill in with more soil, covering the roots. Water thoroughly to settle them in.

Note: It is nearly always better to purchase bare-root plants locally than by mail order because you can actually see "in person" what you are buying.

Balled and burlapped: A balled-and-burlapped plant is grown in a field. When it reaches its desired size, it is dug up with a soilball which will be tightly wrapped with burlap and fastened with nails, wrapped with twine, or placed in a wire basket. When it is dug out of the ground, such a plant loses much or most of its root system and is susceptible to transplant shock. For this reason, balled-and-burlapped plants are best planted during the cooler months of October through March.

Many larger trees and shrubs are sold in this form, although today large trees grown in containers are also available.

Container grown: Container-grown plants are the most common plants for sale. They have well-developed root systems and suffer less transplant shock when planted. For this reason you may plant them virtually year-round, even though it is better to plant them during the milder weather that occurs from October to March.

Avoid planting in the stressful months of June, July, and August whenever possible. Remember, fall is for planting, including trees and shrubs.

Gardening in Texas

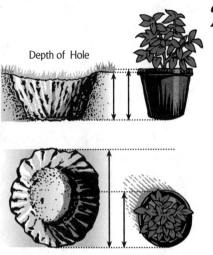

Depth of Hole

Width of Hole

Planting in Individual Holes

Planting trees properly in individual holes is not difficult, but it can make the difference between success and failure.

1 Whether the tree is balled and burlapped or container grown, *dig* the hole at least twice the diameter of the rootball and no deeper than the rootball's height.

2 *Remove* a container-grown tree from its container, and place it gently onto the firm, undisturbed soil in the bottom of the hole. A rootball that is tightly packed with thick encircling roots indicates a rootbound condition. Try to unwrap or open up the rootball to encourage the roots to spread into the surrounding soil. Do not remove the burlap from balled-and-burlapped trees unless it is synthetic burlap (check with the nursery staff when you purchase the tree). Once the tree is in the hole, try to remove any nylon twine or wire basket that may have been used, and fold down the burlap from the top of the rootball. Whether the tree is container grown or balled and burlapped, the top of its rootball should be level with or slightly above the surrounding soil. It is crucial that you do not plant the tree too deep. If planted too deeply, trees, shrubs, and other plants may terminate.

3 *Pulverize* the soil dug out from the hole thoroughly; use this soil, without any additions, to *backfill* around the tree. Research shows that blending amendments such as peat moss or compost into the fill soil slows establishment; it encourages the roots to grow primarily in the planting hole and delays their spread into the soil beyond. As a tree grows, its roots will grow out well beyond the reach of its branches. Since the roots will spend most of the tree's life growing in native soil outside of the planting hole, they might as well get used to it from the beginning.

4 Add soil around the tree until the hole is half full, then *firm* the soil to eliminate air pockets—but do not pack it tight. Finish filling the hole, firm again, and then *water* the tree thoroughly to settle it in. We do not generally add fertilizer to the planting hole, although it is all right to use some premium-quality long-lasting slow-release fertilizer in the upper few inches if you like. We apply a root stimulator after planting trees and shrubs.

5 *Stake* the tree only if it is tall enough to be unstable—otherwise, staking is not necessary. Do not drive the stakes into place directly against the trunk. Two or three stakes should be firmly driven into the ground just beyond the rootball and planting hole. Tie cloth strips, old nylon stockings, or wire (covered with a piece of garden hose where it touches the trunk) to the stakes and then to the trunk of the tree. Leave the support in place for no longer than 9 to 12 months.

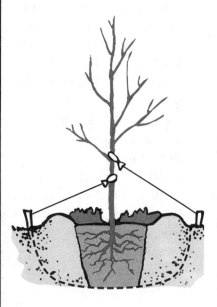

6 It is beneficial to keep the area 1 to 2 feet out from the trunk mulched and free of weeds and grass. This encourages the tree to establish faster by eliminating competition from grass roots. It also prevents lawn mowers and string trimmers from damaging the bark at the base of the tree, which can cause stunting or death. The mulch should be about 4 inches deep.

7 *Water* your tree when the weather is dry. This is the single most important thing you can do to ensure its survival, especially during its first summer. To properly water a tree the first year, turn a hose on to a trickle and lay the end on top of the ground within 6 inches of the trunk. Let the water trickle for about 30 to 45 minutes. This should be done once or twice a week during hot, dry weather. Apply a root stimulator monthly during its first year of growth.

Bed Preparation

Shrubs, ground covers, annuals, and perennials are almost always planted in well-prepared beds. Since their roots are less extensive than trees, amendments are generally added during bed preparation. Soil amendments are materials that are blended with the soil to improve it and can be organic matter (compost, aged manure, finely ground pine bark, peat moss), and sand (for heavy clay soils). Here are the basic steps for preparing the bed.

1 First, do a thorough job of removing unwanted vegetation in the bed. Weeds or turfgrass may be removed physically or eliminated with a weed-control aid (always read and follow label directions).

2 Next, *turn over the soil* to a depth of 8 to 10 inches. Spread any desired soil amendment over the turned soil. We recommend adding 6 inches of organic matter and tilling into the top 6 inches of native soil. (Have a soil test done to find out the specific needs of your soil.)

3 *Blend* the amendments thoroughly into the soil of the bed. A rear-tined tiller works well for heavy soil and organic matter.

4 *Rake* and you're ready to *plant.*

5 *Apply* soil amendments and fertilizer according to label directions when planting each plant. Use premium-quality slow-release granular fertilizers for great results.

Gardening Techniques

The Importance of Fertilization

In conversations with gardeners over the years, we have come to realize that there is, overall, an incomplete understanding of fertilizers—what they are, what they do, and why we use them. To put things in perspective, using fertilizers properly is an important part of gardening—but it is usually not a matter of life and death.

What Are Fertilizers?

First of all, fertilizers are not food. Plants make their own food through photosynthesis, which utilizes the energy of the sun to create sugar from carbon dioxide and water. If you need to think of plants eating something, their food is *light*.

To be healthy, plants also require sixteen known nutrients that are essential to their ability to carry on their life processes. These sixteen essential nutrients are the same for all plants. Plants in laboratory experiments that are completely deprived of any one of the essential nutrients become very sick or die. That, of course, virtually never happens in the garden since at least some of each essential nutrient is always present. There are times, however, when an essential nutrient may not be present in sufficient quantities for a plant to grow and function to its full potential. That's where fertilizers come in—a fertilizer is an aid added to the plant's environment that provides one or more essential nutrients.

Of the sixteen essential nutrients, three of them—carbon, hydrogen, and oxygen—are obtained from water and carbon dioxide. These elements are always available to plants in abundant quantities under normal conditions, and we don't need to be concerned about them. The other thirteen are almost always absorbed by plants from the soil through their roots (some epiphytic and aquatic plants are exceptions).

Why We Use Them

The thirteen essential mineral elements obtained from the soil are divided into three groups, based on the relative amounts of the nutrients used by plants. The micronutrients are used in very tiny amounts and include boron, chlorine, copper, iron, manganese, molybdenum, and zinc. Acid-loving plants often have problems obtaining iron in areas of Texas where the soil is alkaline. Micronutrients are also called trace elements.

The secondary nutrients—calcium, magnesium, and sulfur—are used by plants in larger amounts, and deficiencies can be more common. If your soil is very acid, it is generally going to be low in calcium and possibly magnesium. Gardeners with acidic soils often must add dolomitic lime to their gardens to provide calcium and magnesium and make the soil less acidic.

Nitrogen (N), phosphorus (P), and potassium (K) are the macronutrients, or primary elements. Although they are no more important to plants than any other essential element obtained from the soil, these nutrients are used in the largest quantities and so are most likely to be in short supply. As a result, gardeners focus on them almost exclusively when using fertilizers. Nitrogen (N), phosphorus (P), and potassium (K) are represented by the three numbers on a fertilizer's label, indicating the relative amounts of those nutrients contained in the fertilizer.

Gardening Techniques

In summary, we use fertilizers to correct deficiencies in one or more of the essential nutrients that plants obtain from the soil. The three nutrients most likely to be deficient are nitrogen (N), phosphorous (P), and potassium (K) since they are used in the greatest amounts, and most fertilizers focus on providing those nutrients. You do not need a separate fertilizer for every plant you grow. Despite the bewildering array of fertilizer brands and formulations available, it is not that complicated to fertilize properly. Remember, all plants use the same essential nutrients. However, some plants perform better in soils with high levels of specific nutrients.

The Importance of Pruning

When it comes to gardening, pruning is something that is done to aid plants in obtaining *our* goals. Plants may never grow exactly the way we want them to, and so will need to be shaped. There will be plants that grow larger than we anticipated and need to be regularly pruned to control size. Dead branches, diseased tissue, and insect infestations may be pruned away for the health of the plant. Then there are special situations such as topiary, espalier, and bonsai where careful selective pruning is used to completely alter the plant's normal growth patterns.

The average gardener is often very concerned about pruning. The main reason is that most gardeners feel they don't know what they are doing and are afraid they will damage or kill the plants. You can gain confidence by asking and fully answering two questions before pruning begins.

1 Why, specifically, do I feel this plant needs to be pruned? Or, what specific goal do I want to accomplish and what problem do I need to correct?

2 How, specifically, do I need to prune this plant to accomplish the goal?

There are three basic techniques we use to prune plants: *pinching, heading back,* and *thinning. Deadheading* is another grooming technique that may be placed in the pruning category.

Pinching is done with the thumbnail and forefinger or small garden scissors. The idea is to remove the young, soft growing tip of a shoot.

Pinching encourages branching and produces a fuller, bushier plant.

Pinching

Heading back involves shortening shoots or branches. Like pinching, it stimulates growth and branching. Heading back is often used to control the size of plants, encourage fullness, rejuvenate older plants, and maintain specific shapes as with topiary and espalier.

Often overutilized by gardeners, careless heading back can destroy the natural form of a plant, such as cutting crape myrtles into "flat top" forms.

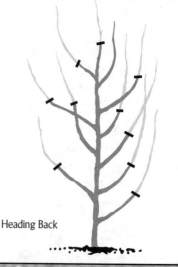

Heading Back

Gardening Techniques

Thinning removes shoots or branches at their point of origin, either back to a branch fork or back to the main trunk. Thinning can control the size and shape of a plant while doing a better job of maintaining the plant's natural shape.

Thinning cuts stimulate growth, and often work with the plant's natural growth patterns to correct problems.

Thinning

Deadheading is a rather morbid gardening term that refers to the continual removal of faded, unattractive flowers. This is done for a variety of reasons, including keeping the plant more attractive, encouraging more flowers, and preventing self-seeding.

Deadheading is usually a tedious process but often worth the effort. Try it on your roses.

It is generally better to prune lightly regularly than to prune severely occasionally. Do not prune plants when they are under stress. Do not prune plants late in the year when the new growth stimulated will not have time to harden off before freezes. If needed, prune spring-flowering trees and shrubs soon after they finish flowering. Prune most summer-flowering trees and shrubs in early fall.

The Importance of Proper Watering

Plants must have a constant and regular supply of water to maintain health. Even though some areas of Texas are not considered dry locations, rainfall does not fall evenly throughout the year. Drought conditions are not uncommon during the hot months of July, August, and September, and gardeners will usually need to irrigate to keep landscape plants in good shape.

Proper watering is a matter of timing and application. Timing is a matter of experience, paying attention to weather conditions, and common sense. Do not allow plants to show water stress (wilting, dull leaf color, burned leaf edges) before you begin watering. During hot weather periods, seven to ten days without rain usually means you should irrigate most plants.

Water must be applied slowly over time to penetrate the soil and thoroughly irrigate a landscape. During especially dry periods, watering landscape plants by hand does not provide enough water. Sprinklers, soaker hoses, and drip irrigation systems are effective devices for delivering water slowly over time for thorough watering.

Plants in the landscape growing in containers need much more frequent watering, sometimes every day during hot weather. For container plants, water generously until water flows from the drainage holes. Water again when the soil feels dry to the touch but before the plants wilt. Small containers may require two waterings per day during our "blast furnace" hot months of July, August, and often September.

Winter Protection

What Does "Winter Hardy" Really Mean?

You'd think that worrying about cold protection would not be necessary during our relatively mild winters. And it wouldn't be if we used only hardy plants in our landscapes. But tender tropicals are, and probably always will be, part of most gardens; container plants in the landscape are often tender tropicals as well.

The gardening term "hardy" refers to the ability of plants to withstand temperatures below freezing (32 degrees Fahrenheit) or colder with little or no damage. There are degrees of hardiness. A plant that can tolerate 10 degrees is hardier than one that is hardy only to 20 degrees. In zone 9 areas of the state, plants hardy to 15 degrees are considered winter hardy because the likelihood of lower temperatures is rare. In zone 8, plants hardy to 10 degrees are considered winter hardy. In zone 7, plants hardy to 0 degrees are considered hardy, and in zone 6, plants hardy to -10 degrees are considered hardy.

The term "tender" indicates plants that will be severely damaged or killed by temperatures below freezing. Factors such as how long the temperature remains below freezing, the moistness of the soil, how far below freezing it goes, and how protected is the plant's location in the landscape or microclimate will all affect the amount of damage that occurs. Cold protection is needed by tender tropicals whenever temperatures are predicted to go into the low 30s or upper 20s. Do not be concerned about wind-chill factors—look at the actual temperatures predicted.

Overwintering Plants–How To

One benefit of our mild winters is that the ground here never freezes. Tropicals and semi-tropicals growing in the ground that produce fleshy underground parts such as bulbs or rhizomes are generally very reliable about coming back even if the tops are killed by freezing temperatures. **Cannas, agapanthus, gingers, callas, elephant ears, caladiums, crinums, clivia,** and **amaryllis** fall into this category in well-drained soils. Do not leave them in the ground in wet or poorly drained soils.

You can help ensure the survival of these below-ground parts by placing 4 to 6 inches of mulch over the soil around the base of the plants for additional protection. Pine straw is one of the best mulches. It stays loose and does not pack, which improves its insulating qualities. Remember, mulches protect only what they cover. They are most useful in protecting below-ground parts or covering low-growing plants. Mulch may help keep the lower stems, crown, and roots of a cold-tender plant alive, but it won't protect the uncovered upper part of the plant. To protect the upper parts of these plants, you must cover them.

Canvas or fabric may be used as covers. There must be enough material to extend all the way to the ground when the plant is covered. If possible, find two or three posts or stakes that are taller than the plant. Drive them into the ground around the plant and they will hold the cover off the foliage. This is particularly important if the weight of the cover might damage the plant.

Texas Winter Hardiness Zone Map

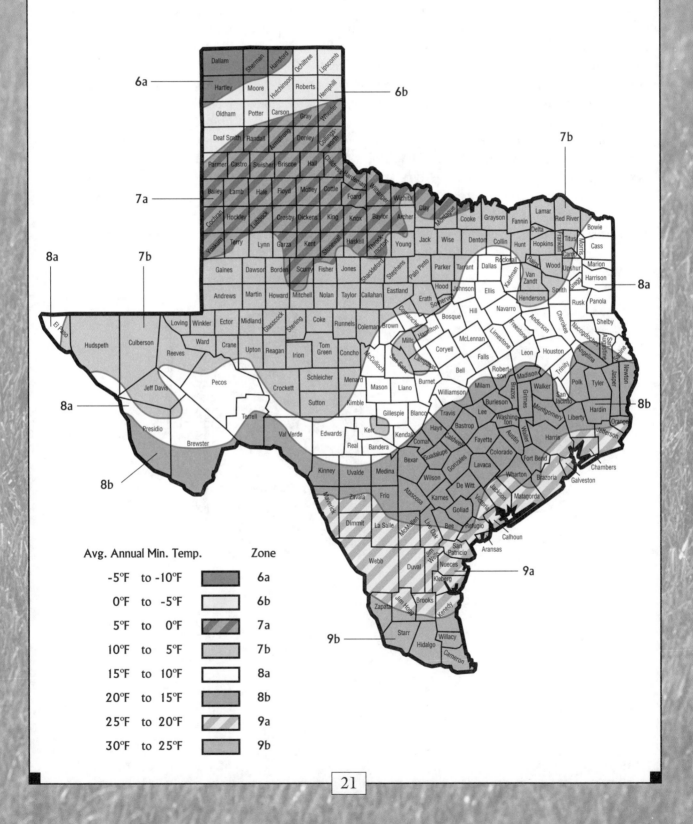

Avg. Annual Min. Temp.	Zone
-5°F to -10°F	6a
0°F to -5°F	6b
5°F to 0°F	7a
10°F to 5°F	7b
15°F to 10°F	8a
20°F to 15°F	8b
25°F to 20°F	9a
30°F to 25°F	9b

Winter Protection

Covering plants works particularly well when temperatures dip into the mid-20s overnight and rise again the following day. Providing a heat source under the cover improves protection when there are more severe freezes or prolonged temperatures below freezing. One of the safest and easiest methods is to wrap or drape the plant with miniature Christmas lights. Not enough heat is generated to damage the plant, but the heat that is given off by the small bulbs can make a big difference in the plant's survival. If you want to use lights, remember a cover is still necessary to trap and hold in the heat. Be sure to use outdoor extension cords. To avoid covering your plants or using lights, always plant winter-hardy selections.

Bringing Plants Indoors

You must also decide what to do with tender plants growing in containers outside. You have three choices. One, leave them outside and let them take their chances (at least gather them together under some protection such as a carport or patio cover). This could be an option with low-value, easily replaced plants. Two, bring them inside and keep them in through the winter. Make sure you put them in a good location that receives plenty of light. Or three, move them inside on those nights when a freeze is predicted and back out again when the freezing episode is over.

Good: Sheets or quilts

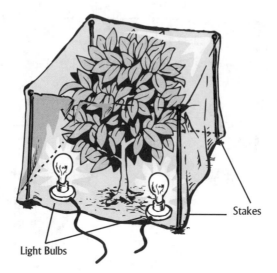

Light Bulbs

Stakes

Better: cloth cover or row cover

Annual Flowering Plants

Annuals are plants that sprout from seeds, grow, mature, flower, set seed, and die in a single growing season. The group is divided into **warm-season annuals** and **cool-season annuals,** with classification depending on cold hardiness and heat tolerance.

Warm-Season Annuals

Warm-season annuals are killed or damaged by freezing temperatures and therefore grow best during the warm to hot months of April to early November. Seeds or transplants may be planted into the garden from late March through August. They usually thrive during the long, hot months, although the performance of some will diminish during the hottest weather in late summer.

Since we have a growing season that is seven months long, it is unusual for true annuals to last from April to November. There is a group of plants called **tender perennials** that do have the stamina to last the entire season. Since they are often killed during winter freezes, and so last for just one season, these plants are grown as warm-season annuals and are generally grouped with them

even though they are perennials. Unlike true annuals, tender perennials are not programmed by their genes to die after flowering and setting seed. Beds planted with tender perennial bedding plants usually will not have to be replanted in July or August as is typical for some true annuals. This makes them a good choice for lower-maintenance landscapes. As a bonus, some tender perennials can survive mild winters and may live to bloom another year. Tender perennials on the Warm-Season Annuals chart (page 25) are marked with single plus marks (+).

Cool-Season Annuals

Flower beds can remain colorful through the winter when planted with cool-season annuals, a wonderful group that will grow and bloom from November to May or whenever it gets warm/hot in the spring. Seeds for most may be planted in flats or direct-seeded from August through November. Transplants should be planted from September through February, depending on which hardiness zone you live in.

Cool-season bedding plants will generally tolerate freezing temperatures into the low 20s and even teens without protection (**nasturtiums** are the exception, as they are damaged by temperatures below 30 degrees Fahrenheit). Some will bloom all winter during mild weather, peaking in March and April. With the onset of hot weather in May, most cool-season annuals are quick to decline. **Pansies** are the most cold-hardy annuals we use in Texas.

There are several hardy perennials that are commonly used as cool-season annuals in Texas. Although **foxglove, delphinium,** and **hollyhock** are reliable perennials in cooler zones, they have a hard time surviving our summers. Transplants are set into the garden from October through February for blooms in April through early June. Planting dates are determined by the zone you live in.

Annual Flowering Plants

Grow Annuals Successfully

Successful annual growth depends on selecting varieties that do well, good bed preparation, planting each type of annual in the growing conditions it prefers, and paying attention to proper care after planting.

Don't scrimp on bed preparation, as this is essential for plants to perform their best. Good bed and soil preparation is the foundation for successful long-term annual growth and bloom.

1 First *remove any weeds or other unwanted plants* from the bed. Growing weeds may be controlled with a non-selective herbicide which does not leave a residue in the soil. Refer to page 291 for a summary of your options. Be sure to follow label directions carefully.

2 *Turn the soil* to a depth of at least 8 inches with a shovel, fork, or tiller.

3 *Spread* a 4-inch layer of compost, rotted leaves, aged manure, finely ground pine bark, or peat moss over the bed. Blend the organic matter into the top 4 inches of soil thoroughly, rake smooth, and then plant. Add small amounts of slow-release fertilizer to each planting hole according to label directions.

Planning the Annual Flower Garden

Before you go to the nursery and buy annuals, *look carefully* at the growing conditions in the area to be planted. Most annuals do best with six to eight hours of sun a day (partial to full sun). Several will do well with two to four hours of direct sun (shade to partial shade). Make sure you select plants that will thrive in the light conditions they will receive. Annuals generally need good drainage, so plant in a raised bed if the area tends to stay damp. Measure the size of the bed and calculate how many plants you will need to create your desired effect. Although spacing varies with the plants' known average spread, about 8 inches can be used for estimating.

It is also a good idea to *make some decisions on the color or colors* that will be used in the flower bed, as well as desirable heights (usually taller plants in the back of beds, shorter in front) and general layout to meet your desire. You can always make changes or adjustments if necessary, but it is a good idea to have developed your ideas as completely as possible before buying plants.

Planting Annuals

When planting annual transplants, make sure you *space them properly.* Too close, and the plants will crowd one another and be less healthy. If planted too far apart, the plants will not grow together to completely fill the bed. Plant transplants so the top of the rootball is level with the soil in the bed. If the roots are in a dense mass, *open the mass* slightly to encourage the roots to grow into the surrounding prepared soil.

Many annuals are easy to direct-seed into the garden—but in this day of instant gratification, many gardeners don't have the patience for this (or only want a few plants of specific types/varieties), and rely on transplants instead. If you have the patience, *plant seeds at the proper depth* in a well-prepared bed and *keep moist* until they come up. When direct-seeding, it is important to thin seedlings so they are spaced properly. Check the seed package for recommendations.

Annuals Planting Chart

Warm-Season Annuals

Ageratum	Geranium
Alyssum	+Impatiens+++
Amaranthus*+++	Marigold*+++
Bachelor's Button/	+Ornamental Pepper*
Gomphrena+*	+Pentas+++
Balsam++	+Periwinkle*
Begonia	Portulaca*+++
+Blue Daze*++++	+Purslane*
Celosia*	Rudbeckia*
Cleome++	+Salvia* (some varieties)
+Coleus+++	+Scaevola+++
Copper Plant*	Sunflower*+++
Cosmos++	Torenia
Dahlberg Daisy++	+Verbena
+Dusty Miller	Zinnia*+++
Gaillardia*	

*   Heat tolerant
+   Tender Perennials
++   Easily direct seeded
+++ Best to buy transplants
At the beginning of the planting season, you can plant seed in flats or directly in beds, or you can use transplants. (Use transplants if you are planting towards the end of an annual's planting season.)

Cool-Season Annuals

Alyssum+	Nasturtium+
Annual Baby's Breath	Nicotiana
Annual Candytuft	Ornamental Cabbage
Annual Phlox+	and Kale
Calendula+	Pansy**+++
Dahlberg Daisy+	Petunia++
Delphinium++	Poppies+
Dianthus	Snapdragon
Dusty Miller	Statice
English Daisy	Stock
Forget-me-not	Sweet Pea+
Larkspur+	Viola

** The most cold-hardy annual we use
+   Easily direct seeded
++   Best to buy transplants
At the beginning of the planting season, you can plant seed in flats or directly in beds, or you can use transplants. (Use transplants if you are planting towards the end of an annual's planting season.)

Although many bedding plants prefer partial sun to full sun (about 6 to 8 hours of direct sun), the following will do well in shade, or even prefer shade to partial shade (about 2 to 4 hours of direct sun).
Warm-season: Balsam•, Cleome•, Coleus•, Impatiens, Pentas•, Salvia• (some varieties), **Torenia•**.
Cool-season: Forget-me-not, Nasturtium•, Nemophila, Nicotiana•.
•Also do well in full sun.

General Care

Proper care of annuals will keep them attractive for a long time. Annual beds may be relatively high maintenance, and this should be remembered when deciding how many beds you want and how large the beds will be. Water as needed and weed if necessary, although both of these jobs can be reduced with the use of a mulch. A 3- to 4-inch layer of pine bark mulch will work well. Thorough watering during dry weather, especially when it's hot, is important to keep annuals growing vigorously and blooming. Soaker hoses, where suitable, are a great way to water without getting the flowers or foliage wet. This can reduce disease problems and damage to open flowers.

Whenever it is practical, remove the old flowers to keep the plants looking attractive and to encourage continued flowering. This practice is called deadheading or tip pruning.

Insect and disease problems may occur, especially with warm-season annuals. Keep a watchful eye out for symptoms and act promptly before significant damage occurs. Some annuals will not recover well if badly damaged. Remember, it is important to properly identify the cause of a problem before taking action.

Planning

Make a New Year's resolution to start a Texas gardening journal.

An important part of planning for the future is remembering what was done in the past.

A favorite pastime of gardeners is to look through the many seed catalogs that arrive in December and January. There is still plenty of time to decide what to plant when the cool-season annuals finish, but it won't hurt to start coming up with some ideas. Look for new cultivars of reliable plants that you'd like to try. Nurseries may or may not carry the newest cultivars, but it is fun to know what's on the cutting edge. You can also consider growing the plants yourself from seed. Note the All-America Selections winners for the new year, as well as past winners. These cultivars have proven themselves in trials all across the country and are usually a good choice.

Planting and Transplanting

In some Texas zones there is still time to *purchase and plant seeds of fast-growing cool-season annuals* such as **alyssum, annual phlox, calendula, forget-me-not,** and **nasturtium.** Although the selection in nurseries may be somewhat skimpy now, you can continue to plant cool-season transplants in January during periods of pleasant weather in zones 7b, 8, and 9.

Care for Your Annuals

Keep beds well mulched to suppress weed growth, retain soil warmth, and conserve soil moisture.

Our coldest weather usually occurs in January. Most bedding plants will not need protection. *Cover nasturtiums* if temperatures below 30 degrees Fahrenheit are predicted. **Pansies, dianthus, ornamental kale and cabbage, viola,** and **snapdragons** are among the most hardy. They survive temperatures below 20 degrees with no problem, so are especially reliable. Protect **sweet peas** if temperatures in the low 20s are predicted. **Pansies** are the most cold-hardy annuals we plant.

Watering

Cool temperatures and normal rainfall generally make watering unnecessary this month. Do *watch rainfall amounts* and if the weather is dry, water thoroughly. Annuals in container plantings will need to be watered regularly.

Fertilizing

Cold temperatures often slow the growth of cool-season bedding plants in January. If the weather has been mild and plants are in active growth, you may decide to *fertilize* them, if fertilizer has not been applied for six to ten weeks. Before deciding to fertilize, check the type of fertilizer you are using to see how long it will last, and evaluate the appearance and condition of the plants.

- If plants are deep green: *don't fertilize.*

- If plants are pale or yellow-green: *fertilize.*

Slow-release granular fertilizers such as 15-5-10 will generally supply nutrients for about six to eight weeks. If a slow-release fertilizer was used at the time of planting, it will generally last the entire growing season. Soluble fertilizers must be applied according to label directions every two weeks during active growth.

Pest Control

Pest problems are relatively few this time of year. *Watch for aphids* if the weather is mild, and *control* with an appropriate insect-control aid. Refer to page 291 for a summary of your options. Be sure to read and follow label directions carefully.

Planning

Purchase seeds of warm-season annuals locally this month. Many seeds can be planted in flats outside or in beds in late March.

Seed packets often contain more seeds than needed to produce enough plants for a garden. Get together with a gardening friend and agree to share packets of seeds (and cost) for those plants you both want to grow. Or you can each grow more transplants than you need of different plants and trade the extras. *Draw simple sketches* of your flower beds and begin to plan what will go into them for the warm season. *Decide on a color scheme and the texture and forms your plantings will have.*

Planting and Transplanting

If you are just getting around to planting cool-season bedding plants or have decided to plant more, it is best to choose transplants in 4-inch pots this late in the season. Do not plant transplants too deeply, especially those that tend to form a crown (rosette of leaves on a short stem), such as **pansy, viola, dusty miller, delphinium, hollyhock, foxglove, English daisy,** and **statice.** Planting too deeply may cause these beauties to terminate.

Care for Your Annuals

Spring is here in zones 8b and 9. Flowering trees and spring bulbs are blooming, but February can still produce bitterly cold weather and most often will. Keep an eye out for extreme cold, but rest assured that most cool-season bedding plants can recover from whatever comes along. If severe weather is predicted, it doesn't hurt to *place some old blankets, sheets, tarps, or grow cover over a bed* if you are concerned about cold damage. Low-growing bedding plants can be covered with several inches of leaves or pine straw for protection. Be sure to remove any cold protection after the danger has passed.

Watering

Rain is usually generous in February, so watering chores are normally minimal. There may be too much rain this time of year, but because of the low temperatures, rot is generally not as much of a problem as would be expected. Still, if beds seem to be staying too wet, *pull back the mulch* to allow water to evaporate. Sometime this year, rework the beds and elevate them to increase drainage.

Fertilizing

If you haven't fertilized since you planted several months ago, you might need to now. Peak flowering on cool-season bedding plants generally occurs in March and April. Encouraging strong, robust growth now is important, especially if the plants do not appear vigorous. At this time, use your choice of soluble or granular fertilizer formulations according to label directions. **Pansies** are especially heavy users of nitrogen, so keep a close watch on them.

Pest Control

Wood sorrel, henbit, chickweed, and annual bluegrass are just a few of the weeds that plague cool-season flower beds. Wood sorrel must be lifted with the roots and bulbs attached, using a trowel or weeding tool. Weed-control aids are effective if you are persistent and make several applications as the weed reappears. Refer to page 291 for a summary listing your options. You must apply these aids only to the foliage of the weeds you want to control. *Do not allow any weed-control aid to contact the foliage of desirable plants nearby.* This is also the time to apply specialized pre-emergent granular aids according to label directions in the beds of established annuals to prevent weeds.

Planning

March is a transitional month. The possibility of frost diminishes greatly in zones 8 and 9, and gardeners begin to think about planting warm-season bedding plants.

At the same time, the cool-season bedding plants are gearing up for their finale, which should last until May or whenever temperatures warm to 80 degrees Fahrenheit during the day and 70 degrees at night. ***Sit back and enjoy.*** Now is a good time to begin to evaluate the performance of the cool-season bedding plants in your garden. Make notes in your Texas gardening journal.

- How well are they blooming?

- Were there any problems?

- What are the good points or bad points?

- Which ones did you and your family enjoy the most?

Keeping good records helps us avoid repeating mistakes and continue our successes. Look at other plantings in private landscapes and public gardens and note plants that you might want to try the next cool season. Take photographs where possible.

Some gardeners who did not plant in the fall may notice the amazing display of **pansies, dianthus,** and **alyssum** in other gardens and just have to go out and buy some for their gardens. If you want to plant cool-season plants, choose well-established plants in 4-inch pots. At this point, it is probably better for most gardeners to leave beds unplanted and focus on planting warm-season bedding plants later this month or in April. It is time for you to seriously begin planning your warm-season flower beds. Make a note in your Texas gardening journal to plant some fall cool-season annuals this year.

Planting

The weather may still be chilly, but in zones 8 and 9 some warm-season bedding plants may be direct-seeded into the garden now, including **cleome, cosmos, Dahlberg daisy, marigold,** and **rudbeckia.** Once the shoots come up, remember to cover them if nighttime lows are predicted to go below the low 30s.

Think about starting some warm-season annual seeds in flats or pots for transplants to be set out in May. Seeds may be started indoors, but light inside is generally insufficient to produce healthy transplants—windowsill seedlings usually end up stretched, weak-stemmed, and floppy.

1 Plant the seeds in containers filled with moist soilless mix following directions on the seed package.

2 As soon as the seeds germinate, move the containers to a location outside where they will receive the light they need.

Seedlings of plants that like full sun should receive direct sun for about 6 hours, and those that prefer shady beds should be placed in a spot that receives sun for about 3 to 4 hours.

3 Watch the weather carefully.

As long as daytime highs are in the 60s and 70s and nighttime lows in the 40s, you may leave the seedlings outside. Bring them in whenever temperatures will be in the 30s, or during windy, chilly weather.

4 Watch for watering needs, as small pots and flats dry rapidly.

Care for Your Annuals

As the days lengthen and grow warmer, cool-season annuals respond by growing faster and blooming more. ***Deadhead*** (remove spent flowers) as often as possible to keep plants looking neat and encourage continued flowering.

This is particularly effective with **annual phlox, calendula, dianthus, pansy, snapdragon,** and **sweet pea.** Do this as the flowers fade but before a seedpod develops.

Watering

Adequate rain generally falls in March, but dry conditions can occur. With warmer temperatures (we occasionally get above 80 degrees Fahrenheit in March, especially in zones 8 and 9 and sometimes in zone 7), plants use water faster. Although cool-season annuals planted in the fall should be well established at this point, *water deeply and thoroughly whenever irrigation is needed.* Newly planted bedding plants should usually receive water more often than well-established plantings if conditions are dry.

If you have started seeds in pots or flats for transplants, watch them carefully. Those in sunny locations, in particular, will dry out rapidly. Plan on checking once a day, maybe even twice. *Do not allow the seedlings to wilt or become dry.*

Fertilizing

If it has been over six weeks since your last application of granular fertilizer, or over two weeks since you last used a soluble fertilizer, *consider fertilizing cool-season annuals now.* Those that were previously fertilized with a slow-release fertilizer should be fine, but if they seem pale or sluggish, an application of your favorite soluble fertilizer will give them a push. If your plants are dark green and growing vigorously but not blooming much, *do not fertilize.* You may have overdone the nitrogen, and it's best to leave them alone.

Pest Control

Weeds, insects, and diseases will take advantage of the warmer weather to attack flower beds with surprising swiftness.

Stay on top of the weeds! Keep beds well mulched. Many gardeners either do not use mulches or do not apply them deep enough. Mulches should be at least 3 inches thick. Pine straw, chopped pine straw, cypress mulch, pine bark, leaves, and dry grass clippings are just some of the suitable, commonly used mulches. Our favorite mulch is pine bark, and we maintain it 3 to 4 inches deep year-round.

Snails and slugs can be a major problem, chewing holes in leaves and flowers, particularly those of low-growing plants like **pansies.**

Use selected baits per label directions to reduce snail and slug populations. Trapping also works if you are persistent, and is a good way to monitor population levels. A trap is easily constructed using a small, disposable bowl and some beer. In the early evening, place several bowls around the garden where snails and slugs have been a problem. Sink the bowls in the soil or mulch up to their rims, and fill half full with fresh beer. Snails and slugs are powerfully attracted by the smell of the beer. They crawl into the bowl, and once the beer washes the slime from their undersides, they cannot crawl out again. Empty the traps every morning, noting how many pests you caught. Continue to put out traps every evening until very few of the pesky critters show up in the beer. Toads are an excellent ally in this fight, and you should welcome them in the garden, even if you are squeamish about them. Actually, toads are very neat if not pretty critters to have in any garden.

Planning

This is the month that cool-season annuals really shine. In the spring, if it doesn't warm early, azaleas and other spring-flowering shrubs put on a spectacular show, and the last of the spring-flowering bulbs and trees chime in for good measure. But with temperatures in the 70s and 80s, April can definitely feel like summer.

Most of the warm-season bedding plants can be planted this month statewide, but many gardeners are too busy enjoying flower beds full of blooming cool-season annuals to start planting yet. This is a great time to make notes in your Texas gardening journal on color schemes you liked (or didn't like) and how all your cool-season annuals performed.

Even if you are not ready to plant your warm-season flower garden, you will notice that nurseries are stocking a good selection of warm-season annual transplants this month. You might want to stop by and get ideas on what to plant later. Don't forget to take a notepad and pen to jot down the names of plants that catch your eye. Then you will be able to look up information on those plants and learn more about them before you decide to purchase.

Planting and Transplanting

Tempting as it may be, *resist buying the cool-season annual transplants that nurseries continue to carry.* Their season is nearing its end. In particular, be aware that some of the **petunias** sold by the truckload in April and May may not bloom through the heat of the summer. The VIP varieties Madness Series and old-fashioned types are the exceptions.

If you started warm-season annual seeds last month in flats, the seedlings of many types may be large enough to *separate into individual cell-packs or small pots.* Tease them apart gently, primarily handling them by their roots to avoid damaging the delicate stems. *Pot them up* in the same soilless mix you used to start them. Give them extra shade for a few days after separation. Make sure you keep them well watered.

Care for Your Annuals

Many cool-season annuals are achieving full size now. Make sure larger plants are not crowding smaller plants around them. *Stake or otherwise support plants that need it.* **Hollyhocks, snapdragons, foxgloves,** and **larkspur** are among the taller-growing plants that may need support. Bamboo, dowel rods, or similar "supports" work well for these applications.

Watering

As the weather warms and the plants grow larger, cool-season annuals growing in containers will need more-frequent watering. *Apply water until it runs from the drainage hole.* This will ensure that the entire rootball has been moistened. If a large part of the water moves quickly through the drainage hole(s), however, this may suggest that the soil has been a bit too dry too long and has shrunk away from the pot's walls. This condition allows the water to bypass the rootball without wetting it. Make sure this is not the case before you're satisfied that the soil mass has been sufficiently moistened. Smaller containers and those planted with a combination of several plants will dry out the fastest. In these cases, fill the container several times until the soil ball is saturated, then allow water to drain.

April may be one of our drier months. *Continue to water beds and pots as needed.* Soaker hoses are good to use where practical. They apply water slowly to allow deep penetration of water into the soil. The foliage and flowers stay dry, however, preventing damage to open blossoms and reducing disease problems.

Fertilizing

If you prefer water-soluble fertilizers, fertilize growing transplants once a week with your favorite at half the recommended rate. Soluble fertilizers are those that should be dissolved in water and applied in liquid form.

Annuals growing in containers need regular fertilization, as constant watering leaches available nutrients quickly. Use a soluble fertilizer regularly, or apply a slow-release fertilizer according to label directions, as needed. We prefer premium-quality long-lasting slow-release granular fertilizers for growing annuals in beds or containers.

Pest Control

Hungry caterpillars are on the prowl. Look for their droppings, which can be the size of a BB or pencil eraser and dark green to black. Look for holes in the leaves as well.

Visit local retail garden centers for help in identifying insect pests, including caterpillar damage. Select appropriate control aids and apply according to label directions. Refer to page 291 for a summary listing your options. Your retail garden center or nursery can help you with these control aids and information on how and when to apply.

MAY

Planning

In May we often see a transition from warm weather to intense heat. Many cool-season annuals are in decline. Daytime highs begin to reach 90 degrees Fahrenheit, and by the end of the month, cool weather is but a memory in the southern one-half to two-thirds of Texas. Still, the weather is pleasant compared to how hot it will be in July . . . so take advantage of it.

May is one of the busiest months in the flower garden. As cool-season annuals become unattractive, the beds should be *cleaned out and replanted with warm-season annuals.* By this time you have probably developed a working plan of how you want your summer gardens to look and what you want to plant. Don't forget that summer heat can make the care of flower beds uncomfortable, to say the least. Keep this in mind when deciding on how many beds you can maintain and how large they can be. Remember, tender perennials are excellent choices (see Warm-Season Annuals chart on page 25).

If you haven't done so, make notes in your Texas gardening journal on what you did and did not do well during the fall, winter, and spring. Also note what you are planting now, rainfall, temperatures, when plants were fertilized, etc. The notes will be a valuable tool when planning future plantings.

Planting and Transplanting

After removing finished cool-season annuals, *put some effort into getting the bed ready for the next crop of flowers.* Careful attention to bed preparation is very important to successful gardening.

1 First *completely remove* any weeds or other unwanted plants from the bed.

2 *Turn the soil* to a depth of at least 8 inches. *Spread* a 4-inch layer of compost, rotted leaves, aged manure, finely ground pine bark, or peat moss over the bed.

3 *Blend* the organic matter thoroughly into the bed, *rake* smooth, and you're ready to plant.

4 After planting is complete and watering is done, *apply* a layer of mulch around and between all transplants. Leave no bare soil. As plants grow in height, increase mulch depth to 3 to 4 inches.

It is best to plant transplants in staggered rows or a checkerboard pattern. Plant the first row at the recommended spacing. Plant the next row at the recommended spacing from the first row, but the plants should be positioned so that they form triangles with the plants of the first row (see diagram). Continue in this way until the bed is planted. This arrangement is more visually pleasing.

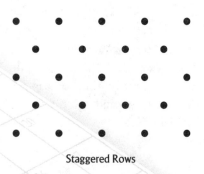

Staggered Rows

If the rootball of a transplant is a solid mass of roots, *loosen the roots* slightly prior to planting to encourage them to spread into the surrounding soil. Do not plant transplants too deep, and make sure they are spaced properly. If anything, annuals have a tendency to grow larger in our climate than their tags predict. *Water-in the transplants with your favorite root stimulator* to get the young plants off to a good start.

Watering

Newly planted flower beds will need thorough watering if the weather is dry. (Do not water lightly every day.) Water deeply as needed. It is generally best to water early in the day so that plants have the water they need when heading into the hot afternoon. Try not to water in early evening.

Fertilizing

Some gardeners use a slow-release fertilizer when planting bedding plants. About one teaspoon can be placed in each planting hole and nutrients will be provided for the entire growing season. This is a rather expensive (slow-release fertilizers cost more than standard granular types) and tedious way to fertilize, but it does save time and labor throughout the summer. You must choose one method to use, however. It is never a good idea, for example, to add a granular fertilizer during bed preparation. Use a slow-release during planting, and then follow up with repeated applications of a soluble fertilizer.

Pest Control

Get ready: here they come. Crawling, hopping, flying, and walking, there are lots of insect pests out there ready to damage your annuals. Fortunately, most of us get by with only occasional major outbreaks of these pests. Do keep a constant eye out and *regularly inspect your plants for early signs of problems.* This practice is perhaps the most important part of pest control. Some damage is inevitable—just don't let it get out of hand.

Note which annuals tend to have the worst problems from year to year, and consider avoiding them in the future. **Celosia,** for instance, are highly susceptible to caterpillars in some plantings. **Marigolds** have problems with spider mites. **Periwinkles** plantings are more and more often devastated by *Phytophthora* fungus in alkaline soils. *Record this type of invaluable information in your Texas gardening journal.* If you don't have a journal started, look for *My Texas Garden: A Gardener's Journal* (Cool Springs Press, 2000) at retailers.

Small pale specks all over leaves are commonly seen this time of year. This damage is the result of sucking pests such as spider mites, lace bugs, leaf hoppers, and plant bugs. Visit local retail nurseries for information

Helpful Hints

If your cool-season annuals are way past their prime and you are not ready or able to replace them, pull them up anyway, improve the soil by adding organic matter to it , and heavily mulch the bed until you can plant. An empty, mulched bed looks much better that one full of dying cool-season annuals.

If you have seen your **periwinkles** wilting and dying, the problem is most likely aerial blight caused by the **Phytophthora** fungus. Research indicates that the **Pacifica** group of periwinkles is the most blight-resistant, and you should wait until May to plant. In acidic soils this problem does not occur.

Don't forget to put all of those dead cool-season annuals in your compost pile.

and help in identifying these problems and how to control them. Just *pull up infected cool-season annuals and replace with warm-season plants.*

Planning

Think of ways to deal with the intense heat of the next three or four months. Try to work on days that are overcast, or work in shady areas of the landscape, moving as the shade moves from one location to another. We enjoy very early morning times. Give them a try.

Evaluate flower plantings and decide if more plants or beds need to be added or reduced. Make sure you have included colorful plants around outdoor living areas like patios where you can enjoy them. Don't overlook the use of containers and hanging baskets planted with warm-season annuals. Tropical color plants often work well in containers, can be relocated as needed, and tolerate our heat. Make notes in your Texas gardening journal on what's doing well.

Planting and Transplanting

Most planting should have been done last month, but our growing season is long enough to continue planting warm-season annuals if you need to. You can also continue to direct-seed warm-season annuals in well-prepared beds, or plant seeds in flats or pots to grow your own transplants.

Watering

Drought stress will be a constant concern over the next few months. *Pay careful attention to the weather and rainfall amounts.* Some areas tend to be either very dry or very soggy—you just have to deal with whatever situation arises. Drought-stressed plants may be more susceptible to pests like spider mites. Keep in mind that light, frequent irrigation promotes a shallow root system, making plants even more drought-susceptible and possibly increasing disease problems. Always water deeply and thoroughly when irrigating.

Vacation plans this summer mean deciding how plants will be watered while you are away. Here are some ideas:

1 Place all your outdoor container plants, including any hanging baskets, in a shady location near the northern side of a building or within the protective cover of a large shade tree or covered patio. Group your plants fairly close together, as this will help slow water loss. Water thoroughly just before you leave.

2 Some container plants outside should be watered almost every day. If you'll be gone for more than two or three days and you can't find a friend to water regularly for you, small inexpensive water timers are available at local nurseries and building supply or hardware stores. They can be hooked up to a sprinkler or drip irrigation system to periodically water your plants while you are gone.

3 Water your home grounds thoroughly prior to leaving, especially if there has been little rainfall. A slow, thorough soaking will provide a lasting supply of moisture. Make sure that you have mulched all flower beds with a 3- to 4-inch layer of pine bark mulch, leaves, pine straw, cypress mulch, or other material to conserve moisture and hold down weeds.

4 To water automatically, attach either soaker hoses or sprinklers to cover various beds with a timer attached to each faucet close to your garden beds. Set the timers to come on twice a week and stay on long enough to thoroughly soak an area. Set the times so each water timer comes on at a different hour and you won't lose water pressure while irrigating. Morning irrigation is preferred.

Fertilizing

Monitor the growth, foliage color, and vigor of your annuals. If plants are pale and low in vigor, *try an application of soluble fertilizer* (use a hose end applicator for faster, easier application). If the plants respond within about a week, either continue to apply a soluble fertilizer per label directions as needed or sprinkle the bed with a 3:1:2 ratio fertilizer appropriate for your area. Follow package directions carefully. Continue to regularly fertilize annuals in containers and hanging baskets as needed.

Overfertilization can lead to lush growth with fewer flowers and even damage to your plants. *Always use fertilizer in moderation.* A little goes a long way. Reading and following label directions is a wise policy.

Pest Control

It is to be hoped that your early efforts have prevented any major pest outbreaks.

Hot, dry weather favors the outbreak of spider mites. These very tiny spider relatives are almost too small to be seen with the naked eye. Damage starts as tiny pale or white speckles on the upper surface of foliage. The foliage may eventually turn faded tan and the infested plants appear very sick. Fine webbing may be seen on plants that have very heavy infestations.

Because of spider mite problems, there are certain annuals, including marigolds, we do not plant. When installing varieties of plants known to have spider mite infestations, visit local retail nurseries for information and aids to control them. Refer to page 291 for a summary listing your options.

All the effort you put into making your annuals grow well will make weeds in the bed grow even faster. Deal with weed problems promptly while weeds are still young and small. They can ruin an annual planting with just a few weeks of inattention.

Handweeding, mulches, and aids are the primary methods of weed control. Use them regularly and use them all for a multi-front approach to weed control.

Pruning

Gardeners rarely think about pruning annuals, but they may need to be shaped or controlled like any other plant in the landscape. Feel free to pinch or snip back plants in flower beds so that everything has enough room to grow. Trimmings from tender perennials generally root easily. Deadheading may help keep plants blooming better.

Enter notes in your Texas gardening journal on temperatures, rain or lack of it, pests, which plants are doing well, and those that are less fortunate.

Helpful Hints

Plants that you know will grow tall may need some sort of support. Plan for this and decide what method would be best in different situations. Have the materials on hand and use them before tall plants lay over. Left alone, they may damage or kill nearby plants. Stakes, cages, and bricks pushed against the base of a plant are some of the more common supports.

Planning

Plan on doing most of your gardening during the early morning or early evening when temperatures are more bearable. Some annuals planted back in March or early April may be winding down toward the end of this month or in early August, especially those that can't handle our heat. Evaluate them and make plans for their replacements as they finish. New plants should do well until cool-season annuals are planted in October or November.

When it's too hot to be outside, spend some time indoors reading a good gardening book. It is especially important to read books and use those written for Texas. Most books written for other parts of the country do not apply in Texas. Make a point of reading one gardening book each summer.

Decide on cool-season annuals you might like to grow from seeds. It's not too early to shop locally for seeds to plant next month or in September to raise your own transplants.

Be sure to make entries in your Texas gardening journal covering which annuals are holding up, temperatures, rainfall, insect problems, and diseases.

Planting and Transplanting

If you need to add color to your landscape, you will find that most nurseries carry a decent selection of warm-season bedding plants through the summer. You can also direct-seed some of the quick, easy annuals such as **amaranthus, cosmos, gaillardia, marigold, portulaca, sunflower,** and **zinnia.**

Since there are still three or four months left of the growing season, you can purchase smaller transplants available in cell-packs, or those in 4-inch pots if you want larger plants.

Watering

High temperatures place great stress on annual flower beds, and this time of the year can be very hot and dry. *Watch the weather and water appropriately.* Newly planted transplants will need more frequent irrigation than plants that are established. Seedbeds will need to be watered frequently enough to maintain a moist soil until the seeds sprout. Annuals in containers may need to be watered twice a day. Check prior to watering by touching the soil and, if needed, water thoroughly.

Fertilizing

July is probably the month we are least likely to fertilize our warm-season annuals. There are generally enough nutrients left in the soil from earlier fertilizer applications to keep plants vigorous. High temperatures can also lower the vigor and slow the growth of many plants, making them less needful of additional nutrients. *Continue to fertilize container plants.*

Pest Control

Over the next three months, be sure to *evaluate and record the performance of your annuals.* You will note striking differences in the amount of pest damage from one type of plant to the next. If you are trying to minimize pest problems in your landscape, plan to *plant more of the relatively pest-free types next time,* avoiding those that were more frequently attacked. Journal notes will help you remember the better plants to use next year.

Planting the same annual in the same bed year after year can lead to a buildup of disease organisms that like that particular plant. Root knot nematodes which attack and damage plant roots and fungus organisms (root rot, stem rot) are the leading culprits. If you have planted a bed with a particular annual successfully for several years and notice the plants are not doing as well as before, it may be time to rotate. It is usually better to *plant different bedding plants in beds every few years,* if not more often. This will also keep you from getting in a rut when it comes to color, types of plants, and planting designs.

In the cool of air-conditioned rooms, make notes and entries in your Texas gardening journal about what was done in your summer annual plantings and what you would like to do next season.

Helpful Hints

Working outside in especially hot weather places extra stresses on the body. Gardeners working outside may lose up to two quarts of water each hour. To prevent dehydration, drink before, during, and after working outside. Drink before you're thirsty, and drink cold liquids because they are absorbed by the body faster. Drink water if you can; if you choose other liquids, make sure they contain only a small amount of sugar, as sugar slows down liquid absorption by the body. Avoid beverages containing alcohol and caffeine.

Work in your garden in the early morning or late afternoon when it is cooler, and stay in shady areas as much as possible. Follow the shade in your landscape as the sun moves across the sky; leave areas as they become sunny and move into areas as they become more shaded.

Wear a hat and loose, comfortable clothing, and use sun screen. Take frequent breaks and try not to stay outside in the heat for extended periods.

Planning

August is a month of evaluation. True annuals planted earlier will often need to be replaced unless they are heat tolerant. Hanging baskets of annuals may also be past their prime, and may need to be replanted. Next year, use more heat-tolerant varieties.

Although milder weather is still about two months off, we should begin to think about the next transition, which will occur in late September or early October. What needs to be done now to make our flower beds look their best until cool-season annuals are planted in late October and November? This may include *cutting back or trimming, deadheading, staking or supporting, replacing plants, pest control, and fertilization.* Reworking and improving existing soil in beds for fall plantings is also a good idea at this time. Don't forget to note in your Texas gardening journal which plants are doing well in the August heat.

Excellent Heat-Tolerant Annuals and Tender Perennials

Under 2 feet:
- Bachelor's Button
- Blue Daze
- Celosia
- Coleus
- Dahlberg Daisy+
- Dusty Miller
- Dwarf Cosmos+
- Gaillardia
- Gomphrena
- Lantana
- Marigold+
- Mexican Heather
- Ornamental Peppers
- Periwinkle
- Portulaca+
- Purslane
- Salvia 'Lady in Red'
- Scaevola
- 'VIP' Petunias
- Wax Begonia
- Zinnia

Over 2 feet:
- Butterfly Weed
- Canna
- Cigar Flower
- Cleome+
- Cosmos+
- Four o'Clock+
- Hardy Hibiscus (Mallow)
- Mexican Sunflower (*Tithonia*)+
- Rudbeckia
- Salvias such as 'Mealy Blue Sage'
- Shrimp Plant
- Sunflower+

+Seeds may be planted in flats or direct-seeded this month where the plants are to grow.

Planting and Transplanting

Plant replacements for annuals that are no longer attractive. Check local nurseries for colorful, heat-tolerant bedding plants. Don't overlook colorful foliage plants such as **ornamental sweet potatoes, copper plant, Joseph's coat, coleus, dusty miller, purple leaf basil, lantana, 'Lady in Red' salvia,** and **blue daze.**

Care for Your Annuals

Larger-growing annuals often lean, sprawl, fall over, or simply grow too large for the plants around them to tolerate. This is especially common in mixed beds where a variety of annuals are planted together. *Stake, support, trim back, or even remove* those that are "overly enthusiastic" to make sure everybody has enough room.

Pruning

Tender perennials grown as annuals are expected to look good until late October, but they may be looking overgrown and/or a little "tired" now. Many will look better over the next two or three months if they are cut back now when warm temperatures will encourage rapid regrowth. Even though they are in bloom, trim them back one-third to one-half their height. It is worth the temporary loss of flowers to have more shapely, attractive plants for the late summer to fall period. *Don't put this off if you want better flowering in the fall.*

Fertilizing

Fertilize those annuals that you have pruned back to encourage regrowth. A light sprinkling of a 3:1:2 ratio premium-quality long-lasting slow-release granular-type will carry them through to the end of the season. If you used a slow-release granular early in the season, no additional fertilizer is needed now. It would still be good, however, to give the plants an application of your favorite soluble fertilizer to give them a little "kick."

Pest Control

It is not unusual to experience frequent afternoon showers along the Coast. These may wash off and reduce the effectiveness of many insect control aids. *Repeat applications as needed.* Damp weather also favors snails and slugs. *Continue to use baits, traps, and barriers as needed. Be on the lookout for insect pests. If they become a problem, get them identified at local nurseries and/or your County Agent's office. When and if control aids are needed, apply according to label directions. Refer to page 291 for a summary listing your options.*

Disease problems are difficult to deal with. While not as common as insect pests, diseases such as root rot or stem rot can be devastating. *Avoid root rot* by making sure beds are well drained and incorporate generous amounts of organic matter, preferably compost, into the bed during preparation. Don't plant transplants too deep or too close together and rotate plantings from year to year. Water deeply and occasionally, not lightly and frequently.

To avoid foliar diseases, *avoid wetting the foliage* when watering, if possible, and *water when the foliage will dry quickly.* Early morning is best. Good air circulation and proper spacing when planting also helps. Disease prevention and control aids are available at local retail nurseries. When selected for use, apply according to label directions.

Planning

Can it be that the hot season is almost over? Often, especially in north Texas, a cool front will come through sometime in September, relieving the intense heat of the last few months. We can begin to look forward to the upcoming mild weather and the cool season that will follow. Cool-season annual seed can be sown this month . . . if you haven't begun to think about plans for the cool-season annual garden yet, perhaps you should. Note in your Texas gardening journal which plants are doing well in September. Knowing which plants survived our heat and which colors you especially liked will aid you in planning for next spring/summer plantings.

Planting and Transplanting

It is too late to plant warm-season and too early to plant cool-season annual transplants in most of the state. Not much should be added to the flower garden now unless it is really necessary. You can still plant transplants of warm-season annuals, but we are getting toward the end of their season. Even a bare area is probably best mulched and held until next month, when cool-season annuals can be planted. In zones 6

and 7a it may cool sufficiently to plant cool-season annuals, as the weather may change from year to year. You can plant seeds of cool-season annuals in flats or small pots to raise for transplants, which will be planted in the garden in November and December. Note temperature requirements for germination; some cool-season annual seeds need cool temperatures to germinate.

Use a soilless potting mix to start seeds.

1 *Pre-moisten* the mix by blending it with some water in a bucket.

2 When moist but not soggy, place it into the seed-starting container and gently *firm* it with your hand.

3 *Plant* the seeds and *cover* to the depth recommended on the package.

4 Keep the container in a completely shaded area outside and make sure the mix stays moist (the container may be covered with clear plastic wrap to retain moisture).

5 When the seeds come up, *remove* any cover and *place* the container in a part-shady or part-sunny location, depending on the type of annual.

6 When seedlings are large enough to handle, gently *separate* them into small individual pots or cell-packs filled with pre-moistened soilless mix.

7 *Plant* when transplants are large enough to plant and when there is space for them in the garden.

Watering

We aren't out of the hot season yet. Continue to *monitor rainfall and water thoroughly when necessary.*

After months of growth, annuals in containers will have filled those containers with roots. Frequent watering is critical to plantings in this condition since the roots will deplete water in the soil rapidly. *Consider repotting into a larger pot* if watering once or twice a day is insufficient. Don't forget to keep your beds of annuals watered as needed.

Fertilizing

Other than making sure that container plantings are receiving adequate nutrients, little or no fertilization chores are needed this month.

Pest Control

Whiteflies are often a major pest on **lantana, hibiscus,** and a variety of other ornamentals. Control is difficult once they get out of hand. The adults are snow-white gnat-sized flies that fly up from the plant when disturbed. The larvae are attached to the underside of the foliage and look like pale green or whitish disks. Visit local retail nurseries for information on control aids. Refer to page 291 for a summary listing your options. After making your selection, apply according to label directions.

When using pest-control aids, read the label carefully and use according to directions.

Continue to deal with weed problems before they get out of control. The intense heat makes it easy to just let the garden go this time of year. Even if only for 10 or 15 minutes in the early morning or evening, spend a little time two or three times a week on weed control. Handweeding, weed-prevention aids, weed-blocking rolled products, and mulching 3 to 4 inches deep will all help keep weeds in annual plantings at a minimum.

Helpful Hints

Continue to make entries in your Texas gardening journal about the performance of your annual plantings. Sketches of bed layouts, lists of varieties used, and comments are all helpful to include in your notes. Photographs are priceless in recording how a garden turned out and are far more effective than words alone. Take pictures of your garden regularly and include them with your records.

Visit local and regional botanical gardens, arboretums, and other public gardens.

Planning

October is another transitional month when reliably milder weather relieves the heat of summer. Along with April, October is considered one of the most pleasant months of the year. Once again, it becomes a pleasure to get into the garden . . . and there's lots to do.

It is time to think about your cool-season annual garden and plants:

- What color schemes will you use in various beds?

- What types of plants will you select?

Look at your notes from the last cool season as you begin to make these plans and decisions.

Planting and Transplanting

Most flower beds are still full of attractive warm-season annuals. If you have some empty spots, some of the more heat-tolerant cool-season annuals may be planted. Select from **pansies, snapdragons, alyssum, annual phlox, calendula, dianthus,** and **nicotiana** (to name a few). *Prepare the beds properly* prior to planting with organic matter blended into the soil. We can have hot, muggy weather in October, particularly in the southern part of the state. If we do, early plantings of the popular **pansy** will often rot and need to be replaced. If you want to play it safe, wait until November to plant **pansies** and **violas** in these hot areas of Texas. In north Texas, start planting **pansies, violas,** and all other cool-season annuals if temperatures are below 70 degrees Fahrenheit during the day.

If you started seeds for transplants in community pots, it may be time to *separate them into cell-packs or individual pots.* Do not allow the seedlings to become too large and overly crowded before separating them.

You can direct-seed **poppies, larkspur, sweet pea, calendula,** and **alyssum** now. **Chrysanthemums** are often planted in flower beds this month. **Marigolds** are becoming a popular substitute—they provide some of the same yellow, gold, orange, and mahogany colors, but bloom longer than mums. *Look for marigold transplants in local nurseries.* These may be marketed as 'Mari-Mums'.

Watering

October may be a relatively dry month. *Water plantings as needed.* Pay special attention to any newly planted areas. It is generally best to water direct-seeded beds frequently enough to make sure the seeds do not dry out.

Fertilizing

When raising your own transplants, it's sometimes necessary to fertilize them. The soilless mixes used to grow transplants contain only enough nutrients for a few weeks. After transplants have been in new pots for about three weeks, begin to *fertilize them with your favorite soluble fertilizer.* Fertilize new plantings in beds at the time they are installed. We prefer premium-quality long-lasting slow-release granular fertilizers. Always apply fertilizer according to label directions.

Pest Control

Caterpillars can be a major problem on annuals now, and moths have had all summer to build up populations. Treat promptly with an approved insect-control aid according to label directions. Refer to page 291 for a summary listing your otpions.

Butterfly gardening has become very popular. Never use insect-control aids around those plants you have planted to attract adult butterflies (nectar plants) or caterpillars (larval food plants).

Planning

Finalize your plans for beds of cool-season bedding plants and plant them.

Have a good idea of the colors, heights and amounts needed, as well as the growing conditions in the areas to be planted, before you go to the nursery. Make notes in your Texas gardening journal so you will know what was planted and where, and which ones you enjoyed.

Planting and Transplanting

Along with May, November is the most active month for planting beds of annuals. Some will bloom well from now through next April (depending on the mildness of the winter), while others will save their best for the spring. **Pansies** are our most cold-hardy annuals and usually produce a colorful show all cool/cold season.

The hard decision now is what to do with the tender perennials that may still be looking attractive in our flower gardens. Tempting as it may be to leave them in the bed, they will eventually have to make way for cool-season plants.

In north Texas, go ahead and remove the tender perennials this

month, and plant the new plants. If you want to pot some of the removed plants, they will usually transplant successfully if they are not too large. In south Texas, leave them in the ground for a few more weeks if you like, but remove them and plant your cool-season annual transplants by early December, at the latest, if you want great cool/cold-season color. If this isn't desired, mulch well, and new color will be enjoyed next season.

Care for Your Annuals

You generally don't need to replace the potting mixture in containers when changing plantings. If the mix seems to be dense and compacted, *blend it with some sifted compost or peat moss along with some vermiculite or perlite*. If you decide to replace the mix, throw the old potting mix in your compost pile or a garden bed.

Watering

If you used soaker hoses to water warm-season annual beds, the hoses can be easily removed from the bed while you prepare it for the next planting. Once the bed is prepared and replanted, lay back the

soaker hose, snaking it throughout the bed area. *Cover the soaker hose with mulch* for a more attractive appearance.

Rain in November is usually adequate, but *water as needed*— especially your new plantings, containers, and transplants.

Fertilizing

Make sure you *add* organic matter during bed preparation. Fertilize transplants at the time of planting. Fertilize containerized color plants as needed.

Pest Control

With the onset of cooler weather, many insect and disease problems are reduced. Snails and slugs always seem to be waiting in the wings for an opportunity—*control as needed with baits, traps, and barriers.*

Wet weather can promote root rot. *Make sure beds are well drained.* If necessary, build up raised beds during bed preparation and add generous amounts of compost or other organic matter, including peat moss and ground bark, if you have had problems in the past.

Planning

Things should be coming together for your cool/cold-season flower beds in early December. Try to get most plantings done well before the holidays. You know you won't have time later. Make notes in your Texas gardening journal on which plants were planted where.

Planting and Transplanting

Continue to plant cool/cold-season annual seeds or transplants. Should temperatures below freezing be predicted, bring flats or pots of transplants that haven't been planted yet into a protected location for the night. Direct-seeded annuals will probably be fine, but if they are newly germinated and temperatures will drop to the mid- to low 20s Fahrenheit, *cover them.*

In beds where direct-seeding was done, remember to thin out the seedlings to the proper spacing before they get too crowded.

Care for Your Annuals

Annual beds should be mulched. Weeds do not take the winter off,

and oxalis, henbit, and chickweed along with many others are growing now. Mulches prevent weed seeds from germinating and can save tremendous amounts of effort and time. Mulches also help retain a considerable amount of the warmth stored in soil from summer. This encourages strong root systems to form on annuals during the cool season before their explosive growth in March. Maintain a mulch 3 to 4 inches deep.

Watering

Cool temperatures and adequate rainfall usually make watering this month less important. Keep an eye on newly planted or seeded beds and plants growing in containers. *Whenever a freeze threatens, water beds thoroughly.* Drought-stressed plants are less able to withstand subfreezing temperatures. When watering, do so thoroughly.

Fertilizing

Fertilize only if plants show deficiency symptoms such as pale leaves, stunted growth, and yellow lower leaves. Premium-quality long-lasting slow-release, and other forms of fertilizers may be used.

Pest Control

It is a relief to see insect and disease problems diminish. Weeds, however, are not so kind. Wood sorrel, a weed that looks like clover but has a sour taste when you bite a stem, is a persistent perennial weed that plagues many gardeners, particularly in south Texas where winters are milder. If you handweed, you must dig down and get the fleshy root or bulb from the ground. Where you can, spray the foliage of the wood sorrel with control aids of your choice. More than one application may be needed, and you must not get these aids on the foliage of nearby desirable plants. Refer to page 291 for a summary listing your options. Visits to retail nurseries will help you to decide which aids you want to use. Remember to always apply according to label directions.

Helpful Hints

We're always looking for nice gifts for the hosts of the parties and gatherings that come with the holiday season. Think about a basket filled with blooming cool/cold-season annuals growing in 4-inch pots, the pots hidden by sphagnum moss or greenery. They can be enjoyed this way inside for a few days, and then planted into the garden where they will continue to bloom for months. And don't forget your favorite gardeners on your list.

Bulbs, Corms, Rhizomes, and Tubers

Gardeners tend to use the term "bulb" for any fleshy, underground organ produced by a plant, and we'll conform to that tradition in this chapter. But the term actually refers to several botanically distinct structures including *true bulbs, corms, rhizomes, tubers,* and *tuberous roots.*

A **true bulb** consists of a compressed stem and a growing point or flower bud enclosed with thick, fleshy, modified leaves. In some bulbs, the fleshy leaves form concentric rings (onions), and in others, they look like thickened, overlapping scales (lilies). Examples of plants that produce true bulbs: **allium, amaryllis, crinum, clivia, garlic chives, hyacinth, lilies, narcissus, oxalis, rain lily** (*Zephyranthes*)**, society garlic, spider lilies** (*Lycoris*)**, tuberose,** and **tulip.**

A **corm** is a compressed, fleshy stem with a growing point on top. Roots grow only from the base. Corms can develop small buds around their base called cormels, which are useful in propagation. Examples of corms: **crocus, freesia** and **gladiolus.**

Rhizomes are fleshy, horizontal, underground stems. Shoots occur along the top and roots grow from the bottom. Plants that produce rhizomes include **canna, calla lily, agapanthus, gingers (hedychium, alpinia, zingiber, curcuma, costus, kaempferia), iris (bearded, Louisiana, Siberian, Japanese),** and **walking iris** (*Neomarica*).

Caladium

Tubers are similar to corms but tend to be more irregular in shape and have more growing points. Both shoots and roots arise from these growing points. Examples of tubers are **caladium** and **Jack-in-the-pulpit** (*Arisaema*).

Tuberous roots are thickened, fleshy roots. Often, as with **dahlias,** a portion of the crown or stem containing buds must be attached to the tuberous root in order for it to grow. Others, such as **sweet potatoes,** are able to grow shoots directly from the tuberous root. Some plants grown from tuberous roots are **dahlia, gloriosa lily, ornamental sweet potato,** and **ranunculus.**

Bulbs are divided into two groups according to their season of growth and bloom: spring or summer. Spring bulbs are planted in the fall and early December (**tulips** and **hyacinths** in late December and early January) and bloom from January through April. Summer bulbs, generally planted between March and May, are in active growth from March through November and bloom at some time during that period.

Planning the Spring Bulb Garden

Unfortunately, most spring-flowering bulbs originate in climates cooler than ours and do not rebloom well in our state, especially in south Texas.

Bulbs, Corms, Rhizomes, and Tubers

Determine where spring bulbs would make a nice addition to the landscape. Since several provide only one season of bloom, it may make better sense economically to use them to embellish rather than to produce lavish displays. Plant groups or drifts of bulbs among existing shrubs, flower beds, and ground covers, especially in areas where they can be appreciated up close.

True Bulb

Bulbs become available in local nurseries as early as September. Go ahead and purchase them, but there is no hurry to plant them. Purchasing early provides you the opportunity to choose from a good selection and get the bulbs you desire.

Selecting Spring Bulbs

Buy the largest bulbs of the best quality your budget will allow. With bulbs, you definitely get what you pay for. When choosing loose bulbs at a local nursery or garden center, pick the plumpest bulbs in the bin. They should be firm with no obvious cuts, soft spots, insects, or disease damage. When purchasing **daffodils,** look for double-nosed bulbs, which look like two bulbs joined together at the base.

Planting Spring Bulbs

Most spring-flowering bulbs require excellent drainage, so avoid low, wet areas, or use raised beds as necessary. Prepare the area for planting:

- Remove any unwanted weeds.

- *Turn* the soil 8 to 10 inches deep.

- *Spread* 4 to 6 inches of organic matter (compost, rotted manure, ground bark, peat moss) over the area and *blend* thoroughly.

- *Rake smooth,* dig appropriate holes, apply slow-release fertilizer, and *plant.*

It is important to plant bulbs at the proper depth. Dig individual holes, or excavate to the recommended depth the entire area to be planted, and plant all the bulbs at once.

Bulbs that are expected to rebloom reliably should be planted in areas that receive at least six hours of direct sunlight. This allows them to build up food reserves for next year's bloom. Bulbs that will be grown for just one season may be planted in shadier locations since they are discarded after blooming, although the same amount of direct sunlight is still preferred.

Care for Your Spring Bulbs

Keep areas planted with spring bulbs mulched and weed-free. Little supplemental watering is needed during our usually rainy winters.

Bulbs grown as annuals may be removed from the bed anytime after they finish flowering. Repeat-blooming bulbs may simply be left in the ground from year to year. This works best in settled situations such as in front of shrubs, at the base of deciduous trees, or in areas of low-growing ground covers. If the bulbs are growing in a location where you intend to plant something else to bloom during the summer, they may be lifted, stored, and replanted in the fall. Another option is to mark the location of the bulbs and plant around them.

In order for repeat-blooming bulbs to bloom the following year, you must allow the foliage to persist after flowering. Do not cut back the leaves until they have turned mostly yellow.

Bulbs, Corms, Rhizomes, and Tubers

Planning Your Summer Bulb Garden

Most summer-flowering bulbs are native to tropical or subtropical climates and will reliably bloom here for many years in zones 8 and 9. Indeed, for some of these plants the trick is not getting them to grow but keeping them under control. In zones 6 and 7, mulch heavily and hope for regrowth or lift, store, and replant each year.

These plants offer a wide variety of uses in the landscape, providing valuable additions to flower beds, perennial borders, ground covers, and containers. Think carefully about the characteristics of each type of bulb and the growing conditions it needs. Then determine where the bulbs will grow and look best before you plant.

Planting Your Summer Bulbs

Generally, dig 2 to 4 inches of organic matter (such as compost, finely ground pine bark, rotted manure, or sphagnum peat moss) into the area before you plant your bulbs. Raise beds to improve drainage if necessary. A light sprinkling of premium-quality long-lasting slow-release granular fertilizer

every six to eight weeks during active growth (beginning in March and ending in August) is sufficient for most summer bulbs. A granular rose fertilizer applied according to label directions usually works well for summer bulbs.

Care for Your Summer Bulbs

Indeed, no matter what situation you have—from shady to sunny and from dry to wet conditions—at least a few kinds of bulbs will thrive there. Most summer bulbs prefer good drainage. **Calla, canna, crinum, spider lily** (*Hymenocallis),* **Louisiana iris, blue flag, yellow flag,** and some **gingers** are a few exceptions. Full to partial sun (six or more hours of direct sunlight) is needed by most of these plants for healthy growth and flowering, although many, such as **achimenes, caladium, gingers,** and **bletilla,** do fine in shadier spots. **Crinum** is one of the most dependable summer-blooming bulb plant groups we grow in Texas.

Many summer bulbs have a dormancy period when foliage dies off and the bulb rests. This period generally occurs during winter. At that time, yellow or brown foliage may be trimmed back to the ground. Place markers where the dormant

bulbs are located so you won't accidentally dig into them later. Avoid removing any of a bulb's foliage when it is healthy and green.

Most summer bulbs are best propagated by dividing the clumps in early March. Some bulbs, such as **bearded iris,** do best when divided every year or two, while others, like **agapanthus,** prefer to be left alone.

The following lists include many of the best summer-flowering bulbs for Texas. Those marked with a plus sign (+) may be better suited to the southern part of the state in zones 8 and 9, but could be grown successfully farther north with a thick winter mulch and well-drained beds.

Summer bulbs for full to partial sun are: **agapanthus, belamcanda, canna, crinum, crocosmia, dahlia, dietes, eucomis+, garlic chives** (*Allium tuberosum*), **gladiolus, gloriosa lily+, habranthus, hymenocallis, iris (bearded, Siberian), lilies, oxalis, tigridia, society garlic** (*Tulbaghia violacea*), **zephyranthes.**

Summer bulbs for partial shade to shade are: *Arum italicum,* **achimenes+, alpinia+, bletilla, caladium, clivia+, crinum, costus, curcuma, globba, hedychium, hymenocallis, kaempferia+, oxalis, walking iris** (*Neomarica*)+.

Spring Bulbs

Name	Plant	Depth	Spacing	Blooms
Allium (Flowering Onion)	Sept. to Dec.	2 in. to 4 in.	4 in. to 12 in.	April to May
Anemone	Oct. to early Dec.	1 in.	6 in. to 8 in.	March to May
Arisaema	Oct. to early Dec.	2 in. to 4 in.	8 in. to 12 in.	March to May
Bletilla (Ground Orchid)	Sept. to April	1 in.	6 in. to 8 in.	March to April
Crocus	Oct. to early Dec.	2 in.	2 in. to 3 in.	Feb. to March
Hippeastrum (Amaryllis)	Sept. to Dec. in pots. April in garden.	Neck of bulb exposed	8 in. to 12 in.	Nov. to Jan. in pots. April in garden.
Hyacinth	late Dec. to early Jan.	3 in. to 4 in.	4 in. to 6 in.	March
Iris, Dutch (bulbous)	Oct. to early Dec.	2 in. to 4 in.	4 in. to 6 in.	March to April
Iris, Louisiana, Siberian, Japanese, Bearded (rhizomatous)	Sept. to Feb.	Just below soil surface	12 in. to 18 in.	March to May
Leucojum (Snowflake)	Oct. to early Dec.	4 in.	4 in. to 6 in.	April
Lily, Easter	Oct. to early Dec.	4 in.	8 in. to 12 in.	April to May
Muscari (Grape Hyacinth)	Oct. to early Dec.	2 in.	2 in. to 4 in.	March to April
Narcissus (including Daffodils)	Oct. to early Dec.	4 in.	4 in. to 6 in.	Jan. to April
Ornithogalum (Star of Bethlehem)	Oct. to early Dec.	4 in.	4 in.	April
Ranunculus	Oct. to early Dec.	1 in.	8 in.	April to May
Spanish Bluebell (*Hyacinthioides hispanicus*)	Oct. to early Dec.	4 in. to 6 in.	4 in.	April
Spring Starflower (*Ipheion Uniflorum*)	Oct. to early Dec.	2 in. to 3 in.	3 in. to 6 in.	March to May
Sisyrinchium (Blue-eyed Grass)	Oct. to early Dec.	2 in.	4 in. to 6 in.	April
Tulip	Late Dec. to early Jan.	4 in. to 6 in.	4 in. to 8 in.	March to April
Zantedeschia (Calla Lily)	Sept. to Nov. (bulbs). March to May (plants).	2 in. to 3 in.	12 in. to 18 in.	April to May

Notes: Because they bloom in the spring, amaryllis, Louisiana iris, calla lily, and bletilla are grouped with the spring bulbs. However, their foliage persists through the summer and they should be handled as summer bulbs.

Check with local nurseries and/or Extension Service/County Agent offices when uncertain of exact planting dates for your garden. Texas has four USDA Plant Hardiness Zones with two subzones in each of these. The planting dates listed usually work for a large part of Texas.

Summer Bulbs

Name	Plant	Depth	Spacing	Blooms
Achimenes	May to June	1 in.	4 in. to 6 in.	June to Oct.
Agapanthus	March to Aug.	1 in.	8 in. to 12 in.	May to June
Alpinia (Shell Ginger)	March to Aug.	1 in.	1 ft. to 5 ft.	May to June
Belamcanda (Blackberry Lily)	March to April	1 in.	8 in. to 12 in.	June to Aug.
Caladium	April to July	1 in. to 2 in.	6 in. to 12 in.	Foliage May to Oct.
Canna	March to Aug.	1 in. to 2 in.	12 in. to 18 in.	May to Nov.
Clivia	March to Aug.	1 in.	18 in. to 24 in.	March to May
Costus (Spril Ginger)	March to Aug.	1 in.	1 ft. to 2 ft.	June to Oct.
Crinum	March to Aug.	Neck of bulb exposed	1 ft. to 3 ft.	April to Oct.
Curcuma (Hidden Lily Ginger)	March to Aug.	1 in. to 2 in.	1 ft. to 2 ft.	May to Aug.
Dahlia	March to May	4 in.	8 in. to 18 in.	May to Oct.
Daylily (*Hemerocallis*)	Oct. to Dec.	4 in.	12 in. to 18 in.	May to June
Dietes (African Iris)	March to Sept.	1 in.	1 ft. to 3 ft.	April to June
Elephant Ear (Colocasia, Alocasia)	April to Aug.	Neck of bulb exposed	2 ft. to 3 ft.	Foliage spring to frost
Eucomia (Pineapple Lily)	Sept. to Nov.	Neck of bulb exposed	18 in.	May
Gladiolus	Feb. to March	4 in. to 6 in.	6 in.	April to June
Globba (Dancing Lady Ginger)	April to Sept.	1 in.	1 ft.	July to Oct.
Gloriosa Lily	March to April	4 in.	8 in. to 12 in.	May to Aug.
Habranthus	Sept. to Dec.	1 in.	8 in.	May to July
Hedychium (Butterfly Ginger)	March to Sept.	1 in.	1 ft. to 2 ft.	May to Nov.
Hymenocallis (Spider Lily)	March to Sept.	Neck of bulb exposed	1 ft. to 3 ft.	June to Aug.
Kaempferia (Peacock Ginger)	April to Aug.	1 in.	8 in. to 12 in.	June to Sept.
Iris (Bearded, Siberian)	Oct. to Feb.	1 in.	12 in.	April to May
Lily (Phillipine, Tiger)	March	4 in. to 6 in.	1 ft.	July to Sept.
Lycoris (Spider Lily, Naked Ladies)	March to Aug.	3 in. to 4 in.	4 in.	Sept. to Oct.
Neomarica (Walking Iris)	March to Aug.	1 in.	8 in. to 12 in.	May
Oxalis (*O. regnellii* and *O. triangularis*)	March to Sept.	1 in. to 2 in.	6 in. to 8 in.	March to Nov.
Sprekelia (Aztec Lily)	March to April	Neck of bulb exposed	8 in. to 12 in.	May
Tigridia (Tiger Flower)	March to May	4 in.	8 in.	May to June
Tuberose (Polianthes)	Feb. to April	1 in. to 2 in.	8 in.	June to July
Tulbaghia (Society Garlic)	March to Sept.	1 in.	10 in.	April to Nov.
Zephyranthes (Rain Lily)	Oct. to Feb.	1 in. to 2 in.	2 in. to 3 in.	Spring to fall
Zingiber (Pine Cone Ginger)	March to Sept.	1 in.	1 ft. to 2 ft.	July to Sept.

Note: Plant dormant bulbs, divisions, or container-grown plants early in the planting time given. Later in the planting time given, it's best to choose container-grown bulbs in active growth.

Texas has four USDA Plant Hardiness Zones; zones 6 through 9 with subzones in each of these. Suggested planting dates listed above usually work for a large portion of Texas. Check with local nurseries and/or your County/Extension Agent's office for exact planting dates for your area.

Planning

Start keeping simple records or a journal of your bulb-gardening efforts. This information is invaluable for future projects. Keep track of where you obtain your bulbs, when they are planted, when they bloom, and their overall performance. Include helpful information such as major pest problems, where the bulbs were planted, height and spread of growth, and weather conditions. Look through catalogs and choose summer bulbs to add to your landscape. Purchase locally if possible. Most summer-blooming bulbs can be planted in March and April, so make sure you select yours in time for timely planting. Try something different like **blackberry lily, gloriosa lily, crinum,** or one of the **gingers. Crinum** is a super bulb for Texas gardens.

If it was not done in December, it's time to get those **tulips** and **hyacinths** out of the refrigerator and plant them. This task needs to be finished by mid-month. Take an inventory of what you have (in case you've forgotten since storing them), and decide where everything is to be planted. A little planning before you get the bulbs out will make planting go faster.

Decide if you want to grow some bulbs in containers. It's not hard to do, and nothing beats a pot of **tulips** or **hyacinths** blooming indoors.

Planting

Plant prechilled **tulips** *and* **hyacinths** *into the garden now.* Both are planted about 4 inches deep in well-prepared beds. In north Texas, where **tulips** and **hyacinths** are more likely to rebloom, plant in an area that receives at least six hours of direct sunlight if you want to use the same bulbs next year. In south Texas, a few poor-quality blooms, if any, will be produced the following year. Since bulbs will be discarded after blooming, you can plant in shadier areas. **Species tulips** are the most dependable tulips available, reblooming successfully annually.

Tulips, hyacinths, and other bulbs you have kept refrigerated for growing in containers should be potted now. Remember, **tulips** and **hyacinths** are the only two common bulb groups that need prechilling before planting.

1 *Fill* a container which has drainage holes about two-thirds with potting soil.

2 Place enough bulbs, pointed end up, on the soil surface to fill the container without the bulbs touching. *Plant* tulip bulbs with the flat sides facing the wall of the pot. The first leaf of each bulb will grow facing the outside, creating a more attractive planting.

3 *Add* slow-release fertilizer.

4 *Add* soil until just the tips of the bulbs show, and *water* thoroughly.

5 Place the containers outside in shade and keep the soil evenly moist.

6 When the sprouts are about 1 inch high, *move the pots* into a sunny location. Continue to water the pots regularly. If temperatures below 28 degrees Fahrenheit are predicted, move the pots to a cool location that will not freeze.

7 *Move the pots* back outside as soon as possible.

8 When the flower buds begin to show color, *move them indoors* and enjoy.

To speed up bloom, leave inside after buds begin to grow. Keep the plants as cool as possible and the flowers will last longer.

Hyacinths may also be planted in bowls filled with pebbles. Bury the bulbs two-thirds deep in pebbles, such as pea gravel, and add enough water to touch the bottoms of the bulbs. Maintain water at that level. Place in west- or south-facing locations and enjoy. Individual **hyacinth** bulbs may also be grown in a special hyacinth vase shaped like an hourglass. **Hyacinths** are incredibly fragrant and wonderful to have indoors.

Care for Your Bulbs

Spring bulbs planted in the fall are up and growing. Do not be concerned about freezing temperatures damaging the leaves. Some early bulbs, such as **paper-white narcissus,** may already be blooming in south Texas. **Paper-white narcissus** are super easy to force indoors. Plant some every two weeks for fra-

grant blooms indoors all winter long. **Narcissus** in the garden will often bloom in December in zones 8 and 9, though the flowers and flower buds are susceptible to cold injury. If a severe freeze threatens blooming bulbs, cut the flowers and put them in vases to enjoy indoors.

Little additional water or fertilizer is needed by most bulbs growing in the landscape. Be sure to keep beds weeded, mulched, and watered when needed.

If the foliage of summer bulbs is frost-damaged and unattractive, cut it to the ground. Make sure tender bulbs have a 6-inch layer of mulch over them for protection, especially in north Texas. Pine straw is ideal; it does not pack down and provides excellent insulation. Pine bark mulch or nuggets, clean hay, and dried leaves also work well for cold protection.

Our ground never freezes in Texas, and some gardeners leave tender summer bulbs in the ground during the winter if their soil drains well. North Texas gardeners might choose to dig and store bulbs in frost-free conditions over the winter, but it is generally not necessary. Bulbs commonly lifted and stored include **caladium** and **gladiolus** because they are prone to rot in wet, cool soil. Check stored bulbs occasionally to make sure they are doing

fine. Zones 8b and 9 are the best zones for leaving the tender summer bulbs in the ground if you desire to do so.

Watering

Pots of spring bulbs should be watered as needed to keep the soil moist. Don't overdo it. Until the bulbs produce roots and begin to grow, the pots will dry out slowly. Soil that is constantly wet will promote rot. Growing in well-drained potting soil also helps because it rapidly drains water away from bulbs.

Planning

If you are still haunting retailers who offer colorful summer bulbs or drooling over catalogs that have pictures of these bulbs, make your decisions soon and purchase locally or send in your order. Make sure you have appropriate locations in your landscape to grow the bulbs you purchase. Although we all do it, wandering around your yard with a bag of bulbs looking for a place to plant them is not the best idea.

If you are unfamiliar with a bulb, get as much information as you can. Purchase just a few to see how well they grow for you before making a major investment.

Next month is a good time to divide most summer bulbs (excluding **Louisiana irises** and **calla lilies,** which are in active growth in zones 8 and 9). It's not too soon to decide which bulbs you want to divide. Plan on what will be done with the extra bulbs, whether they'll be planted in other areas of the landscape, given to friends, traded for other plants, or donated to school or public gardens. Don't forget to make entries in your Texas gardening journal this month.

Early spring bulbs such as **crocus** and early **narcissus** generally bloom this month. Note the times bulbs bloom in your yard in your journal for future reference.

Planting

Resist spring-flowering bulbs that are put on clearance sale. They are unlikely to do well if planted this late. Exceptions are **amaryllis** and **paper-white narcissus.** If you find bulbs in good shape that haven't started to sprout yet, they will usually bloom if they are planted now. The most successful reblooming of **paper-whites** and non-hardy **amaryllis** occurs in zones 8b and 9.

Plant **gladiolus** bulbs starting in February, in south Texas and in March in north Texas. For blooms in May and June, continue to plant groups of gladiolus at two-week intervals through April. It is best for **gladiolus** to bloom before the intense heat arrives, and thrips can be a major problem, damaging flowers later in the summer.

Procrastinator's alert: Shame on you if you haven't planted your refrigerated bulbs by now. They may still do fine. Either plant the bulbs now or throw them away. You cannot hold them until next season for planting.

In mid- to late February for zones 8b and 9 and in late March for zones 6 through 8a, plant **caladium** bulbs in flats of sifted compost or potting soil to get a head start. Individual bulbs may also be planted in 4-inch pots.

1 *Plant* the bulbs about 1 inch deep and keep the soil moist.

2 Place the flats in a warm location.

3 When the bulbs sprout, move the flats to a sunny windowsill, greenhouse, or hot bed where they will receive plenty of light. Plant growing bulbs into the garden after soil temperature is 60+ degrees Fahrenheit.

Care for Your Bulbs

A light application of a premium-quality long-lasting slow-release granular fertilizer is appropriate for **Louisiana iris, calla lily,** and fall-planted spring-flowering bulbs that are in active growth. Check the label and follow the manufacturer's recommendations for the product you choose. In Texas, most of our landscape plant materials do well with granular rose fertilizer or 3:1:2 ratio fertilizers such as 15:5:10.

If a severe freeze threatens, cut any open flowers from blooming bulbs and put them in vases inside, as they are likely to be damaged.

Continue to care for spring bulbs growing in containers outside. Bring them in on nights when temperatures below 28 degrees Fahrenheit are predicted.

Watch spring bulbs that have been overplanted with cool-season annuals. Make sure the bulbs are growing well, and trim the annuals slightly if needed to allow the bulbs room to grow.

Check summer bulbs you have dug up and stored. If any are sprouting, pot them and provide a bright, warm location for growth.

Watering

Natural rainfall is generally plentiful this month. If it is unusually dry, however, thoroughly water bulbs that are actively growing in beds, as needed. *Water bulbs growing in containers as needed. Do not keep bulbs grown in beds or pots wet—"moist" is the key word here.*

Pest Control

Stored **caladiums** occasionally become infested with mealybugs, which appear on bulbs and look like a white, cottony substance. You may *dip* or *spray* the bulbs with approved insect-control aids applied according to label directions. Refer to page 291 for a summary listing your options. Another alternative is to plant them in well-drained relatively warm soil as directed on the previous page under Planting. Mealybugs cannot survive underground.

Pest problems are unlikely at this time on bulbs that are growing outside. If the weather is mild, snails and slugs may be a problem. Control with baits or traps.

Planning

The coldest weather has passed and spring bulbs really begin to "wow" us this month. Don't forget to take notes on the performance of bulbs in your landscape. Take photos and/or make videotapes for an excellent record of how things looked. Do this about once a week during the prime blooming season. Enter your written information in your Texas gardening journal. Include photographs with your written entries.

Make decisions on where to plant summer-flowering bulbs. The location should provide the growing conditions needed for best performance. Decide if established plantings have grown beyond their designated spot. Plan to lift and divide them this month, or in April at the latest.

Purchase summer-flowering bulbs locally if available or from catalogs so you will have them to plant in April and May. Don't let your enthusiasm lead you to buy more bulbs than you have room to plant, and try to have a definite purpose and location in mind for the bulbs you select. Keep records of where and what you purchased locally and/or mail-ordered. Check with your local nursery to find out what kind of summer bulbs they intend to carry and when they will be in. This will allow you to select your bulbs early. It is usually best to look at a bulb "in person" before purchasing.

Planting

Plant summer-flowering bulbs into the garden beginning this month in south Texas and in April for north Texas gardeners.

- *Plant* at the proper depth and spacing (see chart on page 49) into beds or areas where 4 inches of organic matter have been incorporated into the soil.

- Apply premium-quality long-lasting slow-release granular fertilizer according to label directions in each planting hole prior to installing your bulbs.

- *Water in* thoroughly and apply about 2 inches of mulch.

- *Add* more mulch to create a layer 3 or 4 inches thick as the bulbs grow. Don't be alarmed if they don't take off and grow rapidly right away. Most bulbs will wait until April or even early May to produce vigorous growth.

This is also the time to dig, divide, and transplant summer bulbs you already have in your garden. Most bulbs benefit from being divided every two to three years, including **bearded iris.** If you noticed last year that the plants were growing but flower production was not what it had been, consider dividing the clump. Division is an excellent way to create new plants. *Plant* the extras in new areas of the landscape, or share them with friends. Consider donating bulbs (especially if they are rare or unusual) to local public gardens, church fund-raisers, or schools.

Care for Your Bulbs

Remove faded flowers and developing seedpods from spring-flowering bulbs that are to be kept for bloom next year. Do not remove any of the green foliage, and *fertilize* them if you did not do so last month. We prefer long-lasting slow-release granular fertilizers. Spring-flowering bulbs that are being grown as annuals can be pulled up and discarded any time after flowering. Chop them up and put them in your compost pile.

Remove any dead or cold-damaged foliage from summer bulbs before new shoots have grown substantially. This makes the job much easier.

Bring spring-flowering bulbs grown in pots indoors when buds show color or begin to grow. As wonderful as they are in the garden, spring bulbs enliven the indoors with their beauty and fragrance as few other flowers do.

Watering

It is seldom necessary to do much watering of spring-flowering bulbs, but warm, dry weather occasionally makes it necessary. Pay attention to rainfall, and water plants if needed. Newly planted or transplanted summer bulbs will need more attention. Their root systems are not yet well developed, and they will benefit from irrigation as needed if rain does not occur. Continue to water spring bulbs in containers as well as any summer bulbs you've started in pots or flats as needed. When watering any bulbs, do so thoroughly.

Helpful Hint

Sometimes **Louisiana irises** get a little top-heavy when in bloom. Stake them if they begin to lean or fall over. Small bamboo stakes and strips of nylon stockings work well for this.

To extend blooming periods, move potted spring bulbs outside or to a cool garage at night. Warm indoor temperatures shorten the life of the flowers, and exposing them to cooler temperatures at night can help them last a little longer.

Salvage potted **Easter lilies** when they are finished blooming. See April Helpful Hints (page 57) to learn how to do it.

If you grew spring bulbs such as **hybrid tulips** or **hyacinths** in containers, throw them away when they finish. If the bulbs are a type that rebloom reliably in Texas, such as **narcissus,** you can plant them into the garden as soon as they finish flowering. They may skip a year, but should eventually begin to bloom again.

Pest Control

Weeds: Do not let weed problems get ahead of you. *Mild temperatures will encourage weeds to grow.* Many cool-season annual weeds like henbit, chickweed, and annual bluegrass are beginning to bloom and set seed now. Don't let that happen! *Remove* weeds promptly and keep beds mulched 3 to 4 inches deep.

Pests: Snails, slugs, and caterpillars may chew holes in leaves or flowers, but damage is generally minor. Control caterpillars with approved aids. Use baits or traps for snails and slugs. If you see toads while working in the garden, remember that they are excellent predators of slugs.

Visit your local nurseries at this time to review insect pest-control aids. Refer to page 291 for a summary listing your options.

Planning

What a beautiful time of year! Texas gardeners often consider April and October two of our finest gardening months. Mild temperatures and abundant flowers create a gardener's paradise.

Spring-flowering bulbs continue to grace flower beds with their charming beauty. Don't let the season pass without making some notes about the performance of the different bulbs you planted. Take pictures of or videotape your garden for a visual record words could never capture. Enter this information and photographs in your Texas gardening journal.

It is getting late for purchasing or ordering some summer bulbs, so get to it as soon as possible. Always purchase locally if the bulbs you want are available. It's good to visit bulbs "in person" if possible. However, don't rule out sites on the Internet when selecting and ordering bulbs. Many companies that send out catalogs also have a website where you can order bulbs directly, which can speed things up considerably. There is usually growing information as well as lists of other resources available at these sites. Many summer bulbs grow vigorously and make large plants, even during their first year. Keep in mind how tall the plants will grow, along with their projected spread, when planning on where to plant them.

Louisiana irises reach their peak this month in south Texas and next month in north Texas. Now is a good time to assess color combinations and how crowded the plantings are becoming. Write down what you see in your Texas gardening journal. Let this help guide you when it is time to divide and transplant these irises in August, September, or October.

Planting

Check local nurseries and garden centers for summer-flowering bulbs. **Tuberous begonias** tempt many gardeners every year. Unfortunately, they are poorly adapted to our hot summer conditions and performance is disappointing. Otherwise, as the summer bulb chart (page 49) indicates, there are lots of great bulbs to choose from.

It's time to plant bulbs you started in pots or flats. Bulbs such as **achimenes, alpinia, arum, bletilla, caladium, clivia, costus, crinum, curcuma, globba, hedychium, hymenocallis, kaempferia, oxalis,** and **walking iris** may be planted into shady beds that receive two to four hours of direct sunlight.

Good choices for sunnier areas (six to eight hours of direct sunlight) are **agapanthus, belamcanda, canna, crinum, crocosmia, dahlia, dietes, eucomis, garlic chives, gladiolus, gloriosa lily, habranthus, hymenocallis, iris, lilies, oxalis, tigridia, society garlic,** and *Zephyranthes*.

Plant bulbs into well-prepared beds. If you are creating a new bed, follow these steps:

1 *Remove* any unwanted weeds or turf.

2 *Turn* the soil 8 to 10 inches deep.

3 *Spread* 4 inches of organic matter (compost, rotted manure, peat moss) over the area and *blend*.

4 *Combine* soil and organic matter thoroughly, *rake smooth,* add premium-quality long-lasting slow-release granular fertilizer to each planting hole, and *plant.*

When planting into established beds, it's generally sufficient to simply dig in organic matter and a little fertilizer in each planting hole prior to planting. Most summer bulbs are planted close to the soil surface (see summer bulb chart on page 49).

In zones 8b and 9, now is the time to plant cold-tender **amaryllis** bulbs that were purchased in the fall and potted for bloom over the winter. Hardy amaryllis may be planted in all Texas zones. Choose a location that receives partial sun (four to six hours) and afternoon shade. They will bloom beautifully each April and May. You may also continue to grow the cold-tender types in a container.

Care for Your Bulbs

Do not remove the foliage of repeat-blooming spring-flowering bulbs until it is mostly yellow.

Helpful Hint

Summer bulbs make great candidates for container growing. A bronze-leaf **canna** surrounded by white **caladiums** in a large container is a real show-stopper. **Achimenes** are ideal in hanging baskets. Place containers on decks and patios, and at entrances. An added benefit of growing summer bulbs in containers is the ability to move plants around to suit your changing needs or impulses.

Salvage potted **Easter lilies:**

1 As soon as the flowers fade, trim them off. Do not remove any of the green foliage.

2 Plant the **lilies** in a well-drained prepared spot outside that receives morning sun and afternoon shade.

3 The bulbs will go dormant in mid- to late summer, and at that time the yellow foliage may be removed. **Mark** where the bulbs are located. Each year they will begin growth some time in October or November, grow very little over the winter, put on a burst of growth in spring, and bloom again in late April or early May.

Watering

April can be somewhat dry. It is especially important to keep newly planted summer-flowering bulbs watered as they grow and establish their root systems. Mulch beds to conserve moisture and reduce drying. Water established beds as needed to maintain a moist soil in the root zone. When you irrigate, do so thoroughly.

Pest Control

Weeds: Warmer weather increases pest problems. Continue to keep bulb beds mulched 3 to 4 inches deep to prevent weed problems.

Pests: Caterpillars may be a problem, especially the highly destructive canna leaf roller. Treat with the appropriate aid as needed. Refer to page 291 for a summary listing your options. Follow label directions carefully.

Animals: Cats are attracted to freshly turned soil and will use beds as litter boxes. Avoid this by mulching immediately, especially with pine straw. Use commercially available animal-repellant aids in problem areas.

Planning

The foliage of spring-flowering bulbs may be cut back if yellow, and most gardeners are quite ready to do so after watching it gradually flop over and turn yellow. Decide which repeat-blooming spring-flowering bulbs will be left in place and which will be lifted and stored. Lift bulbs from spots where you want to rework the bed and plant colorful summer bedding plants. Enter notes in your Texas gardening journal about the bulbs you enjoyed best.

Do you need more summer bulbs? Continue to look at your landscape and flower beds for possible planting sites. Anticipate the abundant growth summer bulbs such as **canna, gingers,** and **crinum** can produce, and avoid overplanting. *Procrastinator's alert: Last chance to order summer bulbs from catalogs to plant no later than June.* Or purchase and plant those bulbs available at local nurseries.

Planting

Continue to add summer bulbs to the landscape. **Agapanthus** is in bloom this month and the nurseries will have container-grown plants available. When planting summer bulbs that are growing in containers, follow these steps:

1 **Remove** the plant from the container.

2 Slightly *loosen* or untangle the roots if tightly packed.

3 **Dig** hole to accommodate soil-ball size, add premium-quality long-lasting slow-release granular fertilizer, and *plant* so that the top of the rootball is even with the soil in the bed.

4 **Firm the soil** around the roots with your hands.

5 **Water in** to finish settling the soil around the roots and mulch 3 to 4 inches deep.

If you haven't tried some, let us suggest a planting of **dwarf cannas.** They are available in super colors and great foliage. Mass plantings make an outstanding impact in the landscape.

Care for Your Bulbs

Summer bulbs are in vigorous growth now and many have begun to bloom. In bloom this month are **shell gingers, hidden lily gingers, canna, crinum, clivia, dietes, agapanthus, gladiolus, gloriosa lily, Siberian iris, walking iris, tropical crocus (Kaempferia), oxalis, sprekelia, society garlic,** and **rain lilies,** among others. The severity of the previous winter has a substantial influence on how early summer bulbs will begin to bloom. The colder the winter, the later flowers will appear.

As flowers fade, *trim* them off to keep the plant looking neat. With plantings such as **crinum** and **agapanthus,** flowers are produced on a thick stalk. When a stalk finishes flowering, *cut* it back to where it emerges from the leaves. Others, such as **gingers** and **canna,** produce flowers at the top of leafy shoots. Each shoot blooms only once. When the flowers have faded, you can just *cut off* the dead flowers, leaving foliage, or *cut* the entire shoot back down to the ground.

If you dig or lift spring-flowering bulbs, *store* in something that will "breathe." The net bags that onions are purchased in are ideal. Nylon stockings, paper bags, or cardboard boxes with ventilation holes also work well. Do not use plastic bags.

Label the bulbs carefully to prevent confusion when it comes time to plant them next fall. Store the bulbs in cool, dry places with good air circulation. Avoid garages, sheds, and other locations where high temperatures and humidity during the summer make for poor storage conditions.

Watering

As the weather gets hotter, bulbs will usually require more frequent watering if there is not enough rain. It is better to water thoroughly and occasionally than to water lightly and frequently. Use sprinklers or soaker hoses for proper watering. Do not set sprinklers or yourself on any schedule. Do water when needed.

Fertilizing

Fertilize bulbs growing in containers with your favorite soluble fertilizer, dissolved in water and applied as a solution, or use a premium-quality long-lasting slow-release granular fertilizer. When using water-soluble fertilizers, regularly fertilize bulbs in containers, as the constant watering they require rapidly washes out available nutrients. Using premium-quality long-lasting slow-release granular fertilizers will require much less frequent applications than water-soluble types. Bulbs growing in the ground can be fertilized as needed to encourage vigorous growth. It is easiest to use a premium-quality long-lasting slow-release fertilizer once in spring. You can also use a standard 3:1:2 ratio granular fertilizer once every six to eight weeks. *Follow package directions carefully.*

Pest Control

One of the great things about growing summer bulbs is that they are not particularly afflicted by major pest problems. Aphids occasionally infest new growth and flowers buds. **Cannas** are affected the most, as they are prone to the dreaded canna leaf roller. This pest can be so invasive that some gardeners give up trying to grow **cannas.** Leaf miners may attack **irises.** Caterpillars will chew holes in the leaves. They are generally a minor problem on other summer bulbs. All of these pests and others can be controlled by various insect-control aids. Refer to page 291 for a summary listing your options. Visit local retail garden centers for assistance in pest identification and selecting specific control aids. Remember to read and follow label directions when applying any gardening aid.

Planning

Catalogs for spring-flowering bulbs are arriving in the mail. There is no hurry to order, but it is impossible to resist looking through them as soon as they come in. As you flip through the catalogs, it wouldn't hurt to begin to make some notes on who has what on sale, or what new bulbs you might want to try. These photographs also make great reference materials in your Texas gardening journal.

Bulbs in the landscape have pretty much filled in their spaces by now, and you can assess the need for any additional planting. Avoid overcrowding beds. Don't overlook the use of bulbs in containers on patios, decks, porches, and other outdoor areas. Evaluate your plantings and make entries in your Texas gardening journal.

Planting

Most planting now should be done using actively growing bulbs in containers. This is the last month to plant most unsprouted bulbs. Exceptions are fall-flowering bulbs such as **spider lily** (*Lycoris*)—also known as **hurricane lily** or **naked ladies**—and **fall crocus** (*Colchicum*).

Try one of the **ornamental sweet potatoes.** Three commonly available cultivars are 'Blackie', 'Margarita', and 'Tricolor', also known as 'Pink Frost'. 'Blackie' produces very dark purple foliage on a vigorous vine suitable for hanging baskets, containers, ground cover, weaving among other plants in a bed, or training up a support. 'Margarita' has leaves that are a bright yellow-green and can be used in the same manner as 'Blackie'. 'Tricolor' is colorful but subtle, with light-green leaves generously splashed with white and pale pink. It is less vigorous than the other two and looks smashing in hanging baskets or around the edge of a large pot. All do well in full to partial sun and thrive on summer heat.

Cannas and **iris** may also be planted this month.

Care for Your Bulbs

Seedpods will sometimes form after a summer bulb has bloomed. Unless you are breeding the plants or want to grow some from seeds, allowing the seedpods to develop is a waste of the plant's energy. Remove the old flower spikes or developing seedpods as soon as you notice them. Growing most summer bulbs from seed is not especially difficult, but it requires patience, as most will not bloom until they are at least two to three years old.

There are very few summer bulbs that climb. Of those that do, most notable are the **gloriosa lily** and its relatives. Provide a support for them to climb on, such as strings, netting, latticework, or a trellis. Many gardeners simply allow their gloriosa lilies to ramble and weave themselves among shrubs or other plants. They are not rampant growers, so this generally does not bother the other plants—and it looks great.

If needed, *stake* or otherwise support taller-growing summer bulbs such as the larger **gingers** (**alpinia**, **hedychium**, **curcuma**), **gladiolus**, **lilies**, and **dahlias.** Bamboo stakes and nylon stockings work well for this task.

Watering

Typical summer weather patterns emerge in June. That means hot days, warm nights, and possible frequent afternoon rains along the Coast, and dry periods statewide. Rainfall can be very unreliable. It is not unusual for heavy rain to occur in one location and not at all a few miles away. Watch the rainfall your garden receives and water as needed. Water thoroughly when you do irrigate.

Bulbs growing in containers and hanging baskets generally need to be watered frequently. Do not allow them to wilt before watering. This can lead to scorched leaf edges and bud drop.

Fertilizing

Continue to apply soluble fertilizers regularly to container plantings, unless you used a premium-quality long-lasting slow-release granular fertilizer earlier.

Fertilize actively growing bulbs in garden beds with a premium-quality long-lasting slow-release granular fertilizer every six to eight weeks. If the bulbs are growing well, additional fertilizer is optional. Fertilizers with a 3:1:2 ratio usually work well. Apply any fertilizer according to label directions.

Pest Control

Continue to watch for signs of damage from chewing insects such as caterpillars. Generally, damage is slight and control is not necessary. Sucking insects, including aphids and leaf hoppers, may be present in your planting. Thrips may be a problem on **gladiolus.** Apply selected pest-control aids as needed according to label directions.

Weeds grow like crazy this time of year, especially when the soil is kept moist. Here are some tips for controlling them:

- Keep beds mulched 3 to 4 inches deep and *pull* weeds promptly when they appear.

- You must *dig up* the roots, bulbs, or rhizomes of tough perennial weeds such as nutgrass and Bermudagrass.

- If you are careful to apply aids only on the foliage of the weeds without getting any on the foliage of nearby desirable plants, you can use weed-control aids. Refer to page 291 for a summary listing your options. Visit your local retail nursery for assistance in selecting these as well as other aids.

Planning

Heat and humidity make gardening uncomfortable, to say the least. Plan on doing most of your garden chores early in the morning or late in the afternoon. We prefer the early morning because it may remain hot in late afternoon.

Continue to take notes in your Texas gardening journal, keeping records of the growth and performance of your bulbs. It is especially important to note when bulbs bloomed, how long they stayed in bloom, major insect or disease problems, and comments on their overall appearance. Perhaps you will decide to move them to a different location next year or divide them. Comments jotted down now can help with those decisions later on. It is just as—or perhaps even more—important to record failures. Those who don't remember mistakes are bound to repeat them.

Planting

You can still purchase and plant summer bulbs growing in containers. Check local nurseries for new types of ginger. **Peacock ginger** is gaining in popularity as a substitute for **hostas** in shady areas. The large leaves lie close to the ground and are richly patterned in green, dark green, silver, and bronze. There are some with creamy-white variegation as well. Lavender flowers the size of a quarter or larger nestle among the foliage all summer. Plant gingers in beds generously amended with organic matter, and keep them well watered and mulched during the summer. These beauties may not be available at every nursery but are worth the search. You may also find other interesting and fun bulbs to try during your hunt.

Care for Your Bulbs

Tropical bulbs like **ginger, crinum, gloriosa lily, achimenes, oxalis, caladium,** and **society garlic** live it up in the midsummer heat. They certainly enjoy it more than we do. Perhaps you can look out a window from your air-conditioned house and appreciate the show. This is but one reason they should be planted earlier in the season so we can enjoy them now.

Continue to deadhead and groom bulbs. Diseased, insect-damaged, brown, or yellow leaves do not contribute to the appearance of the plant and should be regularly removed. Avoid cutting off any healthy foliage unless absolutely necessary (to relieve a crowded situation, for instance).

Caladiums are grown for their attractive foliage but also send up unusual-looking flowers. These contribute little to the overall appearance of the plants, and should be removed promptly to encourage the bulbs to put more effort into producing leaves. Some varieties do well in shade, full sun, or both, so select specific varieties for your applications.

Bulbs growing in containers may have outgrown their pots by midsummer. Repot into larger containers if necessary. Since the roots will be disturbed, keep the newly repotted bulbs in a shady area for several days to recover before moving them back into the sun. When repotting, use a premium-quality potting soil, not a soil mix from a garden.

When **gladiolus** foliage has turned mostly brown, *lift* the bulbs and lay them in an out-of-the-way area to dry. *Cut off* foliage when it is completely dry, and *break off* the shriveled old bulb from the base. Store in paper bags, cardboard boxes, nylon stockings, or net bags. Try cutting back the foliage, marking the spot, and leaving the bulbs in place if you like. They will often return if the bed is well drained in zones 8b and 9. In all other zones you will be gambling on their return.

Watering

Typically, summer weather tends to be too wet in some spots and too dry statewide. Near-daily afternoon showers are not unusual in coastal areas. The remainder of Texas often bakes in hot, dry conditions. Under the circumstances, the best we can do is watch the weather and water as needed. *Water* thoroughly and deeply as needed if weather conditions are very dry. Remember, do not water on any preset schedule. *Do* water deeply and thoroughly as needed.

Check bulbs growing in containers daily since they dry out rapidly in the heat. Again, water as needed.

Fertilizing

In particular, watch the fertilizer needs of container bulbs. If the need to apply soluble fertilizer every two weeks is too much of a bother, apply a premium-quality slow-release long-lasting fertilizer. Such a fertilizer releases nutrients slowly over the entire growing season over several months with one application. Follow label directions to determine the amount to use per pot.

Pest Control

Leaf spots caused by fungus diseases are an occasional problem on a variety of bulbs when the weather turns wet. Broad-spectrum fungi-control aids will help control these problems should they occur. Refer to page 291 for a summary listing your options. Visit your local nurseries for assistance in selecting specific aids to control plant disease. Remember, always read and follow label directions when applying any gardening aid.

Get ready for snails and slugs if the weather turns rainy. They just love to eat low-growing plants in shady areas. Apply bait according to label directions. Beer traps are an effective way to catch these slimy critters that chew holes in leaves and flowers. Here's how to do it:

- In the early evening, *sink* small plastic bowls up to their rims in areas of the garden where snails and slugs are a problem.

- *Fill* the bowls halfway with fresh beer. The brand does not matter. Snails and slugs are attracted by the yeasty smell of the beer and crawl down into the bowl. Once in the bowl, the beer washes off their slimy coating and they can't crawl back out.

- *Dump* out the trap the next morning.

- Continue to *set out traps* until you catch few or no snails and slugs.

Planning

Since it may be too hot to enjoy working in the garden, except in early morning or late afternoon, get out those spring bulb catalogs. Now is the time to start looking through them for what you want to plant next season. Just looking at those pictures of tulip fields and beds of daffodils can almost convince you that it's not 95 or 100+ degrees Fahrenheit outside.

This is one of those times when your Texas gardening journal entries, pictures, and videos you made last spring will be useful. Review what worked and what didn't. Don't get stuck in a rut, doing exactly the same thing every year. But on the other hand, if it ain't broke, don't fix it.

If you are wishing you had taken more careful notes in the spring, let that inspire you to do a good job now while the summer bulbs are growing in the garden.

The entries in your Texas gardening journal will provide valuable information for future planting and help you avoid less-than-successful experiences. Be sure to record temperatures, rainfall, and sun/clouds, as well as weed, insect, and disease information.

Planting

Wrap up planting container-grown summer bulbs this month, or early next month at the latest. Most summer bulbs are left in the ground over winter in zones 8b and 9 if the soil drains well, and they need time to become well established before cold weather arrives.

For all other Texas zones, if your summer bulbs are left in the ground after their tops die, mulch heavily and keep your fingers crossed. Apply 6 inches of bark mulch or nuggets or 10 to 12 inches of pine straw or clean hay for winter protection.

Last chance to plant dormant bulbs of late summer- and fall-blooming **lycoris** and **fall crocus** (*Colchicum*). They begin to bloom next month.

Care for Your Bulbs

Thin out the shoots of **cannas** and **gingers (hedychium, costus, globba, zingiber)** if the clumps are becoming overly thick. Each shoot produces only one spike of flowers, so you can cut any shoots that have already bloomed to the ground. This will make room for fresh, new shoots to grow and bloom. These plants will continue to grow new shoots and bloom until October or November in zones 8 and 9. They will cease blooming earlier in other Texas zones.

One of the most magnificent and stately of the summer bulbs is the **Philippine lily** (*Lilium philippinense*). Blooming sometime between July and early October, the plants grow 4 to 6 feet tall and produce clusters of large, white trumpets at the top. An established clump produces several flowering stems. Be ready to stake them as the heavy load of buds and flowers form. Also blooming in late summer is the brown-spotted **orange tiger lily** (*Lilium lancifolium*), which grows to about 4 feet.

Dig up, divide, and *transplant* **Louisiana iris** and **calla lily** this month.

Watering

Summer weather can vary from wet to mostly dry, even too dry. Almost daily afternoon showers are not unusual in coastal areas. The remainder of Texas often bakes in hot, dry conditions. Under the circumstances, the best we can do is watch the weather. If weather conditions are very dry, water thoroughly and deeply as needed.

Remember to *check* bulbs growing in containers daily since they dry out rapidly in the heat. Also, do not water on any preset schedule. Do water thoroughly and deeply as needed.

Fertilizing

Make your last application of granular fertilizer to actively growing bulbs in the ground this month. These fertilizers will continue to feed plantings until the end of October when it is time for bulbs to start slowing down. In Texas, 3:1:2 ratio premium-quality long-lasting slow-release fertilizers such as 15:5:10 work well. Remember, read and follow label directions when applying.

Pest Control

Spider mites cause oxalis and other plant foliage to look faded and unhealthy, eventually leading to brown edges. If the condition of the foliage is already bad, cut all of the leaves back to ground level. The new growth will come out healthy and the bulbs don't mind regrowing new foliage. If symptoms begin to appear again, visit your local retail nurseries for assistance in selecting mite-control aids. Apply according to label directions. Don't forget to apply your selected aid under the plant's leaves.

Continue to watch for and control caterpillars with your selected aid. Prune off badly damaged foliage.

Don't let the summer heat keep you from controlling weeds. Work in shady areas during the day, or work during early morning, late afternoon, or early evening. If you have maintained a good layer of mulch in beds, weed problems should be minimal. Weedy vines such as bindweed or wild morning glory, cat's claw, poison ivy, and Virginia creeper can cover a planting in no time. Be very aggressive and persistent when you encounter these weeds. When possible, use weed-control aids available at local nurseries. Refer to page 291 for a summary listing your options. Always read and follow label directions when applying any weed-control aid. Dig out the vine, root and all, when a weed-control aid is impractical.

Planning

Okay, it's time to finalize those spring bulb ideas and visit local retailers to purchase or send off your orders. Bulbs should be in your hands for planting in October or November. Don't let Northern information confuse you. September days frequently go above 90 degrees Fahrenheit, and no one with good Texas or Southern sense goes out to plant bulbs this month. Bulbs are often available at local nurseries now. You can go ahead and purchase them, but there is no hurry to plant them.

Standard or **hybrid tulips** and **hyacinths** may be placed in the bottom of your vegetable crisper for prechilling prior to planting. Normally no other "spring blooming" bulb needs this cold treatment.

Decide on the kind, color, quantity, and location of the spring bulbs you want to plant. Since most provide only one season of bloom, it may makes better economic sense to use them to embellish, rather than to produce lavish displays.

It's generally better not to buy bulbs in mixed colors, as the colors included often clash. Buy individual colors of your choice, then combine them in groups or masses. You may have noticed, however, that bulb suppliers are starting to create special blends of bulbs with colors carefully chosen to look good together. These might be more acceptable than mixes sold in the past.

This is a good time to bring your Texas gardening journal up-to-date. Be sure to include information on which spring bulbs, as well as summer bulbs, did well for you. Also, note which varieties you planted and where they were acquired. Names, addresses, phone and fax numbers, and e-mail information are always good to enter into your Texas gardening journal for future reference.

Planting

Not much is going on this month. It's too late to plant most summer bulbs unless you really have to, and it's too early to plant spring bulbs.

It is time to *divide* and *transplant* **iris** and **calla lily,** as they are dormant now. **Louisiana irises** generally do best when divided every three years or so. Here's how to do it:

1 *Lift* out the iris clumps and set aside.

2 *Divide* if needed.

3 While the irises are out of the ground, *rework* the bed, adding generous amounts of organic matter.

4 *Expand* your planting and/or share with friends, neighbors, family, or fellow gardeners.

5 *Replant* at proper depth with a small amount of fertilizer per plant and water thoroughly.

Note: Granular rose fertilizer usually works well for nourishing bulbs in Texas—3:1:2 ratio premium-quality long-lasting slow-release fertilizers also work well. Always apply according to label directions.

Watering

Cool fronts may begin to make their way into the state sometime this month. The relief from the heat is incredibly welcome. Along with the fronts we often receive good, drenching rains. None of this is guaranteed, however. Water as needed, especially if the weather is hot. Water newly divided and transplanted **irises** generously.

Achimenes in containers and in the garden may begin to lose steam this month. When this occurs, those in containers should be given less water. As we move into late October, dry them out, cut off the brown foliage, and store them for the winter. Mark the location of those growing in the ground in zones 8b and 9, or, for the remainder of Texas, lift and store them indoors at above-freezing temperatures in a cool, dry location where air circulation is good.

Pest Control

Pests that have been a problem all summer are still around, often in greater numbers after a summer of breeding. Don't let your guard down now. Continue to *watch for* and *control* pests as they appear.

Visits to your local nursery and/or County Agent office will help you become more familiar with which insects are pests and which ones aren't. These visits will also help you become more familiar with the insect, disease, and weed-control aids available for us gardeners. Refer to page 291 for a summary listing your options.

Planning

Visions of spring bulbs should be dancing in your head. This may be the last opportunity to mail-order spring bulbs, and you should do it early this month. Check with the suppliers and make sure they can deliver the bulbs by mid-November. This is particularly important for **hybrid tulips** and **hyacinths.** Other bulbs can be planted as late as early December with good results. Since **tulips** and **hyacinths** need to be refrigerated for at least six weeks before planting in late December to early January, they should go into the refrigerator no later than late November.

It is best to have a specific purpose and location in mind when purchasing each kind of bulb you choose. The size of an area to be planted with a particular type of bulb, for example, will determine how many bulbs you need. Choose colors and heights carefully based on where they will be planted and what will be blooming alongside them. There will always be a few "I've-just-got-to-try-this" bulbs. That's fine, just don't base all of your plans on sentiments like: "Oh, I'll find some place in the garden for the bulbs when the time comes to plant them."

It helps to visit the garden and carefully consider where bulbs would make an effective display in the landscape. Take catalogs and photographs outside with you, and as you walk through the landscape, try to imagine where the bulbs that have caught your eye would look perfect. Make notes, sketches, and diagrams of your ideas so that when it is time to plant you will remember what you had in mind when you sent off the order. Entries made in your Texas gardening journal at this time will be very valuable when it is time to purchase and plant next year's spring bulbs.

Local nurseries and garden centers are usally good sources for spring bulbs, and you should take advantage of whatever they have available. It's good to look at bulbs "in person" so you can see and feel them prior to making your personal selections.

Planting

If patience is a virtue, gardeners must be a particularly praiseworthy group. Those who demand instant gratification will find themselves often frustrated. Indeed, gardeners frequently play the role of time travelers in their minds—imagining some glorious future when a planting bursts into flowers or a young tree provides needed shade.

Little else illustrates this better than planting spring-flowering bulbs. Here, the impatient gardener has no choice. The bulbs we purchase and plant in October, November, December, and January will not bloom until spring. But it is so worth the wait.

All bulbs except **tulips** and **hyacinths** may be planted into the garden this month in northwest Texas. Planting depth and spacing are important. Check the Spring Bulb Chart (on page 48) for recommendations. Generally, we plant bulbs shallower than is recommended for the North, so don't be confused if the recommended depths do not agree with other information you may have seen.

Care for Your Bulbs

Caladiums may be dug up in early to mid-October. Don't wait until all of the foliage is dead. When many of the leaves have fallen over and the plants are looking decidedly "tired," it's time to lift them. Leave the foliage attached and lay them in an out-of-the-way area to dry. When the foliage is dry and papery, it will detach from the bulb with a gentle tug. Brush off any dirt clods clinging to the bulbs, and store them in a frost-free location in cardboard boxes, paper bags, nylon stockings, or net bags. Do not store them in plastic bags. You may also choose to leave the bulbs in place if the bed space will not be needed for other plantings. If the bed is well drained and the bulbs are mulched, many gardeners find that they return reliably in zones 8b and 9. In all other Texas zones, it is usually better to dig, dry, store, and replant next season.

Daytime highs can still reach 90 degrees Fahrenheit this month, though 80s and 70s are typical. The nights are cooler, but many summer bulbs are still going strong. Watch for the foliage on **spider lilies** to appear after they finish blooming. It is important not to cut the foliage once it appears.

Watering

October is often one of our drier months, so even though the weather may be cooler, watch the rainfall and water as necessary. **Easter lilies** are waking up and would appreciate some water if weather is dry. **Louisiana irises** are also entering active growth. Remember, do not water on any preset schedule. Do water as needed, deeply and thoroughly.

Fertilizing

Add some fertilizer when planting new bulbs. Summer bulbs may still be growing, but colder weather is in the not-too-distant future. None of them should be fertilized now. Bulbs that are in active growth, such as **Louisiana iris, calla,** and **spider lily** (*Lycoris*), can be fertilized lightly now. Granular rose fertilizer or a 3:1:2 ratio premium-quality slow-release fertilizer works well in these applications. Apply according to label directions.

Pest Control

Less stressful weather conditions contribute to a general reduction in pest problems. Fortunately, most bulbs are not particularly susceptible to major insect or disease problems when grown properly.

Weeds, on the other hand, will flourish in any cultivated situation, no matter what types of plants are being grown. In October, the summer weeds are still growing and the cool-season weeds begin to show up. The use of pre-emergent weed-prevention aids is usually beneficial this month. These aids are applied to weed-free beds in order to prevent the growth of new weeds from seeds. Applied this month, they can reduce or prevent the appearance of such cool-season annual weeds as henbit, chickweed, annual bluegrass, and others. Make sure the product you choose is safe to use around your ornamentals, and follow label directions carefully. Refer to page 291 for a summary listing your options.

Suggestion: Visit retail nurseries this month and become more familiar with all the gardening aids available. You will find controls for insect pests, diseases, and weeds, as well as tools to use for best results.

Planning

As the warm weather subsides, keep up with your Texas gardening journal, including notes and records on the performance of the summer bulbs in your garden. We hope you took lots of pictures of your garden and videotaped it. Sometimes we forget just how great a bed or area of the landscape looked. Notes and photographs help us remember our garden as well as plan future plantings.

Decide now if you would like to grow some of your spring bulbs in containers. Most spring bulbs are readily grown in containers, and it is not that difficult. This practice is not the same as "forcing bulbs," which is inducing them to bloom earlier than their normal season. Spring bulbs bloom relatively early in the South, including Texas, anyway, and bulbs that are prepared and potted bloom concurrently with the same bulbs that were planted in the ground.

Don't forget those favorite gardeners on your holiday shopping list because shopping time is next month for most of us. We suggest three publications as possible gifts:

- *Dale Groom's Texas Gardening Guide* (Cool Springs Press, 1997)

- *My Texas Garden: A Gardener's Journal* (Cool Springs Press, 2000)

- And this book, *Month-by-Month Gardening in Texas* (Cool Springs Press, 2000)

All should be available at your local Texas retailers, booksellers, and garden centers.

Planting

You should finish planting most of your spring bulbs this month. Wrap up in December at the latest. You can plant low-growing cool-season annuals such as **alyssum, violas,** or **pansies** over the bulbs. They will provide flowers before, during, and after the bulbs bloom.

Remember that **hybrid tulips** and **hyacinths** go into paper or net bags or nylon stockings in the lower drawers of your refrigerator. (Be sure to label them: NOT TO BE EATEN.) This seemingly odd practice is necessary because our winters are not cold enough long enough to satisfy the chilling requirements of these bulbs. Without this cold treatment, the bulbs will not bloom properly. Do not place apples, pears, or other fruit in the drawer with the bulbs. Fruit gives off ethylene gas, which can cause the bulbs to bloom abnormally (too short, blasted buds, etc.). Plant in late December or early January. Any spring bulb you would like to grow in containers should be handled in the same way.

Note: Specie types of **tulips** do not need the cold treatment, nor do other bulbs we normally plant in our gardens.

Dormant **amaryllis** bulbs become available in the fall, but they should not be planted into the garden now as the flowers could be damaged by cold weather. They are often available in "kits" with pot, potting soil, and sometimes even fertilizer.

1 *Plant* **amaryllis** bulbs into pots using a well-drained potting soil. The bulb's neck should be above the soil's surface. Use a pot that is large enough so that there is a 1-inch clearance between the pot rim and the bulb. Clay or plastic pots may be used, but since a blooming amaryllis can be somewhat top-heavy, clay pots provide a little more stability. You can also buy amaryllis bulbs pre-planted. They are a bit more costly but make good gifts.

2 *Place the pot* in a sunny window (the more sun, the better), and keep the soil evenly moist.

3 When the flower stalk begins to emerge (some bulbs will produce two), *rotate* the pot $1/2$ turn every few days so it will grow straight. If you provide your **amaryllis** with too little light, the flower stalk will grow excessively tall and may even fall over. Flowering generally occurs in December or early January from bulbs planted now.

Sometime after the flower stalk has emerged, strap-shaped leaves will grow from the top of the bulb. After the flowers have faded, cut the stalk at the point where it emerges from the bulb, but do not cut any foliage. Keep the plant inside and continue to provide plenty of light, or the leaves will be weak. *Water* as needed when the soil begins to feel dry. It is not really necessary to fertilize your **amaryllis** during this time. In zones 8b and 9, *plant* bulbs into the garden in April so they will get into the normal cycle of blooming in April each year. In the remaining zones of Texas, you may plant them too, but they may not produce blooms annually. If you desire dependable amaryllis blooms annually statewide, plant the **hardy amaryllis** (*Hippeastrum* × *johnsonni*).

Paper-white narcissus (and other **Tazetta narcissus,** such as 'Soleil d'Or') may be planted in pots this month and are easily grown for winter bloom as well.

Plantings approximately every two weeks will provide fragrant blooms all winter long . . . and children love to plant and grow them.

Care for Your Bulbs

Some summer bulbs have gone dormant, some are winding down, and some are still growing, especially in south Texas. In north Texas, the first freezes often occur in November, putting an end to the summer bulb season. *Cut back* the foliage that has browned, and *mark* the locations of dormant summer bulbs to avoid digging into them later on. After you cut them back, *mulch* tropical bulbs with 10 to 12 inches of leaves or pine straw to protect them from winter cold.

Spring bulbs require no special care now.

Pest Control

Insects: Watch for insects, especially in south Texas. If insect pests are damaging your plantings, select approved aids and apply according to label directions. In north Texas, insects may or may not be in hiding, depending on the day and night temperatures. It's wise to be vigilant.

Weeds: Winter weeds may be waiting to invade your plantings. Hand-remove any existing weeds, apply a label-approved weed-prevention aid according to label directions, and mulch 3 to 4 inches deep for maximum weed control.

Diseases: Diseases are very few this month, especially in north Texas. However, they could be active in south Texas. Day and night temperatures, rainfall, and humidity are all factors that affect the development of disease. During warm, humid periods, be vigilant. If a disease invades, have it identified to decide which aid to use to control it. Refer to page 291 for a summary listing your options. Remember, always apply any gardening aid according to label directions.

Planning

Go over your Texas gardening journal notes on your spring bulb plantings. Make sure everything has gone according to plan. (You did have a plan, didn't you?) If you simply have to, you may still make some final additions to your bulb plantings early this month. This is a busy time of year, so it's best to have most of the work done by now.

Is it already time to think about summer bulb planting for next spring? There is no hurry, but catalogs do start arriving this month. Put them where you can find them later. When the holiday frenzy is over in January, pull them out and start to dream.

Remember, it's time to shop for favorite gardeners on your holiday shopping list. Family, friends, neighbors, and co-workers who enjoy growing anything always appreciate gardening-related gifts. See November Planning for publications recommended for Texas.

Planting

Begin planting **tulips** and **hyacinths** into the garden this month, or early January. You may also begin potting up bulbs to grow in containers at that time. See January to find out how to do it.

Continue to plant **amaryllis** bulbs indoors in containers.

Paper-white narcissus can also be planted in pots and easily grown for winter bloom. Plant the bulbs with their pointed ends exposed, in pots of well-drained potting soil. Keep the pots in a sunny, cool location (outside if the weather is mild). If grown in a warm location or one with too little light, the leaves and flower stalks will be tall and tend to flop over. **Paper-whites** may also be grown in bowls of pebbles and water. **Amaryllis** and **paper-whites** in bloom make wonderful holiday gifts.

Helpful Hints

Review the list of summer bulbs at the beginning of this chapter. You may not be familiar with all of them. During a quiet winter day when the weather is too rough to go out and work in the garden, try to find out more about the bulbs by looking them up in one of your Texas gardening references. Talk to some friends to see if they have grown any of them successfully. You are sure to discover some wonderful new plants to excite you and your garden next summer.

Care for Your Bulbs

There is not much to do for bulbs planted in the garden. Keep beds mulched and weed-free. Provide proper light and water to bulbs growing in containers indoors. Do not allow the soil to dry out in pots of **tulips, hyacinths,** and other spring-flowering bulbs that are outside forming roots.

Check on any stored summer bulbs occasionally to make sure they are fine.

Houseplants

What is a "houseplant?" You can look far and wide, and nowhere in the world will you find a plant that evolved inside a house. The plants we use as houseplants are adapted to grow in natural, outdoor conditions similar to those we maintain inside our homes—relatively low light and mild temperatures that range from the 60s to the 80s Fahrenheit year-round. Plants native to shady tropical forests provide many of the common, easily grown houseplants. They often have interesting or beautiful features such as colorful or unique foliage or flowers and adapt well to growing in containers.

Planning for Houseplants

People enjoy the presence of plants indoors—they make us feel comfortable. Just look at the considerable expense that is invested to maintain lush indoor landscapes in malls (maybe relaxed people spend more money?).

Growing houseplants successfully starts with understanding their needs. Houseplants contribute to and become part of the interior decor, but they are not furniture or knickknacks. They are alive, and like all living things, they have certain needs that must be met for them to remain healthy.

Most important of these is light. You cannot grow a plant where there is not enough light, no matter how good it looks in the location. Light is the energy plants use to create their food. Houseplants are sometimes spur-of-the-moment purchases, but planning will produce more consistent and satisfactory results. Walk through your home and think about where plants would be appropriate. Focus particularly on areas where the family spends a lot of time, such as the kitchen or living room. Where is there sufficient light? How many plants do you want and how large should they be? Will they sit on a windowsill, rest on the floor, or perhaps hang in a basket?

Buying Houseplants

Houseplants are available from a wide variety of sources, from nurseries and flea markets to chain store garden centers and even grocery stores. Quality is of particular importance—the plants should be vigorous and healthy with good color and shape and no insects or diseases.

A plant's overall condition depends on a strong, healthy root system, and you can slip a plant out of its pot to look at the roots before purchasing it. The rootball should be full of healthy roots but not completely solid. Look at the foliage carefully. Avoid plants with yellow leaves or brown leaf edges or spots which indicate the plant has been poorly cared for. Are there signs of scale, mealybugs, mites, or any other pests which could infest your other plants at home?

Make sure there is a tag in the pot with the name of the plant on it. Without a name you cannot look up or ask someone for information about the plant.

Growing Houseplants

Houseplants need light, water, a container, potting soil, and the right temperature.

Light

Houseplants are generally grouped into high light, medium light, and low light categories. These generic terms have no clear meaning to most people. Here are some helpful guidelines:

- High light levels are provided by unobstructed east- and west-facing windows.

- Medium (summer) to high (winter) light levels are provided by unobstructed south-facing windows.

- North-facing windows provide low light levels. Low light levels may also be provided by plants placed several feet from east-, west- or south-facing windows. Light is most often provided by sunlight shining through windows, but artificial light can also be effectively used to grow indoor plants.

Rarely do you have to worry about plants receiving too much light indoors. Within four to six weeks a plant will tell you if there is a problem. If there are no pests present and the plant has been watered properly, a deteriorating condition usually indicates insufficient light. Move the plant to a brighter location. Scorched spots usually indicate low-light plants in high-light locations.

Water

For the majority of plants it is really quite simple. Stick your finger into the pot. If the soil feels wet or moist, don't water. If the soil feels dry, water. Do not allow plants to wilt before you water them. This stresses them and can cause leaf drop, flower bud drop, and brown leaf edges.

Apply water until some runs out of the pot's drainage holes and into the saucer underneath. That way you know that you have moistened the entire rootball. Do not let the pot sit in a saucer full of water. Remove the water in the saucer if it is still there a few hours later. There, isn't that simple? Important: Do not keep plants wet.

Containers

Houseplant containers should have drainage holes. There must be some way for excess water to drain out of the soil. Otherwise, we run the risk of soil staying saturated, drowning the roots, and encouraging root rot. Choose pots you find attractive and that fit in well with your interior decor. Clay, plastic, and other materials are all appropriate as long as they drain. Containers with draw holes at the bottom of their sides usually work best.

Potting Soil

Select soil that is specifically blended for use in containers, called "potting soil." Do not use topsoil or garden soil products, or soil dug up from outdoor garden beds. Professionals use soilless potting mixes made up of peat moss, perlite, and vermiculite. Soilless mixes are available under many brand names. Most if not all brands will have "Professional Potting Soil" printed

on their containers. Make sure the potting soil or mix you use is loose, drains freely, and does not pack tightly in the pot.

Temperature

Since most of the plants grown as houseplants are native to the tropics, they should not be exposed to freezing temperatures. Generally, avoid temperatures below 45 degrees Fahrenheit. Avoid extremely high temperatures as well (don't leave plants in a parked car with the windows rolled up during the summer or they will cook!). The normal temperatures we maintain inside our homes are just fine for most houseplants.

Planting and Transplanting

Plants growing in containers eventually need to be repotted. When you purchase a new houseplant, don't be in a hurry to repot it. New plants have enough changes to deal with, without having to cope with the root disturbance involved in repotting.

There are several reasons for repotting houseplants. Over time, roots fill and become tightly packed in the container, causing the plant to lose vigor (plants in this condition are called "potbound"). The plant may grow until its size is out of scale with the pot. Potting mixes degrade over time and may need to be

Houseplants

replaced (this is common with **orchids**). Sometimes gardeners repot plants simply to change the appearance of the pot.

Steps for Repotting Houseplants

1 Choose a new pot that is no more than twice as large as the original pot. Generally, 2 and no more than 4 inches larger is recommended.

2 Add a layer of potting mix to the bottom of the new pot. It should be deep enough so that when the plant is placed into the new pot, the top of the rootball is about 1 inch below the pot rim.

3 Remove the plant from the old pot leaving root system intact. If roots are tightly packed, use your fingers to loosen them somewhat. Do not tear the root system apart.

Remove the plant from the pot.

4 Place the plant in its new container. If necessary, add more soil underneath the plant or remove some until the plant is positioned properly.

Position the plant.

5 Add new potting soil in the space between the rootball and the pot. Use your fingers to firm the soil as you add it, but do not pack it tightly. Fill to within 1 inch of the rim.

Firm the soil.

6 Water the newly potted plant thoroughly to finish settling the soil.

Fertilizing

Plants growing indoors need relatively little fertilizer. Actively growing houseplants that are producing new leaves and/or flowers will benefit from regular, light fertilizer applications. Most water-soluble or slow-release commercial houseplant fertilizers work well. Houseplants that are not growing should not be fertilized. This is especially true in the winter.

Pest Control

Pest outbreaks on indoor plants can be devastating. There are no natural predators indoors and the climate is warm, dry, and favorable for insects to reproduce and spread. Some pests come in with new houseplants. If you can, isolate new houseplants for several weeks to make sure no pest problems develop. Inspect your houseplants regularly and treat pest problems aggressively and promptly.

The major insect pests of houseplants are scales, mealybugs, and spider mites. Infested plants should be placed far away from healthy plants. Always wash your hands after working with an infested plant to avoid spreading the problem.

The easiest way to deal with most of these pests is to use a premixed, ready-to-use houseplant insect-control aid. Repeated applications are generally necessary to achieve complete control. Refer to page 291 for a summary listing your options. Visit your local nursery for assistance in selecting insect-control aids. Always read and follow label directions.

Houseplant Chart

Name	Shape	Light	Water
Aeschynanthus spp. Lipstick Vine	Trailing vine, basket	Medium to High	Moist, drier in winter
Aglaonema spp. Chinese Evergreen	Bushy	Low	Semi-moist
Aloe vera Aloe, Burn Plant	Succulent	High	Dry*
Aphelandra squarrosa Zebra Plant	Bushy	Medium	Semi-moist
Araucaria exelsia Norfolk Island Pine	Tree	High	Moist
Asparagus spp. Asparagus Ferns	Trailing/vining, basket	High	Moist
Aspidistra elatior Cast Iron Plant	Bushy	Low to Medium	Moist
Beaucarnea recurvata Ponytail Palm	Tree	Medium to High	Dry*
Begonia spp. Fibrous, Cane, Rex	Bushy	Medium to High	Moist
Bougainvillea spp. Bougainvillea	Trailing, basket	High	Moist; let dry between watering to induce bloom
Brassaia actinophylla Schefflera	Tree	High	Moist
Bromeliads Many types	Generally vase-shaped	Medium	Semi-moist; keep cup formed by the leaves filled
Cactus Many types	Succulent	High	Dry*
Calathea makoyana Peacock Plant	Bushy	Medium	Moist, needs high humidity
Chamaedorea spp. Indoor Palm	Tree	Low to Medium	Moist
Chlorophytum elatum Spider Plant	Trailing, basket	Medium to High	Moist
Cissus rhombifolia Grape Ivy	Trailing/vining, basket	Medium	Moist
Codiaeum spp. Croton	Bushy	High	Moist
Crassula argentea Jade Plant	Bushy succulent	High	Dry*
Dieffenbachia spp. Dumb Cane	Bushy to tree	Medium	Moist
Dizygotheca elegantissima False Aralia	Tree	High	Moist
Dracaena fragrans Cornstalk Plant	Tree	Low to Medium	Moist
Dracaena marginata Dragon Tree	Tree	Medium	Moist
Episcia spp. Flame Violet	Bushy/trailing, basket	Medium to High; do not place outside	Moist

*Water thoroughly and allow to dry before watering thoroughly again.

Houseplant Chart

Name	Shape	Light	Water
Euphorbia spp. Crown of Thorns, Pencil Plant, others	Bushy to tree	High	Dry*
Ferns, Various Boston, Bird's Nest, Dallas	Bushy to trailing, basket	Low to Medium	Moist, high humidity
Ficus spp. Weeping Fig, Rubber Tree Fiddle-leaf Fig	Tree	Medium to High	Moist
Hedera helix English Ivy	Vining/trailing, basket	Medium	Moist
Hibiscus	Bushy, large	High	Moist
Howea forsteriana Kentia Palm	Tree	Low to Medium	Moist
Hoya carnosa Wax Plant	Vine/trailing, basket	High	Dry*
Maranta leuconeura Prayer Plant	Bushy	Medium	Moist
Monstera deliciosa Split-leaf Philodendron	Vine	Low to Medium	Moist
Orchids, Various	Bushy	Medium to High	Various
Peperomia spp. Peperomia	Bushy to trailing, basket	Medium	Dry*
Philodendron Self-heading types	Bushy	Medium	Moist
Pilea cadierei Aluminum Plant	Bushy	Medium	Moist
Plectranthus spp. Swedish Ivy	Trailing vine, basket	Medium to High	Moist
Rhapis excelsa Lady Palm	Small tree, bushy	Medium	Moist
Saintpaulia African Violet	Low rosette	High; do not grow outside	Moist
Sansevieria spp. Mother-in-law Tongue	Low rosette, upright	Medium	Dry*
Scindapsus or *Epipremnum* Pothos, Ivy	Vine/trailing, basket	Low to Medium	Moist
Spathiphyllum Peace Lily	Bushy	Low to Medium (no direct sun)	Constantly moist
Syngonium polypodium Tri-leaf Wonder	Bushy to vining, basket	Low to Medium	Moist
Tradescantia spp. Wandering Jew	Vining/trailing, basket	Medium	Moist
Zygocactus hybrids Holiday Cactus	Bushy succulent	Medium to High	Moist, dry in fall

LIGHT: Low — North window, 75 to 200 foot-candles, no direct sun outdoors; **Medium** — South window in summer, 200 to 500 foot-candles, minimal direct sun outdoors (early morning); **High** — East or West window, South window in winter, 500 to 1000 foot-candles, 4 to 6 hours of direct sun outside, preferably morning

WATER: Moist — allow to dry slightly before watering, feels dry when finger inserted about one inch; **Dry** — allow soil to dry before watering, pencil or chopstick inserted two-thirds into pot is dry

*Water thoroughly and allow to dry before watering thoroughly again.

Planning

This is the time for the arrival of catalogs for mail-order companies that sell tropical houseplants. Take a look, and see if they are offering something you can't live without. There is no hurry to order, as most companies wisely do not ship tender tropicals during the winter. Most tropical houseplant gardeners enjoy selecting plants "in person" so they can see exactly what they are purchasing. Make entries in your Texas gardening journal about your purchases.

Planting and Transplanting

Repotting is not a high priority during the winter. Check plants you purchased last year in small (4- to 6-inch) pots, and, if needed, repot into a larger container. Rooted cuttings may be potted up. If repotting is not necessary, leave your houseplants alone.

Tulips, hyacinths, and other bulbs you have kept chilled in the refrigerator for growing in containers should be potted up now. Here's how to do it:

1   *Fill* a container that has drainage holes about ⅔ with potting soil.

2   Place enough bulbs pointed-end-up on the soil surface to fill the container without the bulbs touching. *Plant* tulip bulbs with the flat side facing the rim of the pot. The first leaf of each bulb will grow facing the outside, creating a more attractive planting.

3   Add soil until the tips of bulbs show, and *water* thoroughly.

4   Place containers in shade outside and keep soil evenly moist.

5   When the sprouts are about an inch high, move the pots to a sunny location.

6   *Water* the pots regularly. If temperatures below 28 degrees Fahrenheit are predicted, move them to a cool location where they will not freeze. Move the pots back to a sunny location as soon as possible.

7   When the flower buds begin to show color, move the pots indoors and enjoy. Keep the plants as cool as possible so the flowers will last longer.

Care for Your Houseplants

When the heat is on, humidity inside our houses tends to be relatively low. Group plants together to raise the humidity around them. Plants in smaller pots may be placed on trays of pebbles with water added. Make sure the water does not cover the pebbles and touch the bottom of the pots (the soil in the pots would stay too wet and could cause root rot). Do not place houseplants where warm air from vents will blow directly on them. Avoid locations where cold drafts will blow on plants, such as by a door.

Our winter weather is sometimes bitterly cold, but the episodes are relatively brief. Long spells of mild weather are common, particularly in the southern part of the state. Do you move container plants outside during the mild weather or leave them indoors until the weather is reliably warm and settled in April and May? It depends. If you found a good spot for them indoors and your plants are doing well, leave them inside. If plants you moved in as the weather cooled in November and December have pitched a big fit (dropping leaves, yellowing—a routine you will know better with experience), you can move them outside during mild weather. If you feel you have them in a good location and don't want to lug them in and out, leave them there and see if they will adjust. Move them into more light if it is available. Applications of anti-transpirants will help with the drying effects of low humidity indoors.

Watering

Plants brought in for the winter will need less water than they did when they were growing outside during summer. Always feel the soil with your finger before watering. On the other hand, plants that spend their time indoors year-round may dry out faster due to lower humidity in the air when central heating systems are running. Rely on your finger and it will be hard to go wrong. Do not allow plants to sit in saucers of water for more than a couple of hours before removing the excess. A turkey baster works well for this. Remember, water plants only when needed. Do not water on any preset schedule.

 ## Fertilizing

Very few houseplants need to be fertilized during the winter. Those in active growth or bloom, such as **African violets** or **orchids,** may be fertilized with a commercial fertilizer according to label directions. Fertilizers high in the middle number work well when growing nearly all tropical blooming plants.

Pest Control

Pests can show up indoors at any time of year. Plants that summered outside should be checked in particular. Insects not noticed before may have hitched a ride inside and can reproduce and spread rapidly. Plants should be carefully inspected. One of the best ways to do this is to wipe the foliage of houseplants with smooth (not hairy) leaves with a soft, damp cloth. This takes some time, so do a couple of plants whenever you can until you have worked through your collection. Another option is to wash the entire plant's foliage with a mild detergent, rinse thoroughly, and allow to dry. The plants will look better, you will have inspected them thoroughly during the process, and wiping can even eliminate some problem insects.

Mealybugs are especially common on houseplants. They look like bits of cottony white material on the stems or leaves. Infesting virtually everything, mealybugs can spread rapidly and cause a lot of damage before they are noticed. They suck the sap from plants, causing yellow leaves, poor vigor, and sometimes death if not treated. Control with repeated applications of insect-control aids available at local retailers. Refer to page 291 for a summary listing your options. Repeat applications until control is achieved. Always read and follow label directions.

Helpful Hints

Now that the holiday season is over, what are you going to do with your **poinsettias**? You certainly should not feel guilty about throwing them into the compost heap (chop them up first). **Poinsettias** are often purchased for special decorating, not to become a permanent part of your houseplant collection. And after Christmas, **poinsettias** can look as out of place as a stocking hanging on the mantel.

If you still enjoy them and they are in good shape and you would like to keep them growing, place your **poinsettias** in a sunny window and do not let them wilt before watering. Otherwise, they will drop their leaves. After all danger of frosts and freezes has passed, you can move them outside and even plant them in the ground. Remember, they are tropical, and must be moved inside before the first freeze in the fall to survive.

Keep all of the **holiday cactus** plants and **Norfolk Island pines** you may have purchased or received as gifts. Place them by a sunny window and allow them to dry slightly before watering.

Planning

Signs of spring may be arriving in south Texas, but the possibility of freezing temperatures is still very real. Houseplants can be purchased and added to your indoor collection at any time of year. If your house isn't too crowded by the addition of plants that have summered outside, look around and see if there are spots where some greenery would be a welcome addition. Look at the potential location for a new plant carefully. Evaluate the light it receives and make sure it is not too close to heaters, or where warm air vents blow. When you go to the nursery, clearly describe the light the location receives and the staff will be better able to help you select the appropriate plant.

With spring flowers popping out in the landscape, consider adding a blooming plant indoors. **Reiger begonias, African violets, bromeliads, kalanchoes,** and many others can be purchased in bloom during this time.

Enter information in your Texas gardening journal concerning purchases, which plants are doing well, and any problems.

Planting

Any spring bulbs left in your refrigerator must be planted immediately. See the January Planting and Transplanting section of the Bulbs chapter to find out how to do it.

Sometimes February weather is cold and rainy for extended periods. Frustrated gardeners can get their hands into the soil and create a garden indoors. Dish gardens are miniature indoor versions of an outdoor garden. Several kinds of plants are combined in one container, sometimes with various accessories, to create a garden that has a theme or style. Containers that are wider than they are deep are generally the most suitable. Bonsai pots in various styles colors from unglazed earth tones to colorful, shiny glazes are readily available and beautiful to use. The containers can be as fancy or plain as your imagination and taste allow.

Choose a theme or style. The plants you use should all enjoy the same growing conditions. Possible themes:

- a desert garden using **cactuses** and succulents, rocks and gravel

- a woodland garden using **ferns, mosses,** rocks, and pieces of wood

- a tropical garden using lush tropical plants

- an oriental-style garden with **mosses,** figurines, and small plants trimmed to look like trees

Designing and constructing the dish garden is very much like designing an outdoor landscape, and can be just as much fun with a lot less work.

Once planted, put the dish garden where it will receive appropriate light (a sunny window for a **cactus** garden, a shady north window for tropical plants or **ferns**). Where you intend to place the garden will certainly influence the style and type of plants used.

Dish gardens often have a limited life. When the plants begin to grow larger, everything can get out of scale. At that point, pot up the plants individually.

Care for Your Houseplants

Grooming is a constant part of houseplant care. Remove any yellow leaves as they appear. Wipe or wash off leaves periodically. Larger tropical plants love to take an occasional shower. As they don't receive natural rainfall, houseplants can accumulate a surprising amount of dust. Here's how to give a plant a shower:

1 Cover the soil with plastic or aluminum foil to keep the water from splashing the soil.

2 Turn on the water and adjust it until it feels tepid, then arrange the plant or showerhead so the plant is under the spray. Make sure the water pressure is not too forceful.

3 Mild detergents may also be used to remove difficult dust. Rinse thoroughly after application.

4 Allow water to spray on the foliage for about five minutes or until it is clean.

5 Let it drain, then place it back in its growing location. You will be amazed at how refreshed the plant looks.

Wipe off leaves periodically.

Check on spring bulbs growing in containers. Don't forget to protect them during freezes, water them as needed, and provide plenty of light. When the flower buds begin to show color, bring the pots indoors.

 Watering

During cold winter weather, water coming out of the tap can be decidedly chilly. When filling up your watering can to water indoor plants, don't just turn on the cold water tap. Turn on both cold and hot water and adjust the temperature until the water feels tepid or barely warm. This is healthier for tropical houseplants and will prevent spotting on **African violet** foliage. Remember, water houseplants when needed. Do not water on any preset schedule.

 Fertilizing

Do not apply granular fertilizers meant to be used on outdoor beds and gardens to your container plants. Those formulations can burn plants in pots unless you are very careful. It is far better to use water-soluble or slow-release formulations labeled for fertilizing houseplants. Always apply fertilizers according to label directions.

Make entries in your Texas gardening journal that tell when you fertilize and which fertlizer you use.

Water-soluble fertilizers are concentrated liquids or, more often, powders that are dissolved in water and then applied to the soil in the pot. Since they are diluted before being applied, they are far less likely to burn plants when mixed properly. You do not need several different fertilizers for your houseplants. One all-purpose houseplant fertilizer will generally do the trick. For blooming plants, fertilizers high in the middle number are usually advised.

Pest Control

Giving your houseplants a shower not only cleans and refreshes them, it is also effective in helping to keep plants pest-free. The spray of water along with a mild detergent can dislodge and wash off such pests as mealybugs and spider mites. It's advised not to rely on the shower to deal with an infestation of either one, but occasional showers can help keep outbreaks from occurring.

Insect-control aids labeled for use on plants in the outdoor landscape are generally not labeled for use indoors. Never use any pest-control aid unless its appropriateness for use indoors is stated clearly on the label. Refer to page 291 for a summary listing your options.

Remember, always read and follow label directions on all pest-control aids.

Planning

Freezing temperatures are all but over in south Texas, and it won't be long before some of your indoor plants can be moved outside statewide. Take stock of what you have and start planning on which ones will spend the summer outside and which will stay in the house. Plants form an important part of our indoor environment, so don't move them all outside unless you want to. Still, note those that have had a particularly difficult time indoors. Look around outside and decide where indoor plants would receive the right growing conditions and add to the beauty of outdoor living areas. If you make some plans and decisions now, it will be easier when it's time to begin moving plants outside later. Note your decisions in your Texas gardening journal.

This month is also a good time to start looking at which plants might need to be repotted, divided, pruned back, and propagated. Spring is an ideal time for those activities. If you will need new pots, check out local nurseries to pick out what you will need. It is so much better to have the pots you need on hand when you decide you want to repot. And stock up on potting soil. Enter notes in your Texas gardening journal concerning plants that were repotted and which potting soil was used. This will prove to be valuable information next season.

Planting and Transplanting

Since the time to repot is almost here, how do you tell if a plant needs to be repotted? Look for a solid mass of roots on the soil surface and roots coming out of the drainage hole.

To check the roots:

- Make sure the soil is *moist* but not wet.

- *Turn* the pot on its side and *strike* the side of the pot with the side of your fist or open hand in several places.

- Grasp the base of the plant and pull outward.

  If the plant does not slide out of the pot, use a long knife and run it around between the sides of the pot and the rootball. The plant should slide out with the rootball intact.

If you see a solid mass of roots, it's time to repot—but not if you want to slow the growth of the plant. A rootbound condition tends to slow down a plant's growth. This sounds bad, but if the plant is about as big as you want it to be, it may be an advantage. A rootbound plant requires that you water more often and fertilize occasionally, but if the plant is healthy and looks good, repotting is optional. Eventually,

the rootbound condition may begin to affect the overall health of the plant, and you may notice yellowing of older leaves and little new growth to replace them. At that time, repotting may be the only option.

Plants that you are trying to encourage to grow should be repotted as soon as a rootbound condition is reached.

Care for Your Houseplants

In most of Texas, indoor plants could be moved outdoors in the later part of this month, but the possibility of late cold snaps and the trouble of moving everything back in makes next month a better time. If you are eager to move them outside, go ahead. If nighttime lows will go below 45 degrees Fahrenheit, move them back inside, especially if a freeze or frost is possible. Plants need time to adjust to changes in light intensity. Light outdoors is much brighter than inside your house. Always move plants outside to an area that receives no direct sun initially. The north side of your house, under a large tree, under a patio cover, or in a carport are a few suitable locations.

Watering

Some tropical plants go semi-dormant or take a rest when moved inside for the winter, especially if they are not provided with abundant light. **Plumeria, bougainvillea, hibiscus,** and **croton,** among others, may drop most or all of their leaves. During this period they require much less water, so don't allow the soil to stay wet. Water only as needed. They may begin new growth this month. Watch for it, and increase water when you see new leaves emerging (if the soil dictates the need).

Most tropical **orchids** grown as houseplants are **epiphytes** that grow on the trunks and branches of trees. When grown in containers, they are potted in a special orchid mix that is very different from regular potting soil. Orchid mixes are generally based on chopped fir bark these days. Many **orchids** should be potted in a medium-grade bark or medium-fine bark mix (medium bark with perlite and chopped sphagnum moss added). Others need a coarser bark mix with large-grade perlite and charcoal, and some are grown on slabs of cork or wood, or in wooden baskets with no mix at all.

These special mixes greatly influence the way we water **orchids.** To properly water orchids, you should run water through the mix or soak in containers of water until it absorbs the moisture. This gives the roots of the orchids chance to absorb water. This is often done indoors at the sink, allowing warm water to flow through the mix until it is thoroughly moistened. Outside, just use a hose. Many beginning **orchid** growers, unfamiliar with growing plants in these mixes, tend to keep their orchids too dry. Remember, water as needed.

Fertilizing

Orchid mixes also contain very little in the way of nutrients. To keep your **orchids** growing vigorously, fertilize them often from spring to early fall with a soluble fertilizer high in the middle number, according to label directions.

These same fertilizers work well for nourishing all types of blooming plants.

As usual, fertilize any houseplants in active growth. Most plants will wait until the longer days of April to begin growing vigorously. Fertilization will become increasingly appropriate as plants are moved outside. Use a slow-release granular formulation labeled for houseplants this spring or a houseplant fertilizer spike and you won't have to fertilize again for months.

Pest Control

Tiny insects that live in the soil called springtails are generally harmless to plants. They are common in soils or mixes high in organic matter that are kept moist (especially in terrariums). When the soil is disturbed, you may see them moving rapidly. They feed on decaying organic matter. If they bother you, try allowing the soil in the pot to get drier before you water. Fungus gnats are often controlled by this same method.

Check for insect pests, and if present, have them identified and control if needed. Refer to page 291 for a summary listing your options. Visits to your local retailers can help identify pests and offer various control aids. Remember, always apply pest-control aids according to label directions.

Planning

April is a busy gardening month, and this includes working with houseplants. *It is an excellent time to repot houseplants, as the favorable growing conditions of summer will stimulate growth.*

- As you shift one plant into a larger container, you can repot another houseplant into the now-available pot.

- Houseplants may be moved to locations outside for the summer, or just for a few weeks of vacation.

  Determine which ones you will move and where they will go.

- Evaluate how well houseplants have been growing in various locations in your house. Have some done poorly because they were not getting enough light?

  Plan on replacing them with another type of plant that would do well in the spot.

- Now is a good time to study the shape, size, and condition of your houseplants and plan on which need to be pruned.

Make notes of all the above in your Texas gardening journal.

Planting and Transplanting

Winter-blooming **orchids** are often repotted in spring when new growth begins. If the plant is growing out of its pot, consider shifting it into a larger one. Make sure you use an appropriate orchid mix when repotting. **Orchids** really enjoy spending the summer outside. The excellent light, air circulation, and nighttime temperature drops encourage strong healthy growth and increase the chances of the plant blooming.

Poinsettias you saved can be planted into the landscape in areas of the state that are in zone 9. They make large and spectacular winter-blooming shrubs. Cut the plant back halfway and plant in a sunny location on the south side of a house or fence where it will be sheltered from north wind. Make sure the plant is not close to a streetlight, floodlight, or porchlight, as light at night will prevent these plants from blooming. Some years they will freeze to the ground but reliably return from the roots.

To grow your **poinsettia** in a container, cut the plant back halfway and repot it into a pot 2 to 4 inches larger than that in which it was originally growing.

Place the plant in a location outside where it will receive sun

most of the day. Water as needed and fertilize with a water-soluble or slow-release fertilizer labeled for houseplants or tropicals according to label directions. Pinch out new growth in July or August if the plants grow too tall and leggy. Do not prune or pinch after September 1. After that date, the plants should receive no artificial light at night. They need ten hours per day of uninterrupted dark periods to trigger flowering. Leave them outside unless a freeze threatens. By early December the plants should show color. Bring them in to display for the holidays. The results will generally not be as attractive as greenhouse-grown poinsettias, but at least you can say you did it yourself.

Care for Your Houseplants

Moving houseplants outside can be tricky. The plants became acclimated to lower light conditions while indoors. First move them outside to shady locations where they receive no direct sunlight. Plants that like low-light conditions can stay in those locations all summer. Others that prefer more light can be gradually introduced into direct sun over the next couple of weeks. Sun-loving houseplants like bougainvillea, hibiscus, plumeria, alamanda, cactuses, and some orchids can eventually be placed in locations that get six hours or more of direct sun. Even sun-loving houseplants may burn if put in a sunny location too soon after they come out of the house.

Once outside, most houseplants enjoy a good rinsing with the garden hose. Months of indoor dust can be cleaned away by doing this.

Watering

Houseplants that are moved outside will need to be watered more frequently than they were when they were indoors. Air movement, brighter light, and faster growth all contribute to faster water usage by plants in containers. Feel the soil often and monitor soil moisture carefully. Water as needed. You may need to water even more frequently as temperatures rise. Daily watering is not unusual, especially for plants in smaller containers. Always check prior to watering to determine if it's needed.

Plants that have been repotted, on the other hand, may need to be watered less often. The additional soil space will not dry out as rapidly as when the plant was potbound. Once again, monitor the plant carefully and water as needed. Do not water on preset schedules.

Fertilizing

Watch for new growth to begin on houseplants indoors and outside. This signals the time to begin fertilizing.

Use your favorite soluble fertilizer—one with a 20-20-20 or similar analysis is good for just about every plant grown for foliage. These generally are applied every two weeks throughout the growing season. Slow-release granular and houseplant spike formulations feed slowly over a long period and do not have to be reapplied constantly as the solubles. Solubles are great for gardeners who like to "tend" their plants more often, and slow-release granulars labeled for houseplants for those who would rather not have to remember to fertilize every two weeks. Remember, always fertilize according to label directions.

Pest Control

Houseplant pest problems are less likely to appear outside than inside. Weather, rain, temperatures, and natural predators all work against most of the major indoor pests such as mealybugs, spider mites, and scale. Still, they can and do occur. Applying pest-control aids outside is easier than applying them inside. Keep a close watch for any pest damage.

Caterpillars can eat holes in leaves and should also be controlled. Visit your local retailer, who can help you choose specific control aids. Refer to page 291 for a summary listing your options. Always apply according to label directions.

Pruning

Prune back plants such as hibiscus, bougainvillea (unless it's blooming), and other woody tropicals if needed. Don't wait until later. When they begin to bloom, you will not want to cut them back, and by the end of the summer they may be larger than you want.

Helpful Hint

Fertilization is especially important for plants that are growing in soilless potting mixes, are potbound, or that seem pale and lack vigor, along with those you want to encourage to grow larger. It is generally optional to fertilize plants that are healthy, vigorous, and already as large as you want them to be.

Planning

If you are like some gardeners, it may seem as if you aren't able to get done what you intended to do in April. There is just so much going on. *In May there is still time to repot and prune. Go over what still needs attention and plan on getting it done this month.*

This is a great month to shop local retailers to add more tropical houseplants to your collection. Visit nurseries, garden centers, and any local retailer to "get your hands on" exactly the plant for your application.

Planting and Transplanting

Some houseplants grow from crowns or shoots that multiply, increasing the number growing in a pot over time. Plants such as **ferns** (the popular **Boston** and **Dallas**), **spider plants, bromeliads,** many succulents (**aloe, hen-and-chicks**), **Chinese evergreen, cymbidium orchids,** and many others grow this way. They eventually become crowded in their pot. Instead of shifting them into a larger pot, you may decide to divide them. Here's how to divide a houseplant:

1 Study the plant carefully, noting how many crowns or shoots there are, along with their location. Decide how to divide it. Generally a plant is divided into smaller clumps—dividing the original mass in half, thirds, or fourths, for instance. If you are trying to propagate more of the plant, you may choose to divide it into individual crowns or shoots. The resulting plants are smaller, but you get more of them. Some plants, such as bromeliads, are often grown with a single crown to a pot and should be divided into single crowns.

2 Once you have decided how to divide it, *remove* it from its pot and use a large knife to cut it into pieces. If this is your first division, be brave. It looks like you are tearing the plant up, but it will be healthier in the long run.

3 Immediately *repot* the divisions into pots suitable to their sizes. Do not let their roots dry out.

4 Keep the new divisions in a shady location for a couple of weeks (outside where the humidity is high would be good) and *water as needed.* Move back into appropriate light when they recover.

Another method of propagation is to root cuttings. Most houseplants root easily from 4-inch cuttings taken from the tips of branches. The lower end of the cutting should terminate at a node (where the leaf joins the stem).

1 *Remove* the leaves from the lower two-thirds of the stem and *dip* it in rooting hormone (powders or liquids are available at your local nursery).

2 *Fill* a pot with damp rooting medium. Popular choices include sharp sand, half sand and half peat moss, perlite, vermiculite, half perlite and half vermiculite, or lightweight potting soil.

3 *Make a hole* in the medium with your finger, pencil, or dowel rod and stick the cutting one-half to two-thirds its length into the medium. *Firm* the medium around it. Several cuttings may be stuck in one pot to make care more convenient.

4 Keep the medium moist, and *place* the cuttings outside in a completely shaded location or in a bright window. *Cover* with a clear plastic bag for added humidity (especially recommended if the cuttings are inside). Plastic from the dry cleaners, food wrap, food bags, and most other readily available clear plastics work well for this. Most cuttings will root in four to six weeks. A few houseplants, including **African violet,**

peperomia, **sansevieria,** and some **begonias,** will root from a leaf.

Plant some **achimenes** bulbs in pots or hanging baskets. They bloom nicely in a sunny window indoors or in a shady area outside.

Watering

It is difficult to overwater houseplants if they are potted in a light mix that drains well. Still, if plants are kept wet, the root system will suffer. Roots need abundant oxygen in the soil, and if water constantly fills the air spaces, the roots will drown and rot. Never water a plant if the soil feels moist. If a plant appears wilted but the soil feels wet or damp, the plant probably has root rot. Do not water it. That will only make matters worse. The next time water is applied you may wish to also apply a root stimulator according to label directions. This aid often helps to establish root systems. Root stimulators are widely available at local retailers.

If the plant propagates easily from cuttings, take a few and put them in water until they are no longer wilted. Root them as described above. If the original plant is lost, you will still have the rooted cuttings. Use a knitting needle or pencil to loosen the soil in the pot

to get oxygen to the roots. Do not water until the soil feels dry. Once its roots begin to rot, a plant rarely recovers. To avoid this calamity, do not keep plants wet or allow them to sit in saucers of water for extended periods. The key word is "moist," not wet. Remember, water your houseplants as needed and never water by preset schedules.

Fertilizing

Many houseplants may be taking off with wonderful spurts of growth this month, and most should be. If yours aren't performing well and water, light, and all other cultural and environmental factors are correct, your plants most likely need to be fertilized. Visit local retailers and determine which fertilizer type(s) you like best. Always apply plant-nutrition aids according to label directions.

Pest Control

Keep a sharp eye out for pest problems on new houseplants brought home in the last few weeks. Plants purchased at garage sales or flea markets in particular may have pests. Amateur growers may not be as scrupulous about pest control as are professionals.

Spider mites are common on a wide variety of houseplants. These very tiny spider relatives are not readily visible to the naked eye (it's a good idea to have a magnifying glass on hand to diagnose pest problems on plants) and so go unnoticed until a large population builds up and damage has occurred. Spider mites suck the sap from leaves, and infested foliage is often faded, dusty looking, unhealthy, and smaller than normal. In extreme cases, fine webbing may be seen between the leaf and the stem.

If plants are outside and you have the time, spray daily with a forceful stream of water directed under the leaves for a week. This simple technique that doesn't use pest-control aids may be effective. There is a wide assortment of pest-control aids, including specific ones for spider mites, at your local nurseries. Refer to page 291 for a summary listing your options. Direct your applications under the leaves where the spider mites tend to live.

Helpful Hint

Plants tend to grow in the direction of the brightest light. Indoors, this is often toward the closest window, and plants may become lopsided and less attractive. Rotate the plants occasionally to prevent this from happening.

Planning

It is usually very hot and humid for the rest of the summer. Most houseplants are native to the tropics, though, and they thrive in this kind of weather. If you are planning a party or special event in your home, think about moving some of the houseplants that are spending the summer outside back into the house. They will really dress things up, especially those that are blooming. Use them as decorations, and place them without regard to light or windows. Return plants outside promptly after the event, or move them to appropriate light conditions indoors. Make entries in your Texas gardening journal, including which plants were used and comments made by guests on your houseplants.

Planting and Transplanting

You may continue to repot houseplants despite the heat.

Steps for repotting houseplants:

1 *Choose* a new pot. Generally one that is 2 inches, but no greater than 4 inches large, is recommended.

2 *Add* a layer of potting mix to the bottom of the new pot. It should be deep enough that when the plant is placed into the new pot, the top of the rootball is no more than 1 inch below the pot rim.

3 *Remove* the plant from the old pot. Try to slide it out leaving the root system intact.

4 If the roots are tightly packed together, use your fingers to loosen them somewhat. Do not tear the root system apart. If the soil or mix has degraded substantially, *remove* most of it from the roots prior to planting in the new pot.

5 *Place* the plant in its new container. If necessary, *add* more soil underneath the plant or *remove* some until the plant is positioned properly.

6 *Add* new potting soil in the space between the rootball and the pot. Use your fingers to *firm* the soil as you add it, but do not pack it in tightly. Fill to no higher than 1 inch from the rim.

7 *Water* the newly potted plant thoroughly to finish settling the soil. If desired at this time, a root stimulator may also be applied according to label directions.

Should you put gravel or other materials in the bottom of the container for drainage? It really is not necessary. Water drains quite well through a loose mix and out the drainage holes in the bottom of the pot without a layer of drainage material. When you repot a plant purchased at a nursery you will find that professionals, who rely on well-grown healthy plants for their income, do not put drainage materials in the pots. If they don't do something, it is usually not essential that you do it.

Should you place a shard of broken pot over the drainage hole? This is sometimes done to keep soil from washing out but is also generally not necessary. Most potting soils and soilless mixes will not wash out of the drainage hole in appreciable amounts. If you find it is a problem with the mix you use, the drainage hole may be covered with a wad of sphagnum moss, a piece cut from an old nylon stocking, or a small piece of screen wire.

Care for Your Houseplants

"Groom" houseplants regularly to keep them looking their best. Promptly remove dead growth, yellow or brown leaves, and faded flower stalks. While grooming, look carefully for any beginning signs of pest problems. Yellow or browning leaves can be caused by pests such as aphids, whiteflies, spider mites, or scale.

Watering

Summer is the time when people commonly take their longest vacations. If you are going to be away from home for more than a few days, you may return to find lack of water has caused substantial damage to houseplants.

The ideal solution is to ask a friend who is knowledgeable about plants to check on your plants regularly and water them when necessary. Be sure to give written instructions on the needs of each plant, since your friend is not as familiar with them as you are. Try not to make the instructions too complicated, though.

If the plants will be on their own, move those growing indoors away from sunny, bright windows so they use water less rapidly. They still need moderate light, however, to stay healthy while you're gone. Thoroughly water all of your indoor plants right before leaving for your trip. Even allow some water to stand in the saucers beneath the plants' containers, something we normally would not do.

Plants in small pots will dry out the fastest. Enclose these plants (pot and all) in clear plastic bags to retain moisture and prevent drying out. Plants in plastic bags should receive bright light but no direct sun, which could cause excessive heat buildup inside the plastic.

Plants outside need to be watered almost every day. Place all of your outdoor container plants, including any hanging baskets, in a shady location near the northern side of a building or under the protective cover of a large shade tree or covered patio. Group plants fairly close together as this, along with the shady location, will help slow water loss.

If you can't find someone to water for you, inexpensive water timers—available at local nurseries and hardware stores—can work very well hooked up to an irrigation system. A battery-operated or electrical unit attaches to an outside faucet. All you do is set the timer for when you want the water to come on (based on how often you generally have to water the plants) and for how long, and it will water your plants automatically. It's probably easier to use a sprinkler to water a grouping of your container plants. If you want to be more sophisticated, drip systems are also available.

Fertilizing

Do not overdo it with fertilizers. Only relatively small amounts are needed by plants to be healthy. Never apply fertilizers stronger than is recommended on the label. "If a little is good, more is better" is not a phrase that applies to fertilizers.

Pest Control

Snails and slugs will crawl up pot sides and feast on some houseplants spending the summer outside.

Check under the pots regularly during the day. Snails and slugs will often be found hiding there and can be collected and disposed of. If the problem is bad, sprinkle some bait pellets around the bottoms of the pots. Additional pest-control aids are available at local retailers for: slugs, snails, mealybugs, aphids, scale, or any pest which visits your houseplants inside or outside. Refer to page 291 for a summary listing your options. Remember, always read and follow label directions when using any pest-control aid.

Planning

Gardeners are always on the lookout for interesting new houseplants, but there are some factors you may need to consider before you buy. You will hear experienced gardeners say "I wish I had room for that" or "I wish I had suitable growing conditions for that." They have learned that if you can't give a plant the space and growing conditions it needs, it is better not to buy it no matter how desirable. Well, at least try to resist.

Plan to check young, rapidly growing plants in small pots. They may need to be repotted into larger containers. Check the rootballs occasionally and repot if necessary. Enter in your Texas gardening journal which plants needed repotting and those not yet ready for new containers. Include pot types, potting soil mix used, where purchased, temperatures, humidity, hours of sun, wind, rain, and pests if present.

Planting and Transplanting

When you bring new houseplants home, do not repot them right away, even if they appear to be potbound. Allow the plants to get used to their new surroundings for a few weeks. A new houseplant sometimes languishes after you have had it a couple of weeks, but this condition is generally related to insufficient light or improper watering. Give the plant more light and check your watering. Repotting the plant will not help.

Midsummer is a good time to air-layer houseplants such as **dracaena, dieffenbachia, rubber trees** and other **ficus, crotons,** and **hibiscus.** Air-layering allows you to root much larger pieces than are used in cuttings. The stem is induced to produce roots while still attached to the plant. It is a great way to reduce the size of a large plant and create a new one at the same time. Here's how to do it:

1 Decide on how large a piece you want to root. *Wound* the stem by removing a ring of bark about 1 inch wide, cut a notch about one-third of the way through the stem, or make an upward slanting cut about halfway through the stem.

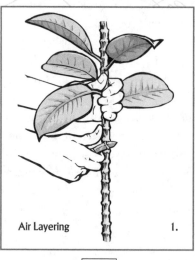

Air Layering   1.

2 *Dust* the wound with a rooting hormone powder. If you chose to make an upward slanting cut, *wedge* it open with some damp sphagnum moss, a toothpick, or wooden match pieces.

2.

3 *Wrap* wound with a large handful of damp sphagnum moss.

4 *Wrap* the sphagnum moss with plastic wrap. Seal the upper and lower ends with tape or twist ties. Do not let the moss dry out during the rooting process.

3.

5 When you see several roots through the plastic, *cut* the stem below the roots and *pot up* the rooted piece. Rooting generally takes two to four months.

Care for Your Houseplants

Plumerias are bold tropical plants that grow into small trees and produce colorful flowers that are very fragrant. They may be planted from their pot into the ground in full sun (acclimate them first). They will grow and bloom all summer. In early November to early December (before any first freeze arrives), dig them up, shake off the soil from their roots, and store them in a frost/freeze-free location. All the leaves will drop off and the plants will stay dormant until next spring.

Bougainvilleas are popular flowering container plants, but once they stop blooming it is sometimes difficult to get them to bloom again. Here are some tips:

- **Bougainvilleas** need direct sun at least four to six hours a day, and more is better.

- They bloom better if they are potbound, so keep them in pots relatively small for their size. Large pots lead to large, vigorously growing plants that will be reluctant to bloom until the pots are full of roots.

- *Water* as needed and *fertilize* according to label directions with fertilizers of your choosing.

- If everything is right and the plant still won't bloom, try this: Allow the plant to wilt slightly before you water. Continue this until you see small flower buds, usually four to six weeks after you begin letting it wilt, then *water* as needed. **Bougainvilleas** do not bloom constantly, but produce flowers in flushes.

Spring to early summer and fall to early winter are the seasons **bougainvilleas** *are most likely to bloom—but they bloom anytime.*

Lightly trim your **poinsettias** if they are too tall and leggy. This will make them more compact and bushy when starting to bloom.

Regularly groom and wash off the foliage of plants outside. Indoor plants will appreciate a rinsing off in the shower (or outside)—or wipe their leaves with a damp cloth.

Watering

It is best if pots on wooden decks are supported off the wood. The constant moisture under the pot can cause damage to the wood. Use three or four small wood blocks, pieces of brick, or terra-cotta pot supports made for that purpose. There needs to be an inch or two of clearance under the pot. Make sure it is stable. Apply water as needed, but the pots may need to be checked daily in our typical Texas July heat.

Fertilizing

Plants that were fertilized with slow-release fertilizers labeled for houseplants earlier may not need to be fertilized again during the summer. Do not overfertilize. Always read and follow label directions.

Pest Control

Weeds are often a problem in pots growing outdoors. Pull them out as soon as they appear. A mulch over the soil in the pot can help, but that makes knowing when the soil looks dry more difficult. Check plants frequently for insect pests.

Helpful Hints

Tropical **hibiscus** flowers last only one day before wilting. This disappoints some gardeners, but the plants produce new flowers continuously. There are almost always open flowers on the plants all summer.

Planning

High temperatures usually continue this month. You may still take cuttings from, divide, or repot houseplants now. Dividing and repotting at this time of year is more stressful to the plants because of the hot weather and because plants are also in active growth. You have to be careful and plan on giving the plants a lot of "TLC" afterwards.

If you have gotten a little carried away with your propagation efforts and find that you have lots of new plants, it may be decision time. Decide on how many you can reasonably find room for inside this winter, and give the rest away. Or plan on donating them to a church or organization fund-raiser.

Enter notes into your Texas gardening journal: which plants rooted successfully, what was used to root them, temperatures (day and night), humidity, rain or lack of rain, wind, sun/clouds, pests if present and how they were controlled, plus any comments from visitors.

Planting and Transplanting

Ask container gardeners about potting mixes and you will hear as many recommendations and recipes as you would if you asked a group of cooks how to bake a chocolate cake. There is not, in fact, one best potting mix (or chocolate cake recipe, for that matter). Different groups of plants need different types of mixes. **Cactuses** and **succulents** need coarse, gritty mixes rich in sand. **Ferns** prefer generous amounts of organic matter. **Epiphytic orchids** grow in chopped fir bark.

Beginning gardeners should generally rely on commercially available lightweight potting soil mixes for growing most types of houseplants. There are a lot of brands out there, however, and not all of them are especially good. In particular, avoid heavy black potting soils. If the bag feels dense and heavy for its size, put it back. The best potting mixes include soil, peat moss, vermiculite, and perlite in proportions that create a fairly light, loose mix that water penetrates readily and drains from rapidly. Make sure the potting soil has been pasteurized to kill disease organisms and weed seeds. These types of mixes often have the word "Professional" somewhere on their front labels. When in doubt, ask your local retailer for assistance.

Soilless mixes, as their name implies, do not contain any soil. They are mostly a blend of peat moss, vermiculite, and perlite which drains well yet retains moisture and is very light in weight. Excellent for growing most houseplants, they are especially useful in hanging baskets and other situations where weight is a concern. Soilless mixes are free from disease organisms and weed seeds. Fertilization is needed, as these mixes contain few available nutrients, and they do dry out faster than other potting soils.

Sifted homemade compost is an excellent addition to potting soils, lightweight potting soil mixes, or soilless mixes. Generally, a compost-to-potting-mix ratio of about 1:2 or 1:1 is blended together.

Continue to root cuttings and make air layers this month while they have time to form roots and get established before the weather turns cold (air layering: see July Planting and Transplanting).

Care for Your Houseplants

Many hanging basket houseplants grow in a way that leaves the pot rather skimpy and all the best growth hanging below. *Trim* these back to stimulate growth closer to the pot. *Root* some of the cuttings and insert those into the pot to provide attractive growth there. As an alternative, some of the longer stems can be coiled up in the pot to provide attractive foliage and a fuller appearance. Trimming or pruning alone may stimulate sufficient new growth to fill in bare spots.

Watering

Water meters with probes are used by some gardeners to help them determine when they should water. These devices can be inaccurate when used improperly. Do not wait to water until the meter reads "dry" to the bottom of the pot. At that point the plant may be stressed and, in the case of mixes high in organic matter, the soil may be hard to rewet. Water when the probe reads "dry" when inserted about halfway into the rootball.

Mixes high in organic matter, especially soilless mixes, can actually repel water if you let them get very dry before you water. These mixes shrink away from the sides of the pot when they get very dry, and when water is applied it runs down the sides instead of wetting the rootball. When this happens, water must be applied generously until the mix begins to absorb it. You can also hold the pot down in a bucket or tub of water until the mix absorbs the water.

Remember, check plants frequently for water needs during August, but water only if needed. Water thoroughly when irrigating.

Note: Small containers may need water daily, but check first before applying.

Fertilizing

Some houseplants will have done most of their growing early in the summer. Fertilize those plants that seem to be slowing down. Others may continue to grow vigorously. If they are healthy and dark green, fertilization is optional or unnecessary. Always read and follow label directions when applying fertilizers.

Pest Control

Aphids as well as scale insects feed by sucking the sap out of the plant, excreting some of the sugary sap as a material called honeydew. This honeydew accumulates on leaves, causing them to appear shiny and feel sticky. It will also get on floors and furniture around the plant. Soft brown scale is common on indoor plants such as **ficus, schefflera, dieffenbachia,** and **palms.** The insects cover themselves with a brown shell-like covering and are immobile once they are big enough to notice. As a result, most gardeners do not realize they are not a natural part of the plant. Because of the protective covering, some insect-control aids may not work well to control these pests. Refer to page 291 for a summary listing your options. Visit your local retailer for specific aids that are effective in controlling scale on tropical houseplants. After you decide which aid to purchase and use, be sure to follow label instructions/directions. You can move an inside plant outside to a shady area to treat it, or treat it in place.

Do not use oil sprays on **ferns.**

Helpful Hints

Bromeliads are popular, easy-care houseplants. Once a plant blooms, it slowly loses vigor and dies. Don't despair. Before that happens the plant will produce side shoots from its base called "pups." When they reach about one-third to one-half the size of the original plant, they can be cut from the plant with a knife and potted up. With good care, they will bloom in a year or two.

Check your air layers and make sure the sphagnum moss is staying moist. Add water if necessary. Do not let the moss dry out completely or it will be very difficult to remoisten.

Planning

Notice how the days are getting shorter? Cooler weather is on the way, and it is not too early to make plans for moving houseplants back inside. Finish up any repotting so the plants have a chance to recover before being brought back inside. Finish up any pruning, also. Look at the size of the plants and imagine them inside. If their size needs to be reduced, do it now so they will have time to make some new growth under favorable conditions before going indoors.

This is a good time to think about giving a friend, neighbor, relative, or someone else you know who likes plants a gift from your growing experiences this season. Enter notes in your Texas gardening journal on who receives which plants, how successful you were in propagation and growing this season, when you fertilized and which aid was used, how often water was applied, temperatures, hours of sun, and your overall enjoyment of growing tropical houseplants.

Planting and Transplanting

Think carefully about pot size before repotting this month. If you shift the plant into a larger container, will it still be convenient to move inside, or will the larger pot make the plant unwieldy and too heavy to move easily? "Plant dollies" are available at local retailers and they make it easy to move large houseplants almost anywhere. These plant-moving aids often look like plant saucers with casters fastened to them. If you are interested in moving large houseplants with relative ease, give these devices a try. You do have the option of keeping a plant in the same size pot and correcting a rootbound condition (kind of like having your cake and eating it, too). But if it's time to repot:

1 *Remove* the plant from the pot.

2 *Trim off* one-quarter to one-third of the lower part of the rootball if needed.

3 *Add* enough fresh potting mix to the bottom of the original container equal to the amount of rootball removed.

4 Place the plant back in the pot, *water* well, and keep in lower light conditions for a few weeks to recover.

5 This would be a good time to do some pruning to the upper part of the plant as well. Do this to outside plants now so they will have a chance to recover before being brought back inside.

Care for Your Houseplants

Houseplants need to be acclimated to lower light conditions before they are moved back inside. Houseplants growing outside in sunny or partly sunny locations should be moved to shady areas now. This will help them adjust to lower light conditions when they are moved inside in October or early November.

Houseplants indoors generally rely on the sun shining through windows to provide the light they need. Windows obstructed by hedges, tree branches, and screens allow less light to enter. If more light is desired, trim hedges and tree branches to give houseplants access to more light. Screens can be removed from windows that are not normally opened to let in fresh air. Even washing a window can remove dust and grime that cut down on the amount of light entering.

On the other hand, sometimes you may want to reduce the amount of light coming through the window. Sheer curtains are one of the most effective and attractive means of accomplishing this. Another solution would be to move the plants back farther from the window, or move them to a window that receives less light.

Remember not to cut back your **poinsettias** after the first of this month, and make sure they receive absolutely no artificial light at night. This is most easily accomplished by growing the plants outside where the naturally lengthening nights will trigger them to bloom. Move inside if cool temperatures are likely.

Another popular holiday houseplant is the **holiday cactus.** (Once called Thanksgiving and Christmas cactuses, these plants have been hybridized and their bloom times overlap so much that we now tend to put them in one category). They are triggered to bloom by long nights as well as by chilly temperatures. Grown indoors, with constantly warm temperatures and lights on at night, they generally fail to bloom. If the plant is inside, move it outside this month into a shady spot (a little morning sun is fine). Allow it to stay outside until you see little flower buds forming. Bring it back inside, place it in a nice, bright window, and watch the spectacular show.

Watering

Plants growing outside still need watering even if the weather turns cooler. But as always, make sure plants need it before applying water. Cool, rainy weather will reduce the frequency of watering needed.

When watering, always apply water until you see some come out of the drainage holes. This indicates you have moistened the entire rootball. Roots will grow only where there is sufficient moisture. If you get into the habit of applying only enough water to wet the upper part of the soil, the roots will grow only there and not take advantage of soil deeper in the pot.

Fertilizing

Fertilization becomes less important for some plants as the summer season begins to reach its end. Some plants, such as **bougainvillea** and **bird-of-paradise,** put on their best flower show in the fall. How well they bloom depends more on the care you have given them through the summer than fertilizer applications made now. If you used slow-release fertilizers labeled for houseplants back in April, they should still be providing some nutrients. The only plants that should be fertilized are those that are pale or stunted, or show other signs of nutrient deficiencies.

Pest Control

Pests have had all summer to infest and build up populations on your houseplants outside. You will want to get all of those problems taken care of before you bring plants inside for the winter. It is far better and more convenient to use pest-control aids outside than indoors. Begin to inspect plants carefully, looking for signs of scale, snails and slugs, caterpillars, spider mites, or mealybugs. Refer to page 291 for a summary listing your options. Pull any weeds that may have found their way into pots.

Helpful Hint

This is a good month to go shopping at local retailers for that "special" or unusual houseplant for your collection. This will provide sufficient time for your new arrivals to become acclimated to their new locations before cold weather and winter arrives, plus they may be on sale. What a deal! Most gardeners enjoy the "hands on" selection process, being able to actually look at and inspect tropical houseplants prior to purchasing them.

Planning

October is the month houseplants outside may need to be adapted for the move back indoors. Planning will make the process go smoother. Determine which plants will spend the winter inside, which will stay outside and take their chances, which will stay outside and be moved in on those nights when it will freeze, and last, which plants you want to give away or donate for a plant sale. Where will particular plants go inside based on their light preferences and where will your favorites be placed? Is there room for everything? Have any plants gotten too big to move back inside? Those plants may have to take their chances outside (if the winter is mild in zone 9, they often make it with some protection). Another alternative would be to check and see if a local botanical garden or conservatory would take them as a donation. Or trade your large ones for smaller plants.

Planting and Transplanting

Repotting generally should have been done by now. If you have some plants that absolutely need to be repotted, go ahead and do it.

Air layers done earlier should be rooted by now. Check the plastic for roots growing in the sphagnum moss. If the roots are at least 1 inch long (longer is better), the layer can be cut. Cut the stem or branch an inch or two below the original wound where the roots will have formed. Pot up the rooted stem in an appropriate-sized pot using a good-quality lightweight potting soil or a soilless mix. Keep it in a shady area until you bring it inside. Watch your watering—do not keep the soil wet or allow it to dry out. Water as needed.

Rooted cuttings should also be potted up now if you have not already done so. Generally, a 4-inch pot is large enough for newly rooted cuttings. If the cuttings have grown for a while after rooting, choose a pot you feel is the appropriate size. Use the same types of soils/growing mixes as you would use for repotting plants or rooted air layers as described above.

Care for Your Houseplants

Before outside houseplants are moved indoors, they must be acclimated to the lower light conditions inside. If you move a **ficus tree** growing outside in a sunny location indoors, it will pitch a big fit no matter how sunny the window

inside is. Yellow leaves will rain down in countless numbers. Move plants in sunny areas outside to very shaded locations such as under a tree, carport, covered patio, or porch. This should be done three to four weeks before you intend to move them inside.

Move plants inside before you have to turn on constant heat. They can adjust to indoor conditions better before the extra stress of warm, dry air is added to the situation. Expect many of the plants to still be unhappy about the move. The better you acclimate your plants and the more light you are able to provide for them indoors, the less leaf drop you should see.

Leave **poinsettias** and **holiday cactuses** outside until blooms or buds are formed. Do not, however, leave them out on nights when a freeze or frost is predicted.

Houseplants that spent the summer outside should also be groomed so they will look their best, and you will be less likely to bring pests inside with the plants.

- *Clean* the outside of containers using a brush and a mild solution of dishwashing liquid and water.

- *Remove* dust and debris from the foliage and where leaves join the stems. *Hose down* the plants and *wipe* the foliage clean

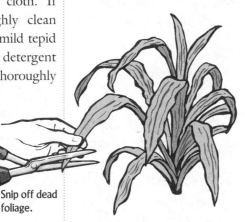

with a soft, damp cloth. If needed to thoroughly clean your plant's foliage, mild tepid water and liquid detergent may be used. Rinse thoroughly after using.

Snip off dead foliage.

- *Remove* all dead or yellow foliage, old flower stalks, and dead or injured branches and stems.

Do not repot immediately prior to moving plants indoors. Repotting should be done four to six weeks before bringing them inside.

Ironically, plants that spend all of their time indoors may actually dry out faster in the winter due to the warm, dry air and lower humidity produced by heating systems. Monitor plants carefully. Remember, water only when needed. Do not water by preset schecules.

Watering

Once they are moved inside for the winter, houseplants will need to be watered less often. How much less is what you will have to determine. Feel the soil regularly with your finger and water when it feels dry, but before the plants wilt. In time, you will establish a routine to check for watering the plants indoors. Remember, it is better to underwater than to overwater and cause root rot. **Cactuses** and **succulents** are particularly vulnerable to overwatering. Be especially careful with them.

Fertilizing

With everything else going on this month, it's nice to know you don't have to worry much about fertilizing now. Use your judgment when it comes to fertilizing or not and determining which aid to use. In winter, plants usually slow down their activities inside as do plants outside. Little nutrition in the form of fertilizers is needed while they are "resting" through our normally cooler months.

Pest Control

Do a good, thorough job of pest control before you bring houseplants inside. You'll be glad you did.

Gardeners are sometimes surprised to find ants have taken up residence in the soil of a container plant outside over the summer. Control them before bringing the plant inside by drenching the soil with a solution of a pest-control aid mixed according to label directions. This will also rid the soil of other undesirables such as earwigs, centipedes, grubs, and fungus gnats.

Be on the lookout for critters such as frogs, toads, and lizards that may hitch a ride inside with the plants. These beneficial animals should be carefully removed from the plant or pot, and released unharmed.

Thoroughly clean all snails and slugs from the bottoms of pots and dispose of them.

Before the plants are brought inside, control pests on plants infested with aphids, spider mites, whiteflies, or thrips with pest-control aids labeled for these purposes. Refer to page 291 for a summary listing your options.

Planning

There are a few fun winter projects you can do indoors with some planning. Two bulbs, **amaryllis** and **paper-white narcissus,** are easy to force for bloom during the holidays. Light setups are wonderful spots of life, and during the winter can be used to start seeds or cuttings of houseplants. Have you ever considered putting up a greenhouse? With the mild climate in south Texas, greenhouses are not as common as in north Texas, but they can provide the serious gardener wonderful opportunities for growing plants over the winter.

This is an excellent month to reflect on your year so far, enter your observations into your Texas gardening journal, and plan holiday shopping for the favorite gardeners on your list. Nearly all gardeners enjoy receiving publications as gifts. Here are three suggested possibilities to consider:

* A copy of this book, *Month-by-Month Gardening in Texas* (Cool Springs Press, 2000)

* The 424-page *Dale Groom's Texas Gardening Guide* (Cool Springs Press, 1997)

* *My Texas Garden: A Gardener's Journal* (Cool Springs Press, 2000)

All these publications should be available at local bookstores and garden centers.

Planting and Transplanting

Plant bulbs of **amaryllis** in pots just big enough to hold the bulb with about 1 inch of clearance to the pot rim. Use a well-drained lightweight potting soil, and plant so the neck and upper quarter of the bulb are exposed. You may also purchase **amaryllis** bulbs prepotted in kits.

* Place the potted bulb in a sunny window and keep the soil moist.

Turn the pot as the flower scape or stalk grows to keep it from bending toward the window. Its flowers are among the most spectacular of the bulbs and always brighten up an indoor plant collection.

* Cut the flower stem back to the bulb once blooms have faded.

Leaves will have begun to grow. Keep the plant in a sunny window and water when the soil begins to feel dry.

Pulleys

Timer

Fluorescent
Lights

Weights

Seed-Starter Tray in
10x20" Flat Tray

- You may plant the bulb into the garden in a well-drained spot with morning sun in April. These bulbs are known to do well in zone 9 and maybe in zone 8b. For the remainder of the state, they are "risky." To have dependable **amaryllis** blooms in the landscape throughout Texas, plant the hardy types.

Plant **paper-white narcissus** in pots of soil with the points showing.

- Place the pots outside in a sunny location and keep well watered.

    Leave the pots outside unless a freeze threatens and place pots back out when the freeze is over. Cool temperatures produce stockier, more attractive plants.

- When the buds show white, bring the plants indoors for display.

- **Paper-whites** can also be planted with the bulbs buried half deep in a bowl full of pebbles or gravel.

Fill with water to the base of the bulbs and maintain it at that level. Follow the directions above.

An alternative to placing bulbs outside is to place them in sunny windowsills after potting as above.

Care for Your Houseplants

Move outdoor houseplants inside this month if you have not already done so. Do not wait for a freeze or frost to threaten and move them all inside in a panic. For those plants left outside, watch the weather carefully and move them to a protected area (such as a garage or shed) if a frost or freeze threatens.

Watering and Fertilizing

Water houseplants only when the soil begins to feel dry. It is easy to overwater if you are not careful. Do not let pots sit in saucers of water for long periods. Little or no fertilizer is required this month, unless a plant is in active growth and/or flowering.

Pest Control

Monitor plants carefully, especially those moved in from outside. Treat pest outbreaks promptly and aggressively. Isolate an infested plant so it will not affect healthy ones—even if you have to move it back outside.

Helpful Hint

Think about growing some of your indoor plants under artificial lights. It can be very rewarding and allows you to grow plants where there would otherwise not be enough light. Attractive light stands are available through mail-order, or sometimes locally (check the classifieds, sometimes you find used ones for sale).

Planning

The hectic holiday season is here. Seasonal plants such as **poinsettias, holiday cactuses, decorated Norfolk Island pines, cyclamens,** and others add joy and beauty to the inside of our homes. Before you purchase them, plan on their placement to contribute to home decorations, while still providing for their needs.

If heating systems are causing low humidity, try misting your plants a couple of times a day, grouping plants together, placing them on trays of pebbles with water, applying an anti-transpirant according to label directions, and/or placing small plants in terrariums.

This is the month for holiday gift-giving, and gardeners as well as want-to-be gardeners will enjoy plants, books, tools, and all types of gardening-related gifts. So plan one or more shopping trips for them.

Planting and Transplanting

In late December, plant the spring-flowering bulbs you have stored in the vegetable bin of your refrigerator since October. **Hyacinths** are easy to grow and very fragrant. See January Planting and Transplanting for directions. You may also con-

tinue to plant **amaryllis** and **paper-white** bulbs. Since they do not have to be prechilled before planting, you can buy and plant them right away.

You will often find a stray **ivy** runner or piece of **wandering Jew** that has broken off and can be rooted in a container with potting soil.

Care for Your Houseplants

On cold nights, bring all outside tender houseplants into a protected location. It takes only one good freeze or frost to destroy a beautiful plant. Generally, we find that tropicals are tougher than they are given credit for. Most will be okay as long as temperatures stay above 35 degrees Fahrenheit. Be cautious: anytime temperatures are predicted to drop below 40 to 45 degrees, move plants in. A few especially tender tropicals may be damaged by temperatures below 50.

Holiday plants require good care to stay attractive as long as possible. This starts when bringing them home. **Poinsettias** are quite brittle and branches break off easily. Have the plant sleeved for protection (placed in a piece of paper or cellophane shaped like a funnel) at the place you purchase it. Do not stop and shop on the way home. On a cold day, the temperature in

the car can get low enough to damage holiday plants.

Place your holiday plants where you can enjoy them, but remember their needs as living plants. Ideally, they should receive some light from a window. Avoid locations where hot or cold drafts will blow on the plants. Check the soil with your finger daily, and water when it begins to feel dry. If the pot is covered in decorative foil, punch holes so excess water can drain into a saucer underneath.

Watering and Fertilizing

Water houseplants as needed, being careful not to keep the soil wet so as not to encourage root or stem rot. Fertilize very little, or in most cases, not at all, unless plants are in excellent growing conditions and active growth.

Pest Control

Pests do not take the winter off and can spread rapidly in a crowded indoor garden. Spider mites thrive in warmth. Watch for pests and *treat promptly.* Be ready. Have a commercial premixed houseplant insect pest-control spray on hand, just in case. Refer to page 291 for a summary listing your options

Lawns

Almost every landscape includes a lawn. These areas of mowed grass provide important spaces for outdoor activities and a restful contrast to beds of flowers and shrubs. For some, the lawn is a source of pride and is lavished with as much attention as a prized rose garden. For others, the lawn is just something that has to be mowed—as long as it's mostly green, they're happy. Most of us fall somewhere in-between.

Lawn care does not have to be complicated, but there are certain necessary elements. Knowing how to select the right grass, providing the right care at the right time, and dealing appropriately with problems that may arise are all important to success.

Our relatively mild climate and long, hot summers dictate the types of lawngrasses that will grow here. The warm-season grasses we use grow vigorously at 80 to 95 degrees Fahrenheit in spring, summer, and fall. They typically go dormant and turn brown with the first frost, greening up again as the weather warms in March and April. Properly maintained, they are long-lived and rarely need to be replaced. The primary warm-season turfgrasses include **common Bermuda, hybrid Bermuda, centipede, St. Augustine,** and **zoysia.**

Cool-season grasses are also planted, but not to create permanent lawns as they are in the northern United States. They are used to overseed warm-season lawns in the fall, maintaining a green lawn during the winter when those grasses are brown and dormant. The cool-season grasses are temporary residents in the lawn and die during the early-summer heat. The cool-season grasses generally used for overseeding are **annual ryegrass** and **perennial ryegrass.**

Selecting the Right Grass

New homeowners rarely change the type of grass in an existing lawn, but occasionally will if sufficient reasons arise. New construction generally allows you to decide which type of grass you want to plant. The choice of grass and how it is planted is a matter of taste, available labor, growing conditions, predicted use, and economics.

Historically, **St. Augustine** has been the most popular lawngrass, and it is still the most commonly seen in yards around the state. **Centipede** has become increasingly popular for new lawn installation (especially in east Texas with its acidic soils), owing primarily to its lower maintenance needs. It requires less mowing and fertilization, and has fewer insect and disease problems than **St. Augustine.** However, **centipede** is not a grass for alkaline or prairie soils. The following chart will briefly acquaint you with the warm-season grasses appropriate for planting in Texas.

Planting a Lawn

Have a soil test done through your local Texas Cooperative Extension Service office or the Stephen F. Austin State University soil testing lab to determine needed fertilizer, lime, sulfur, etc. Remove any weeds growing in the area and debris (especially important around newly constructed homes). Till the soil 4 to 6 inches deep. Apply soil amendments recommended by the soil test and work into the soil. Establish the grade and rake smooth. Use the planting method of your choice.

Lawns

The following are the most commonly used lawn planting methods:

Seeding:

1 *Broadcast* half the seed walking east to west, the other half north to south, to ensure even coverage. (See illustration on opposite page.)

2 Let the soil cover the seeds when initial irrigation occurs.

3 *Water* lightly every day until seeds come up, then as needed to maintain a moist soil until the plants are established.

Plant **Bermuda** *April through August and* **centipede** *April through July.*

Plugging:

1 *Plant* 2- to 4-inch-diameter plugs 6 to 12 inches apart (greater spacing may be used, but coverage will take longer).

2 Once planted, *step* on them to firm them in place.

3 *Water* lightly every day for one week, every other day for another week, then less frequently but more thoroughly, especially if weather is dry.

Plugging is best done April through August.

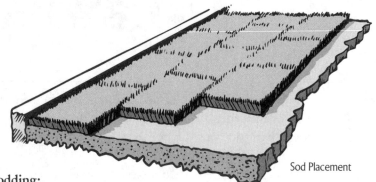
Sod Placement

Sodding:

1 *Lay* the sod in a brick pattern (alternate ends and middles) with the seams pressed tightly together.

2 *Roll* the area to firm the sod into the soil if needed.

3 *Water* lightly every day for a week, every other day for another week, then less frequently but more thoroughly, especially if weather is dry.

Sodding is best done April through September.

Care for Your Lawn

Regular mowing is important during the growing season. This may mean mowing every five to seven days during hot and rainy summer weather. Mow often enough so that no more than one-third of the grass blade is removed each time. Mowing height is very important and your mower blades must be sharp. Set your mower to the following recommended heights:

Common Bermuda: 1 to $1^{1}/_{2}$ inches (rotary or reel mower)

Hybrid Bermuda: $^{1}/_{2}$ to 1 inch (reel mower recommended)

Centipede: 1 to 2 inches (rotary or reel mower)

St. Augustine: 2 to 3 inches (rotary or reel mower)

Zoysia: $^{1}/_{2}$ to $1^{1}/_{2}$ inches (rotary or reel mower)

Irrigation is generally needed only during hot, dry weather, but when necessary, it is very important. Water deeply and thoroughly, applying $^{1}/_{2}$ to 1 inch of water. Lawns are generally fertilized in April, June, and August for maximum growth and quality. Fertilize **centipede** lightly in April and July. Insect and disease problems are most common during the summer growing season (although brown patch fungus attacks in spring and fall). Watch carefully for damage, get an accurate diagnosis, and treat appropriately. Practice good weed control when necessary.

Lawngrass Chart

Types of Grass	Characteristics	Strengths	Weaknesses
Common Bermuda	Fine texture, dark green color; used on athletic fields; coarser texture than hybrids; new, improved named varieties becoming available. Plant seed, sod or plugs.	Rapid establishment rate; excellent wear tolerance; good ability to recover from damage; excellent drought tolerance; good salt tolerance; can be seeded.	Poor shade tolerance; high to medium maintenance.
Hybrid Bermuda	Very fine texture; dark green; excellent quality; used extensively on golf courses and athletic fields; high fertility requirements. Plant sod or plugs.	Rapid establishment rate; excellent wear tolerance; good ability to recover from damage; excellent drought tolerance; good salt tolerance.	Very poor shade tolerance; very high maintenance; should use reel mower.
Centipede	Medium texture; slow growth; low fertility requirements; requires acid soils; popular for home lawns. Plant sod, plugs, or seed.	Good disease and insect resistance; low maintenance; fair tolerance to part shade. Advantages over St. Augustine: finer leaf texture, better cold tolerance, better resistance to chinch bugs and brown patch, can be seeded.	Poor wear tolerance; quality can decline if over fertilized; lighter green leaf color; poor drought tolerance; poor salt tolerance; seed is slow to establish for acidic soils only.
St. Augustine	Coarse texture; rich green color; popular for home lawns. Generally, plant sod or plugs, seed occasionally available, but not best quality.	Best grass for part-shade; excellent salt tolerance; medium maintenance; establishes fairly quickly.	Poor cold tolerance; very susceptible to chinch bugs, brown patch; coarse texture.
Zoysia	Several species and cultivars; medium fine to fine texture; dark green color; very dense growth; used on golf courses and home lawns. Plant sod or plugs.	Excellent wear tolerance; good tolerance to part shade ('Emerald' and 'El Toro' varieties); excellent cold tolerance.	Slow establishment rate; accumulates thatch readily requiring removal; medium to high maintenance.

Seed Spreading

JANUARY

Planning

Relax while there is not much to do. Plan on repairing any damage that may have occurred during the late summer (chinch bugs) or fall (brown patch) to your **St. Augustine** lawn. The grass may return from brown patch, but chinch bugs kill the grass outright and those areas will need to be replaced in spring.

Chinch Bug

Care for Your Lawn

Mow overseeded lawns as needed. If the weather is moist and mild, this could be every week. If the weather is cold, the grass will grow more slowly. **Ryegrass** is mowed to a height of 1 to 2 inches, so it should be cut when it has grown 1½ to 3 inches tall. Clippings may be bagged or not. Don't send bagged clippings to the landfill. Put bagged clippings in your compost pile. Do not bag if you use a mulching mower.

Fertilizer

In south Texas, cool-season grasses should have been fertilized last month and can be fertilized again in early February. In north Texas, fertilizer may be applied in late November (once the warm-season grass goes dormant) and again around the middle of this month.

Pest Control

Winter weeds may be growing in the lawn now. Mow them back if you like.

Planting and Transplanting

Gardeners in the southern part of the state can still overseed dormant lawns with **ryegrass** or a blend this month, but it is risky if severe cold weather occurs before the grass has had a chance to establish. If it hasn't been done by now, it's probably not worth it. More seed may be spread over lawns overseeded earlier to thicken up sparse areas. Overseeding with a cool-season grass means, of course, that mowing should continue through the winter.

Watering

Cool, moist weather generally makes irrigation unnecessary this month. Water as needed.

Helpful Hint

Areas of bare soil will wash away during heavy winter rains. Loosen the soil and scatter ryegrass seeds over the area to stabilize soil and prevent erosion.

Planning

The weather is cold and lawn care is easy. Review the notes you made last year on the performance of the lawn, and make decisions on what needs to be done this spring. If you don't have any notes from last year, don't you wish you did? Plan to keep at least a few simple records in your Texas gardening journal this year for future reference.

Planting and Transplanting

Save all that energy for later. Now is not the time to plant either cool-season grass seed or worry about planting warm-season grasses. Dormant sodding is occasionally done. If you have new construction and need to lay sod to stabilize the bare ground, some companies will lay dormant sod for you. The turf will be brown when planted, but should green up nicely in March or April. There is a risk that severe freezing temperatures can damage vulnerable newly laid sod. Cool, moist weather and a dormant condition mean you don't have to be concerned about watering the new sod.

Care for Your Lawn

Overseeded lawns are a rich emerald green and provide a beautiful setting for the spring flowers beginning to bloom. Mow overseeded lawns as needed. If the weather is moist and mild, this could be every week. If the weather is cold, the grass will grow more slowly. **Ryegrass** falls over, matts, and looks unattractive if allowed to grow too tall.

Watering

Cool, moist weather this month and the fact that warm-season grasses are dormant make the need to water unlikely. Still, if the weather does turn dry and you have **ryegrass** growing, irrigation may be necessary.

Fertilizing

In south Texas, overseeded lawns may be fertilized early this month. A light application of a 3:1:2 ratio fertilizer such as 15-5-10 (six pounds per 1000 square feet) will do the trick. Water-in fertilizer immediately after application.

Pest Control

Mild weather will encourage enthusiastic growth from cool-season weeds in the lawn. Since the lawngrass is dormant and you are not mowing, green weeds are really noticeable against the tan-colored turf. Do not reach for a bag of weed-and-feed (fertilizer combined with a weedkiller). It is far too early to fertilize warm-season grasses. After all, they're dormant. Use a weed-control aid/product to eliminate broadleaf weeds. One group of products/aids to accomplish this is post-emergent herbicides. When using any herbicide, always read and follow label directions. During warm, moist weather, Pythium blight may attack **ryegrass,** causing areas to "melt." Treat with fungus-control aids/products. These fungicides are available at your local retailers. When utilizing fungicides, follow label directions for their uses. Refer to page 291 for a summary listing your weed- and fungus-control aids.

Planning

Regular mowing is just around the corner, and you may need to begin mowing occasionally any time now. Plan on getting your lawn mower in good repair for the coming season. If you are handy with small engines, service your mower according to the manufacturer's directions. Otherwise, take your mower to a local shop that can service it for you. It is very important to have them sharpen the blades while they have the mower. All the mowing last summer dulled the blades, and dull blades produce a poor-quality cut, leaving the grass blade tips brown. As the lawn greens up, begin to evaluate the condition of the grass.

- Note bare areas, areas that are not greening up, and areas of thin grass.

- Plan to renovate (where necessary) by seeding, plugging, or sodding.

- Try to identify what caused the problem and take steps to correct it if necessary. Don't be too hasty in this early evaluation as grass will continue to recover into May. **St. Augustine** damaged by brown patch last fall, for instance, will green up more slowly, but it often recovers by late May.

Planting and Transplanting

This transitional period is not a particularly good time to plant warm-season grasses. The weather is still cool and unsettled, with the possibility of freezes lingering in the northern part of the state. Planting warm-season grasses should be delayed until at least next month.

Care for Your Lawn

During late winter and early spring, the root systems of warm-season grasses actually decline, and as spring progresses, new vigorous roots grow. This month is a particularly critical time in the process, and care needs to be taken not to interfere with the reestablishment of a strong root system. The performance of the turf through the coming summer depends a great deal on what you do now. Do not disturb or stress the grass this month. This would not be a good time to aerate, fill over, or dethatch the lawn.

Watering

Warm days and dry weather may make watering necessary as turf wakes up from winter dormancy. If needed, *water thoroughly.* This encourages roots to grow deep into the soil, increasing drought tolerance this summer. Irrigating this month is generally not required, though, as sufficient rain usually falls.

Fertilizing

As the grass begins to grow, some gardeners are just itching to fertilize. Generally, it is better to wait. Warm-season turfgrasses are just waking up this month and reestablishing a strong root system. They tend to perform better when the first fertilizer application is made in early to mid-April. Early fertilization stimulates leafy vegetative growth at the expense of a strong root system. Brown patch disease is also more likely to occur on **St. Augustine** if it has been fertilized early with quick-release nitrogen (N) fertilizers. When fertilizing, use premium-quality long-lasting slow-release fertilizers. If you haven't had your lawn's soil tested in the past two years, now is a good time. Contact your County Agent's office or the Stephen F. Austin State University soil testing lab in Nacogdoches for information or instruction sheets for this service.

Pest Control

Cool-season weeds such as henbit, chickweed, and annual blue grass continue to flourish in the mild weather. The use of broadleaf weed-killers including herbicides or other weed killing aids may be questionable at this time. The warm-season grasses are more vulnerable while waking up from winter dormancy. Use weedkillers this month with caution.

On the other hand, warm-season weeds are not apparent at this time, but the seeds will soon start to germinate. To prevent a problem with summer weeds, *apply a weed-preventing aid/product such as a pre-emergent. Refer to page 291 for a summary listing your options.* This aid is applied before weeds become a problem and prevent the seeds from growing. This month is the ideal time for applications of pre-emergents in north Texas. They should be applied during February in south Texas for summer annual weed control. Before purchasing and applying pre-emergents, be sure you understand the product's capabilities. Do not apply to areas where you later intend to plant seeds of a warm-season grass.

Refer to page 291

Helpful Hint

One of the most popular shade trees around the state is the **live oak.** It drops lots of leaves in late February and early March, and they should be raked or mowed (with a bag attached) from the lawn promptly. If left on the lawn, they will cover the turfgrass as it begins to grow, and this could cause problems. Those leaves make a great addition to the compost pile instead of the landfill.

Brown patch thrives in the cool, moist weather this month. **St. Augustine** is particularly vulnerable, although **centipede** is occasionally damaged by this fungal disease. Look for areas of green grass turning tan with a slight orange cast. These areas may rapidly enlarge if the weather is moist. Brown patch will often show up in low, moist areas of the lawn. One course of action is to treat with an approved aid/product called fungicide which is labeled to control brown patch in lawns.

Mowing

After a winter of not mowing, many of us are reluctant to get out the lawn mower and start. Watch the lawn, and if sufficient growth occurs, you should mow. It is unhealthy to let the grass get too tall before mowing. Some people have the mistaken idea that they should mow grass especially short the first few times. Scalping the lawn is not recommended and can actually lead to a weakened root system that will affect the turf negatively all summer.

APRIL

Planning

It's finally time to get up and get busy. April is full of lawn care activities that require some planning for best results. Do you want or need to fertilize? How much lawn renovation is necessary, and why did the grass die? Are there signs of diseases that need to be controlled? How about weeds? If you are planting a new lawn, what kind of grass will you plant and how will you establish it?

There's plenty of excellent free information available at your local county office of the Texas Cooperative Extension Service. County Agents can talk to you about lawn decisions you need to make and provide you with free literature on lawn maintenance, grass selection, and pest control specifically for our state.

Planting and Transplanting

This month begins the prime planting season for warm-season grasses, which runs until August or September. With the exception of **common Bermuda,** solid sodding is the preferred method of establishing a lawn whenever possible. Although more expensive and labor intensive at the beginning, solid

sodding more than makes up for it in advantages:

- It provides an instant lawn.

  In this age of instant gratification, that is no small thing. Other methods may take an entire growing season or more before solid coverage is achieved. Traffic on the lawn area must be minimized during this entire period.

- Weed problems are minimized.

  When seeding or plugging, weeds grow easily in the bare-soil areas and compete with the establishing grass. Hand-weeding is often the only way to deal with the situation, as weed-control aids/products are not generally used on young, establishing grass.

- Solid sodding is the most reliable method of establishing most warm-season grasses.

  Plugs are the next most reliable method. Seeds must be carefully watered and nurtured as they establish. Seeds are also subject to loss from birds, washing away by rain, and other factors that can reduce a stand. **Common Bermuda,** *on the other hand, establishes readily and easily from seeds. Seeds lost to birds or washed away are still possible concerns. Careful watering is*

needed, but **Bermuda** *seedlings grow vigorously and can cover a lawn area in six to eight weeks.*

Care for Your Lawn

Ideally, wait until next month to do filling, aerification, or dethatching, when the grass is growing more vigorously.

Watering

April can be one of the drier months, though mild weather generally keeps the grass from getting too stressed. Watch the weather, and if things get too dry, *water* thoroughly and deeply as needed.

Fertilizing

Fertilization is often critical to producing optimal growth in the lawn. Without it, the lawn will not be as lush, vigorous, or dark green. On the other hand, fertilization is not a matter of life and death, and many lawns get along well enough without it. Lawns that have been damaged or are in low vigor certainly should be considered for fertilization.

- Choose a commercial lawn fertilizer that has some of its nitrogen in a slow-release form. This will provide nitrogen to the grass over a longer period, preventing excessive early growth.

- Reams of research data have shown 4:1:2 and 3:1:2 ratio lawn fertilizers work well on Texas lawns. These include 21-7-14, 18-6-12, 16-4-8, and 15-5-10. Determine the ratio of a fertilizer analysis by dividing each number by the smallest number in the analysis. A fertilizer with an analysis of 16-4-8, for instance, has a ratio of 4:1:2.

- Do not apply lawn fertilizer by hand. The results will be uneven and can damage the grass if you aren't careful. Use a broadcast or centrifuge-type spreader to evenly distribute the fertilizer at the recommended rate.

- Do not guess. Follow the label directions carefully.

- Ideally, *apply* fertilizer to a freshly mowed lawn, as this allows the granules to fall to the soil more easily.

- The grass blades should not be wet, so wait for the dew to dry.

- *Water* the lawn immediately after application to wash the fertilizer down to the soil and off the blades of grass.

- If weeds are a problem, apply a post-emergent weed-control aid after the lawn has regrown for 3 or 4 days. One of the preferred devices to apply liquid post-emergents is the compression or pump-up sprayer. Plastic and stainless steel sprayers are known to be the most durable materials and provide trouble-free service for years.

These aids/products contain compounds that may damage the lawn, trees growing in the lawn, and other ornamental plants if applied improperly.

Pest Control

Apply broadleaf weedkillers now and next month. Summer weeds are young and vulnerable, and mild temperatures make using weed-control aids/products easier on the grass. Choose a product that is labeled as safe to use on the type of grass you have. Products suitable for **Bermuda** and **zoysia** may damage or kill **St. Augustine** and **centipede.** Be sure to read the label for tolerant grasses and application rates. There are a number of products that combine several different weed-control aids/products in one formulation which makes them effective in controlling a wide variety of weeds. Refer to page 291 for a summary listing your options.

Brown patch disease may still be active. Treat with a lawn disease-control aid/product labeled to control brown patch promptly before extensive damage occurs.

Mowing

    Mowing becomes a regular job this month, though not as often as will be needed during midsummer. One of the consequences of fertilization is increased growth, which means more frequent mowing will be needed. Make sure your mower blades are sharp and *mow as needed.*

Planning

Plan on doing any needed filling this month. You may also begin topdressing, dethatching, or aerification. Continue to apply weed-control aids/products. Evaluate your lawn now. Are there areas that did not green up or recover well from the winter that need to be renovated? Talk to your local County Extension Agent or local retailers and try to decide what may be the cause or causes before you begin work. Decide what needs to be done and correct any problems.

Planting and Transplanting

Planting warm-season grasses may be done through August or September. Planting lawns now has the advantage of allowing the grass to grow and establish over the long summer months. This is especially important when choosing seeding, sprigging, or plugging to establish your lawn. Grass planted in early summer will also better endure the cold of its first winter, should the weather become severe.

Here are the steps to lawn planting:

1 Have a soil test done through your local Texas Cooperative Extension Service office or the soil testing lab at Stephen F. Austin State University in Nacogdoches to determine needed fertilizer, lime, sulfur, etc.

2 *Remove* any debris, especially important around newly constructed homes.

3 *Eliminate* weeds growing in the area.

4 *Till* soil 4 to 6 inches deep.

5 *Apply* nutrients/fertilizers recommended by the soil test and work into the soil.

6 Establish the grade and *rake* smooth.

7 Use the planting method of your choice. The following are most commonly used:

- **Seeding:** *Broadcast* half the seed walking east to west, the other half walking north to south to ensure even coverage. *Water* lightly every day until sprouts come up, then regularly until the young plants are established. Plant **Bermuda** May through August, **centipede** May through July.

- **Plugging:** *Plant* 2- to 4-inch diameter plugs 6 to 12 inches apart (greater spacing may be used, but coverage will take longer). Once planted, *step* on them to firm them in place. *Water* lightly every day for one week, every other day for another week, then less frequently but more thoroughly, especially if weather is dry.

- **Sodding:** *Lay* the sod in a brick pattern (alternate ends and middles) with the seams pressed tightly together. *Water* lightly every day for a week, every other day for another week, then less frequently but more thoroughly, especially if weather is dry. Best done by September.

MAY

Care for Your Lawn

If your lawn has some low places in it, now is a good time to correct this situation. To accomplish this activity:

1 Choose a soil which matches your native soil for the fill. For example, do not use light sandy soils to fill areas where the native soil is heavy clay.

2 *Mow* and fertilize the lawn prior to applying your selected soil fill.

3 If applying soil deeper than 2 inches, *remove* the sod, *apply* the fill, and then *replace* the sod. Another option is to simply plant new sod, seed, or plugs after the filled areas are leveled.

4 After the grass is established, *mow, water,* and *fertilize* according to your total lawn maintenance activities.

Watering

Temperatures in the 90s Fahrenheit generally make their debut this month. Calibrate your sprinkler system to apply $1/2$ to 1 inch when irrigation becomes necessary. Here's how:

1 *Set out* several cans in the spray pattern of the sprinkler you use to water the lawn.

2 Turn on the water and check the time.

3 Check cans every 15 minutes.

4 When 1 inch of water has accumulated in most of the cans, *check the time.* That is how long it takes your sprinkler to apply 1 inch of water to your lawn ($1/2$ inch would take half as long).

Water in the morning or early enough in the day so that the lawn does not go into the evening wet. Late watering can encourage fungal diseases.

Fertilizing

This should have been done last month, but if you didn't, you may still do so. Do not be in a hurry to fertilize newly planted sod. There is not much root system left when the sod is harvested, so there are few roots with which the sod can absorb nutrients. Generally, wait about six to eight weeks after the sod is laid before fertilizing it.

Pest Control

This month is the last chance to apply broadleaf weedkillers before the weather becomes hot.

Mowing

Mowing is one of the most critical parts of proper lawn care. It must be done regularly before the grass gets too high. Ideally, no more than the top third of the grass blades should be cut each time you mow. Do not wait too long before mowing, especially as the rate of growth speeds up during summer.

Helpful Hint

Button weed is particularly troublesome around the state. This low, mat-forming weed has 1-inch pointed leaves and small four-petaled white flowers. Most people don't notice it until July, but it is beginning to grow now. When using a weed killer to eliminate it, aids/products containing more than one active ingredient are more effective when the weeds are young.

Planning

Lawns that feel too spongy when you walk on them may have developed a thick layer of thatch. Thatch is dead grass material that accumulates between the green leaf blades and the soil, and some is present and desirable in every lawn. But excess thatch reduces water penetration, creates shallow-rooted turf, encourages insect and disease infestations, and makes mowing difficult. Excessive fertilization, mowing infrequently, and mowing too high encourage this problem. Plan on dethatching with a vertical mower, or core aerification this summer if your lawn has this problem.

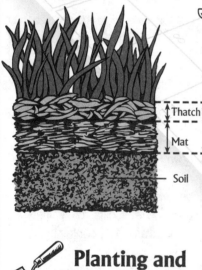

Thatch Layer

Thatch
Mat
Soil

Planting and Transplanting

Continue to plant warm-season grasses throughout the summer. The earlier you get them in, the longer they have to grow and get established before winter. Choose the type of grass for your lawn carefully. The chart on page 103 is a good start. Talk to friends and neighbors about their experiences with different types of grass, and contact your local office of the Texas Cooperative Extension Service for free literature on lawn selection. Repair small bare spots by digging plugs from thick, healthy parts of the lawn and planting them where needed (or purchase plugs). *Loosen the soil in the area and rake it smooth* before planting the plugs. *Water frequently* until the plugs begin to run.

Care for Your Lawn

Deal with excessive thatch buildup during the summer.

Core aerification is effective, and is especially recommended if there is also a problem with soil compaction. The machine used for this process creates small holes in the turf and upper layer of soil with hollow tines, and deposits soil on the surface. The holes reduce compaction and improve air content in the soil.

Heavy thatch buildup may need to be corrected by vertical mowing. Vertical mowers, or dethatchers, have numerous blades mounted vertically on a rod, and pull out the thatch when run over the lawn. This is the most traumatic method. Core aerification and dethatching with a vertical mower are best handled by a professional lawn care company.

Watering

Water newly laid sod for 15 to 20 minutes every day for a week. The roots are mostly lost when sod is harvested, and the sod easily dries and will die if not kept moist. During the next 7 to 10 days, water the sod every other day if it does not rain. Finally, apply $1/2$ inch of water to the lawn twice a week for several weeks if the weather is dry while the sod finishes establishing.

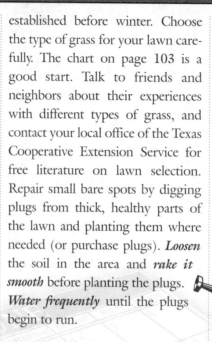

Vertical Mower

JUNE

Do not continue to water the lawn every day for more than a week or you will increase the risk of fungus diseases damaging the new turf. Water established turf only as needed during hot, dry weather. Drought-stressed turf will look pale or slightly grayish, the leaves will roll lengthwise, and footprints will show on the grass for several minutes after you walk across the lawn. Water thoroughly if you observe these symptoms.

Fertilizing

Lawns (other than **centipede**) that were fertilized in April may be fertilized again this month. This is more important in situations where a high degree of quality and vigorous growth are desired. Also, fertilize lawns sodded in April or early May. Many gardeners find it acceptable to fertilize once in April to get the grass off to a good start and leave it at that.

Pest Control

Be cautious about using weed-killers for the rest of the summer. Many could damage the lawn if temperatures are high.

Insect problems like chinch bugs and mole crickets may need to be dealt with this month. Chinch bugs suck the sap out of grass and are especially damaging during periods of hot, dry weather. Look for areas of dead, straw-like grass starting in sunny, hot areas of the lawn. Treat with insect-control aids/products labeled to control chinch bugs in lawns.

When using any pest-control aid/product, always read the label carefully and follow the directions exactly. Refer to page 291 for a summary listing your options.

Mowing

Given our long growing season, it is not a bad idea to sharpen mower blades again in midsummer. Dull mower blades tear the grass blades leaving ragged, brown tips that make the lawn look less attractive. Set your mower to the following recommended heights:

Common Bermuda: 1 to $1^1/_2$ inches (rotary or reel mower)

Hybrid Bermuda: $^1/_2$ to 1 inch (reel mower recommended)

Centipede: 1 to 2 inches (rotary or reel mower)

St. Augustine: 2 to 3 inches (rotary or reel mower)

Zoysia: $^1/_2$ to $1^1/_2$ inches (rotary or reel mower)

JULY

Planning

Mow, edge, and deal with pest problems before you go on vacation. Plan on having your lawn mowed if you will be on vacation longer than seven days. Lawngrass grows rapidly and if left uncut, will show that no one is home. The heat index in Texas will top 100 most days in July and August. Do yard work in the early morning or late evening when temperatures are not so hot. Drink plenty of water and take frequent breaks.

Planting and Transplanting

You may continue to plant lawns despite the heat. Watering newly plugged, sprigged, or sodded lawns is especially critical when it is this hot. Check sod carefully before laying it. Ask the nursery or dealer how long it has been since it was harvested. Ideally, sod should be planted within a day or two of being harvested. It is very perishable in summer heat. This is the last month to seed **centipede** and allow it ample time to establish before winter.

Care for Your Lawn

As landscapes mature, shade trees begin to do what they were planted to do—shade the yard. Lawngrasses eventually receive more shade than they can tolerate and will begin to thin and disappear when that happens.

Increase the amount of sunlight reaching the turf by selectively pruning the trees in your landscape. *Prune* the lower branches and some of the inner branches to allow more light to reach the lawn below (often best done by a professional arborist). This is a temporary solution, as the trees will continue to grow.

St. Augustine (varieties such as 'Raleigh') will tolerate the most shade. **Centipede** and **zoysia** varieties 'Meyers', 'Emerald', and 'El Toro' are also considered fairly shade tolerant. Don't expect any of them to grow in heavy shade. Set your mower at the highest recommended mowing height. **St. Augustine** can be mowed at a height of 3 inches, **centipede** can be allowed to grow to 2$\frac{1}{2}$ inches, and **zoysia** mowed at 1$\frac{1}{2}$ inches. Avoid excessive fertilization as grass in the shade does not grow as fast. If after these efforts you still can't get grass to grow under your tree, it's time to accept the situation (as we gardeners often must do) and stop wasting your effort and money trying to make grass grow where it can't. Unless cutting down the tree is an option, your next step is to plant shade-loving ground covers such as **ferns, monkey grass, liriope, Asiatic jasmine,** or **cast-iron plants (aspidistra).**

Watering

Do not water needlessly. Overwatering your lawn wastes water and promotes disease problems. Wait at least 7 to 10 days after the last good rain before you consider irrigation. Even then, look at the grass and dig into the soil. If the grass is not showing drought stress and there is still some moisture in the soil, wait a while longer to water. Do not water lightly every day, a practice which encourages diseases and creates a shallow root system. Do apply sufficient water when irrigating to reach a depth of 6 to 8 inches.

Fertilizing

If you last fertilized in April you might fertilize again this month, especially if the grass is not growing fast enough and you would like to mow more often. Fertilizer will create a deeper green color along with faster growth. For most lawns, two fertilizer applications, one in April and another this month, produce acceptable color and growth. A second light application of lawn fertilizer could be applied to **centipede** now as well. This grass will actually decline in vigor and fade away if you fertilize it too much. A slight yellow tint to the green color of the blades is normal for this grass. Remember, **centipede** grass is for acidic soils only. Do not grow it in highly alkaline prairie soils.

Pest Control

This is prime chinch bug season for **St. Augustine,** especially if the weather turns dry. Watch for tan strawlike dead areas that enlarge over several days. Do not delay controlling this pest. It kills the grass outright, and extensive damage means a lot of turf replacement.

The most effective weed control should have taken place in late spring and early summer. *Handpull and spot-treat* weeds now. Wait until the weather is not so hot to use most broadleaf weedkillers. Common summer weed problems include button weed, dallisgrass, goosegrass, and nutgrass. Spot-treat button weed, dallisgrass, and goosegrass with a weed-control aid/ product. Refer to page 291 for a summary listing your options. *Spray* directly on the weed, minimizing contact with the lawngrass (it will kill it). *Control* nutgrass with specialized aids/products, which may be used on all warm-season turfgrasses.

Mowing

Mow regularly at recommended heights. Mulching mowers prevent the need to bag clippings. The clippings return nutrients to the lawn, lowering the need for fertilizers. If you don't have a mulching mower, mow frequently so that the clippings are small—that works just about as well. If you do bag clippings, make sure you compost them for use in garden beds instead of the landfill.

Planning

This is a good month to evaluate your lawn. If it's in poor shape, try to identify the problems and plan on how to do a better job preventing them. Make some notes of what you would do differently next year. Earlier and better weed control is a good example. Learn from your experiences and record them for future reference in your Texas gardening journal.

Planting and Transplanting

Finish up seeding common **Bermudagrass** this month. As fast as it grows, expect good coverage before cool fall temperatures slow it down. ***Lay sod*** and ***plant plugs*** if possible. Every week of delay now is one less week of growing season for the turf to establish. This is particularly true for plugs.

Care for Your Lawn

Areas of your lawn that still need to be renovated should also be handled now. Remove any weeds, loosen the soil, and plug or sod new turf into the area. Keep the grass adequately watered and keep pets and people away until it has established.

Watering

These long, hot days coming at the end of a long, hot summer are especially stressful. Watering continues to be important. There is no way to predict the amount of rainfall that will occur. It could be very dry or we could see almost daily rain. Do not be fooled by quick thundershowers. Unless at least $1/2$ inch of rain falls, it should not be considered a "good rain." Water early in the day if possible. Avoid watering in the early evening, which does not give the grass time to dry before nightfall, encouraging disease problems.

Fertilizing

Those who want maximum quality and growth should make their third and last fertilizer application this month. Use fertilizers with an approximate 4:1:2 or 3:1:2 ratio analysis. Basically, look for a fertilizer that has a high first number, a low second number, and a third number somewhere in between. ***Apply fertilizer evenly*** with a broadcast or centrifuge type spreader and water it in immediately after application.

Pest Control

Fleas are insects that infest lawns. Although they don't damage the grass, they sure pester people. ***Treat*** the lawn with insect-control aids/products labeled for flea control in lawns. Several applications will be necessary, and don't forget to treat any pets according to your vet's advice.

Fire ants are other lawn pests that don't damage the grass, but bother us. ***Treat individual mounds*** with label approved fire ant-control aids/products. Refer to page 291 for a summary listing your options. Contact your Extension Service Agent for fact/tip sheets on identifying and controlling fire ants. Baits are effective when spread over the yard, though slower acting.

Planning

This month, relief from the heat is possible, but not guaranteed. Still, the heat is generally not so intense. Lawns are in active growth, but cooler weather in October and November will finally begin to slow them down. With that in mind, plan to finish up sodding, dethatching, and aerification early this month.

Planting and Transplanting

It's late for planting plugs and really too late to plant seeds of **centipede** or even fast-growing **Bermuda.** You may continue to lay sod this month. Don't forget that newly laid sod must be watered regularly to keep it from drying out while the roots establish. In north Texas, **ryegrass** seed may be planted later this month. There is no hurry, and if the weather is hot the **ryegrass** will not appreciate it. Warm-season lawns are still nice and green and there is really no need to plant seed this early.

Care for Your Lawn

Repair dead areas caused by chinch bugs this month:

1 *Remove* any dead grass plaguing your lawn. *Turn* the soil and *rake* it smooth.

2 *Lay* sod, or at least *plant* some plugs in the area.

3 Keep thoroughly watered during establishment. You will feel better next spring not seeing the dead spots in an otherwise green lawn, and your lawn will be more attractive this fall.

September is a prime month for hurricanes (the season runs from June to October). If a hurricane threatens your area, pick up and store all loose objects in the lawn, including sprinklers, tools, lawn ornaments, and anything else that could be picked up by 100-mile-per-hour winds. Should a hurricane hit your area, rake and hose off debris and mud from your lawngrass as soon as possible after the storm. If it stays covered for several days, significant damage can occur. If the area was covered by salt or brackish water, **St. Augustine** and **Bermuda** have good tolerance. Rinse the salt water away with fresh water as soon as possible.

Watering

Water as needed, especially newly laid lawns or lawns that are recovering from dethatching or aerification.

Fertilizing

This month or the first week of October is the time to winterize your Texas lawn. The same ratio and analysis we often use throughout our long growing season work well now. These include 21-7-14, 18-6-12, 16-4-8, and 15-5-10. Apply according to label directions with a broadcast or rotary spreader. Water thoroughly after application is complete.

Pest Control

Watch for caterpillars such as army worms or sod webworms. They chew grass blades and can make the lawn look terrible. *Control* with insect-control aids/products labeled for sod webworms. Refer to page 291 for a summary listing your options. Always read and follow label directions carefully. The grass will generally recover well from the damage.

Mowing

You may not have to mow quite as often as the weather turns cooler, but don't let your grass get overgrown before mowing.

Planning

As we move into the cool dormant season for our warm-season grasses, plan on whether or not you want to overseed with a cool-season grass. Remember, you will have to continue to mow throughout the winter if you do.

Planting and Transplanting

Plant **ryegrass** seed this month and in November. Annual **ryegrass** is the least expensive, most readily available, and most commonly used.

1 *Spread* the seeds evenly over a mown lawn using a spreader.

2 *Apply* half the seeds walking east to west, half walking north to south. Use about 5 to 10 pounds per 1000 square feet. Use the higher rate for an extra thick stand of **ryegrass**.

3 *Water* the seeds lightly every day for the 7 to 10 days it takes them to germinate. **Ryegrass** usually fills in about four to five weeks after it comes up. For higher quality, use **perennial ryegrass** or a **perennial ryegrass** blend. The color will be darker, the texture finer, and will last longer into the spring. It is, of course, more expensive.

Care for Your Lawn

Some gardeners are afraid that overseeding existing warm-season turf will damage it. *Don't worry.* Overseeding will not harm any of the commonly used warm-season grasses. In fact, overseeding tends to reduce competition from cool-season weeds since the lawn is mowed and maintained throughout the winter.

Watering

The weather now makes this one of the most enjoyable months of the year. It is, however, usually dry. Do not allow turfgrass to go into dormancy when it is drought stressed. *Water deeply and thoroughly* if a good rain does not occur for 10 to 14 days. Overseeded lawns will need more frequent watering while the ryegrass establishes.

Fertilizing

If you didn't winterize your lawn during September, the first week of this month is the time to do so, especially in north Texas. Anytime in October works well for south Texas lawns. The same analysis used during our growing season works well to winterize your lawn. Some numbers to look for are 21-7-14, 18-6-12, 16-4-8, and 15-5-10. Use a rotary or broadcast spreader to apply the fertilizer and water thoroughly after the application is complete.

Pest Control

If the weather is unusually wet, brown patch may appear on **St. Augustine.** Watch for it and *treat if necessary.* Apply weed prevention aids to the lawn this month to control cool-season annual weeds such as henbit, chickweed, and annual blue grass. These aids/products which prevent weeds from growing must be applied before the weeds show up in the lawn. Refer to page 291 for a summary listing your options.

Mowing

Do not mow an overseeded lawn until the **ryegrass** seed germinates and you see the green blades. Mowing newly overseeded lawns can suck up the seeds or otherwise damage them.

Planning

In the northern part of the state, warm-season grasses are going dormant with the first freeze. Down south, mowing is greatly reduced as the weather cools. Cool fronts bring rain. This is a good time to review successes and failures of the past season. What would you do differently? Write brief entries in your Texas gardening journal for next year at the proper times when lawn maintenance jobs will need to be done. The journal will provide you with a handy guide and remind you when things like fertilization, weed control, and planting need to be completed.

Planting and Transplanting

Continue to overseed **ryegrass** if you have not already done so. The look of **ryegrass** is outstandingly beautiful throughout the winter. The rich green is nicer than any of the warm-season grasses. You will need to continue mowing throughout the winter, but many people think it is worth it. If you have bare areas where soil might wash away during the winter, use **ryegrass** seed to stabilize the soil until spring.

Ryegrass can also be planted around newly constructed homes to stabilize the soil until it is time to lay sod next season.

Care for Your Lawn

After a long growing season, it is nice to be able to slow down. Little needs to be done to warm-season grasses other than watch them slow down and go dormant. **Zoysia, Bermuda,** and **centipede** go off color (turn tan) relatively early. This increases their hardiness, as they are quite dormant if and when severe freezes occur. **St. Augustine** is not so inclined to go dormant, especially in south Texas, and may stay fairly green well into December, and even into January if no hard freezes occur. This may make it more likely to sustain freeze injury during a sudden drop to the low 20s or teens.

Watering and Fertilizing

Cool, moist weather and a dormant condition make the need for irrigating warm-season grasses unlikely for the rest of the cool season. In north Texas, *fertilize* **ryegrass** planted in October in late November after the warm-season grass in your lawn has gone dormant.

Pest Control

Apply a preemergence herbicide early this month if you did not do so in October. In south Texas, watch for brown patch on **St. Augustine,** and *treat promptly* with an appropriate brown patch control aid/product. Refer to page 291 for a summary listing your options.

Mowing

Mow **ryegrass** regularly. Set the mower to a height of 1 to 2 inches.

Planning

Unless you overseeded with ryegrass, lawns are wonderfully care-free this time of the year. Review your notes and make sure you have recorded everything you need to do in your Texas gardening journal before you forget. Before you store your lawn mower, be sure to service it properly (check the manufacturer's instruction booklet) or take it to your local lawn mower shop for servicing.

Planting and Transplanting

In the warmest parts of the state, **ryegrass** is often planted successfully through the winter. If the winter is mild, there is no problem. If temperatures in the teens occur while the grass is getting established, however, the grass can be damaged. If there are some areas of the lawn where the **ryegrass** seems a little thin, feel free to scatter some seed to thicken up those spots a bit. Dormant sodding of warm-season grasses is done during the winter but is not very popular. The grass goes in dormant and brown, which is a bit disconcerting, and

there is some risk involved during particularly cold winters—the turf is more susceptible to freeze injury. Laying sod during the winter has no real advantage other than to stabilize soil around new construction. The grass will not begin to grow and establish until the weather warms up next March or early spring.

Care for Your Lawn

Honestly . . . you really can ignore the lawn this time of the year and devote more time to other gardening activities such as planting trees and shrubs.

Watering

Cool to cold weather and a dormant condition make watering warm-season grasses unnecessary during this month. Continue to *irrigate* lawns overseeded with **ryegrass** as needed if the weather is mild and dry. Mixed in with the freezes, temperatures in the 70s are not unusual in December.

Fertilizing

Fertilize **ryegrass** around the middle of this month after warm-season grasses go dormant. This will make the **ryegrass** darker green and encourage vigorous growth.

Pest Control

As with other aspects of lawn care, pest control is minimal this time of the year. Cool-season weeds should not be a problem if you applied a weed preventer in October or early November.

Mowing

Mow **ryegrass** regularly. A height of 2 inches is used for **ryegrass** overseeded on **Bermuda** or **zoysia**. Mow **ryegrass** at a height of 2 inches if it was used to overseed **centipede** or **St. Augustine**.

Perennials

Perennials are a flower gardener's delight. Though showy and colorful like annuals, their longer lives make them a less transient part of the garden. The ability of some varieties to live for years allows them to become old friends that can provide you with beauty for many seasons. As with annuals, though, perennial beds and borders can be a high-maintenance part of the landscape.

Perennials are plants that live for three years or longer. Unlike annuals and biennials, perennials do not die after flowering and setting seed. Technically, trees, shrubs, lawn-grasses, and bulbs are all perennials, but gardeners use the term "perennial" as an abbreviation for "hardy, herbaceous perennial"—a group of non-woody, hardy plants grown for their attractive flowers or foliage. Some herbaceous perennials are evergreen and never go completely dormant, while others go dormant, lose their leaves, and essentially disappear at certain times of the year, usually winter.

Success with perennials in Texas depends largely on proper selection, beginning with a rejection of perennials that only grow well north of zone 6. To survive here, perennials must be able to endure the summer heat, humidity, and rain or lack of rain, along with the diseases that may visit. Stop planting perennials recommended in books written for the rest of the country and focus on those that will thrive in our climate. You will discover that not only is perennial gardening possible here, but we can plant beds that rival those in any part of the world.

Planning the Perennial Garden

Gardening with perennials is something that gardeners often develop an interest in as they become more experienced. When you finally reach that "been there, done that" stage with annuals, perennials offer exciting challenges and great fun. Utilizing perennials effectively does, however, require learning and careful planning to achieve best results.

Different perennials have various seasons of bloom—some over a long period, some for just a few weeks. Utilizing a variety of perennials that bloom at different times can keep your perennial garden blooming throughout much of the year. Some other important questions you need to answer about the perennials you want to use:

- What species or cultivars are best for Texas?

- How tall will the plants grow?

- What colors are the flowers?

- What light conditions does the plant prefer—full or part sun, part shade or shady?

- Do they need excellent drainage?

- Are they evergreen? If they go dormant—when?

- How fast will they spread?

With some thoughtful planning, perennials can serve many purposes and attractively embellish the landscape in a variety of ways. They are impressive in perennial borders or mixed borders (which could include annuals, bulbs, shrubs, and even small trees). Tucked in pockets among shrubs they can brighten up an area when the shrubs are not in bloom. Many perennials make outstanding specimens in containers.

Perennials

Planting and Transplanting

The first step in planting perennials is excellent bed preparation. It is important to do a good job at each of the following stages:

1 **Remove** weeds and other unwanted plants from the bed. Growing weeds may be eliminated with a non-selective weed-control aid that does not leave residue in the soil. Refer to page 291 for a summary listing your options.

2 **Turn the soil** to a depth of at least 8 to 12 inches.

3 **Spread** a 4-inch layer of compost, rotted leaves, aged manure, finely ground pine bark, or sphagnum peat moss over the bed. If needed, add sand, lime, or sulfur at this stage. Have your soil tested through your county office of the Texas Cooperative Extension Service to learn more about what will improve your soil's fertility.

4 Thoroughly **blend** the amendments into the top 4 to 6 inches, **rake** smooth, and you're ready to plant.

Perennials are most often planted using purchased transplants or divisions. Transplants may be purchased in 4-inch to gallon-sized or larger pots. Generally, spring- and early summer–flowering perennials are planted in October through early December, and late summer– or fall-flowering perennials are planted from February through early April (they may also be planted in fall). Many gardeners plant perennials throughout the winter when weather is mild, especially in the south part of Texas.

Planting Transplants

1 Space plants according to label information, references, or local advice. Most perennials will grow considerably larger than the size of the transplant. Do not crowd them.

2 Plant transplants with the top of the rootball even with or slightly above the soil. Many perennials will rot if planted too deeply. If the roots are in a tightly packed mass, separate before planting. A small amount of granular slow-release fertilizer may be placed in each planting hole. Firm the soil around the plant once you have finished planting.

3 **Water** newly planted transplants thoroughly. A root stimulator may be applied according to label directions.

4 Mulch the bed 3 to 4 inches deep to control weeds.

Some perennials are relatively easy to grow from seed. Seeds are generally planted directly into garden beds or in containers outside to raise transplants. This is best done after the danger of frost or freeze is past, and early enough for the plants to become established before winter—April through August.

Care for Your Perennials

Perennial beds require watering, fertilizing, grooming, staking, cutting back, dividing, transplanting, weeding, and mulching. Do not plant more beds of perennials than your time will allow you to properly care for.

Supporting tall-growing perennials is important and often neglected by gardeners. Sprawling perennials may be unattractive and can damage the plants around them. Plan to stake, cage, tie up, or otherwise support perennials that need it early, before they fall over.

Perennials

Watering

Watering is most critical for newly planted perennials, especially during hot, dry summer weather. *Water* deeply and thoroughly by applying water slowly over a period of time. Sprinklers may be used, but water can damage flowers and encourage leaf diseases. Soaker hoses provide an excellent alternative. The use of 3 to 4 inches of mulch in perennial gardens will conserve moisture and reduce the need for irrigation.

Fertilization

A small amount of granular slow-release fertilizer can be added to the planting hole at planting. Always apply any fertilizer according to label directions. During the growing season, fertilize established perennials beginning in March or early April and then every six to eight weeks using a general-purpose premium-quality long-lasting slow-release fertilizer appropriate for your area. Follow package directions. Scatter the fertilizer granules evenly throughout the bed, and water-in to wash the fertilizer off the foliage and into the soil. In Texas, premium-quality granular rose fertilizers and multi-purpose 3:1:2 ratio fertilizers (including 21-7-14, 15-5-10 and 18-6-12) work well in perennial plantings.

Pest Control

Pest control is usually a part of perennial gardening, but the use of tough, well-adapted perennials will minimize problems. Remember, when using pest-control aids, *always read the label thoroughly before purchase and use.* Refer to page 291 for a summary listing your options.

Insects: Caterpillars damage plants by chewing holes in leaves. The whitefly can be a difficult insect to control, especially in mid- to late summer when populations can get way out of hand. The adults are small, snow-whiteflies; the larvae appear as small disks under the leaves. Aphids cluster on new growth and flower buds, sucking the sap from the plant. They are relatively easy to control but may return, requiring additional applications of pest-control aids. Various

Spreading Fertilizer

sucking insects, such as leaf hoppers, thrips, and plant bugs, cause small white flecks to appear on the foliage of many perennials. The damage is generally little more than cosmetic, but can weaken the plant if extensive.

Other pests: Spider mites can be devastating, especially during hot, dry weather on some plants. Snails and slugs love hostas and other plants that have succulent leaves and grow in shady areas. Control with baits used according to label directions, handpicking, or traps.

Diseases: Well-adapted perennials planted in the right location generally have minor problems with diseases. Leaf spots caused by various fungi and powdery mildew will sometimes occur and can be treated with fungus-control aids. Root and crown rot may occur if drainage is inadequate, during periods of excessive rain, or if perennials not well-adapted to Texas are planted.

Perennials for Texas

Name	Light*	Type and Size	Flowers	Comments
Achillea millefolium Yarrow	Full sun to part shade	Evergreen in mild winters; 12 inches	Flat clusters of various colors on stalks to 24 inches; early summer	Ferny, aromatic foliage; very easy to grow; flowers dry well; **native** and non natives
Artemisia ludoviciana A. 'Powis Castle' Artemisia	Full to part sun	Semi-dormant in winter; 2 to 3 feet	Not significant	Outstanding silvery foliage; cut back late winter/spring
Asarum spp. Wild Ginger	Part shade to shade	Evergreen; 6 to 8 inches	Small, brown, not significant	Shiny kidney-shaped dark green leaves
Asclepias curassavica A. tuberosa Butterfly Weed	Full to part sun	Dormant in winter; 1 to 3 feet	Showy orange flowers in summer	Excellent nectar food for butterflies, larval food for Monarchs; **native**
Asparagus densiflorus 'Sprengeri' Asparagus Fern	Full sun to shade	Evergreen, dormant if low 20s occur; 1 to 2 feet (**zone 9 only**)	Tiny, white to pale pink, summer; scarlet pea-size fruit	Tough, indestructible in the garden or in containers; mulch crown in winter
Aspidistra elatior Cast Iron Plant	Shade to full shade	Evergreen; 2¹/₂ feet	Not significant	Prune out unattractive leaves as necessary; tough; easy to grow
Aster spp. and hybrids Aster	Full to part sun	Dormant in winter; 1 to 5 feet depending on type	Showy, daisy-like in clusters, many colors; late summer, fall	Excellent for late-season color; cut back hard after blooming; **native** and non natives
Canna × generalis Canna	Full sun to part shade	Dormant in winter; 18 inches to 7 feet tall, depending on varieties planted	Spikes or stems with several blooms in yellow, orange, pink, red, coral, and cream	Dwarf to tall varieties are available and very easy to grow
Centaurea cineraria spp. *cineraria* Dusty Miller	Full to part sun	Dormant evergreen, depending upon the winter	Colorful, prune as needed, gray foliage	Virtually pest-free
Chlrophytum comosum 'Variegatum' Spider Plant	Part shade to full shade	Evergreen, dormant if low 20s occur; 1 foot (**zone 9 only**)	Not significant; remove flower stalks to keep the plants looking neat	Normally thought of as a houseplant; the roots will survive the low teens
Coreopsis lanceolata Coreopsis; Tickseed	Full to part sun	Dormant in winter; 24 inches	Yellow, gold, mahogany daisy-like flower; early to midsummer	Very showy flowers and easy to grow from seed; **native**
Cuphea micropetala Cigar Plant	Full to part sun	Dormant after first freezes; 2 to 5 feet	Yellow and red-orange; fall to winter, and spring if the winter is mild; early to midsummer	Cut back hard after freezes brown the foliage; can spread aggressively

*
Full sun: 8 hours or more of direct sun   Part shade: About 4 hours of direct sun   Full shade: Little or no direct sun
Part sun: About 6 hours of direct sun   Shade: About 2 hours of direct sun

Perennials for Texas

Name	Light*	Type and Size	Flowers	Comments
Dendranthema × morifolium cultivars **Garden Mums**	Full to part sun	Dormant in winter; 1 to 2 feet	Showy, daisy-like flowers in many colors; fall	Cut back hard in winter; divide in early spring
Echinacea purpurea **Purple Coneflower**	Full to part sun	Dormant in winter; 2 feet	Purple or white daisy-like flowers with a prominent cone; summer	Cut back after flowering; easily grown **native**
Eupatorium coelestinum **Wild or Hardy Ageratum**	Full sun to part shade	Dormant in winter; 2 to 3 feet	Soft lavender-blue fluffy flowers, primarily in fall; some blooms in early summer	Spreads rapidly; **native;** Joe-Pye Weed (*E. maculatum* and *E. purpureum*) are also good
Hemerocallis hybrids **Daylily**	Full to part sun	Semi-dormant in winter; 1½ to 3 feet in bloom	Large flowers on stalks in many colors; early to late summer	Reliable, easy perennial; divide in Sept. or Oct.
Hibiscus moscheutos **Hardy Hibiscus**	Full to part sun	Dormant in winter; 2 to 4 feet	Very large plate-sized blooms in white, pink, or red; early to late summer	Reliable; spectacular in bloom; easy to grow from seed; cut back in fall
Hosta spp. and hybrids **Hosta; Plantain Lily**	Part shade to shade	Dormant in winter; 6 to 24 inches	Lavender or white, bell-shaped flowers on stalks to 3 feet, some fragrant; summer	Excellent for shady areas; snails and slugs may be a major problem
Leucanthemum × superbum **Shasta Daisy**	Full sun to part shade	Dormant in winter; 24 inches in bloom	White daisy flowers with yellow centers; spring	Problems with rotting out in summer increase closer to the coast; provide good drainage
Ligularia tussilaginea **Ligularia**	Part shade to shade	Evergreen; 18 inches	Clusters of 1-inch yellow daisy-like flowers; late summer or fall	Excellent texture plant for shady beds; leaves look like lily pads
Mirabilis jalapa **Four-o-Clocks**	Full sun to part shade	Dormant in winter; 3 to 4 feet tall and 3 feet wide	Dark green foliage with white, pink, salmon, lavender, yellow, and blended lightly fragrant blooms	Old favorite in Texas; a "can't miss" perennial; may be invasive
Monarda fistulosa *M. didyma* **Beebalm**	Full to part sun	Dormant in winter; 2 to 3 feet	Flower heads in various colors, primarily pink, rose, and purple; summer	Cut back hard after flowering for repeat bloom; aromatic foliage
Phlox divaricata **Blue Phlox** or **Louisiana Phlox**	Full sun to part shade	Dormant in winter; 12 inches	Lavender-blue to purple flower clusters; spring	Flowers occur about four weeks; trim back when finished

*
Full sun: 8 hours or more of direct sun
Part sun: About 6 hours of direct sun

Part shade: About 4 hours of direct sun
Shade: About 2 hours of direct sun

Full shade: Little or no direct sun

Perennials for Texas

Name	Light*	Type and Size	Flowers	Comments
Phlox paniculata Garden Phlox (Summer or Border)	Full to part sun	Dormant in winter; 2 to 3 feet	Various colors; early to late summer; most varieties will not thrive here in zones 8 and 9	Those with magenta flowers, such as 'Robert Poore', are most reliable
Physostegia virginiana Obedient Plant	Full to part sun	Dormant in winter; 2 to 3 feet	Spikes of rosy purple or white; midsummer	Staking is recommended; spreads rapidly
Rudbeckia hirta 'Angustifolia' Black-Eyed Susan	Full to part sun	Dormant in winter; 2 feet	Golden daisies with dark brown centers; midsummer	Reliable, long-lived, and easy; cut back after flowering; **native**
Ruellia brittoniana Ruellia; **Summer** or Mexican Petunia	Full sun to part shade	Dormant after first freezes; 1 to 5 feet depending on cultivar	Lavender, purple, or pink; very long bloom period— spring to early winter	Very easy and reliable; self-seeds readily; new cultivars include dwarfs and variegated foliage; **native** and non natives
Salvia spp. and hybrids Salvia; Sage	Full sun to part shade	Evergreen in some areas if winter is mild; 1 to 6 feet, depending on type	Spikes in various colors, especially purples, reds, and blues; spring, summer, and especially fall	A large group that includes many excellent plants for Texas gardens; trim in late summer and cut back in late winter; **native** and non natives
Saxifraga stolonifera Strawberry Begonia	Shade	Evergreen; 4 inches	Airy panicles of small white flowers; spring	Attractive foliage, dark green with silver veins
Sedum spp. Sedum; Stonecrop	Full to part sun	Usually evergreen succulent; 4 to 12 inches	Various colors of star-shaped flowers generally in clusters	Many types; some do better than others; needs well-drained soil
Solidago spp. and hybrids Goldenrod	Full to part sun	Dormant in winter; 2 to 6 feet, depending on type	Spikes of golden yellow; late summer to fall	Does not cause hayfever; excellent tough **natives** for late-season color
Stokesia laevis Stokes' Aster	Full to part sun	Dormant in winter; 1 to 2 feet in bloom	Showy lavender-blue flowers in early summer	Reliable, easy, long-lived **native**
Tradescantia virginiana Spiderwort	Full sun to part shade	Dormant in winter; 1 to 2½ feet	Clusters of purple, blue, rose, or pink; spring/early summer	**Native** wildflower tolerates damp conditions; easy and reliable; may be invasive
Veronica spicata Veronica; Speedwell	Full to part sun	Dormant in winter; 1 to 2 feet	Spikes of purple, blue, or rose in early to midsummer	Cut back faded flower spikes to encourage more bloom
Viola odorata Violet	Part shade to shade	Evergreen; 4 inches	Small, fragrant purple flowers; spring	Nice for edging or detail plants in shady beds

*
Full sun: 8 hours or more of direct sun
Part sun: About 6 hours of direct sun

Part shade: About 4 hours of direct sun
Shade: About 2 hours of direct sun

Full shade: Little or no direct sun

Planning

Visit your local nurseries. Become familiar with which perennials they have on hand in January and ask when additional perennials will be available. If you have specific types or varieties you are searching for, let the manager or owner know. Many local nurseries will stock their stores based on customers' requests and even order special types/varieties for individuals. When possible, it is nearly always better to look at plants "in person" prior to purchasing.

If the perennials you are looking for aren't currently available locally and will not be this season, visit nurseries in other cities and/or review mail-order or Internet sources. When purchasing plants out of your area, make sure they are hardy in your zone and can handle the Texas heat.

Planting and Transplanting

Gardeners frequently move perennials, trying to find a location where they will look and grow best, or just to try out a different combination. Often we are unfamiliar with what a perennial will do for us until we have grown it in our own garden. After a year or two, a gardener may realize that another location for the plant would be better. Now would be a good time to move it.

Care for Your Perennials

Apply mulch over the crowns and roots of some of the less hardy perennials during the coldest part of winter. This will help prevent cold damage. Pine straw, clean hay, pine bark mulch, dry leaves, pine bark nuggets, and shredded hardwood bark all work well for this purpose. Mulch perennials such as **asparagus fern, spider plant, ruellia, salvias,** and any others which are known to be "tender" in your area.

Watering

Cool to cold temperatures, typical rainy weather, and the dormant condition of many perennials generally make watering unnecessary. If the weather turns mild and/or dry, *water* beds containing perennials as needed. Do not water on any preset schedule.

Fertilizing

Few herbaceous perennials are in active growth during the winter, and January is not the best time to fertilize them. Dormant perennials do not need fertilizer.

Pest Control

Insect and disease problems are at a minimum this time of year. Cool-season weeds, however, will be in active growth any time a stretch of mild weather occurs. Keep beds mulched 3 to 4 inches deep and promptly pull up any weeds as they appear. If the temperatures rise above 65 degrees Fahrenheit, tough weeds, like wood sorrel, may be treated with a weed-control aid. Refer to page 291 for a summary listing your options. Since you should be careful not to get any on the foliage of desirable plants, it is easier to use when the perennials are mostly dormant and there is little or no foliage present.

Pruning

Cut back and remove old, dead upper portions of dormant perennials. This will keep the garden looking more attractive. Chop up the material and put it in your compost pile. Some perennials don't go dormant until the first freezes hit, and in the southern part of the state freezes may not occur until late December or January (or sometimes not at all in the Rio Grande Valley area). Sharp "bypass" types of hand pruners usually work well for all types or perennial pruning.

Planning

Part of the fun of using perennials is planning. It's like choreographing a dance, each member of the troupe with a role to play. There are supporting cast members, soloists that enliven the dance at various times, and even prima donnas. Throw a bunch of dancers on the stage without a carefully-thought-out plan, and the result will be chaos that may even lead to injuries. Purchase and plant perennials without carefully designing the composition, and the result may be chaos in the garden and disappointing results.

Planning begins with the site, not the perennials themselves. Just as a choreographer looks at the size of the stage, where the audience will be, the lighting available, and the backdrops, you should study the site where the planting will be located. How large is the bed? From which direction will it be viewed? How much light does the area receive? Is the drainage good? What existing trees, shrubs, or other features will contribute to the composition?

Next, develop your ideas on what characteristics the perennials must have to create the composition you imagine.

- Is the bed location sunny or shady? Dry or damp? Choose perennials that will thrive in the growing conditions of the area.

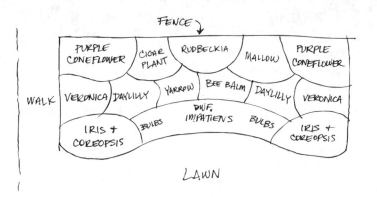

- Flower colors are important—they should blend, harmonize, or contrast attractively with one another. Decide on a visual scheme and which colors you will use to achieve your goal.

- Time of bloom should be considered. Selecting perennials that bloom at various times is wise.

- Height should be noted and decided. How tall do you want the tallest perennials to be? They are normally placed toward the back of a bed from the direction it will be viewed, or toward the middle of a bed to be viewed from all sides. The tallest perennials will guide the height of shorter perennials to be used in the bed.

- Choose perennials with a variety of textures (coarse-textured plants have large leaves, fine-textured plants have small or thin leaves, and medium-textured plants fall somewhere in-between) and growth habits (upright, bushy, mounding) to create interest and contrast in the composition.

Make a sketch of the bed and section it off into areas indicating where the tall, intermediate, and short plants will go.

Begin to make lists of perennials you like that have the characteristics you are searching for. Beside each name indicate briefly the major features of the plant (height, bloom time, color). Use the lists to make your final perennial choices, and place the names and number of plants needed into areas on your sketch. Depending on the size of the bed and how large a perennial will grow, it is generally best to plant perennials in groups, masses, or drifts of the same variety rather than as a lot of different individual plants. Try not to fall into the "I'll take one of each" and create a hodgepodge planting, unless this is the desired goal.

Purchase locally if available or order the selected plants, plant them into the garden, and watch the magic of the dance that careful planning creates. Note your decisions in your Texas gardening journal.

Planting and Transplanting

It's time to gear up for major planting this month and in March. Although a fall planting is preferred for most spring/summer-blooming selections, it is especially important to get spring and early-summer perennials planted as soon as possible. Perennials such as **canna, daylily, blue phlox,** and **daisy** are in this group.

Work on getting beds ready and in shape for planting. *Eliminate* any weeds in existing beds, and remove turf from new beds. *Turn the soil*, add 4 to 6 inches of organic matter, and blend with the soil 4 to 6 inches deep. Beds may be prepared several weeks prior to planting. Newly prepared beds may be heavily mulched until you are ready to plant them.

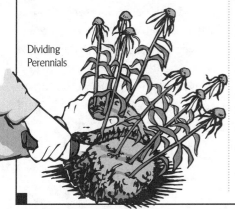

Dividing
Perennials

If you need to dig up and move or divide perennials, get started now. This activity needs to be finished by late March (in south Texas) or early April (in north Texas).

Care for Your Perennials

Watch for new growth on dormant perennials, and be careful. They are easily damaged by hoeing or digging. **Hostas** are late sleepers and often do not wake up until April or later. Note where dormant perennials are located (it is hoped that you marked them with small stakes in the fall as they went dormant), and do not damage them while digging. Note their locations in your Texas gardening journal.

Watering

Cool, moist weather usually means that little watering will need to be done. Water-in newly planted perennials thoroughly, and continue watering as needed. Perennials growing in containers will need watering, especially if they are in a location where they do not receive rain, such as on a covered patio. Check containers frequently but water only as needed.

Fertilizing

In south Texas, perennials that are in active growth may be fertilized in late February. It's generally best to wait a few weeks until mid-March, just in case a late cold snap hits. North Texas gardeners should certainly wait, perhaps until as late as April.

A little slow-release granular fertilizer may be placed in the planting hole when planting perennial transplants. Apply any fertilizer aid according to label directions

Pest Control

There are generally no major insect or disease problems in February. If the winter has been mild, aphids may be seen on new growth. Use a pest-control aid as needed. Refer to page 291 for a summary listing your options. Continue to control weeds.

Pruning

Remove old, dead growth on perennials as soon as possible if you have not already done so. It will become increasingly difficult to remove dead stalks without damaging the new growth as it grows taller.

Planning

Visit your local nurseries because they should have selections in stock this month for your spring/ summer gardens. Remember, always select the best varieties for your area which will meet your goals. Should you decide to order plants through the mail or over the Internet, you will find they are often shipped bare root or are fairly small (a 4-inch pot size is common), and will need as much time as possible to become established before the heat of summer.

Before purchasing locally or ordering perennials, plan on where they will be planted based on the growing conditions they need and how they grow. Avoid perennials that have little chance of thriving in the growing conditions you are able to provide. It is a wise, experienced gardener who can say, "I'd really love to grow that, but I just don't have the right spot.", or "It doesn't do well here."

Avoid the temptation of buying more new perennials than you have room to plant, or dig up and give away perennials you've grown for some time to make way for the new ones. Enter your decisions in your Texas gardening journal.

Planting and Transplanting

Finish up transplanting and dividing perennials as soon as possible. If they are transplanted now, most perennials will barely miss a beat if moved with most of their roots. Later on, warmer weather makes it more likely that perennials will suffer transplant shock.

Divide clumps of perennials that need it. Some are best divided every two to three years, but most can be left alone for longer. Dividing helps control the size of the plant and the space it occupies, as well as rejuvenating it. Dividing perennials is also a good way to propagate many of them. To divide perennials:

1 *Lift* the entire clump while the soil is moist.

2 Study the clump carefully. Note the crowns or shoots present.

3 Decide how many pieces to divide the clump into. Generally, each division should have several crowns or shoots.

4 Decide where to make the cuts. Avoid cutting through crowns or damaging shoots.

5 *Cut apart* the clump with a large, sharp knife. Be careful. Wear leather gloves.

6 *Replant* or *pot up* the divisions immediately.

Perennials may not look like much when you purchase them this month. This is a reason newer gardeners, accustomed to buying annuals in full bloom, are slow to appreciate perennials. Just imagine how they will look when they bloom in two or three months—or even at the end of the summer—to value them in March.

Growers have overcome this to some extent by producing perennials in gallon containers. These container-grown selections are often found at local retailers and can be planted later since the perennials have more room to develop a strong root system. This allows gardeners to purchase plants in bloom. Buy and plant perennials in smaller containers now, and it may be these plants in your garden that will grow to be as attractive as the gallon-sized perennials available later.

Plant perennials into beds so that the tops of the rootballs are level with or slightly above the soil of the bed. Many perennials are more likely to suffer crown rot if planted too deeply. If you see that the rootball is tightly packed when you remove the perennial from the container, pull it apart and spread out the roots a little when planting.

Care for Your Perennials

Watch the weather carefully. March is an unsettled month and periods of warm temperatures can be followed by a sudden freeze, particularly in north Texas. It is unlikely that you will need to protect hardy perennials. Tender new growth, however, is more susceptible to sudden freezes. Mulch, fabric sheets, or cloth may be placed over perennials you think might be vulnerable. Promptly *remove* coverings when freezing temperatures have ended.

Watering

Warmer temperatures and active growth make watering increasingly important if regular rainfall does not occur. *Apply* slowly over time with a sprinkler or soaker hose to ensure a deep, thorough watering. It is far better for the health of the perennials to water them thoroughly as needed than to water lightly and frequently.

Newly planted perennial beds will need special attention. Until new perennials have a chance to grow a strong root system into the surrounding soil, they are vulnerable to drying out. *Water* new plantings to maintain moist but not wet soil conditions.

Fertilizing

Established perennials should be fertilized this month. This is most efficiently and economically done using a granular fertilizer applied evenly throughout the bed. If your soil has adequate phosphorus, choose a premium-quality long-lasting slow-release fertilizer with a 3:1:2 ratio, such as 15-5-10. For soils that test low in phosphorus, select an analysis to meet the soil-test recommendations. Follow label directions when applying all fertilizers.

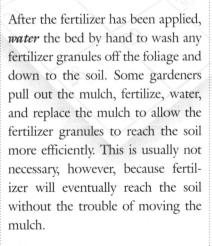

Spreading Fertilizer

After the fertilizer has been applied, *water* the bed by hand to wash any fertilizer granules off the foliage and down to the soil. Some gardeners pull out the mulch, fertilize, water, and replace the mulch to allow the fertilizer granules to reach the soil more efficiently. This is usually not necessary, however, because fertilizer will eventually reach the soil without the trouble of moving the mulch.

Pest Control

Make notes of pest problems in your Texas gardening journal.

Snails and slugs may be active in some zones during mild weather. Get an early start on control and don't let their populations build. Various baits and traps, and hand-picking, will help reduce populations. **Hostas,** which generally begin to grow in late March, April, or later, are particularly vulnerable. Control aphids, caterpillars, and any other insect pests with approved aids if needed. Keep most pest-control aids away from your butterfly garden area.

Whoever said, "A job well done doesn't have to be done again," may have never weeded a flower bed. Pre-emergent weed-control aids may be applied now in weeded beds to prevent the growth of new weeds from seeds. *Check* the label carefully, and make sure the aids you select are appropriate to use around the ornamental plants growing in the bed. Always follow label directions when applying any gardening aid. Refer to page 291 for a summary listing your options.

Planning

The nurseries are full of plants, and if you never quite got around to visiting your local or area retailers earlier this year, you can find out what's new at the nursery now. Choose larger plants in larger containers for planting this late, if possible.

No one said that a plan cannot allow for some spontaneity or change. "I saw it and just had to have it" is often reason enough for a purchase. But it is difficult to create a planting that really comes together effectively if you make that the primary way you choose your plants. Entries at this time in your Texas gardening journal will prove to be valuable information for future decisions. Include in your notes: varieties and types of perennials purchased, where purchased, when and where planted, weather conditions including rainfall, temperatures, wind, and sun/clouds, and pests.

Planting and Transplanting

Pay careful attention to spacing when planting perennials. If you are accustomed to planting annuals, you may be tempted to plant the perennials too close. Most perenni-

als grow considerably larger than the small transplants you set out. Remember as well that these plants will grow in that location for several years, getting larger every year. The full look you see in beautiful photographs of perennial borders happens after the perennials have been growing for some time—don't expect your bed to look like that a couple of months after planting. Despite our long growing season, it will take most perennials more than one season to reach full size.

If you would like to try your hand at growing perennials from seed, now is a good month to start. Since many perennials will not bloom until their second year, most gardeners plant seeds in containers to raise transplants which can be planted into the garden in the fall or early the next spring.

1 *Fill* a flat or pot with moistened soilless potting mix or lightweight potting soil.

2 *Plant* seeds thickly at the recommended depth, and gently *water* the flat to settle them in.

3 *Cover* the flat with clear plastic wrap and place it in full shade.

4 *Check* the mix frequently and do not allow it to dry out or stay wet—*moist* is the desired soil condition here. With the plastic cover, you may not need

to add more water. If the mix stays too wet, vent or remove the plastic for a few hours.

5 When the seeds begin to germinate, *remove* the plastic and immediately move the flat to a location that receives about six hours of sun early in the day for sun-loving perennials. Place the flat in part shade to shade if you are growing perennials that prefer those conditions. *Water* as needed to maintain a moist soil.

6 When the seedlings begin to look crowded, gently *separate* them (try to handle them by their leaves rather than their stems) and *plant* into cellpacks, or individually in 4-inch pots using moistened soilless mix or lightweight potting soil.

7 *Water* the growing transplants daily, if necessary, to keep the soil moist. *Fertilize* weekly with half-strength high-middle-number soluble fertilizer.

8 *Repot* into larger containers as needed.

9 *Plant* in the landscape during October or November, or even during the summer if the plants get big enough.

Care for Your Perennials

Some perennials, such as **butterfly weed, Shasta daisy,** and **blue phlox,** are in bloom this month, especially in the southern part of the state. **Blue phlox** (also known as **Louisiana phlox**) is particularly beautiful. *Deadhead* (remove the faded flowers) regularly to keep plants attractive and, in some cases, encourage more flowers. Some perennials will generally send up a few more blooms if the faded flower cluster at the shoot tip is pinched off.

As perennials grow, make sure your layer of mulch is at least 3 inches thick. Add more mulch to beds if necessary. A proper layer of mulch will keep soil cooler as the weather heats up, conserve soil moisture, and prevent weeds, as well as make perennial plantings look more attractive. Many Texas perennials gardeners maintain mulch layers 3 to 4 inches deep year-round in their plantings.

Watering

Deep watering is especially important this time of year if sufficient rain does not fall. It will encourage your perennials to develop a deep root system that will make them stronger and more drought resistant later in the summer. Always water deeply and thoroughly when irrigating perennials, and only as needed. Do not water lightly, frequently, or on a preset schedule.

Fertilizing

Fertilize perennial plantings if you have not done so. Finish up this month. Don't overlook perennials growing in containers. One of the easiest ways to fertilize them is to apply a premium-quality long-lasting slow-release granular fertilizer in the container according to label directions. You will not need to fertilize again all summer.

Pest Control

Pest problems will likely become more numerous from now on.

Insects: Watch out for caterpillars and beetles, which chew holes in the leaves, and aphids.

Diseases: Look for a white, powdery coating on the leaves of perennials in your garden. Powdery mildew is a common disease that may attack a variety of ornamentals.

Treat with a fungus-control aid. Gray mold (Botrytis) may attack flowers and foliage during cool, wet weather, causing tissue to brown and rot with a gray fuzzy growth on it.

Weeds: Cool-season weeds are still around, but warm-season weeds are beginning to grow. Do not let them get out of hand.

If you haven't already done so, this is a good month to visit local retailers and become familiar with the various types of gardening aids they stock. Gardening aids include fertilizers plus insect-, disease-, and weed-control products. Refer to page 291 for a summary listing your options. Ask for assistance in selecting and using the aids that will help you achieve your goals. Remember, read and follow label directions when using/applying any gardening aid.

Helpful Hint

Perennials easily grown from seed include **yarrow, butterfly weed** (*A. curassavica*), **asparagus fern** (zone 9), **aster, coreopsis, purple coneflower, daylily, mallow, rudbeckia, wild petunia, salvia, goldenrod,** and **spiderwort.** Many of these perennials will bloom the first year if seeds are started early.

Planning

Summer arrives this month as we move into the warm season and daytime highs in the 90s may begin (unfortunately) to occur. Often perennials are growing vigorously and happily.

Vigorous growth of many perennials leads to plants that need support. Some supports are less noticeable and more effective when used earlier rather than later. Short tomato cages are useful and effective. They are less conspicuous when spray-painted dark green prior to use. Commercial plant supports in many designs are available, and many will work well only if the plant grows through them early in the season. Keep in mind that excessive fertilization with quick-release fertilizers can cause overly vigorous, weak growth, which increases the need for supports.

As the growth and development of your perennials accelerate, make sure you keep up with entries in your Texas gardening journal. Evaluate and enter comments on the spring-blooming perennials as they finish. Also include when plants were fertilized and with what, weather conditions, and any pest problems and how they were controlled.

Planting and Transplanting

If you're just getting around to planting a perennial garden with transplants, you're late. If you are willing to put in extra effort to get them established in the heat, however, you should be successful. If you just want to add a few more perennials to existing beds, choose transplants in larger containers for best results. Perennials in small pots are often rootbound and stunted this late in the planting season.

It is very risky to dig and transplant or divide perennials this late. If you absolutely must transplant a perennial, lift it with as much of a rootball as you can and replant it immediately in its new location. *Water* it in and keep it well watered until it recovers from the shock. There is a high probability that the plant will be stunted and sulk the rest of the season, but you never know—it may not miss a beat. Planting healthy container-grown selections from pots 1 gallon or larger is a good way to help ensure establishment of perennials planted this time of year in Texas.

Care for Your Perennials

Continue to care for the perennial seeds you may have planted. Although not a lot of work, they do require frequent monitoring for water. As soon as they are large enough to handle, begin transplanting seedlings into cell-packs or 4-inch pots. Their stems are delicate and easily broken. A broken stem kills the seedling. Handle seedlings by leaf to avoid damaging stems. Provide newly transplanted seedlings with shadier conditions for several days, then move them back into their original location.

Cut back **blue or Louisiana phlox** about halfway after it finishes flowering.

Watering

Soaker hoses are an effective way to water perennial beds without getting water on the flowers and foliage. Flowers are sometimes damaged by water spraying on them, and foliage that stays dry is less likely to develop disease problems. Snake the soaker hose through the bed to cover the entire area. Remember, always water deeply and thoroughly when irrigating. Do not water frequently, lightly, or on preset schedules.

Water does not move a great distance from the hose, so it is important to make sure all the plants in the bed are receiving water. Mulch may be placed over the soaker hose so no one even knows it's there. To determine how long to leave it on in order to thoroughly water the bed:

1 *Turn on* the soaker hose and check the time.

2 After 30 minutes, *turn off* the hose and go check the bed. *Dig* in several places with a trowel to determine how deep the water has penetrated, and how far out from the hose. Note any dry areas and readjust the hose if necessary.

Soaker hoses not only place water into a plant's root zone but also save up to 50 percent on water usage.

3 If sufficient water was applied to soak most of the bed 4 to 6 inches down, you know to leave it on 30 minutes. If not, leave the hose on for another 20 to 30 minutes, and check the soil. Continue to water and check until the bed is properly watered. Note the time it takes.

It's a bit of a bother, but you only have to do it once.

Fertilizing

Most of your fertilizer applications should be finished by now. If for some reason you haven't fertilized yet—better late than never. *Apply* a premium-quality long-lasting slow-release granular fertilizer appropriate for your area at the rate recommended on the label. *Spread* the fertilizer evenly and water-in immediately by hand to wash the granules off the foliage and down to the soil. In Texas, most of our plants respond well to 3:1:2 ratio fertilizers. Examples of this ratio include 21-7-14, 18-6-12, and 15-5-10. Use premium quality, long-lasting slow-release types according to label directions for best results.

Pest Control

Most perennial plantings are not constantly plagued by pests. Carefully chosen, well-adapted, and cared-for perennials generally need only occasional help with pest problems. Watch your plants and try to eliminate pests before they do too much damage. On the other hand, don't reach for the spray bottle every time you see a hole in a leaf.

Helpful Hints

Take some time to notice the wildflowers blooming along the highways in late spring and early summer. Many are the ancestors of perennials growing in your garden. **Blue or Louisiana phlox, Indian paintbrush, Mexican primrose (*Oenothera speciosa*), verbena, salvia,** and **mallow** are just a few garden perennials that are derived from plants native to this state.

Planning

Most activity in the perennial garden now centers on care and maintenance and recording notes in your Texas gardening journal. Take some pictures throughout the summer as the garden grows and develops. Video is also a great way to record your gardens throughout the season. Digital cameras allow you to store pictures in your computer, and photo processors will put pictures taken with regular film on diskettes these days. Dated pictures are an invaluable way to record how things looked at particular times, when plants bloomed, problems with color schemes, the performance of plants, and a myriad of other details. Writing in your Texas gardening journal helps to support any photos and/or videos you have shot of your plantings. There's nothing like written records in gardening.

Planting and Transplanting

Perennial transplants growing in containers can be planted now, but it's harder for them to establish when it is hot. Container-grown perennials may be potbound this time of the year. *Check* the roots before you purchase the plants, slipping them out of the pot. If the plant does not look vigorous and the root system is a tightly packed solid mass, put it back. Generally, avoid planting during the hottest months of the year—unless you really want to and will be able to provide the care and attention required. However, vigorously growing, healthy transplants you raised yourself from seed can be planted now if they are large enough. Disturb the roots as little as possible and keep them well watered for the first several weeks while they get established.

Do not transplant perennials growing in the ground until the weather cools in October.

Watering

These next three or four months are the most stressful of the year. The weather is bound to be too wet or too dry at various times (usually dry). Excessive rain will rot out perennials, especially those not well-adapted to Texas and the Deep South.

In a surprisingly short time, 95-degree-Fahrenheit days and 75-degree nights can dry out the soil. *Water* deeply and thoroughly as needed when rain has not occurred. Always water deeply and thoroughly when irrigating. Do not water on preset schedules.

Perennials grown as container specimens may need daily watering. Check first and water if needed. Transplants you've grown from seed will also need regular attention to watering.

Fertilizing

Another application of fertilizer may be made to beds last fertilized in March or April. Evaluate the plants before you do. If they are growing vigorously (or too vigorously) and have a rich green color and plenty of flowers, fertilization is optional.

If your soil has adequate phosphorus, choose a premium-quality slow-release long-lasting fertilizer with a 3:1:2 or 4:1:2 ratio, such as 15-5-10 or 16-4-8. For soils that test low in phosphorus, select a fertilizer higher in the middle number, or add extra phosphorus to 3:1:2 fertilizers. Follow label directions.

After the fertilizer is applied, *water* the bed by hand to wash any fertilizer granules off the foliage and down to the soil.

Pest Control

Pest problems abound at this time of the year, but we hope that not too many have found your gardens.

Insects: Caterpillars are common and damage plants by chewing holes in leaves.

The whitefly can be a difficult insect to control, especially in mid- to late summer if populations get way out of hand. The adults are small, snow-whiteflies; the larvae appear as small disks under the leaves.

Aphids cluster on new growth and flower buds sucking the sap from the plant. They are relatively easy to kill, but may return, requiring additional applications of pest-control aids/products.

Various sucking insects, such as leaf hoppers, thrips, and plant bugs, cause small white flecks to appear on the foliage of many perennials. The damage is generally little more than cosmetic, but it can weaken the plant if extensive.

Other pests: Spider mites can be devastating, especially during hot, dry weather.

Snails and slugs love **hostas** and other plants that have succulent leaves and grow in shady areas.

Control snails and slugs with baits used according to label directions, by handpicking, or with traps. Check under pots where they like to hide during the day. Collect and dispose of them.

Diseases: Well-adapted perennials planted in the right location and well cared for generally have minor problems with diseases. Leaf spots caused by various fungi and powdery mildew will sometimes occur and can be treated with a fungus-control aid. Root and crown rot may occur if drainage is inadequate, especially during periods of excessive rain, or if perennials not well adapted to Texas are planted. Remove the affected plant and improve soil drainage.

When using any pest-control aid, always read the label thoroughly before purchase and use. Make sure the problem has been properly identified. Check with your local office of the Texas Cooperative Agricultural Extension Service for help with diagnosing a problem. You may also contact your local retailers for assistance and suggestions on various methods and aids to prevent and/or control pest problems including insects, diseases, and weeds. Refer to page 291 for a summary listing your options.

Planning

Plan on getting most of your gardening work done during the cooler morning and evening hours. The heat this time of year is brutal. Perennials that aren't going to make it should be showing signs of stress by now. Excessive rain or lack of rain combined with high temperatures can be deadly to all but the best-adapted perennials. Don't forget to record failures as well as successes in your Texas gardening journal. These types of notes help all of us become more successful gardeners.

Planting and Transplanting

Most Texas gardeners wouldn't want to go out and dig up a bed to plant perennials this time of year, so you may be glad it's not a good time to plant anyway. If the perennial transplants you started from seed have outgrown their containers, shift into larger containers that will hold them until fall. It is important for the plants not to become root-bound, so they will continue to grow vigorously. If you would like to plant into the garden, plant with as little root disturbance as possible and keep well watered until they get established. Applying a root stimu-lator at planting time according to label directions should aid in root establishment.

Care for Your Perennials

Take some time now to cruise through your landscape. The more you do it, the better. During these walks you can mark gaps and note which plants are doing poorly. Make plans and decide on which plants might need to be transplanted or replaced this fall. You can see the beginnings of pest and disease attacks, the onset of weed problems, the need for water, the overgrown plants that might need to be pruned back or supported, and the faded flowers which need to be removed. If you catch these problems early, you will have a much easier time correcting them, and the plants will be better off as a result.

Most important, it should give you a chance to savor and appreciate what your efforts have accomplished. Don't let life's hectic pace keep you from enjoying what you have worked to create. Take the time to enjoy the goals you have met.

The gardener's most valuable tools are these moments of undivided attention you give to your garden. You may find they benefit you as much as they do the garden. After a visit through your landscape, it is usually a good time to note your observations in your Texas gardening journal.

Watering

Proper watering is critical during this stressful time of year. Do not think watering perennial beds by hand is adequate. We usually apply water by hand too fast and over too short a period for it to deeply penetrate the soil. As relaxing and therapeutic as it may be for some gardeners, it is not good for your plants. Use soaker hoses, drip irrigation, or sprinklers, and leave them on long enough for the water to moisten the soil about 4 to 6 inches down. Morning is the preferred time to water so plants are well supplied with water going into the hottest time of the day. Late-afternoon or early-evening watering with sprinklers is less desirable. The foliage goes into the night wet, which can encourage fungal diseases on some plants.

Remember, water deeply and thoroughly but only when needed. *Do not water lightly and often.*

Fertilizing

Only perennials in active growth should be fertilized, and only if needed. Those that have already bloomed or are finishing should be left alone. High temperatures stress plants and can actually slow down the growth of many perennials. If you're not sure, or you fertilized last month, don't fertilize.

Always read and follow label directions when fertilizing any plants including perennials.

If you haven't had your soil tested within the past two years, now is a good time to have it done. Contact the Stephen F. Austin State University soil-testing lab, Box 13000, Nacogdoches, TX 75962 or your County Agent's office for forms and soil sample containers.

Pest Control

"Melting out" means that a herbaceous plant suddenly collapses, withers up, and dies. Sometimes the dead tissue is slimy to the touch. This condition is common in perennials poorly suited to our growing conditions or growing in improperly drained beds. There is little you can do other than record what happened in your Texas gardening journal. Check with gardening friends and references. If other people have had success, try the plant again in another location with better drainage, and perhaps some afternoon shade. You may find, however, that everybody else has had the same problem with the plant. You might have even known that, but just had to give the plant a try yourself.

Weeds: If desired, the judicious use of a nonselective weed-control aid (which should be available at local retailers) can be helpful in controlling tough weeds such as crabgrass, Bermudagrass, grass/sand burs, nut grass, and other label-listed weeds. Refer to page 291 for a summary listing your options.

The spray must be applied to the foliage of the weeds only. If any gets on the foliage of a desirable plant, wash it off immediately. Use a piece of cardboard as a shield, along with a hand-held pump-up or compression sprayer, when spraying close to desirable plants. An alternative method of application is the "high tech" coffee can method. Screw off the end of your spray nozzle and locate a drill bit the same size as the "attaching" end of the nozzle. Drill a hole in the center bottom of an empty 1-pound or smaller can. Slide the nozzle into the drilled hole from the bottom. Screw the spray nozzle end on to the sprayer. You now have a "high tech" coffee can sprayer which, when placed over undesirable weeds at ground level with the top of the can, should provide great safety when applying weed-control aids.

Planning

The fall perennial planting season is still a couple of months off, but it's not too early to visit local nurseries and other retailers to see what is currently available and ask what will be available in September, October, and November. This should help you in planning fall plantings. If you let your wants be known, many nurseries will call you when the plants arrive at their stores. The proper way to plan a perennial garden and select the plants for it is covered in February Planning. This is highly recommended if you are just getting into perennial gardening.

Experienced gardeners should also use the planning and perennial selection process, especially when designing new beds or extensively redesigning old ones. There is, however, a less formal way of choosing perennials that all of us succumb to sooner or later. It's called the "I gotta have this and I'll worry about where to plant it later" technique of garden design. Most of us have wandered around the garden holding a plant purchased on a whim or given to us by a friend, looking for some place to plant it. Gardening should be fun, or why bother? These plants, however, may end up planted in some random, empty spot where the growing conditions are not suitable, or where they do not combine well with adjacent plants. Try to keep this type of planting to a minimum. The occasional "jewel" is found, however, so don't completely eliminate this activity. Be sure to enter notes in your Texas gardening journal about your observations and decisions.

Planting and Transplanting

You can continue to plant perennial seeds throughout the summer to raise your own transplants, but you should finish up this month. If planted now, seeds should still have time to germinate and grow into reasonably-sized transplants before winter. If they are still too small to plant in the garden by November, they can be grown outside in containers over the winter. Bring them indoors only on those nights when temperatures below the upper 20s Fahrenheit are predicted.

Buy and plant **salvias** now if you can find plants in the nurseries and have some open spots in the garden. Most **salvias** put on a wonderful display of flowers in the fall and early winter—well into December if the weather stays mild, especially in south Texas. Since the weather is still so hot, disturb the roots of the **salvias** as little as possible when planting them, and keep them well watered for the first few weeks to help them get established. A few of the more reliable and outstanding perennial **salvias** for Texas gardens include:

- Perennial *Salvia coccinea* (**Texas sage** or **red sage,** especially **'Lady in Red'**)

- *S. farinacea* (**mealycup sage,** especially **'Victoria'**)

- *S. gregii* (**autumn sage**—a **native** Texas plant)

- *S. leucantha* (**Mexican bush sage**)

- *S. madrensis* (**forsythia sage**— yellow, an unusual color for salvias)

- *S.* **'Indigo Spires'**

- *S. guaranitica* (**anise sage**— **'Argentine Skies'** is pale sky-blue)

- *S. miniata* (**Belize sage**)

Keep the base of these plants mulched 3 to 4 inches deep during the winter.

Care for Your Perennials

Our long growing season combined with plentiful rainfall (along the coast) or adequate watering (in the rest of Texas) can produce abundant and even rampant growth during the summer. Now would be a good time to look over your perennial beds and evaluate how things are growing. A gardener must often play the role of referee. Tall plants can shade out, or fall over onto, smaller plants. Plants will spread into areas where they were not intended to grow. Note these observations in your Texas gardening journal and make decisions about what to remove, divide, or transplant this fall. In the meantime:

- *Prune back* overgrown perennials, especially those that bloom over a long period and well into the fall (**Artemisia, butterfly weed, cigar plant, wild ageratum, four-o-clocks, ruellia, salvias**).

- *Stake* or otherwise support larger perennials that need it. If young children will be playing around the garden, the stakes should be taller to avoid injury. Be sure to inform children of their presence.

- *Straighten* a leaning plant and *wedge* a piece of brick or stone at the base. This will support the plant without being visible.

- Many perennials spread by underground stems, some fast, some slow. Promptly *dig out* unwanted growth outside the area allotted to the plant, *pot it up, replant* somewhere else, or give to a fellow gardener. Barriers extending 8 to 12 inches down in the ground

around aggressive spreaders can help keep them under control.

Watering

Even one week without a good rain will create dry conditions in August heat. Spring-planted perennials should be well established by this time, but may still need to be watered deeply once or twice a week during dry periods. If you notice plants wilting, you are waiting too long before watering your garden. Check daily if needed and apply water when necessary. Water deeply and thoroughly when irrigating.

Fertilizing

Salvias are heavy feeders, and as they gear up for their outstanding fall blooming season, a light fertilizer application will encourage vigorous growth and abundant October flowers. Other fall-blooming perennials, such as **chrysanthemums,** may also be fertilized now. Generally, however, it should not be necessary to fertilize most other perennials. Most plants in Texas respond well to premium-quality long-lasting 3:1:2 or 4:1:2 ratio granular fertilizers applied according to label directions.

Pest Control

Whiteflies can be a major problem in late summer.

You will need repeated applications of whatever you use, and spray under the foliage thoroughly. Consider cutting back heavily infested plants.

Spider mites thrive in hot, dry late-summer conditions.

It is important to spray under the foliage where the spider mites live. A strong spray of water under the leaves every day for a week is often an aid in controlling them. Additional controls for spider mites and other pests are available at your local retailers.

Refer to page 291 for a summary listing your options for pest-control aids.

Pruning

Continue to *cut back and remove* dead flower stalks and unattractive growth on perennials. Look for vigorous new growth at the base of many perennials, and when you see it, cut back the plant hard. *Deadhead* regularly.

Planning

Make lists of perennials you would like to plant this fall. Some local nurseries, unfortunately, may not offer as large a selection of perennials in the fall as they do in spring. Now is a good time to check with your local nurseries to see what, if any, perennials they will have available. Ask them to stock the types and varieties you want to plant. Many will also order specific plants for you from growers.

Evaluate the performance of your perennials this summer and record information in your Texas gardening journal.

This is also a good time to think about the amount of care your perennial gardens required. Did they become a burden? Were you able to keep up with the weeding and general maintenance? Look at ways to reduce maintenance if you need to. Plant part or all of a bed with low-maintenance shrubs and ground covers. Eliminate some beds altogether and replant the spaces with lawngrass. Do not allow your landscape to demand more time than you have to give it—redesign it to fit your needs. Evaluate your goals and determine if they were realized and if not, why, and what you wish you had done differently.

Planting and Transplanting

It is still too hot to transplant or divide most perennials. **Daylilies** and **iris** may be divided now. This is also a good time to divide your **Louisiana irises** (included in the Bulbs chapter, but often thought of as perennials).

Daylily

Perennial transplants started from seeds earlier this summer are probably large enough to go into the garden now, if there is room. You should have already decided where they will be planted. If you raised more than you can use (and we almost always do), share some with friends, donate some to a fund-raiser like a church fair, or sell them at a garage sale.

Care for Your Perennials

Most of the summer-blooming perennials are finished or are finishing up their floral display for the year. Cut back the flower stalks and old faded flowers to keep the plants looking attractive.

It's a good idea to carry a pair of garden shears or hand pruners whenever you walk through the garden. Grooming plants is an important part of flower gardening. These colorful beds are meant to draw attention, and must be kept as attractive as possible at all times. Make sure the setting is just as nice for the late-blooming perennials as it was for the ones that bloomed earlier. No matter how stunning a perennial in bloom may be, if it is surrounded by plants with brown stalks, faded leaves, and dead flowers, the effect is diminished.

Mulches may have decayed and thinned out over the summer. Replenish mulch layers with fresh material to maintain at least a 3-inch thickness. Ideally, use what you can get for free. Stockpile leaves in bags when you rake them up this fall. Pine straw is an excellent material for mulching and is readily available at no charge if you have pine trees in your yard. It is also available in bales at some local nurseries, and is one of the least expensive of the commercially available mulches. You can also find chopped or shredded pine straw available in bags. Other popular materials for mulches are cypress mulch, pine bark mulch, clean hay, pine bark nuggets, and other agricultural by-products.

Check specimen perennials growing in containers. If they have become rootbound, transplant them into larger containers now. This will give them time to get established in their new pots before winter. Use lightweight professional potting soil mixes when repotting perennials.

Watering

We often get some relief from the heat this month, especially in the northern part of the state. Cool fronts are so very welcome after the long, hot summer, and often bring needed rain. Daytime highs in the 90s Fahrenheit still occur in September, and the month can be dry. Continue to *water* as needed using sprinklers, soaker hoses, or drip irrigation.

Fertilizing

Be cautious fertilizing this late. Few perennials grow actively throughout the winter, nor should they be encouraged to do so with late fertilizer applications. Perennials that have finished blooming for the year and those that are slowing down should not be fertilized. Perennials showing nutrient deficiencies may be fertilized, but use a soluble fertilizer to deliver available nutrients immediately. Soluble fertilizers feed for a short time and should not continue to stimulate growth into fall and winter.

Pest Control

Pests have had all summer to build up population levels.

Inspect plants frequently. There are many excellent broad-spectrum insect-control aids for a wide variety of insect problems. Refer to page 291 for a summary listing your options. Spray only infested plants to minimize the impact on beneficial insects. Apply only when and if needed.

Visit local retail nurseries for assistance in selecting and information on how and when to use pest-control aids for insects, mites, diseases, and weeds. Effective insect-control aids are available to control chewing insects such as caterpillars and beetles, sucking insects such as aphids, whiteflies, scale, and insect eggs.

When using lightweight summer horticultural oil, apply in the early morning hours according to label directions. Repeat applications as needed according to label directions.

Other pests: Damp weather favors snails and slugs.

Continue to use baits, traps, and barriers, or other controls as needed. Beer traps are effective and popular.

Diseases: Disease problems are difficult to deal with. While usually not as common as insect pests, diseases such as root rot or stem rot can be devastating.

Avoid root rot by making sure beds are well drained. Incorporate generous amounts of organic matter, including compost, ground pine bark, and sphagnum peat moss into the bed during preparation; don't plant transplants too deep or too close together; and water deeply and thoroughly as needed.

For foliar diseases, avoid wetting the foliage when watering (if practical) and water at a time when the foliage will dry quickly. Early morning is the best time.

Good air circulation and proper spacing when planting also helps. Broad-spectrum fungus-control aids can be used if needed.

Planning

The prime fall planting season for perennials runs from October through early November in north Texas and December in south Texas. Make sure you have appropriate locations in your garden for any new perennials you decide to plant. Check your local nurseries to see what they have available. In areas of the state with milder winters, such as zones 8 and 9, planting can continue throughout the winter months. Local nurseries are always good places to order specific types and/or varieties of plants you want to install.

Planting and Transplanting

Now is the time to begin putting all of that summer planning to work. Dig and prepare new beds for fall planting. Before you do, decide if you have the additional time that the maintenance of more beds will require. For information on bed preparation, see the Planting and Transplanting section in the introduction to this chapter (page 122).

Many perennials can be dug and transplanted over the next couple of months. Now you can correct problems with plants in the wrong location you noticed this summer. Do not move perennials that are in bloom now or will be later on this fall.

Most perennials can be dug and divided over the next couple of months as well. This is especially important for fast-growing or rampant perennials in order to keep them under control. Do not divide perennials that are in bloom now or will be later on this fall. For information on dividing perennials see the Planting and Transplanting section of November.

Plant perennial transplants in the garden now. These could be transplants you grew yourself, divisions from friends, or transplants purchased from local nurseries or mail-order companies.

1 *Space* plants according to information on the label, references, or local advice. Most perennials will grow considerably larger than the size of the transplant. Do not crowd them, even if the bed looks relatively empty when you finish.

2 *Set* transplants so that the top of the rootball is even with or slightly above the soil of the bed. Many perennials will rot if planted too deeply. If the roots are in a tightly packed mass, *pull apart* and *spread* the roots when planting. A small amount of premium-quality slow-release fertilizer may be placed in the planting hole. *Firm* the soil around the plant once you have finished planting.

3 *Water* newly planted transplants thoroughly. A root stimulator may be used to help establish your new transplant's root system.

4 *Mulch* the bed 3 to 4 inches deep to control weeds, but do not cover the perennial plants.

Blooming **chrysanthemums** are available now. Plant a few if you need to "punch up" the color in some of your flower beds, or develop entire beds of garden mums.

Enter notes in your Texas gardening journal to record your purchases, divisions, and plantings.

Care for Your Perennials

As perennials finish and are cut back, *remove* stakes, cages, and other supports when they are no longer needed. Clean them up and store them out of the way. How well did they work? Can you think of a better way to support the plants? Note in your Texas gardening journal which perennials needed support so you can be prepared to provide it next year.

Enjoy the flowers of such late-season bloomers as **wild ageratum, narrow-leaf sunflower, butterfly weed, salvias, chrysanthemum, cigar plant, ruellia**, and **goldenrod**. *Deadhead* these plants as needed to keep them looking attractive.

Helpful Hints

If you are growing **butterfly weed,** watch for the appearance of monarch butterflies. They migrate through Texas on their way back to Mexico each fall, and will stop to feed on nectar and lay eggs on your butterfly weed. The monarch caterpillars are large and striped black, white, and yellow. **Do not spray** with insect-control aids. They should be allowed to feed on your butterfly weed to their heart's content. The plants will recover, and everyone will enjoy the beautiful butterflies they grow up to be.

Take a few photographs of your fall garden for your Texas gardening journal, and make sure you have updated your entries for the summer. This is a valuable source of information for next year's plantings.

Watering

October could be one of our driest months. Cooler weather relieves the stress on perennials to some degree, but watering is still needed if it does not rain. In particular, pay careful attention to watering newly planted, moved, or divided perennials, and those that are blooming or in active growth. Water deeply and thoroughly as needed.

Fertilizing

Slow-release premium-quality fertilizer is not added to the planting hole of fall-planted perennials that will be dormant over the winter. It is sufficient to water-in newly planted perennials with a soluble fertilizer mixed half strength.

Pest Control

Cooler, drier weather greatly reduces the incidence of diseases. They should not be a worry until next summer.

Weeds: Cool-season weed seeds will be germinating soon.

Keep beds mulched 3 to 4 inches deep. Pre-emergent weed-control aids may be applied now to help prevent the weeds from appearing. Refer to page 291 for a summary listing your options. Check the label carefully. Make sure they are appropriate to use around the types of plants you have in the bed. Always read and follow label directions when using any gardening aid, including those which control weeds.

Other pests: Armyworms are large, dark caterpillars that can chew up a perennial planting in no time. Common in September and October, they feed during the day and are easily seen if you look carefully.

Control as needed with appropriate aids.

Planning

Fall-blooming perennials continue to put on a show. November weather can run from delightful to downright chilly. If freezes threaten in north Texas, plan on covering some of the blooming perennials that could be damaged. The plants will survive without protection, but it would be a shame to lose out on some of the flowers. Perennials you might consider covering include **butterfly weed, cigar plant, ruellia,** and the **salvias.** If the weather stays mild, these plants can bloom well into December, especially in south Texas and perhaps in north Texas as well. It often varies year to year.

Planting and Transplanting

Continue to plant and transplant perennials in the garden:

1 When digging up and transplanting a perennial, get as much of the root system as possible.

2 If the soil falls away, immediately *wet the roots* and *wrap* them with plastic to keep them from drying out. Replant the plant immediately after removing the plastic.

3 If the plant will stay out of the ground for an extended period, *pot it up* in a container large enough to hold the rootball. *Add* some potting soil if necessary. *Place* the potted plant in a shady area and keep it well watered. *Plant* as soon as possible.

Garden mums are still available at local nurseries. Buy plants that have few open flowers and mostly buds. The plant will be attractive longer. Do not buy mums if all the flowers are fully open, especially if some of them have begun to fade. Plant in a sunny to partially sunny location and keep well watered. *Deadhead* regularly, and when all of the flow-

Good: Sheets, quilt spun fiber, or fabric

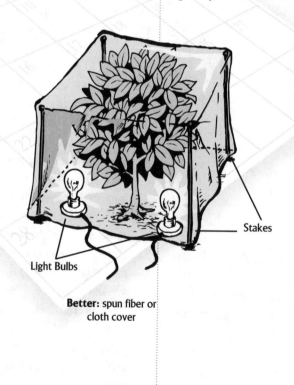

Light Bulbs

Stakes

Better: spun fiber or cloth cover

NOVEMBER

ers have faded, cut the plant back by about one-third. Sometimes we get a few more flowers. Cut them back hard in late January or after the first hard freeze hits in your area and they will bloom again next fall, or pull the plants up and put them in the compost pile if they were planted for temporary color.

Care for Your Perennials

Continue to keep things neat. Tall-growing, fall-blooming perennials, like **narrow-leaf sunflower, gold-enrod,** and **cigar plant,** may need to be staked. Remember how windy some of those cold fronts can be. *Deadhead* perennials that are in bloom as needed. After they finish

flowering, most should be cut back hard. ***Cut back and remove*** dead flower stalks and unattractive foliage from perennials winding down for the year. Mark each spot where perennials are growing that go totally dormant and disappear. This will keep you from accidentally digging into the plant later.

Watering

Cool to cold weather and regular rainfall generally allow us to ease up on this chore. Other than for newly planted, transplanted, and divided perennials, little or no irrigation should be necessary. *Water* these plants as needed to maintain a moist soil if weather is dry.

Fertilizing

Fertilizer is usually not needed at this time of year.

Pest Control

Few, if any, pests bother perennials in November. Watch for caterpillars, aphids, snails, and slugs, and treat if necessary. Weed gardens regularly and maintain a good layer of mulch 3 to 4 inches deep to keep weeds under control.

Planning

Although gardening does not stop in winter, it does slow down. This is a good time to take inventory of your gardening tools. How many were broken or lost last summer? In what condition are the rest? What needs to be replaced? Are there tools you need that you don't have? With gift-giving season right around the corner, now would be a good time to pick out some new tools, and let those gift-givers know what you want. While you're at it, ask for:

- *Dale Groom's Texas Gardening Guide* (Cool Springs Press, 1997). Its 424 pages cover when, where, and how to plant in Texas.

- More copies of this book, *Month-by-Month Gardening in Texas* (Cool Springs Press, 2000).

- *My Texas Garden: A Gardener's Journal* (Cool Springs Press, 2000).

Planting and Transplanting

Try to finish things up early this month. You know how hectic it can get around the holidays.

Care for Your Perennials

Cut back fall-blooming perennials that have finished blooming. If freezes have killed back the foliage of **salvias, cigar plant,** or **ruellia,** cut them back and mulch 3 to 4 inches deep over the roots and base of the plant.

Watering

Water-in newly planted, transplanted, or divided perennials as soon as they are in the ground. Cool weather and regular rainfall make the need for additional irrigation unlikely. If mild, dry weather does occur, give them a good soaking. Established perennials usually need little or no additional irrigation beyond natural rainfall. When irrigation is needed, apply water deeply and thoroughly.

Fertilizing

No fertilizer is required by perennials this month. Even if the weather has been mild and late-flowering perennials like **salvias** are still in bloom, don't fertilize them. Winter is on its way and little of the fertilizer would be used effectively.

Later fertilizer applications may also decrease the hardiness of perennials by stimulating growth.

Pest Control

Most perennials go dormant in the winter, so there is little pests can do to them. A few evergreen perennials like **strawberry begonia** may have problems with snails and slugs eating holes in their leaves.

One method of developing a trap: Sink a plastic bowl up to its rim in the soil, fill it half-full of beer, and you will trap lots of the critters. Dump out the bowl out every morning and continue to set out traps until you catch very few in a night. Baits are also effective and available at your local retailers.

Helpful Hints

Collect, clean, and store stakes, cages, and other supports used in the perennial garden. Make a note in your Texas gardening journal if you think you will need more next year. While you're at it, update your journal with what happened in the fall perennial garden.

Roses

People have been cultivating roses for several thousand years. It's even possible that very early humans appreciated the edible and medicinal qualities of the hips and delighted in the color and fragrance of the flowers. This long history (as well as the flower's extraordinary beauty) has created a special relationship between gardeners and roses. Indeed, it would be difficult to find a flower as universally loved. The rose is now our nation's floral emblem.

The original garden roses were tough, resilient plants that could pretty much take care of themselves. A strong focus on perfecting flower form and color in the late 1800s and early 1900s led to the modern roses that are so popular today. The use of pest-control aids that became available in the early to mid-1900s allowed breeders to overlook disease resistance in their pursuit of the perfect flower. As a result, some varieties of **modern roses,** such as the **hybrid teas, grandifloras,** and **floribundas,** have reduced resistance to diseases. With their outstanding beauty, however, these types have dominated the rose scene since they were introduced.

In the late 1900s, gardeners began to rediscover the beauty, fragrance, and durability of the **old garden roses.** Although **modern roses** are still the most commonly planted and grown, the popularity of **old garden roses** is steadily increasing in some corners. Today's rose breeders have been strongly influenced by current trends. New cultivars, **landscape roses,** and other **shrub roses** share many traits with the **old garden roses,** including flower form, fragrance, attractive growth habit, and increased disease resistance in certain varieties.

Planning

First decide how you want to use roses in the landscape and why you intend to grow them. The trend these days is to incorporate roses into landscape plantings just like any other shrub. This works particularly well with the **old garden, shrub, polyanthas, floribundas, climbers, grandifloras, miniatures,** and **species.**

If you want to grow roses with perfect flowers on long stems for cutting, you will probably choose the **hybrid teas** and **grandifloras.** These rosebushes often have rather unusual shapes that do not combine easily with other plants. That, along with their cultural requirements, is why they are often grown in separate beds.

If you want to train roses on a trellis, arbor, or fence, you'll want to grow rose cultivars from the **climbers, ramblers,** and **old garden roses** that produce long vigorous canes.

Hybrid teas, grandifloras, and **floribundas,** the most popular and widely available groups of roses, can be relatively high-maintenance plants. Keep this in mind when planning how many roses you want to include in your landscape and where you want to plant them.

When purchasing roses from nurseries or mail-order firms, note whether the bushes you are buying are grafted (budded) or growing on their own roots. Most roses are grafted onto a rootstock to increase their vigor. This part of the plant is located below the large knob on the lower part of the bush. Never allow shoots from below the graft union to grow—*prune* them off as soon as they're discovered. **Old garden roses** are often sold growing on their own roots, and **miniatures** almost always are. Low sprouts may be allowed to grow if roses are on their own roots.

Roses

Planting

Do not plant roses in shady areas. They must have at least six to eight hours of sun daily to perform up to your expectations. Any shade they receive should ideally come in the afternoon. Morning sun helps dry the foliage early, reducing disease problems. Roses need excellent drainage; avoid low areas that stay wet.

Bed preparation is important:

1 **Remove** unwanted vegetation from the area. If this is a new bed, remove the sod or eliminate it with a weed- control aid. Refer to page 291 for a summary listing your options. In an existing bed, remove weeds.

2 **Turn the soil** at least 8 to 10 inches deep.

3 **Spread** amendments over the turned soil. Add at least 4 inches of organic matter such as compost, sphagnum peat moss, rotted manure, or finely ground pine bark. If the soil is heavy clay, a 2- to 3-inch layer of sand should be spread next. Sulfur should be applied if the soil's pH is over 7. Lime is needed if the pH is lower than 5.5 and calcium levels are low. To find out what your soil needs, have it tested through your local county office of the Texas Agricultural Cooperative Extension Service, which we often call the County Agent's Office.

4 Thoroughly **blend** the amendments into the existing soil and **rake** smooth.

Roses are sold in containers or bare root, and generally become available at nurseries around January or February. Buy the highest-quality bushes available, preferably 1 or 1¹/₂ grade. It is well worth the extra investment for a healthy, vigorous plant that will produce lots of flowers. Purchase and plant roses in late winter or early spring so they can become established before beginning to bloom. Do not purchase bare-root roses after February. Container roses can be planted as late as May with acceptable results, but an earlier planting is much better.

To plant roses:

1 **Dig** a hole in a well-prepared bed as deep and wide as the roots or rootball. In a clay soil, use a mixture of 25 percent soil and 75 percent organic matter to fill the hole. In a sandy soil, a 50:50 mixture of soil and organic matter works well. These are also ideal mixes to use when you are constructing a complete rose bed.

2 For bare-root roses, place a cone of soil in the hole, **remove** the roots from the wrapper, position the plant over the cone, and **spread** the roots out over it. Hold the plant in place so the graft union (large knob on lower part of plant) is about 2 inches higher than the soil of the bed. Use your other hand to push and firm soil into the hole to cover the roots. Make sure the graft union remains 2 inches above soil level.

3 For container roses, slide the plant out of the container. Put the rootball in the hole. Its top should be level with the soil of the bed. Make sure the graft union is 2 inches above soil level. **Fill in** around the rootball and **firm** with your hand.

4 **Water** plants in thoroughly to finish settling the soil.

5 A root stimulator may be applied according to label directions.

6 Mulch the plants 3 to 4 inches deep, filling in all space between them with your favorite bark mulch. Maintain this mulch year-round.

Roses

Watering

Irrigation will be necessary when rain does not occur regularly, especially in the warm to hot months of April through November. An occasional thorough soaking is preferred to light, frequent irrigation. If done properly, irrigation should not be necessary more than once or twice a week during dry periods. Use soaker hoses if practical. They apply water without wetting the foliage, which helps reduce disease problems.

A 3- to 4-inch layer of mulch, like cypress mulch, or pine bark, or 4 to 6 inches of pine needles, clean hay, or dry leaves will help retain soil moisture and reduce the need for irrigation by preventing surface evaporation.

During our long growing seasons, roses usually need 1 to $1^1/_2$ inches of water per week. If this isn't supplied by rain, it's up to the gardener to irrigate as needed.

Fertilization

Roses require an adequate supply of available nutrients to produce vigorous bushes and high-quality flowers. Begin to fertilize in mid- to late February or early March in zones 8b and 9. In zones 8a, 7b, 7a, and 6, start fertilizing in late March/early April or as new growth begins and all dangers of frost have passed. In areas where the phosphorus levels in the soil are high, choose a premium-quality slow-release granular fertilizer with about a 3:1:2 ratio, such as 15-5-10. Where phosphorus levels are low, use a premium-quality granular rose fertilizer according to label directions. If needed, apply granular fertilizers every six to eight weeks throughout the growing season until late August or early September.

If you wish to fine-tune your fertilization program, follow the recommendations from a soil test.

Pest Control

If you want to minimize the use of pest-control aids in your landscape, roses may not be your best choice. Texas's hot, humid to dry climate creates perfect conditions for a variety of insects and diseases that attack roses.

For roses in general, **hybrid teas, grandifloras,** and **floribundas** in particular, controlling the fungal disease blackspot may require weekly spraying from late March to November. Other fungal diseases you may see are powdery mildew and stem canker, while downy mildew and rust are less common. To control these diseases by preventing them, it is advised that a spray program be started early and continued on a regular basis. There are many fungus disease-control aids available at your local retailers. Visit them for assistance in selecting specific aids based on your needs and goals. Refer to page 291 for a summary lising your options. Remember, always read and follow label directions.

Insects are not generally as destructive as fungus, and control can be provided on an as-needed basis. Thrips damage flowers in April through October. Aphids attack new growth and flower buds in spring, early summer, and any other time tender new growth and flower buds arise. Leaf-cutter bees cut neat, round holes from the edges of rose leaves to line their nests. Beetles and caterpillars are occasional problems.

Spider mites attack rose foliage and are generally worst during hot, dry weather.

As with diseases, wide selections of aids to control insect pests are available at local retailers, including nurseries and garden centers. After making your decisions on which aids to purchase, be sure to follow label directions.

Pruning

In Texas, roses may be pruned twice a year—in early to mid-February,

Roses

rather severely, and again, lightly, in mid-August to early September. The classic pruning technique for **hybrid teas** and **grandifloras** is designed to encourage the production of high-quality flowers with long stems for cutting. This involves rather hard pruning, back to 18 to 24 inches or as much as $\frac{1}{2}$ the plant's height in the late winter, and 30 to 36 inches or less in the late summer. **Floribundas, shrub roses, miniatures, old garden roses,** and others require only moderate pruning to shape them.

Roses are pruned primarily to:

- remove dead wood.

- stimulate new growth.

- control size and shape.

Cut the bush back to the desired height. Remove all dead wood, diseased canes, and twiggy growth. Cut each remaining cane back to just above a bud (preferably one facing away from the middle of the bush).

Some rose cultivars (**ramblers, some climbers,** and **old garden roses**) bloom prolifically in the spring and early summer, and then stop. These roses bloom on growth they made the summer before and generally are not as popular as repeat-blooming roses that bloom all summer. They should be pruned as needed in early to midsummer soon after they finish their bloom season.

Most roses look and bloom better if they are regularly deadheaded. *Prune* off faded flowers back to the first five-leaflet leaf on the stem. The exception is roses that produce attractive "hips" or fruit after flowering. Gardeners may allow these bright orange or red structures to develop for their ornamental qualities and for wildlife food. Some gardeners use these "hips" when brewing rose hip teas.

Pruning Roses

Types of Roses

The following is not a complete list of all the many types of roses, but includes some of the more popular types, and some of those that will do well in our state.

Modern Roses

(Types developed after 1867, the year the first hybrid tea was introduced.)

Hybrid Tea
Large, exquisitely shaped flowers (generally produced singly on long stems) and an amazing range of colors are the hallmarks of hybrid teas. The flowers of many cultivars are richly fragrant. The plants range in size from 3 to more than 6 feet, and can be leggy and awkward in appearance. Some varieties may be highly susceptible to blackspot; these roses generally require regular spraying and pruning to remain healthy and vigorous. Repeat-flowering.

Polyantha
Excellent in landscape plantings, polyanthas are vigorously-growing bushy plants that produce small flowers in large clusters or sprays. Most are relatively disease resistant, and they are some of the more reliable and easy-to-grow roses in our state. Many cultivars are fairly small, staying around 3 feet, while others can get quite a bit larger. Repeat-flowering.

Grandiflora
Tall plants (up to 7 feet) produce hybrid tea–like flowers singly or in clusters on long stems. Comparable to hybrid teas, they may also require similar care. Repeat-flowering.

Floribunda
A useful type of rose for landscape planting, the floribunda's shrubby growth is less ungainly than that of hybrid teas. The flowers are small, often brightly colored, and produced in clusters. Fragrance is light or lacking entirely. Repeat-flowering.

Climbers and Ramblers
Many types of roses will produce long canes that can be tied or trained on a support. Some roses have been bred to climb while others are vigorous mutations of bush roses. Climbing roses generally do not "climb" the way vines do and must be tied or woven onto supports.

Miniatures
Tiny to small bushes generally under 2 feet, miniature roses are delightful in containers. They are very hardy and will easily tolerate winter weather when planted in the ground. On a small scale (less than an inch), the flowers are similar to hybrid teas and come in many colors. Repeat-flowering.

Shrub Roses
A catchall name for roses that tend to be bushy and useful for landscape planting. Includes English roses, groundcover roses, landscape roses, hedge roses, and others. Repeat-flowering.

Old Garden Roses

(Types developed before 1867. The term "old garden rose" is used for many distinctly different types, and some types and varieties grow better in Texas than others. The following are just a few of the many types.)

China
The first repeat-blooming roses, the flowers are produced constantly and have thin, delicate petals. The foliage is neat, dark green, pointed, and rarely bothered by blackspot. These roses have a bushy, twiggy growth habit that fits in well with other landscape plantings. Repeat-flowering.

Tea
Wonderful roses for Texas, teas produce relatively large flowers in pastel shades and light reds. The fragrant flowers are produced continuously on robust bushes that are rugged and disease resistant. Repeat-flowering.

Noisette
Mostly climbers, although a few are robust shrubs, these roses thrive in the Deep South. The pastel-colored flowers are fragrant and produced in clusters that hang down from the canes. Repeat-flowering.

Bourbon
Though more susceptible to blackspot than the previously mentioned old garden roses, many of the Bourbons will thrive in our climate. The flowers are usually quite fragrant and produced on large, robust shrubs. Many are repeat-flowering.

Noteworthy Species Roses

(The following species roses are excellent, tough roses for Texas landscapes.)

Lady Banks Rose (*Rosa banksiae,* white; *R. banksiae* 'Lutea', yellow)
Cherokee Rose (*Rosa laevigata*)
Swamp Rose (*Rosa palustris scandens*)
Chestnut Rose (*Rosa roxburghii*)
Musk Rose (*Rosa moschata*)

JANUARY

Planning

Rose catalogs are wonderful to look through, and it's fun to dream about all the offered roses growing to perfection in your garden. Local nurseries should be getting in their roses sometime this month. Call around or stop by and see what types they will carry.

Make decisions on how many roses and which types and cultivars you want to add to your landscape, as well as where you want to add them. Early planting, this month or next month, is especially important for bare-root roses.

Keep records of your efforts to grow roses. Notes jotted in your Texas gardening journal on a regular basis create an important tool to help you grow roses better. Record the cultivar names and types of roses you're growing, where you bought them, and where they are located in the landscape. Note times of bloom, best bloom periods, pest problems, and overall performance. Try to make an entry at least once a week.

Planting and Transplanting

Late December through early February is the best time to transplant roses. To move a bush to a new location, *prune* it back appro-

priately, *dig* it with as much of the roots as possible, and *plant* immediately. It is critical that the roots not dry out. If the bush cannot be planted immediately, *wrap* the roots with plastic or temporarily *pot up* the plant. This is also an excellent time to plant roses.

Care for Your Roses

Roses may continue to bloom during mild winters, especially in south Texas. Still, very little is done to them this time of the year other than enjoying the flowers, if any, and deadheading. Even if they are not dormant, you do not have to be concerned about freezes.

Watering

It is unlikely that you will need to water your roses this month unless the winter is dry. They are probably dormant, but even if still blooming, natural rainfall this time of the year is generally adequate.

Fertilizing

No fertilizer should be applied to roses this month.

Pest Control

Blackspot may be active if the weather is mild and the roses have not gone dormant. Most gardeners take a break from spraying this time of the year. Defoliation is not as debilitating now as it would be during the summer. Mulching 3 to 4 inches deep usually supresses winter/cool-season weeds. If any "pop up," handpull while small.

Pruning

Repeat-blooming roses should be pruned in early to mid-February. Do not prune **climbers, ramblers,** or **bush roses** that bloom heavily in the spring and early summer and then stop—unless they have become monsters and you need to reclaim the space or wish to "train" them. These roses bloom on last year's growth. Pruning them heavily now will remove much or all of the flowering wood, and the roses will bloom very little, if at all, this spring.

Helpful Hint

When pruning roses, be sure you have the right tools handy: sharp bypass-type handpruners for canes the size of your finger or smaller; sharp bypass-type loppers for larger canes; leather gloves and long sleeves to protect your hands from thorns.

Planning

When planning the location of roses in the landscape, keep in mind the extraordinary fragrance of many cultivars. Plantings of fragrant roses are especially nice around porches, patios and at entrances. Some fragrant cultivars are 'Blush Noisette' (light-pink **noisette**), 'Chrysler Imperial' (deep-red **hybrid tea**), 'Double Delight' (bicolor **hybrid tea**), 'Fragrant Cloud' (coral **hybrid tea**), 'Sombreuil' (creamy-white **tea**), 'Mrs. B. R. Cant' (silvery, dark-pink **tea**), 'Summer Fashion' (yellow **floribunda**), and 'Don Juan' (dark-red **climber**).

Planting and Transplanting

This is a good month for both planting and transplanting roses. Finish transplanting in the early part of the month, especially in the southern part of the state.

Plant rosebushes in well-prepared beds with good drainage and plenty of sun. It is important for the graft union to be 2 inches above the soil of the bed. If you are planting container roses, this was taken care of when the nursery planted the rose in the container. Just plant the bush so the top of the rootball is level with the soil of the bed. In the case of bare-root roses, you must see to this yourself during the planting. See page 150 for complete directions on bed preparation and planting roses.

Care for Your Roses

Roses generally do better with good air circulation. Make sure they are not crowded. When they are used in mixed plantings, nearby shrubs, vines, and even large perennials should not be allowed to crowd the rosebushes. While pruning your rosebushes, *trim* or *snip back* shoots or branches from nearby plants that are growing into the roses' space.

Watering

It is unlikely that you will need to water established roses. Newly planted roses should be watered in thoroughly. If there is no rain and the soil in the bed becomes dry, *soak* the soil of the rose bed. Maintain a moist soil.

Fertilizing

Established roses can be fertilized in the latter part of this month in south Texas, but there is no hurry.

Pest Control

If your roses have blackspot, collect and dispose of leaves as they yellow and fall. Continue this sanitary practice throughout the growing season.

Pruning

Finish pruning during the early to middle part of this month. Cut **hybrid teas, grandifloras,** and **floribundas** back to a height of 2 to 3 feet, or at least cut the bush back to about one-third to one-half its height. Some gardeners even favor more severe pruning, back to 18 inches. This produces fewer but larger flowers on long stems for cutting.

Old garden roses, shrub roses, miniatures, and repeat-blooming **climbers** can be pruned more to the preferences of the gardener. They generally are not pruned severely unless to control their size. *Prune* out any dead wood or canes infected with canker, and shorten excessively long shoots and anything else needed to produce a pleasing, balanced shape.

Planning

If you plan to regularly spray your roses, check out your supply of pest-control aids this month. Spraying should begin soon and you will need materials on hand when the time comes. Make entries in your Texas gardening journal about which, if any, pests are active and how you will control them.

Watering

Watering should not be a major concern this month. Warmer weather and new growth, however, make it important for you to watch the rainfall and water if beds begin to dry too much. Newly planted roses need particular attention. Maintain a moist soil condition, not wet or dry.

beginning to open. Other types of roses will also get blackspot to some degree, sometimes just as bad. If you want to keep those roses free from blackspot, you will also have to spray any of them that have problems with this disease. Visits to your local retailers help you decide which aids, if any, you wish to utilize in your disease-, insect-, and weed-control activites. Refer to page 291 for a summary listing your options.

Planting and Transplanting

Continue to plant roses purchased in containers. If you are still expecting a mail-order shipment of bare-root roses, hope they will arrive soon; *plant* them immediately. You might still give unsprouted bare-root bushes a try.

Fertilizing

Roses throughout the state should be fertilized this month when new growth begins. In areas where the phosphorus levels in the soil are high, choose a premium-quality long-lasting slow-release lawn fertilizer with a 3:1:2 ratio, such as 15-5-10, 18-6-12, 19-5-9, or 21-7-14. Where phosphorus levels are low, use a premium-quality rose fertilizer. *Follow label directions.* If you have a favorite rose fertilizer that has worked well for you in the past, by all means continue to use it.

Pruning

Prune immediately if you have not already done so. Pruning this late will not hurt your bushes, but your roses will bloom later.

Helpful Hint

Keep in mind that running roses are supposed to RUN, so do minimal pruning, if any, on them. If they have overgrown their spaces and/or you wish for them to grow in specific patterns or directions, prune as necessary to reach your goals. Always prune with sharp pruning tools which "fit" your hand well and are comfortable to use. Small files and/or sharpening stones used correctly will keep your pruning tools sharp.

Care for Your Roses

Evaluate your roses carefully. They will begin active growth this month. Any bushes that are dead, sprouting poorly, or have only a few weak living canes may need to be replaced. Evaluate the location to make sure it is good for roses. Note your decisions and evaluations in your Texas gardening journal.

Pest Control

Regular spray programs for blackspot should begin as soon as **hybrid teas, floribundas,** and **grandifloras** have new leaves

Planning

Take a few moments to make some notes in your Texas gardening journal about when various roses started blooming. Note how many weeks had passed since you pruned. You can manipulate, to some degree, when your roses bloom by pruning earlier or later within the recommended period.

Planting and Transplanting

Blooming roses are available in containers at local nurseries. You can pick out the color, shape, fragrance, and size of the flowers you want. There is a price, however. Planting roses now means they have to establish themselves while blooming.

Care for Your Roses

The grafted roses we grow are composed of two genetically different roses joined together at the graft union to form a single, functioning plant. The part that provides the roots is called the *stock.* It makes a great root system but should never be allowed to sprout and grow. The upper part that produces beautiful flowers is the *scion.* It is nurtured and trained into the ornamental part of the plant. The *graft union* is the large knob at the base of the plant.

Watering

Supplemental water is usually needed this month. *Water* until the soil is moistened at least 5 to 6 inches down. Leave sprinklers on long enough to provide 1 to 1$\frac{1}{2}$ inches of water weekly if not supplied by rain. Ideally, use a watering method that does not wet the foliage. Soaker hoses work very well and are inexpensive and easy to use. Place them so that a hose lies about 6 inches from each bush. Maintaining a mulch of 3 to 4 inches deep will reduce the required frequency of watering.

Fertilizing

If you fertilized last month, no additional fertilizer is needed at this time. (If not, fertilize now . . .) Use a granular rose fertilizer or a premium-quality long-lasting slow-release granular 3:1:2 or 4:1:2 ratio fertilizer. Follow label directions.

Pest Control

Diseases: You should not wait for blackspot to occur before you start spraying. Begin spraying as soon as possible, and spray every seven to ten days through November. Powdery mildew appears as a white powdery coating on flower buds, new growth, and leaves. Both these diseases (and others) can be controlled.

Insects: Aphids are relatively small insects that congregate in large numbers on flower buds and new growth.

Many rose gardeners use products that combine two or three pest-control aids for effective control of diseases, insects, and mites. These are usually great. Several combination aid products are available and especially labeled for roses. Refer to page 291 for a summary of your options.

Weeds: Keep rose beds well mulched to control weeds. Hand-pull small weeds. Visit local retailers for "first-hand" assistance in selecting appropriate control aids.

Pruning

Roses are in bloom now and should not be cut back. *Deadhead* faded flowers regularly by cutting the stems back to the first or second five-leaflet leaf.

Planning

Stop and smell the roses. Forgive the cliché, but this is one of our best rose-blooming months. Record comments on each type of rose you are growing in your Texas gardening journal. In particular, note which cultivars seem to be susceptible to disease and which do not seem to be affected much. Careful records will help tremendously when, at the end of the growing season, you are deciding which roses to keep and which just did not live up to expectations or were highly susceptible to pest problems. Also record which varieties are fragrant, the colors of the roses, and comments from visitors especially children. If your little ones enjoy roses, you can let them plant roses with you the next planting season. It's a great activity both you and your young gardeners will enjoy and remember.

Planting and Transplanting

This is the very last month many gardeners plant roses from containers. Do not disturb the roots of container-grown roses when you plant them, even if the root system looks potbound. They will not tolerate any root damage when in active growth and when temperatures are hot. It is much better to plant roses earlier in the year.

Do not transplant any roses now.

Care for Your Roses

Ramblers and **climbers** should be in full bloom. Pay attention to training and tying these roses to the arbor, fence, trellis, or other structure they are to grow on. **Climbing roses** are not like most vines, and generally cannot climb or hold on to structures well on their own. New growth will continue throughout the summer, and these types of roses can easily get out of control. Regular efforts to train them produce far better results than letting them go and dealing with an overgrown mess or monster.

Watering

More heat means that the need for water is more likely. Watch the weather closely. From now on, a week or ten days without a good rain means turning on the irrigation. If dry weather continues, *water thoroughly* once or twice a week. Avoid wetting the foliage, or plan to water when the foliage will dry rapidly such as early morning.

Roses usually need 1 to 1½ inches of water per week. If this is not supplied by rain, it should be supplied by irrigation. Maintain a moist but not wet or dry soil during our long growing season.

Fertilizing

You can fertilize again this month (six to eight weeks after your spring fertilizer application). Use your favorite rose fertilizer according to label directions, or a premium-quality long-lasting slow-release 3:1:2 or 4:1:2 ratio fertilizer appropriate for your area. Be moderate. Overfertilization can damage plant roots or lead to lush, rapid growth that makes a plant more susceptible to pest problems.

Pest Control

Diseases: Are you spraying regularly? If not, expect to see blackspot on virtually every type of rose.

Many old garden roses will lose some to most of their leaves, look weak, then recover without spraying. This may happen several times during the summer. Notice which roses seem to be more disease resistant. 'Lady Banks' rose and many of the

Chinas, teas, polyanthas, *and* **noisettes** *are less susceptible to blackspot, even if not sprayed.*

Note your observations in your Texas gardening journal.

Mites: Spider mites may occur if the weather is hot and dry.

Mite controls are available at local nurseries.

Continue a regular spray program with a combination product to keep pests under control.

May is usually a super blooming month for rose growers in Texas, and most want their plantings to be relatively disease-, insect pest-, and weed-free or at a minimum. If this is also your goal, visits to your local retailers can help you become a better informed rose-growing consumer/gardener. Refer to page 291 for a summary listing your options. After you have secured all the information you need, decide what your goals are, acquire specific aids, and you should be able to realize your goals.

Texas is a great rose-growing state, and May is a good month to visit public gardens and plantings. See for yourself what other rose growers are doing.

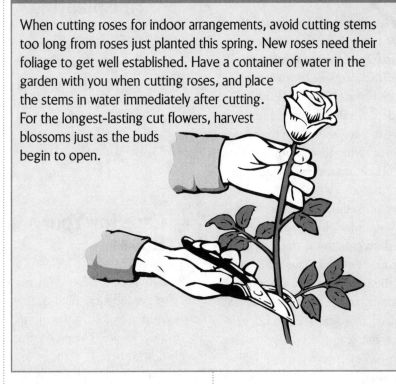

Helpful Hints

When cutting roses for indoor arrangements, avoid cutting stems too long from roses just planted this spring. New roses need their foliage to get well established. Have a container of water in the garden with you when cutting roses, and place the stems in water immediately after cutting. For the longest-lasting cut flowers, harvest blossoms just as the buds begin to open.

Pruning

Other than deadheading and pruning off suckers from below the graft union, no pruning is required this month.

Planning

Roses are entering the most stressful time of the year this month. Plan for the efforts you will make to help them come through in the best shape possible. Watering as needed, mulching, deadheading, and insect, weed, and disease control will all continue to be important in caring for your roses.

The outstanding spring and early-summer bloom season may be drawing to a close. Don't despair. With good care throughout the summer, many varieties will continue to bloom, though often at reduced frequencies. The fall rose-blooming season can be just as (or even more) spectacular for repeat-blooming roses. October is another super blooming month for roses in Texas. This is one reason the Texas Rose Festival is held each October in Tyler. Make plans now to attend a great Texas event.

Enter notes in your Texas gardening journal on which varieties continue to bloom, their bloom frequency, any pest problems, and which varieties are growing well in June.

Planting and Transplanting

The intense heat this time of year stresses roses too much to make this a good time to plant them. To transplant a rose in this heat would almost certainly kill it or set it back significantly.

Care for Your Roses

Despite your best efforts, do not expect to get the same high-quality flowers during mid- to late summer that you did earlier. The problem is the heat, and there is nothing you can do to make it go away. It is still important to take proper care of your roses. Rose cultivars that are susceptible to blackspot will yellow and drop their leaves almost as fast as they can grow them without a regular spray program. By the end of the summer, the bushes will be too weak to produce the outstanding flowers we expect in the fall. Removing fallen diseased leaves from the planting areas is advised at this time.

Watering

The intense heat this time of year can dry out beds surprisingly fast. Roses planted this year need a deep watering whenever we go five to seven days without a good rain (a "good rain" means receiving 1 to $1^{1}/_{2}$ inches of rain—do not count brief showers). Older, more established plants should be watered seven to ten days after the last good rain if 1 to $1^{1}/_{2}$ inches of rain was not received. During exceptionally dry periods when rain has not fallen for two weeks or more, water roses in the landscape once or twice a week as needed.

"Bottom line"—maintain a *moist* but not wet or dry soil during the active growing season. And water as needed to maintain this moist condition. Roses will not do well in dry or wet soils, so moist soil conditions are important for the overall health of your roses.

As always, avoid wetting the foliage if possible by using a bubbler hose attachment, drip irrigation, soaker hoses, or another irrigation system that sprays water below the foliage. If you must wet the foliage, irrigate during the morning or whenever the foliage will dry rapidly.

Fertilizing

If you did not fertilize last month, you may this month. Use your favorite rose fertilizer according to label directions, or a premium-quality long-lasting slow-release 3:1:2 or 4:1:2 fertilizer appropriate for your area. Read and follow label directions when applying any gardening aid, including fertilizers.

Pest Control

Although it may seem as if your roses have pest problems no matter what you do, don't give up.

Diseases and insects: A regular weekly spraying with a combination product that includes a fungus-control aid for blackspot and an insect-control aid for insect pests is important. Frequent rains can make this job difficult, but stick with it. Blackspot may still occur on very susceptible cultivars, but less than if you were not spraying.

Mites: Hot, dry weather may encourage spider mites to attack.

If you use a combination pest-control aid, make sure it will control mites as well as the other pests. If not, secure a mite-control aid if and when needed at your local retailers. Always apply any gardening aid according to label directions. Refer to page 291 for a summary listing your options.

Weeds: Keep weeds under control by regular handpulling and mulching 3 to 4 inches deep.

Do NOT get weed-control aids on the stems or leaves of the roses.

Pruning

This is a good month to prune roses that are not repeat-blooming types. These roses, which bloom heavily in the spring and early summer and then not at all or very little the rest of the year, will bloom next year on growth they produce this summer. *Prune* appropriately now.

Always prune with sharp pruning tools. Good-quality leather gloves and long sleeves are recommended when giving your rose planting a "haircut" or pruning.

Climbers and **ramblers** may need to have excessively long shoots shortened, old, low-vigor canes pruned back hard, and growth in areas where it is not wanted removed. The structure on which you are training these roses and the effect you are trying to achieve will have a great influence on how you prune them. Non-repeat-blooming **bush roses** are simply pruned to shape them and remove dead or weak growth.

Helpful Hint

Regularly collect and dispose of diseased leaves that yellow and drop from your rosebushes. This may help reduce blackspot problems. And it helps to make the entire planting area look better.

JULY

Planning

Plan on gardening during the cooler early-morning and late-afternoon hours. Heat is brutal this time of year for gardens and gardeners alike.

Before you forget, make sure you have made entries in your Texas gardening journal on the performance of roses during the early bloom season. Note which roses have the most difficult time with the heat and pest problems this summer.

Planting and Transplanting

The intense heat of midsummer stresses roses too much to make this a good time to plant them. To transplant a rose in this heat would almost certainly kill it or set it back significantly.

Care for Your Roses

Daytime highs in the mid-90s to 100+ Fahrenheit and nighttime lows in the mid- to upper 70s and 80s actually lower the vigor of many roses. Despite your best efforts at proper care, you will notice the flowers your rosebushes produce now are often smaller with less-vivid colors. The flowers seem to fade almost as soon as they open. Hang in there and don't give up! Continue regular care. It is important to get your roses through the summer in the best shape possible so they will be able to produce a wonderful crop of flowers during the fall blooming season. This is one of the reasons you want to plant only the best adapted varieties of roses for Texas. See *Dale Groom's Texas Gardening Guide* (Cool Springs Press, 1997) for information on the best-adapted rose varieties for Texas.

Watering

Keep roses watered as needed to maintain a moist soil. Do not keep the soil dry or wet. Soil in beds can dry out surprisingly fast when weather is this hot. Do not allow your roses to wilt before you water them. *Water thoroughly* to moisten the soil at least 4 to 6 inches down. Avoid wetting the foliage if possible. Mulching 3 to 4 inches deep with your favorite bark mulch and maintaining it through the summer reduces the required frequency of irrigating, conserves soil moisture, reduces weed populations, and moderates soil temperatures. All these functions are desirable, especially during our "blast furnace" summer heat.

Fertilizing

July is generally not a good month to fertilize roses. High temperatures reduce vigor, and roses may actually grow less than they did earlier. If you fertilized in May or early June, no fertilizer is required now.

Pest Control

Blackspot, spider mites, leaf-cutter bees, caterpillars, beetles, and weeds are the most common problems this time of the year. *See the introduction to this chapter for information on controlling these pests.*

Pruning

Other than deadheading and pruning out diseased or dead growth, no pruning is required this month.

Helpful Hint

If you find that the fungus-control aid you have been using for blackspot does not seem to be working well, try switching to another recommended aid, or even better, alternate between two different aids in your spray program. Always read and follow label directions.

Planning

While we are in the middle of the worst part of the summer, it's time look ahead to the fall blooming season and its beautiful flowers. With that in mind, plan on fertilizing and pruning late this month.

This is also a good time to evaluate how your roses did over the summer. By now, roses will show how well they endured the heat, drought, rain, and humidity of a Texas summer. Make some notes in your Texas gardening journal. A rose that performs poorly for two seasons should probably be replaced with another cultivar.

Planting and Transplanting

Don't even think about planting or transplanting roses this month. Cooler weather may be on the horizon, but it's not here yet.

Care for Your Roses

Tell your roses to hold on for just a few more weeks. Cool fronts often make their way through the state in late September, particularly in north Texas. In the meantime, care this time of the year looks ahead to the fall blooming period. Roses need to be fertilized, pruned, and otherwise groomed.

Fertilizing

Fertilizing during late summer is second in importance only to the spring fertilization. Extra nutrients provided now will encourage vigorous growth and flowering over the next three months.

- Use a rose fertilizer, 3:1:2 or 4:1:2 premium-quality long-lasting fertilizer such as 21-7-14, 19-5-9, 18-6-12, or 15-5-10, following label directions.

- Fertilizer should be applied immediately after you prune your roses.

- If using granular rose fertilizers, follow label directions.

Pruning

It is important to *prune roses now* to get them in shape for the fall blooming season. After a long summer of growth, most roses are rather overgrown. Top the bush back to the desired height (usually 2 to 3 feet for **hybrid teas** and **grandifloras**). *Remove* all dead wood, diseased canes, and twiggy growth. Cut each remaining cane back to just above a bud (preferably facing away from the center of the bush).

The **ramblers,** many **climbers,** and some of the **old garden roses** bloom prolifically in spring and early summer and then stop. These roses bloom on growth they made the summer before. They should have been pruned as needed in early to midsummer after they finished their bloom season. *Prune now* if absolutely necessary, but do so right away.

Pest Control

Diseases: Blackspot continues to be the number-one problem.

Keep yellow, fallen leaves raked or picked up from rose beds. These fallen, infected leaves often serve as a continuing source of disease. As new growth begins to emerge on newly pruned roses, continue a regular spray program to control blackspot.

Insects: Leaf-cutter bees may chew round holes from the edges of rose leaves. The damage is generally little more than cosmetic, but it can be rather extensive. *Controls for these and other insect pests are available at local retailers. Refer to page 291 for a summary listing your options.*

Planning

When a bed of hybrid tea roses is planted, it often functions as a collection of different cultivars. Flower color is chosen for individual beauty—little consideration is given to how well the different colors will complement one another.

If you are using roses in the landscape, however, the colors should be thought out carefully. Many of the modern **hybrid teas** and **floribundas** have brilliantly colored flowers that may overpower some of the pastel shades common in **old garden roses.** Take a critical look at the colors you have combined and make sure they work for you.

Planting and Transplanting

Have you identified a rose that is having problems with its growing conditions? Perhaps the spot is shadier than you thought and the rose is languishing. You will want to move it, but it is still too soon to transplant roses. *Note the location of the plant and perhaps even tag it and wait at least until early December to transplant.*

It is also too hot to plant roses. *Plant no sooner than late October for south Texas, and anytime in October for north Texas.*

Care for Your Roses

It has been a long growing season, and well-grown roses have certainly needed their share of your gardening time. Don't slow down yet! Continue to keep your roses watered as needed and keep pest problems from getting out of control. Over the next two months, some of the finest flowers of the year will be produced in great abundance from healthy rosebushes.

Watering

Summer rainfall is unpredictable. By this time, we might be cursing a drought or perhaps dreading the next downpour. Although roses need good drainage, they are not very drought tolerant. During this growing period before their fall bloom, pay careful attention to rainfall amounts; *water* roses if 1 to 1½ inches of rain has not fallen for about a week. Water thoroughly as needed.

Fertilizing

If fertilizing this month, use the same types/ratio/analysis as used earlier this season. This is the last fertilization required for this season.

Pest Control

Most common pests of roses stay active through the fall. An exception is thrips. These insects, so destructive to the spring and early-summer flowers, are rarely a problem in the fall. Blackspot, powdery mildew, spider mites, aphids, and various other pests often mean keeping up with that once-a-week spray schedule. Refer to page 291 for a summary listing your options. If you want great-looking roses and healthy plants, it is necessary to follow a program.

Pruning

Roses that were not cut back in late August should be cut back in early September. Pruning roses later generally means they will come into bloom a little later.

Helpful Hints

Rose hips make great wildlife food and various types are used to make jelly. Rose hips are very high in vitamin C. Rose petals are also edible. Use petals or hips only from flowers that have not been sprayed with pest-control aids.

Planning

Plan on enjoying all the beautiful roses blooming this month. Pleasant weather makes it a delight to be outside. Fall planting is certainly possible in Texas. Roses are hardy and will not mind winter's cold. Look around the landscape and determine if and where you want to plant more roses. If you don't have room for standard-size roses, think about **miniatures.** A row of **miniature roses** in matching containers looks great on a low wall, bench, or small outside table.

Planting and Transplanting

Container-grown roses can be planted into the ground from late October through winter. These roses have likely been growing in their pots for some time and have gotten potbound.

1 *Remove* the rosebush from pot.

2 If needed, use your fingers to pull apart the rootball a little. This will help the roots grow and spread into the adjacent soil.

3 *Plant* the rosebush in a well-prepared spot with organic matter added. The top of the

rootball should be level with the soil of the bed, and the graft union should be about 2 inches above ground.

4 *Firm* the soil around the rose's roots with your hands, and *water* thoroughly to finish settling the soil. After watering, a root stimulator may be applied using label directions. Mulch the planting area 3 to 4 inches deep with bark mulch and maintain year-round. *The weather must be cool for the plant to tolerate the pulling apart of its rootball. If October is warm, wait for the more reliably cool month of November to plant.*

Care for Your Roses

Now that flower production has resumed, it's time to start deadheading again.

Watering

Although the weather is mild to cool, October can be one of our driest months. *Water roses deeply* as needed, based on rainfall. Avoid wetting the foliage as this encourages blackspot. If you must wet the

foliage, water in the morning when the leaves will dry quickly. Maintain a *moist* soil condition.

Fertilizing

No fertilizer is needed for the rest of the growing season.

Pest Control

Diseases: Cooler, drier weather will reduce blackspot.

If the weather cooperates, reduce spray frequency to once every ten days or more. If the weather is warm and wet, spray weekly.

Weeds: Cool-season weeds start to show up next month.

Prevent them with 3 to 4 inches of mulch, 6 inches of pine straw, or clean hay placed over the soil of the bed. A pre-emergent weed-prevention aid may also be used on the soil prior to mulching.

Helpful Hint

Be sure to use weed-control aids labeled for roses. Refer to page 291 for a summary listing your options.

Planning

Roses continue in full bloom. Many rose gardeners consider these fall flowers the finest of the year. Roses will continue to bloom well into December, or longer, usually in south Texas. In years where the first killing frost/freezes are late, they will also continue to bloom in north Texas. Bloom for the year/season usually stops when the first hard killing freeze/ frost occurs in your area.

Little has to be done to prepare roses for the coming winter. Mild winters in south Texas often prevent roses from going dormant at all, and they may still be blooming when it is time to cut them back in February. Full dormancy is most likely in north Texas.

Planning for winter primarily means refraining from fertilizing this late. Late fertilization would make the roses even less likely to go dormant.

Planting and Transplanting

Planting roses in fall is a good idea for most of Texas because it allows a plant to grow roots and become established during the cool season. Fall-planted roses are more likely to be stronger and more vigorous during their first summer. The container roses available at local nurseries may be left over from last spring.

1 *Remove* the rosebush from pot.

2 If needed, use your fingers to pull apart the rootball a little. This will help the roots grow and spread into the adjacent soil.

3 *Plant* the rosebush in a well-prepared spot with organic matter added. The top of the rootball should be level with the soil of the bed, and the graft union should be about 2 inches above ground.

4 *Firm* the soil around the rose's roots with your hands, and *water* thoroughly to finish settling the soil. After watering, a root stimulator may be applied using label directions. Mulch the planting area 3 to 4 inches deep with bark mulch and maintain year-round. *The weather must be cool for the plant to tolerate the pulling apart of its rootball.*

If you need to move a rosebush, wait until December or January. They could be moved in late November, but since they may still be in full bloom, it would be a shame to disturb them. Roses may be transplanted at any time after they go dormant (through late February).

Cutting a Rose

Care for Your Roses

Rose flowers provide a great deal of pleasure when cut and brought indoors.

- **Cut** roses just as the buds start to open with stems long enough for arranging.

  Feel free to take longer stems, 8 to 12 inches, from the more-vigorous bushes. Limit stem length to 6 to 8 inches on less-vigorous cultivars.

- Make your cut just above a five-leaflet leaf with sharp by-pass hand pruners.

  Immediately after cutting, place the rose stems in a bucket of tepid water.

- When you have gathered enough roses, bring inside to arrange them. *Strip off* any foliage that would be underwater in the vase, and *recut* the stem of the rose while holding it under water.

  Arrange in a container filled with water or with wet florist foam. Enjoy!

Watering

Cool to chilly weather and normal rainfall make it unlikely that you will have to water much this month. Dry, mild weather can occur, and irrigation during those periods is important. Try to use a watering method that applies water directly to the roots, such as soaker hoses or irrigation systems that spray the water onto the soil below the foliage. Water as needed to maintain a *moist* soil.

Fertilizing

No fertilizer is needed for the rest of the growing season.

Pest Control

You may finally begin to relax. Most gardeners do not continue to spray their roses after this month, but for now, spray roses as you have done throughout the growing season. Blackspot is still active and aphids may show up on flower buds or new growth. Overall, pest problems are diminishing.

Pruning

Avoid heavy pruning that would stimulate new growth. Other than deadheading, no pruning is needed now. Some rose cultivars reliably produce attractive fruit called "hips." They turn red or red-orange when mature, and can add color to the winter landscape. If you grow rose cultivars that produce hips, do not deadhead.

Tie up and otherwise train **ramblers** and **climbers.** Only limited pruning should be done, if absolutely necessary, as you tie them to their supports.

Planning

Need more roses? Check out the new catalogs to see what new roses are being offered. Rose breeders are always coming up with beautiful new cultivars. Look for roses that offer attractively shaped plants and disease resistance as well as beautiful flowers. These are excellent to use in the landscape as you would any flowering shrub (but they still may need to be sprayed regularly to control blackspot).

If you order roses instead of visiting your selections "in person" at local nurseries, specify that you need to receive them for planting in January (south Texas) or in January or February (north Texas).

Plan and conduct a shopping trip for the favorite gardeners on your holiday gift list early in the month.

Planting and Transplanting

Early to mid-December after a killing freeze or frost is a good time to transplant roses to a new location. If you aren't in a hurry and the bushes are still blooming, this can be done anytime from now to late February. To move a bush to a new location, ***dig*** it with as much of the root system as possible and ***plant*** immediately. It is crucial to keep roots from drying out in the process. If the bush cannot be planted immediately, ***wrap*** the roots with plastic or temporarily ***pot up*** the plant. Do not prune it back hard until early to mid-February. Many gardeners wait to transplant roses until then since the pruned roses are smaller and easier to handle in the move.

Continue to plant container-grown rosebushes purchased from local nurseries.

Watering

Slower growth, cool to cold temperatures, and abundant rainfall generally make watering unnecessary this month. Newly planted or transplanted roses, however, should be watered as needed if sufficient rain does not occur.

Fertilizing

No fertilizer is needed this month.

Pest Control

Most gardeners have put away the sprayers by now. Although roses may continue to grow and bloom, and blackspot can occur during the winter, it does not hurt the rosebushes enough to merit continued spraying. Keep beds mulched and weeded.

Pruning

No pruning will be needed until next month.

Helpful Hint

Update your Texas gardening journal. List all the pests you encountered and which cultivars seemed to have the worst problems. How effective were pest-control efforts, and how might they be improved? Determine the causes for other problems you might have experienced. Make sure all your bushes have labels with their proper names still stuck in the ground at their base. It's a good idea to keep track of the cultivar names and types.

Shrubs

Shrubs are woody perennial plants that produce multiple stems from the soil or multiple branching close to the ground, and grow very low, or no taller than 20 feet. They may be evergreen or deciduous. In Texas, relatively mild winters allow us to grow a wide variety of evergreen shrubs, and a few deciduous shrubs which are really popular. Shrubs are generally grown for their colorful flowers or attractive foliage, but they may also provide fragrance and ornamental or edible fruit.

Planning

Shrubs are a fundamental and essential part of most landscape designs. They are the primary plant material used to shape spaces, create structure in the landscape, enhance the home and other buildings, provide privacy, screen views, and guide traffic patterns. See the introduction (pages 12–14) for information on how to develop a landscape design.

Planting the right shrub in the right location is critical to the plant's health and your happiness with the planting. Every gardener has favorite shrubs he or she wants to plant in the landscape. By all means, choose shrubs you like, but it is also important that you consider the growing conditions of the area, size limitations, the purpose of the planting, and the characteristics you want the shrubs to have.

First evaluate the site. Is it shady or sunny? Well drained or damp? Is the soil acid or alkaline? You must choose shrubs that will thrive in the growing conditions in which they will be planted.

Next consider the purpose of the planting. Is it to beautify the house, screen a view, provide colorful flowers, create privacy, or another of the many reasons for which shrubs are planted?

List the characteristics the shrubs must have to satisfy your taste and the purpose they will serve. Decide on the mature size needed, between evergreen or deciduous, whether or not you want flowers (and if so, what color and when), and any other features you feel are important.

Finally, choose the shrubs that will most closely fit the growing conditions, purpose, and desired characteristics. Choose your favorite shrub if it's the best choice, but if not, plant another shrub. Planting a shrub that will grow too large for its location is the most common mistake gardeners make. Always ask about or find out the mature size of the shrubs you intend to plant. If someone says, "You can always keep it pruned to whatever size you want," walk away and choose a smaller-growing shrub.

Planting Shrubs

The ideal planting season for shrubs in Texas is October through March. Fall planting in October through early December is especially good. Roots grow readily at that time of year. Shrubs then have until May to make root growth and get established before hot weather. Shrubs are almost always sold as container-grown plants. On occasion, larger specimens are available balled and burlapped. Shrubs are generally planted into well-prepared beds.

Bed Preparation

1 *Remove* unwanted vegetation from the bed area. Weeds or turfgrass may be removed physically, or eliminated with a weed-control aid (follow label directions carefully) and turned under. Refer to page 291 for a summary listing your options.

Shrubs

2 *Turn the soil* to a depth of at least 8 to 10 inches with a shovel, spade, or garden fork.

3 *Spread* any desired amendments over the turned soil. Have your soil tested through your local extension service office to find out what it needs. You should always add 4 to 6 inches of organic matter, such as compost, sphagnum peat moss, rotted manure, or finely ground pine bark. Depending on your soil and the type of shrubs that will be planted, additional materials might include sand, lime, or sulfur.

4 Thoroughly *blend* the amendments into the soil, *rake* the bed smooth, and *shape* the edges. The level of the soil in the bed will be higher than it was before. This is good, as it will improve drainage.

Planting

1 Place shrubs in their containers atop the soil where they will be planted. Make sure the spacing and arrangement are proper before going to the next step.

2 *Push down* slightly on a pot to make a shallow depression, and *set* the shrub—in its container—aside.

3 *Dig* a hole into the depression deep enough to accommodate the rootball and a little wider.

4 *Remove* the shrub from the container. If the roots are tightly packed in a solid mass, *cut* or *pull apart* the root system slightly. This will encourage the roots to grow into the surrounding soil.

5 Place the rootball into the hole. It is crucial for the top of the rootball to be level with or slightly above the soil surface.

6 Use your hands to push and firm soil into the space between the rootball and the sides of the hole.

7 After planting all the shrubs in the bed, *water* them in thoroughly by hand to finish settling the soil.

8 Apply a root stimulator according to label directions now.

9 Finally, *mulch* the bed 3 to 4 inches deep.

Care for Your Shrubs

Carefully chosen shrubs that are well adapted to Texas's climate are relatively easy to take care of. Which shrubs you choose and where you plant them will greatly influence the amount of maintenance required. Pruning is sometimes needed to control the shape or size of shrubs. Fertilization is required to stimulate growth or provide needed nutrients. Well-established shrubs can thrive with irrigation only during the hottest, driest periods. Pest problems do occur, but most shrubs are only occasionally bothered with outbreaks that would require treatment. In south Texas, the use of less-hardy shrubs such as **yesterday-today-and-tomorrow,** or **daisy shrub,** may require efforts at cold protection. Overall, shrub beds require far less maintenance than beds of annuals, perennials, or lawns.

Watering

Newly planted shrubs will need careful attention to watering the first year after planting. Water as needed during hot summer weather if adequate rain does not occur. Established shrubs will need supplemental irrigation only during the hottest, driest weather. It is important to water thoroughly enough to moisten the soil 4 to 6 inches down. This is best accomplished with sprinklers or soaker hoses.

Fertilizing

Shrubs are best fertilized in early spring and, where rapid growth is desired, again in late spring. Standard granular fertilizers will feed for about six to eight weeks. Applied in early spring, they supply nutrients to shrubs during their primary growth period from spring to early summer. This is adequate in most circumstances. Young shrubs that are being encouraged to grow rapidly, or shrubs in low vigor, may be fertilized again in midsummer or early fall.

A premium-quality long-lasting slow-release granular fertilizer is fine for most situations. Fertilizers with a 3:1:2 ratio, such as 15-5-10, 18-6-12, or 21-7-14, work well. Always read and follow label directions when applying fertilizers.

Acid-loving shrubs, such as **azaleas, camellias,** and **gardenias,** will occasionally have problems with iron deficiencies, and may require fertilizers rich in available or chelated (KEY lay ted) iron.

Pest Control

Insects are an occasional problem on some shrubs. A few popular shrubs have fairly common pest problems, lacebugs on **azaleas** and whiteflies on **gardenias,** for instance, but most of the time we simply monitor shrubs and deal with pest problems as they occur. Common insect pests on shrubs are lacebugs, scale, whiteflies, caterpillars, and aphids. Insect-control aids commonly used to control those pests are widely available at local retailers.

Spider mites are an occasional problem during hot, dry weather.

Diseases can be very destructive, particularly root rots. The best defense against root rot is choosing well-adapted plants and providing good drainage. Leaf spots are not uncommon, but generally are not severe enough for you to worry about spraying if shrubs are vigorous and otherwise healthy. Powdery mildew creates a thin, white, powdery film on the foliage of certain shrubs. It can be fairly easily controlled with fungus disease-control aids and/or by planting in locations where the air movement is good.

Weeds must be dealt with in any garden situation, including shrub beds. The use of 3- to 4-inch-deep mulches will minimize weed problems. Pre-emergent weed-prevention aids can be used in certain situations. When weeds do occur, deal with them regularly and quickly to prevent major problems. Handweeding and spot treatment with a nonselective weed-control aid will take care of weeds that do crop up. Weeding is an ongoing part of shrub care. Refer to page 291 for a summary listing your insect-, disease-, and weed-control options.

Pruning

Pruning is a regular part of shrub care. Done primarily to keep shrubs

attractively shaped, make them bushier and fuller, rejuvenate old, overgrown specimens, or control size, pruning can be minimized with careful plant selection.

Specially shaped shrubs, such as topiary and clipped hedges, require the most pruning. Shrubs that grow too large for their location may require almost constant pruning to keep the right size. Do not plant shrubs that will grow significantly larger than needed for a location.

Hedges, topiaries, and shrubs not grown for flowers can be pruned anytime between mid-March and September. Prune hedges so that the base is slightly wider than the top. This will keep the hedge full at the bottom.

Shrubs that bloom from January through April should be pruned after they finish flowering, but before late June. Shrubs that bloom from May through September should be pruned January through March (except **hydrangeas** and **gardenias,** which are pruned right after they finish flowering in June or July).

Prune flowering shrubs at the wrong time and you may prevent them from flowering during the ensuing growing season.

Shrubs for Texas

Name	Size (H × W) and Type	Light	Flowers and Comments
American Beautyberryscape *Callicarpa americana*	6 by 4 feet; deciduous.	Full to part sun.	**Native** shrub suitable for relaxed land- styles; purple berries in clusters along stems in late summer.
Aucuba *Aucuba japonica* 'Variegata'	5 by 3 feet; evergreen.	Shade.	Dark green and yellow variegation, coarse texture. Looks tropical but is quite hardy.
Azaleas *Rhododendron* spp. and cultivars	2 by 2 to 10 by 10 feet, depending on cultivar; mostly evergreen.	Part shade to sun, depending on cultivar.	Many different cultivars of this very popular spring-flowering shrub exist. Indica types are largest and easy to grow. Azalea cultivars that bloom at times other than spring are becoming more popular.
Banana Shrub *Michelia figo*	15 by 6 feet; evergreen.	Full sun to part shade.	Very fragrant, banana scented, creamy yellow flowers in April.
Barberry *Berberis thunbergii*	1½ by 2 to 6 by 7 feet; mostly deciduous, depending on variety.	Full to part sun.	Colorful leaves during the growing season and in the fall.
Boxwood *Buxus microphylla*	1 by 1½ to 20 by 6 feet; evergreen.	Part sun to shade.	Bright-green to dark-green leaves depending on variety. Great as formal hedges.
Butterfly Bush *Buddleia alternifolia* and *B. davidii*	6 by 6 feet to 10 feet by 10 feet; deciduous.	Full to part sun.	Long summer blooming season; spikes of fragrant purple, pink, or white flowers are attractive to butterflies; tends to be short-lived. **Native** and non-native varieties.
Camellia *Camellia japonica*	12 by 8 feet; evergreen.	Part sun to part shade.	Large flowers of striking beauty in shades of red, pink, or white December to March. Acid-loving, depending on variety.
Cherry Laurel *Prunus laurocerasus*	1½ by 3 to 25 by 16 feet; evergreen	Full to part sun.	Dark, glossy green leaves and fragrant white blooms; good screening plant.
Chinese Holly *Ilex cornuta* and many cultivars	3 by 3 to 12 by 10 feet, depending on cultivar; evergreen.	Full sun to part shade.	Most cultivars produce bright red berries fall to spring. Leaves are prickly. Watch for white scale insects, especially on the back sides of leaves.

Shrubs for Texas

Name	Size (H × W) and Type	Light	Flowers and Comments
Chinese Mahonia *Mahonia fortunei*	3 by 3 feet; evergreen.	Part morning shade to shade.	Excellent small shrub for shady areas; flowers are not significant.
Cleyera *Ternstroemia gymnanthera*	8 by 5 feet; evergreen.	Morning sun to part shade.	Slow growth; good for a hedge in part shade; new growth is burgundy; flowers not significant; best in acidic soils.
Crapemyrtle *Lageratroemia indica*	1½ by 3 to 25 by by 25 feet; deciduous.	Full sun.	Medium-green leaves, many bloom colors. Great as accents, specimens, and hedges.
Dwarf Yaupon *Ilex vomitoria* 'Nana'	3 by 3 feet; evergreen.	Sun to part shade.	Tough, widely planted shrub with small leaves and a neat growth habit; no berries are generally produced.
Fatsia *Fatsia japonica*	5 by 4 feet; evergreen.	Part shade to shade.	Large tropical leaves on a plant hardy to the mid- to low teens; striking large clusters of small white flowers in early December.
Flowering Quince *Chaenomeles speciosa*	8 by 6 feet; deciduous.	Full to part sun.	Showy flowers in shades of red, coral, pink, or white produced in late winter/early spring before the foliage; often called "Japonicas."
Gardenia *Gardenia jasminoides*	6 by 5 feet; evergreen.	Morning full to part sun.	Very fragrant, white flowers in May; some flowers in fall; acid-loving; watch for whiteflies.
Glossy Abelia *Abelia × grandiflora*	3 by 3 to 10 by 10, depending on cultivar; semi-evergreen.	Full to part sun.	Long summer blooming season, small white flowers in clusters; pest-free; evergreen in all but the coldest winters.
Hydrangea *Hydrangea macrophylla*	4 by 4 feet; deciduous.	Part shade to shade; no afternoon sun.	Large, showy flower clusters in shades of blue, lavender, or pink in May; prune before the end of July; blue in acidic soils, pink in alkaline soils.
Indian Hawthorne *Raphiolepsis indica*	2 by 2 to 5 by 4, depending on cultivar; evergreen.	Part sun to full sun.	Clusters of pink or white flowers in April. White cultivars generally more resistant to fireblight; watch for scale.
Japanese Viburnum *Viburnum japonicum*	12 by 6 feet; evergreen.	Full sun to part shade.	Excellent hedge plant; watch for thrips during summer; flowers not significant.

Shrubs for Texas

	Size (H × W) and Type	Light	Flowers and Comments
Japanese Yew *Podocarpus macrophyllus*	15 by 6 feet; evergreen.	Full sun to part shade.	Useful as a hedge or screen; grows well in part shade; flowers not significant.
Junipers *Juniperus* spp. and cultivars	1 by 3 to 10 by 10, depending on type; evergreen.	Full sun.	Large group of plants of various sizes and growth habits; full sun and good drainage are important; spider mites are common.
Mock Orange *Philadelphus coronarius*	10 by 6 feet; deciduous.	Full sun to part shade.	Large, arching branches produce showy fragrant, white flowers in late spring.
Nandina *Nandina domestica*	2 by 2 to 6 by 4, depending on cultivar; evergreen.	Full sun to part shade.	Tough, adaptable shrub that is essentially pest-free. Several varieties. Great shrub for Texas landscapes.
Oakleaf Hydrangea *Hydrangea quercifolia*	8 by 5 feet; deciduous.	Part sun to part shade.	Large spikes of white flowers in early summer age to old rose by fall; beautiful bark shows well during the leafless winter period; **native.**
Oleander *Nerium oleander*	15 by 10 feet; evergreen.	Full to part sun.	Large shrub with a long summer blooming season, flowers red, pink, white, or peach; watch for aphids and scale. Subject to freeze injury by temperatures in low 20s Fahrenheit.
Pineapple Guava *Feijoa sellowiana*	10 by 8 feet; evergreen.	Full to part sun.	Attractive white and red flowers in early summer followed by green, edible fruit ripening in September.
Pittosporum *Pittosporum tobira*	12 by 10 feet; evergreen.	Full sun to part shade.	Often planted where a smaller shrub would be more appropriate; very fragrant creamy white flowers in early summer. Dwarf cultivars are susceptible to root rot. Grow in zones 8b and 9.
Pomegranate, Dwarf *Punica granatum* 'Nana'	3 by 2 feet; deciduous.	Full sun to part shade.	Bright orange double flowers in early to midsummer, attractive fruit. The standard pomegranate grows to 10+ feet and the cultivar 'Wonderful' produces edible fruit.
Pyracantha *Pyracantha coccinea*	12 by 10 feet; evergreen.	Full to part sun.	Showy white flowers in spring, bright orange-red fruit in fall and winter; very thorny; prone to a variety of insect and disease problems.

Shrubs for Texas

Name	Size (H × W) and Type	Light	Flowers and Comments
Rose of Sharon, Althea *Hibiscus syriacus*	10 by 5 feet; deciduous.	Full sun to part shade.	Showy flowers like small hibiscus in white, pink, rose, or lavender in summer over several months; tall upright shrub; easily trained into a small tree form.
Sasanqua *Camellia sasanqua*	10 by 8 feet; evergreen.	Full sun to part shade.	Showy, fragrant flowers in October through December; good for hedges or screens.
Sweet Olive *Osmanthus fragrans*	15 by 10 feet; evergreen.	Full sun to part shade.	A "must have" for gardeners looking for fragrance; will slowly grow into a small tree; tiny, creamy white flowers are produced from fall to spring. Grow in zones 8b and 9.
Spirea, Bridal Wreath *Spirea × vanhoutei*	6 by 5 feet; deciduous.	Full to part sun.	Often planted where a smaller shrub would be a better choice; beautiful fountain of white flowers in April.
Virginia Willow *Itea virginica*	5 by 4 feet; deciduous.	Full sun to part shade.	Spikes of small white flowers in late spring and outstanding burgundy red fall foliage make this native shrub worth planting.
Wax-leaf Ligustrum *Ligustrum japonicum*	15 by 10 feet; evergreen.	Full sun to part shade.	Fast-growing shrub popular for hedges and screens; clusters of fragrant white flowers in summer. Grow in zones 8b and 9.

Planning

Many gardeners focus on spring to do major planting in the landscape, but the best season for planting shrubs is October through March. You still have time to make decisions and choices before the end of the ideal planting season, but do not put it off. Decide where and what kind of shrubs you want to plant. When choosing a shrub, consider the following questions:

- What are the growing conditions where the shrubs will be planted?

- What purpose will the shrubs serve—decorative, screen, hedge, privacy?

- What mature size would be desirable for the shrubs?

- What characteristics do you want the shrub to have—evergreen or deciduous, flowers (color, season of bloom, fragrance), decorative fruit, freedom from pests, growth rate, shape (low, mounding, upright)?

Draw simple sketches of the areas you intend to plant. How many of each type of shrub should you plant? You need to know before you go to the nursery. Here's how to find out.

Measure the space to be planted, and draw it out on a piece of graph paper, allowing one square (or more if you like) to equal a foot.

When you have selected the shrub you want to plant in that area, look at the shrub planting chart or another reference to see how wide it spreads. *Dale Groom's Texas Gardening Guide* (Cool Springs Press, 1997) contains 424 pages of landscape plants specific for Texas and includes the height and spread of many plants that can be grown in Texas.

Draw circles, representing the shrubs, on the graph paper. The diameter of each circle should be the number of squares needed to equal the spread of the shrub in feet: if one square equals a foot in your sketch, a shrub that spreads three feet would be represented by a circle three squares in diameter.

See how many circles you can fit into the area, allowing them to overlap only slightly. Remember to locate shrubs an appropriate distance from the house, patios, walks, and driveways.

Enter notes covering your decisions in your Texas gardening journal.

Planting and Transplanting

This is an excellent month for planting and transplanting shrubs.

- Do not plant immediately after rainy weather. Soil is often difficult to dig and will compact if worked while wet.

- If possible, do not plant immediately before a freeze in the teens. This cannot always be predicted, and the shrubs you are planting should take the cold, but keep it in mind.

- Shrubs are as dormant as they will get this month, and the weather is cool to cold and moist. That makes it an ideal time to transplant.

- Don't fight a shrub that has grown too large for where it is planted. Move it to a new location where its size is more appropriate, and plant a smaller-growing shrub in its place. Lift the shrub with as many roots as possible and replant it in its new location immediately. Do not allow the roots to dry before planting.

JANUARY

Care for Your Shrubs

Extremely cold weather is stressful to shrubs, especially when following a spell of mild weather. The hardy shrubs we use in our landscapes, however, usually make it through. If temperatures reach the low teens, some shrubs (such as certain varieties of **azaleas** and **pittosporum**) may experience bark splitting. Check your shrubs a week or two after a severe freeze for splits in the branch bark. The planting of hardy shrubs adapted to your Texas zone is the best way to ensure winter survival with little or no freeze damage.

Watering

There is generally no need to water established shrubs in January. Newly planted shrubs should be watered in thoroughly, but may not need to be watered thereafter if rainfall is regular. Should the weather be dry and mild, water newly planted shrubs as needed to maintain a moist soil. If a hard freeze is expected and the soil is dry, water thoroughly before the freeze arrives.

Fertilizing

No shrubs should be fertilized this month.

Pest Control

Winter is an excellent time to apply horticultural oil sprays to shrubs that are prone to scale. These include **camellias, hollies, magnolias, euonymus, privets,** and **cleyera.** Spray **gardenias** with oil for whiteflies. Check over these and other shrubs in your landscape and treat if necessary. Do not spray with oil if the nighttime low is predicted below 40 degrees Fahrenheit.

Refer to page 291 for a summary listing your options.

Pruning

Not much pruning is done this month, although in zones 8 and 9 you may prune just about anything except spring-flowering shrubs if you like. Some of the earliest-flowering shrubs, such as **flowering quince,** may bloom during January in south Texas. Cut a few branches and place them in a vase in your home to be enjoyed and to help herald the coming of spring.

Planning

Continue to develop your ideas for shrub planting. Remember that all parts of a landscape should work together. Shrub plantings should also take into consideration flower beds, areas of ground covers, outdoor living areas, and structures in the landscape.

Descriptions of plants in books sometimes do them justice, but you might want to pay visits to nurseries or public gardens, where you can see the plants "in person." Look at the shrubs you are thinking about planting. Once you see them, you might like them even better, or you may decide not to plant them (do not wait to find this out the day you go the nursery to purchase the shrubs).

Talk to local nursery staffs and/or your County Agent about your choices. They can provide additional information based on experience and observation to make sure you are selecting appropriate shrubs.

Planting and Transplanting

It would be great to finish up planting shrubs this month, giving them even more time to get established before hot weather arrives. Remember, next month ends the ideal planting season in south Texas.

Shrubs should be planted into well-prepared beds. Have your soil tested through the local county office of the Texas Cooperative Extension Service. The cost is nominal, and the information it provides is very helpful when it comes time to fertilize plants.

If your soil is heavy clay, the addition of several inches of sharp sand is recommended after 4 to 6 inches of organic matter has been added. If your soil has a pH below 5.5 and is low in calcium, add lime into the bed (if the soil is also low in magnesium, use dolomitic lime). If your soil test shows a pH above 7 and you are planting acid-loving shrubs, add sulfur, copperas, or aluminum sulfate during bed preparation to make the soil more acid. It is more effective to make these additions during bed preparation than after the shrubs have been planted.

Follow the steps below for bed preparation:

1 *Remove* unwanted vegetation from the bed area. Weeds or turfgrass may be removed physically, or eliminated with a weed-control aid and turned under. Refer to page 291 for a summary listing your options.

2 *Turn the soil* to a depth of at least 8 to 10 inches with a shovel, spade, or garden fork.

3 *Spread* any desired amendments over the turned soil. You should add about 4 to 6 inches of organic matter such as compost, sphagnum peat moss, composted manure, or finely ground pine bark.

4 Thoroughly *blend* the amendments into the soil, *rake* the bed smooth, and *shape* the edges. The level of the soil in the bed will be higher than it was before. This is good as it will improve drainage.

Note: In most situations, rear-tined tillers work well when preparing Texas shrub beds.

Bed preparation may be done several weeks prior to planting; it's great to have the bed already completed when you are ready to plant. Mulch the bed about 4 inches deep to keep rain from packing the soil back down and also to prevent weed growth. Plant through the mulch, or move the mulch off the bed, plant, and replace the mulch.

Care for Your Shrubs

February can have spells of bitter cold. Make sure shrubs are well watered prior to a freeze if the ground is dry. Should you have tender shrubs, such as **hibiscus** or **Mexican heather,** planted in your landscape, cover and protect them during temperatures in the mid- to low 20s Fahrenheit. See the section on cold protection in the introduction for more information.

Watering

Little additional water is needed by shrubs this time of year. Shrubs are mostly dormant and the weather is cool with adequate rain.

Fertilizing

It is still a little early for fertilizing most shrubs. Although shrubs like **camellias, star magnolia,** and **flowering quince** may be blooming, encouraging new growth with fertilizer may cause plants to be damaged by a late freeze.

Pest Control

Diseases are rarely a problem during the winter.

Insects: During the early part of this month, apply oil sprays to shrubs to control scale and whiteflies if this was not done in January.

Weeds: Winter weeds will take advantage of moist, mild weather and grow . . . like weeds!

Keep beds mulched 3 to 4 inches deep, pull weeds promptly, and spot-treat with weed-control aids. Refer to page 291 for a summary listing your options.

Pruning

Prune summer-flowering shrubs now if you need to (do not prune **gardenias** or **hydrangeas** now). The fact that it is time to prune does not mean you must. Prune with a definite purpose in mind. Study the shrub carefully, decide specifically what needs to be done, and prune accordingly. Take your time. Until you build your confidence, do a little, wait a few days, and do some more until you are satisfied.

MARCH

Planning

Plan on getting your shrub planting finished up this month in south Texas. Don't panic. Shrubs may be planted from containers throughout the year, but they like it so much better when they have a chance to make some root growth before the hot weather arrives. From March on, the later you plant, the more you will have to pamper new plantings, and the greater the chance that some of the shrubs will not survive.

Evaluate your established landscape for areas where shrubs are needed. The unattractive view you have always wanted to screen, for instance, would be such a spot.

Planting and Transplanting

Proper planting will get your shrubs off to a good start. Here's how to plant in a well-prepared bed.

1 Place shrubs in their containers on top of the soil where they will be planted. Make sure the spacing and arrangement are proper before going on to the next step.

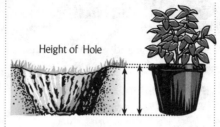

Height of Hole

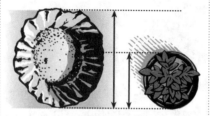

Width of Hole

2 ***Push down*** slightly on a pot to make a shallow depression, then set the shrub—in its container—aside.

3 ***Dig*** a hole into the depression deep enough to accommodate, and a little wider than, the rootball. Do not dig any deeper than soilball depth.

4 ***Remove*** the shrub from the container. If the roots are tightly packed in a solid mass, ***cut*** into the ball in several places or ***pull apart*** the root system somewhat. This will encourage the roots to grow into the surrounding soil.

Removing Container

5 ***Place*** the shrub's rootball into the hole. It is critical for the top of the rootball to be level with or slightly above the soil surface of the bed.

6 Use your hands to push and ***firm*** soil into the space between the rootball and the sides of the hole.

7 After planting all the shrubs in the bed, ***water*** them in thoroughly by hand to finish settling the soil around their roots.

8 Apply root stimulators according to label directions.

9 Finally, ***mulch*** the bed 3 to 4 inches deep.

Follow the same procedure for balled-and-burlapped shrubs. Larger sizes are sometimes sold that way. After you set the rootball into the hole, remove any twine, nails, or wire securing the burlap. Remove the burlap (use a knife or scissors), being careful not to break the rootball.

Care for Your Shrubs

Many shrubs begin to wake up and grow this month. Watch out for insect and disease problems. Late freezes may nip back new growth, but hardy shrubs will recover.

MARCH

Check the mulch situation in your shrub beds. If it has broken down and gotten thin over time, now is a good time to replenish it. There is no need to remove the old mulch; just add new mulch on top of it—a 4-inch layer is recommended.

Watering

Established shrubs rarely need water except in hot, dry weather. Water newly planted shrubs thoroughly if the weather is dry and warm this month. The advantage of planting shrubs during the cool season is not having to fuss over them as much.

Fertilizing

This is the month to fertilize shrubs in your landscape. Granular fertilizers provide an easy and economical way to feed shrubs. You usually will not need a separate fertilizer for the different types of shrubs you are growing. Acid-loving plants may be fed with a fertilizer formulated for them, especially where soils are alkaline. But otherwise, don't make fertilizing too complicated.

Most shrubs respond well to 3:1:2 or 4:1:2 ratio fertilizers, like 15-5-10, 18-6-12, 9-5-9, and 21-7-14. Use premium-quality long-lasting slow-release granular fertilizers for good results.

Apply your selected fertilizer evenly around the plants and water it in. Fertilizers can be applied directly over the mulch, or you can pull back the mulch, apply the fertilizer and replace the mulch.

Apply aluminum sulfate around the roots of **hydrangeas** now if they are pink and you want them to be blue. It may take a couple of years for the color change to occur.

Pest Control

Pests become a problem in Texas with mild weather.

Insects: Aphids are fairly common on the new growth of a variety of shrubs. Fortunately, they are easy to control.

Diseases: Leaf spo_ attack new growth on some _

Watch carefully for the first signs and treat with a fungus-control aid if necessary. Refer to page 291 for a summary listing your pest- and fungus-control aids.

Pruning

Finish up pruning summer-flowering shrubs such as **althea, oleander,** and **crapemyrtle** by the end of this month. **Oleanders** and **dwarf crapemyrtles** are often cut back to stimulate bushy new growth. Have a definite purpose in mind when pruning.

Do not be too hasty to prune growth that has been damaged by winter freezes. Wait until the shrub has begun to grow and look at which branches are sprouting. Some branches that look dead may have only lost their leaves to the cold and will resprout.

APRIL

Planning

Take some time to appreciate the abundant flowers produced by spring-flowering shrubs this month. **Azaleas** in particular really put on a show. This would be a good time to check out the combinations of colors you have created. Sometimes colors we thought would look good together, don't. Make notes to move or replace shrubs in November if you need to change or refine color combinations in your landscape.

When you go to nurseries and see the crowds this month, you'll be glad you bought and planted your shrubs months ago when the staff had more time to help you with questions. Enter notes in your Texas gardening journal about shrub colors, growth, weeds, pests, and weather conditions.

Planting and Transplanting

You may continue planting shrubs from containers. If you choose to plant balled-and-burlapped shrubs, do so in early April. Hot weather is just around the corner and there is little time for them to make root growth before the heat arrives. When shrubs are planted this late, you should pay very careful attention to their water needs in the coming summer.

It is too late to transplant shrubs unless absolutely necessary. Even then you are taking a substantial risk. Transplant as soon as possible with as many roots as you can dig, keep the plants well watered, and cross your fingers.

Care for Your Shrubs

In order to do well, shrubs must be planted in the growing conditions they prefer. The wrong location can mean constant problems:

- Too much shade produces leggy, low-vigor shrubs that bloom poorly or not at all and are more susceptible to disease problems.

- Too much sun can cause a shrub to appear stunted, with bleached-out, burned foliage.

- Poor drainage leads to root rot.

- Soil that stays too dry can cause excessive wilting, scorched leaves, and even termination.

Observe your shrubs carefully throughout the year. Those that are not thriving may be in the wrong location or not properly cared for.

Watering

Newly planted shrub beds may need to be watered once or twice a week if five to seven days pass without a good rain ($\frac{1}{2}$ to 1 inch). These plants do not have well-established root systems growing out into the soil and are very susceptible to drought stress. Plantings that are two or more years old will not need as much attention. The first summer after planting is always the most critical time for newly planted shrubs.

When you water, water thoroughly so that the soil is moistened 4 to 6 inches down. Apply an inch of water with a sprinkler or use a soaker hose. To calibrate your sprinkler to apply 1 inch of water, place several cans in the area the sprinkler covers. Turn on the sprinkler and check the time. When one inch of water has accumulated in most of the cans, check the time again. That's how long it takes your sprinkler to apply an inch of water.

If you use a soaker hose, make sure it passes within several inches of the base of each shrub in the bed. Water does not move a great distance from the soaker hose and it needs to be fairly close to a plant in order to properly water its roots. Water as needed to maintain a moist soil.

Fertilizing

Fertilize now if you did not do so last month. Your shrubs will need the extra nutrients during the next six to eight weeks when they do much of their growing for the year. If you are fighting with a shrub that wants to be bigger than you want it to be, don't fertilize it—you will just be encouraging it to grow faster. Generally, if a shrub is growing well and has good color and vigor, fertilization is optional.

Premium-quality slow-release granular fertilizers are more expensive initially than quick-release granular fertilizers, but they feed over a much longer period of time. Slow-release fertilizers allow you to skip the summer fertilizer application since they will still be releasing nutrients 3 to 8 months (or longer) after application. Always apply fertilizers according to label directions.

Pest Control

Insects become more common as warmer weather settles in.

Insects: Watch for aphids clustering on new growth and flower buds.

The leading pest afflicting **azaleas** is the azalea lacebug. Look for tiny white spots on the upper surface of the leaves. Turn a leaf over and you will see dark brown specks on the back.

Treat promptly before the damage becomes too severe. Once heavily damaged, the foliage will not regain its attractive color. Spray, especially under the leaves, with appropriately labeled insect-control aids. Make applications every ten days until June. Follow label directions.

Caterpillars will chew holes in new foliage.

The damage is generally not serious, but if necessary, treat with appropriate control aids.

Diseases: Powdery mildew may show up on a variety of shrubs if the weather is warm and humid. Look for a fine, white powdery coating on the foliage.

Powdery mildew may be controlled with specific fungus-control aids.

Insect pest-, disease-, and weed-control aids are available at local nurseries. Visit them for assistance in selecting the appropriate aids. Refer to page 291 for a summary listing your options. Always read and follow label directions when using any gardening aids.

Pruning

Prune spring-flowering shrubs any-time after they finish flowering. Unless you are creating special shapes, such as clipped hedges or topiary, try to work with and pre-serve the natural form of the shrub when you are pruning. This can be best accomplished by using hand pruners (preferably bypass-type) rather than shears. When used repeatedly, shears turn shrubs into mounds, boxes, spheres, and other geometrical shapes. Unless this is how you want your shrubs to look, don't use them.

Heading Back

MAY

Planning

We often think of May as late spring, but it can be really quite hot and summery this month. If the winter was mild, **oleanders** will begin to enliven landscapes with clusters of red, pink, white, or rose flowers. One of the most fragrant flowers, the **gardenia,** opens white flowers that perfume the air and fade to a buttery yellow. **Hydrangeas** brighten shady plantings with cotton-candy heads of blue, pink, rose, or lavender flowers. Careful planning shows in how well shrubs thrive, fit in their location, and provide needed color, privacy, screening, or beauty.

Shrubs are a long-term commitment in the landscape; mistakes will not just go away. Constantly evaluate how well shrubs are living up to your expectations, and plan on changes to refine shrub plantings. Most of us inherit a landscape when we purchase a home. Spend a year getting to know your site and the existing plant materials. If shrub plantings do not function the way you want, if the previous owner made mistakes (you know, the giant holly hiding the picture window), or if there are shrubs that are not doing well, feel free to make the changes needed to create the landscape you and your family want.

Note your decisions and evaluations in your Texas gardening journal.

Planting and Transplanting

Although planting shrubs from containers may continue, increasingly stressful weather conditions mean that extra care will be needed. The chance of problems with newly planted shrubs increases as the weather gets hotter. If you do plant shrubs now, do not disturb the root system, even if it is rootbound. Shrubs will not tolerate damage to their root systems when it is hot.

Care for Your Shrubs

In an effort to make a planting look full from the beginning, shrubs are often planted too close together. Even professionals do this. Eventually, the shrubs begin to crowd one another. Overcrowding can create stress through competition and increases insect and disease problems. In extreme cases, it might be necessary to remove some of the shrubs to make room for the rest. Sometimes regular pruning can keep things from getting out of hand. Avoid this problem by spacing shrubs properly at the beginning, even if the bed doesn't look full.

Watering

As temperatures rise, shrubs absorb water faster from the soil. Enough rain usually falls to meet the needs of established shrubs. Shrubs planted within the last six months, however, may need to be watered once or twice a week whenever beds are dry and rainfall is scarce. Water as needed to maintain a moist soil condition.

Fertilizing

Acid-loving plants can develop a disease called iron chlorosis, caused by a deficiency of iron. The symptoms are found mostly in new growth. Leaves turn a yellow-green color, while the veins of the leaves stay dark green. **Azaleas, gardenias, roses, blueberries,** and **camellias** are a few plants in which this condition occurs, especially when they are grown in alkaline soil. Treat with a fertilizer rich in chelated iron, following label directions, and acidify the soil with sulfur, copperas, aluminum sulfate, or a liquid soil acidifier.

Pest Control

Continue to spray for azalea lace-bugs. Watch for signs of other pest problems. Identify the problem and use the appropriate pest-control aid, if necessary. Refer to page 291 for a summary listing your options. Fortunately, gardeners can go for years without seeing a major outbreak of pests on their shrubs. If you need help identifying a problem, contact your local County Agent, talk to local nursery staff, or use another reference.

Pruning

This is a major month to prune spring-flowering shrubs that need it. About the only shrubs you wouldn't prune now are those that bloom in summer. Prune with a definite vision of what you are trying to accomplish. Ask, and fully answer, two questions before pruning begins:

1 Why, specifically, do I feel this plant needs to be pruned? (Or, what specific goal do I want to accomplish; what problem do I need to correct?)

2 How do I need to prune this plant to accomplish the goal?

There are two basic techniques we use to prune shrubs: heading back and thinning out.

Heading back involves shortening shoots or branches. It stimulates growth and branching. Heading back is often used to control the size of shrubs, encourage fullness, rejuvenate older shrubs, and maintain specific shapes, as with topiary and espalier. Shearing is a form of heading back. Often overutilized by gardeners, careless shearing can destroy the natural form of a plant.

Thinning out removes shoots or branches at their point of origin, either back to a branch fork or the main trunk. Thinning cuts can control the size and shape of a plant while doing a better job of maintaining its natural shape. Thinning cuts do not stimulate as much growth, and often work more with the plant's natural growth patterns to correct problems.

Thinning Out

Heading Back

Planning

Keeping records about plants in your landscape is a great way to learn from past experiences. Shrubs aren't as finicky as other types of plants, and are long-lived when selected and cared for properly. You might think that keeping records is not very important, but pest problems, treatments that were effective or ineffective, blooming times, when shrubs were planted, and where they were purchased are all valuable bits of information. Keep your Texas gardening journal handy to jot down quick observations. As time goes by you'll be surprised at how helpful the notes can be.

Planting and Transplanting

The intense heat of the next three months will make it more difficult for shrubs planted now to survive and become established. If at all possible, avoid this hottest time of the year for planting shrubs, and wait for cooler weather this fall.

Transplanting shrubs should not be attempted. Plants use water faster when it is hot and they are in active growth. To damage the roots now would reduce the plants' abilities to absorb water just when they need it most.

Care for Your Shrubs

Most summer-flowering shrubs bloom over a relatively long period, compared to spring-flowering shrubs. Faded flowers often linger as new ones are being produced, detracting from the attractiveness of the display. *Pull or trim off* faded flowers as they occur. In the case of **dwarf crapemyrtles, oleanders,** and others, trimming off the faded flowers will encourage more blooms to form.

Hot weather makes it less pleasant to be outside. Use the early morning or early evening hours to walk around the landscape and check out your shrub plantings. Look for plants that need to be pruned, pest problems getting started, weeds that need to be pulled, and other assorted jobs. All gardeners eventually learn that these problems are much easier to deal with if handled sooner rather than later.

Watering

Watch carefully for drought stress on shrubs planted within the last six months, especially those planted after March. Symptoms to look for include wilting, scorched leaf edges, or dull, brown, or dropping leaves. Water deeply and thoroughly once or twice a week when adequate rain does not fall.

Ironically, you may be watering properly but your shrubs are still showing signs of drought stress. Newly planted shrubs have a restricted root system that has not grown extensively into the soil of the bed. A shrub can pull all the water out of its rootball and get desperately thirsty even when the soil of the bed feels moist. Stick your fingers directly into the rootball under a shrub rather than in the soil of the bed to see if it is dry.

When irrigating new shrubs, make sure their rootballs are thoroughly watered, not just the soil around them.

JUNE

If you see drought symptoms even though you are watering, turn a hose on trickle and lay it at the base of each shrub for about 10 minutes (or longer) to provide water directly to the shrub's roots where it is needed. This situation is generally more common when sprinklers are used to irrigate and less of a problem when soaker hoses are used.

Young shrubs, in their second year after planting, may be fertilized in June or July to encourage additional growth. Use about the same rate you did in the spring or less. Generally, avoid fertilizing shrubs planted in the past eight months. They should not be pushed to grow while they are establishing.

Control whiteflies on **gardenias, citrus trees,** and any other shrubs as needed, with aids specifically labeled to control them. Follow label directions. Make three applications ten days apart, and spray during the cooler early-morning hours. Refer to page 291 for a summary listing your fungus- and pest-control aids.

Fertilizing

Most spring-flowering and other shrubs have finished their primary growth period and by following our recommendation the fertilizer you provided in March was sufficient. Unless you cut them back, little or no growth will occur throughout the rest of the summer. Fertilizing established shrubs that are about as big as you want them to be is of little benefit. If you have problems controlling the size of shrubs in your landscape, fertilizing them will just make matters worse.

Pest Control

Control powdery mildew on your shrubs with fungus-control aids labeled to control powdery mildew on ornamentals.

Pruning

You should finish any extensive pruning that needs to be done on spring-flowering shrubs this month, or early July by the latest.

JULY

Planning

Is there a bland sameness to your shrub plantings? Many shrubs have a medium texture that can look uninteresting if there are no contrasts nearby. Plant shrubs with a variety of textures (coarse-textured plants have large leaves, fine-textured plants have small or thin leaves, and medium-textured plants fall somewhere in-between) and growth habits (upright, bushy, mounding) to create interest and contrast. Groups of herbaceous perennials, annuals, bulbs, and ornamental grasses can also be included in shrub plantings. Make plans to plant or rearrange shrubs this fall if needed. Enter your notes, observations, and plans in your Texas gardening journal.

Planting and Transplanting

Although planting can continue through the summer with container-grown shrubs, think carefully before you decide to plant now. It is far better to wait for the weather to cool. Remember, fall is for planting all types of shrubs, trees, vines and other landscape plants in Texas.

If you are in a new house without any landscaping and need to do something, plant beds of heat-tolerant blooming plants now instead of shrubs. Good choices are **pentas, lantana, blue daze, dusty miller, purslane, periwinkle, torenia,** and **salvia** for sunny areas, and **coleus** and **wax-leaf begonias** for shade. These plants will grow, bloom, and thrive in midsummer heat through November or until the first killing freeze/frost. At that time, they can be pulled up and replaced with permanent shrub plantings.

Watering

Even well-established shrubs will need to be watered if rain does not occur for several days. Intense heat stresses shrubs, and they need an adequate supply of water to deal with it. On the other hand, frequent rains may occur, particularly in south Texas along the coast, making irrigation unnecessary. Watch the weather and *water when needed.* **Azaleas** are shallow-rooted and one of the most drought-vulnerable shrubs we grow.

A good policy is to maintain a soil that is *moist,* and not wet or dry. Maintaining a 3- to 4-inch-deep mulch year-round will help conserve soil moisture, moderate soil temperatures, and reduce weed populations.

Fertilizing

You may *fertilize* established shrubs that were last fed in the spring. This is recommended for shrubs you want to grow as much and as fast as possible. This is not recommended for shrubs that have already outgrown their space and have to be cut back frequently. Use a premium-quality long-lasting slow-release 3:1:2 or 4:1:2 ratio granular fertilizer appropriate for your area at the rate recommended on the label (or less).

Apply a fertilizer containing chelated iron to acid-loving plants such as **azaleas, gardenias, blueberries, camellias,** and others that show an iron deficiency. Young leaves will appear yellow-green with dark green veins. Apply a soil acidifier to lower the pH and make iron more readily available.

Care for Your Shrubs

Shrubs should not require a great deal of care in your landscape. Other than occasional pruning, watering, and dealing with infrequent pest problems, shrubs normally do not demand a lot of time. Shrubs that always seem to have something wrong or need constant work to be kept attractive may not have been good choices for your landscape. Decide if there is a problem that can be corrected, or replace those shrubs with lower-maintenance types this fall.

Pest Control

Insects: A black deposit on foliage is a fungus called "sooty mold" that indicates the presence of sucking insects. It is not attacking the shrub, but living off sugary excretions produced by the sucking insects. Sucking insects that commonly produce this sugary substance (called honeydew) include aphids, whiteflies, and scales.

Caterpillars and beetles can chew holes in shrub leaves.

All can be controlled with applications of various insect pest-control aids available at your local nurseries and garden centers. Refer to page 291 for a summary listing your options. During July, early morning is usually the best time to apply insect pest-control aids. Remember, always read and follow label directions when using any gardening aid.

Diseases: Rainy weather encourages leaf spot diseases, but they rarely warrant spraying.

Generally, by the time you notice the spots, the damage is already done.

Wet soil also encourages root rot diseases in late summer. Established shrubs that are otherwise healthy may show dead or wilted branches. Fungal infections have generally killed a portion of the root system that provided water to that section of the shrub. A shrub may wilt completely and die. Often only one or a few shrubs in a planting are affected.

There is little that can be done. Pull back the mulch and loosen the soil slightly to increase air spaces and allow soil to dry out. To avoid the problem, make sure beds drain well when they are being prepared. And don't over-water— keep the soil moist.

Pruning

Finish pruning spring-flowering shrubs early this month. Do not prune **camellias**; their flowerbuds for fall and winter bloom are already set. *Prune* hedges as needed to keep them neat and thick. Remember that the base of the hedge should be slightly wider than the top. This prevents lower portions of the hedge from being shaded and thinning out.

Planning

These hot weeks of a long, hot summer are particularly stressful to shrubs in the landscape (as well as to the gardener). Carefully chosen shrubs, well adapted to our climate and planted in the proper growing conditions, however, should have no difficulty getting through this most trying time of the year.

The fall planting season begins in a couple of months, and it's not too soon to make plans. Check out local botanical gardens and gardens open to the public, as well as local nurseries. Shrubs that are thriving in the heat of August make good choices for your landscape. Shrubs in public gardens and nurseries are generally well labeled, so it is not difficult to identify a shrub you are not familiar with. Once a shrub catches your eye, spend some time researching the plant.

Enter your observations, places visited and future plans in your Texas gardening journal. Also note which plants are holding up well, the weather conditions, and any pest problems.

Planting and Transplanting

This is not a good month for planting or transplanting shrubs in the landscape. The intense heat of this month is hard enough for an established shrub to endure. New plantings are especially vulnerable. If you do plant, proper watering is crucial. And try to plant heat-tolerant, well-rooted, container-grown selections.

Care for Your Shrubs

Late-summer stress can occasionally cause shrubs to drop some of their older leaves. This is generally not a major problem and no cause for alarm.

Keep beds mulched to a depth of 3 to 4 inches. Not only does this help control weeds and conserve soil moisture, but it also helps prevent the soil from building up so much heat. In older plantings where the shrubs have grown enough to shade the soil of the bed, this is less critical. But in new plantings where the ground is still exposed, a 3- to 4-inch layer of mulch is very beneficial.

Choose a mulch that suits your taste, but try to use what is available for free. Pine straw, shade tree leaves (saved from the fall), dry grass clippings, and partially finished compost are all excellent. You may also purchase mulch such as pine bark, cypress mulch, pine straw, pine bark nuggets, and hardwood bark.

Watering

August can be very hot and dry. Provide deep, thorough irrigation with sprinklers or soaker hoses. *Water* as needed if rain has not occurred in the last five to seven days for new plantings, in the last ten days for established plantings. Maintain a *moist* soil, not dry or wet.

AUGUST

Fertilizing

If your plants were fertilized earlier in the growing season and are now growing well with good leaf color, they generally will not need any additional applications this growing season. For plants with off color and/or limited growth, September is usually a good month to fertilize one last time during the active growing season. Make applications of 3:1:2 or 4:1:2 ratio premium-quality slow-release granular fertlizer according to label directions in late August/early September. Do not fertilize with quick-release aids.

Pest Control

Mites: Spider mites can be a problem on shrubs such as **azaleas** and **junipers** during hot, dry weather. Spider mites are generally too tiny to see without magnification, but the foliage will become faded and tan as they feed.

Insects: Azalea lacebugs become more active in the late summer and fall. Watch for new damage.

If needed, continue to treat for caterpillars and beetles, which chew holes in the leaves of a variety of shrubs.

If the damage is light, control is usually not necessary.

Pest-control aids are available at your local retailer along with instructions on the proper uses of them. Refer to page 291 for a summary listing your options. After your choices are made, remember to read and follow label directions when applying any gardening aids, including fertilizers and aids that control insect pests, diseases, and weeds.

Pruning

Finish shearing hedges or pruning shrubs not grown for flowers. Pruning after August will stimulate new growth which will not have time to harden off before winter, making the plant more susceptible to freeze injury.

If you prune spring-flowering shrubs this month or later, you will remove flower buds from next year's display.

Keep your pruning tool *sharp* for best results and clean cuts.

SEPTEMBER

Planning

This month usually brings some relief from the heat. **Sweet olives** will often burst into bloom with the first cool front. The small, inconspicuous, creamy-white flowers produce one of the most delightful fragrances of any shrub. Fragrance is an often-overlooked aspect of flowering shrubs, but it can add so much to the enjoyment of our gardens in zones 8b and 9. Plan to include some fragrant shrubs in your landscape. Good choices include **butterfly bush** (*Buddleia*), **sweet shrub** (*Calycanthus*), **sasanqua, gardenia, winter honeysuckle** (*Lonicera fragrantissima*), **star magnolia** (*Magnolia stellata*), and **native azalea** (*Rhododendron canescens*).

Remember, always plant the best locally adapted and hardy plant for your zone of Texas. Refer to the Texas hardiness zone map on page 21 if you aren't sure which plant hardiness zone you live in.

Planning on planting some shrubs this fall? If we do get some beautiful cool weather and you feel like digging in the garden, go ahead and start preparing beds now for planting shrubs next month.

Enter your plant information, observations, and thoughts in your Texas gardening journal.

Planting and Transplanting

Wait until next month to begin planting. The weather will be more pleasant for you to get out and dig beds, and the shrubs will appreciate the cooler temperatures, too.

Care for Your Shrubs

Now that the hottest weather is probably coming to an end, take time to evaluate the shrubs growing in your landscape. What would you do differently regarding pest control? Sometimes we decide to let a problem go untreated, then regret the decision when a lot of damage occurs. Make a note in your Texas gardening journal to treat if the problem should show up again next summer. You might decide to prune some shrubs differently. Perhaps you should have cut them back sooner or later, more than you did or less.

If we do not take the time to look at what we have done and remember the results, we may continue to make the same mistakes or forget something that worked well.

Watering

Although temperatures may become milder, September weather can also be sweltering and dry. If your new shrub plantings are still alive, you've been doing an excellent job of watering. *Keep up the good work.* Apply water as needed to maintain a *moist* soil.

Fertilizing

This is usually the last month we fertilize shrubs in most of Texas. If you live in the Rio Grande Valley, fertilization may take place even later. Always apply fertilizers according to label directions.

Pest Control

Insects: The same pests that have been around all summer may continue this month. Insect pests to control include whiteflies (especially on **gardenias**), lacebugs (especially on **azaleas**), scales (especially on **camellias, hollies,** and **euonymus**), and aphids (especially on **oleanders**). Pest-control aids and information on their proper uses are available at your local nurseries, garden centers, and other retailers who carry gardening aids.

Diseases: Disease problems generally begin to diminish as weather grows cooler, especially if September is relatively dry. If the summer has been very wet, root rot may have taken its toll on some shrub plantings.

Wait until fall to replace dead shrubs. Before planting new shrubs, dig generous amounts of organic matter into the area. Plant the shrubs slightly higher to ensure better drainage.

Weeds: If you let weeds get the upper hand during the hot weather of summer, get out on cooler days and try to get them under control.

You may elect to pull, dig, or spot-treat with selective weed-control aids. Although you can use some of them very close to desirable plants, do not allow them to get on the foliage or stems of your shrubs. Use a piece of cardboard or other material as a shield, cover nearby shrubs with plastic bags, or otherwise prevent spray from getting on the shrubs. Selective weed-control aids will kill grassy weeds, but not the ornamentals listed on their labels. These aids may be helpful in situations where it would be impossible to spray the weed without getting the aid on the shrub. Refer to page 291 for a summary listing your pest- and weed-control options.

Maintaining a 3- to 4-inch layer of bark much year-round will greatly cut down on weed problems in shrub beds.

Pruning

The only pruning that would be appropriate from now on would be thinning (see the May pruning information). It may be done just about anytime. Remember: spring-flowering shrubs such as **gardenias, hydrangeas,** and **camellias** already have their flower buds set. Any pruning now will remove flower buds and reduce the spring display.

When pruning shrubs, keep your shears, handpruners, loppers, and saws sharp to help ensure clean, smooth cuts.

Planning

Shrub planting can begin this month, but there is no hurry. If you need to plant a new landscape, or extensively redesign an existing one, take some time to think about what you want to plant and where it will be located. An attractive, functional landscape doesn't just happen. You cannot go to the nursery one Saturday morning, buy a bunch of shrubs that catch your eye (or happen to be on sale), bring them home, plant them here and there, and expect the landscape to turn out the way you wanted. But you probably know better than that by now.

Take time to consider your needs and develop a plan for a landscape that will be attractive, functional, and successful. See "Planning the Garden" (page 12) for more information on how to do this, and the introduction to this chapter for information on how to select shrubs. You have plenty of time to do this—the planting season runs from now until March for much of Texas. In zones 6 and 7, plant only very winter hardy shrubs during January, our coldest month. In these zones, February, March, and April are nearly always great planting months in addition to October, November, and December. November through early December, however, is a particularly good time for landscape installation.

Enter notes on your plans, decisions, and observations in your Texas gardening journal.

Planning and Transplanting

It's still too early to transplant, but you can begin to plant container-grown shrubs. Proper bed preparation is the first step to successfully growing shrubs.

Follow the steps below for bed preparation:

1 *Remove* unwanted vegetation from the bed area. Weeds or turfgrass may be removed physically or eliminated with selective weed-control aids (follow label directions carefully) and turned under. Refer to page 291 for a summary listing your options.

2 *Turn the soil* to a depth of at least 8 to 10 inches with a shovel, spade, garden fork, or rear-tined tiller.

3 *Spread* any desired amendments over the turned soil. You should always add about 4 to 6 inches of organic matter such as compost, sphagnum peat moss, rotted manure, or finely ground pine bark. Most experienced gardeners apply two or more types of organic matter when constructing planting beds in Texas. Have your soil tested through the county office of the Texas Cooperative Extension Service to determine soil pH and which nutrients may be added to nourish your plants when installing them.

4 Thoroughly *blend* your selected amendments into the soil of the bed, *rake* smooth, and *shape* the edges. The level of the soil in the bed will be higher than it was before. This is good, as it will improve drainage.

OCTOBER

If you don't intend to plant right away, apply a 3- to 4-inch layer of mulch over the prepared bed. This will keep the soil loose and prevent weeds from growing until you plant. At that time you can pull off the mulch, plant, then replace it, or simply plant through the existing mulch.

Watering

Although cooler, October can be one of our driest months. Established shrubs probably will not need much attention, but continue to water shrubs planted in the past year as needed if expected rainfall does not occur.

Remember, irrigate as needed to maintain a soil that is *moist,* not wet or dry.

Fertilizing

Apply fertilizer during plant installation, but usually no fertilizer is applied to existing shrub plantings this month.

Pest Control

Azalea lacebugs will be active through November. These insects feed from the underside of the leaves, causing small, white dots on the upper side of the leaves and dark-brown spots on the back.

Do not let a lot of damage occur before you treat. Once the damage occurs, the leaves will not turn green again, even if you control the lacebugs. Spray under the leaves with pest-control aids labeled for lacebugs on azaleas as needed. Refer to page 291 for a summary listing your options. Always read and follow label directions when applying any pest-control aid.

Pruning

This is normally not a good time of year to prune shrubs. If absolutely necessary, thinning may be used to correct problems that can't wait.

Planning

Even if they have gardened in our state for a long time, some Texas gardeners still have a hard time resisting the feeling that this is the end of the gardening year—that it's time to put up the tools, watch the plants go dormant, and wait for a blanket of snow to cover the land-scape. But this is not the end (and we rarely get snow, except in the Panhandle and the High Plains). In fact, it's a prime time for planting in most of our state. So much can be planted now, including shrubs.

Although the ideal planting season for shrubs runs from now through March for most of Texas, planting in November and early December is particularly recommended. The weather is generally mild and pleas-ant, and shrubs planted in late fall and early winter benefit in several ways:

- The plants are dormant, or "resting," during this time and therefore less likely to suffer transplant shock.

  This is especially important for balled-and-burlapped shrubs.

- The mild weather and rainfall typical of our winters allow the new plantings to settle in and adjust with little stress (and less work for you).

- Planting shrubs now also allows them to become well established prior to spring growth and the intense heat of summer.

Research shows that the roots of plants can continue to grow and develop during our rela-tively mild winters, even though the top is dormant. Shrubs planted now will develop well-established root systems and are better able to absorb water than spring-planted shrubs. This increases their ability to survive that first stressful summer after planting.

If you were looking for a break, think again. It's time to get out your shovels and *start planting.*

Planting and Transplanting

A tremendous advantage of plant-ing shrubs during this time of year is that the nurseries are much less busy than they were in the spring, when most people headed to the nurseries. Now that you know bet-ter, enjoy the time and attention that nursery staffs can give you as you make your shrub purchases. Plant shrubs in well-prepared beds. Avoid preparing beds and planting

if the soil is wet. Wait a couple of days after a heavy rain before dig-ging in the soil. Working wet soil damages its structure and can lead to soil compaction.

1 Place shrubs in their containers on top of the soil where they will be planted. Make sure the spacing and arrangement are the way you want them before going on to the next step.

2 *Push down* slightly on a pot to make a shallow depression, and set the shrub—in its con-tainer—aside.

3 *Dig* a hole into the depression deep enough to accommodate, and a little wider than, the rootball.

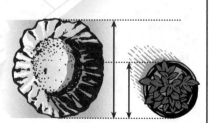

Height of Hole

Width of Hole

4 *Remove* the shrub from the container. If the roots are tightly packed in a solid mass, cut into the ball in several places or pull apart the root system somewhat. This will encourage the roots to grow into the surrounding soil.

Removing Container

5 Place the shrub's rootball into the hole. It is critical for the top of the rootball to be level with or slightly above the soil surface of the bed.

6 Use your hands to push and *firm* soil into the space between the rootball and the sides of the hole.

7 After planting all the shrubs, *water* them in thoroughly by hand to finish settling the soil around their roots.

8 A root stimulator should be applied at the time according to label directions.

9 Finally, *mulch* the bed 3 to 4 inches deep.

You can follow the same procedure for balled-and-burlapped shrubs. Larger-sized shrubs are sometimes sold that way. After you set the rootball into the hole, remove any twine, nails, or wire securing the burlap. Pull down or remove the burlap (use a knife or scissors), being careful not to break the rootball. (The "burlap" may actually be a synthetic material that resists decay. If you're not sure if the wrapping is true burlap that will rot or is the look-alike material, remove it completely from the hole.)

Watering

Established shrubs should not need to be watered during this time of the year. Water-in newly planted shrubs thoroughly, watering as needed thereafter if the weather is mild and dry.

Thinning Out

Fertilizing

No fertilizer should be applied to shrubs this month.

Pest Control

Few pest problems will plague your shrubs from here on out. If you notice scale on **camellias, hollies, euonymus,** or other plants, the cool season is an ideal time to treat with oil sprays. During cooler temperatures, heavier oils are safe to use. Refer to page 291 for a summary listing your options.

Pruning

Be very cautious about what you prune and how. November can be relatively mild, and shrubs often do not get a strong signal to go dormant. Shearing or heading back shrubs might still stimulate growth, which is not a good idea just before winter. Spring-flowering shrubs have set their buds and should not be pruned extensively until after they bloom next spring. Light, selective pruning may be done if absolutely necessary. Try to use thinning cuts to correct any problems.

Planning

Although gardeners usually purchase shrubs from local nurseries, which are most often the best sources of locally adapted plants, shrubs are also available through mail-order companies, who may have more unusual cultivars than are available locally. Be cautious and selective. Try cultivars of a shrub you already know will do well in Texas.

Planting and Transplanting

If planted now, shrubs will have about five months to get established before dealing with high temperatures next summer. This makes them better prepared to survive their first Texas summer in the ground.

Transplanting or moving shrubs in your landscape to a new location can also begin now. If you plan on moving a deciduous shrub, wait until it has dropped its leaves to move it. Transplanting may be done from now until the end of February.

When transplanting, dig the shrub with as much of the root system as you can manage. Roots spread out more than they grow down, so it is more important for you to take a rootball that is wider than it is deep. Replant shrubs immediately in holes you have already dug and

prepared. Do not allow the roots to dry out once the shrub is out of the ground. Wrap in plastic or place in a container if the shrub cannot be replanted immediately. Water-in thoroughly once planted, and water during the winter if needed. A root stimulator should be applied according to label directions. Continue to treat the transplanted shrubs as new plantings next summer, and pay careful attention to water needs.

Care for Your Shrubs

In south Texas along the coast, gardeners often plant various tropical shrubs. The chance of severe injury or loss during cold winters makes it generally unwise to include too many tropicals in landscape plantings. For more information on protecting tender plants in winter, see pages 20–22.

Watering

Cool to cold weather and generally abundant rainfall usually make watering established shrubs unnecessary. Water newly planted shrubs and those that have been transplanted if the weather turns dry and mild. Keep the soil moist.

Fertilizing

Fertilizer should not be applied to shrubs this month.

Pest Control

Other than applying controls for scale, little pest control is necessary in December.

Pruning

By mid-December, shrubs are pretty much dormant, and pruning them now will not stimulate new growth. Feel free to *trim* hedges and other shrubs, unless they bloom in the spring.

Helpful Hints

Did you ever stop to think that outdoor plants make good holiday gifts? Since this month is an excellent planting month, drop a few hints to family members or friends about the kinds of shrubs you would like in your landscape. Growing plants continue to increase in value with proper care, and a plant received as a gift can make a lasting impression.

Trees

Trees are a vital part of most landscapes. They provide shade, privacy, windbreaks, fruit or nuts, and flowers, and can increase real-estate value as well. Select them carefully. They will be around for a long time. Proper placement is very important, as mistakes are not easily corrected later on when trees are large.

Planning

There is no one perfect tree for all of Texas. Trees have advantages and disadvantages, depending on their planting locations and desired characteristics. Here are some points you need to consider:

1 Select a tree that will mature at a size right for its site. This cannot be stressed too much. Planting trees that will grow too large for their locations is one of the most common mistakes people make (along with planting too many trees). Generally, small trees are those that grow from 15 to 25 feet tall, medium-sized trees grow from 30 to 55 feet tall, and large trees are those that grow 60 feet or taller.

Make use of different types of trees in your landscape.

2 Think about the purpose of the tree and why you feel it is needed. This will help you determine what characteristics the tree should have, such as its shape, size, and rate of growth. Ornamental features such as flowers, attractive berries, brightly colored fall foliage, or unusual bark should also be considered .

3 Decide if you want a tree that retains its foliage year-round (evergreen) or loses its leaves in the winter (deciduous). Deciduous trees are particularly useful where you want shade in the summer and sun in the winter.

4 Choose trees that are well adapted to our growing conditions. They must be able to tolerate long, hot summers and mild/cold winters. A number of northern species of **beech, maple, conifers,** and others you might see in catalogs are often unsuitable for our state. Trees that are not completely hardy are not good choices either.

5 *Check* the location of overhead power lines, and if you must plant under them, use small, low-growing trees. Consider underground water lines and septic tanks as well as walks,

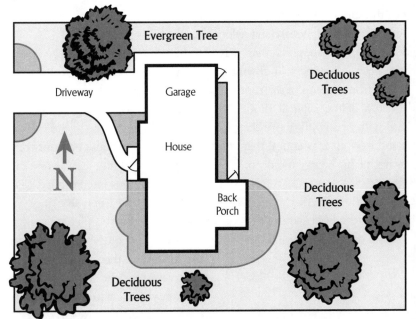

drives, and paved surfaces that may be damaged by the roots of large trees. Locate large trees at least 15 to 25 feet away from your house.

Planting and Transplanting

Planting trees properly can make the difference between success and failure. Whether the tree is balled and burlapped or container grown, *dig the hole* at least twice the diameter of the rootball, and no deeper than the height of the rootball.

Remove the tree from the container and place it gently in the hole. A rootball tightly packed with thick, encircling roots indicates a root-bound condition. Try to unwrap or open up or even cut some of the roots to encourage them to spread into the surrounding soil. Once the tree is in the hole, *remove* any nylon twine or wire supports that may have been used, and fold down the burlap from the top of the rootball. The top of the rootball should be level with or slightly above the surrounding soil. It is critical that you do not plant the tree too deep.

Thoroughly pulverize the soil dug out from the hole and use this soil, without any additions, to backfill

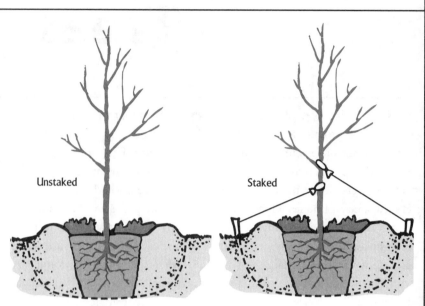

Unstaked   Staked

around the tree. Add soil around the tree until the hole is half full, then firm the soil to eliminate air pockets—but do not pack it tight. Finish filling the hole, firm again, and then *water* the tree thoroughly to settle it in. Generally, we do not add fertilizer to the planting hole. The use of a root-stimulator solution is optional.

If the tree is tall enough to be unstable, it should be staked—otherwise, it's not necessary. Do not drive the stake into place directly against the trunk and then tie the tree to it. Two or three stakes should be firmly driven into the ground just beyond the rootball as illustrated above. Tie cloth strips, old nylon stockings, or wire (covered with a piece of garden hose where it touches the trunk) to the stakes and then to the trunk of the tree. Leave the support in place no more than nine to twelve months.

Care for Your Trees

Keep the area one to two feet out from the trunk of a newly planted tree mulched and free from weeds and grass. This will encourage the tree to establish faster by eliminating competition from grass roots. It also prevents lawn mowers and string trimmers from damaging the bark at the base of the tree, which can cause stunting or death. The mulch should be about 4 inches deep.

People tend to think of established trees as almost indestructible. Trees do not need a great deal of care compared to other plants in the landscape, but they do occasionally need water, fertilizer, and pest control.

Trees

Perhaps the greatest threat to trees is people. A common misconception is that tree roots are located deep in the soil and so are well protected from damage. Actually, tree roots are remarkably shallow. The majority of the root system responsible for absorbing water and minerals is located in the upper 18 inches of soil, and it spreads out at least twice as far as the branches. As a result, many people damage or kill their trees in a variety of ways. Tree roots are vulnerable to damage from soil compaction caused by excessive foot traffic or vehicular traffic. Whether building a new home on a lot with existing trees, an addition to an existing home, or a new patio, construction work kills lots of trees. Even repairing driveways, sidewalks, and streets may cause extensive damage to tree roots. If filling is needed, no more than 2 inches of fill per year should be spread over a tree's root system.

Watering

Water a newly planted or transplanted tree whenever the soil is dry. This is the single most important thing you can do to ensure its survival, especially during the first summer after planting. To properly water a tree its first year, turn a hose on trickle and lay the end on top of the ground within 6 inches of the trunk. Let the water trickle for about 30 to 45 minutes. This should be done as needed during hot, dry weather.

Older, established trees rarely have to be watered, but exceptionally dry weather during the months of July, August, and September may place enough stress on trees to make watering necessary. Lawn sprinklers are good devices for watering the expansive root systems of established trees. Set the sprinkler to apply about an inch of water, and water about once a week until sufficient rain occurs.

Fertilizing

In the first five to ten years after planting, young trees can be encouraged to grow significantly faster if fertilized annually. Older trees can be fertilized less often. In fact, for older trees with good vigor, color, and rate of growth, fertilization is optional.

Trees are generally fertilized in late February in south Texas in anticipation of growth beginning in February or March. In north Texas, fertilize two to four weeks later.

Pest Control

Although they require less pest control than other plants in the landscape, trees do occasionally have pest problems that need to be controlled. The best trees are relatively free from pest problems, or will not be badly damaged or killed by pests that do attack them. This is fortunate, as the average gardener does not have the proper equipment to spray a large tree.

When selecting a tree for your landscape and before purchasing, be sure you are familiar with its potential pest problems: how serious they tend to be and how often they are likely to occur.

Pruning

For a variety of reasons, virtually all trees are pruned at some time. Lower branches are gradually removed from a young, growing tree to lift its canopy to an appropriate height. Dead or diseased branches should occasionally be removed. Fruit trees are pruned in a variety of specialized forms. Problems with poorly placed branches or an unattractive shape may need to be fixed.

Pruning needs to be done correctly. Except for certain types of fruit trees, pruning is generally kept to a minimum, but should certainly not be avoided when necessary.

Trees for Texas

Name	Type	Height × Width	Comments
American Holly *Ilex opaca*	Evergreen	40 to 50 by 15 to 30 feet	Excellent medium-sized tree; red berries on females in winter are eaten by birds; **native;** 'Savannah' is a popular smaller-growing hybrid cultivar. Great in eastern one-third of Texas.
Bald Cypress *Taxodium distichum*	Deciduous	50 to 100 by 20 to 50 feet	Narrow cone shape when young; knees rarely produced in cultivation, remove if desired; an unusual conifer that drops its needles in winter; **native.**
Cabbage Palm *Sabal palmetto*	Evergreen	25 by 6 feet	Hardy in zones 8b and 9; may be damaged or killed by temperatures below 15 degrees; slow rate of growth. A palm for the coast and Rio Grande Valley.
Cedar *Juniperus virginiana*	Evergreen	20 to 40 by 20 by 30 feet	Attractive fine-textured conifer; trunk with peeling bark has great character; good source of wildlife food; spider mites and bag worms may occur; **native.**
Cedar Elm *Ulmus crassifolia*	Deciduous	60 to 80 by 40 to 50 feet	Dark-green 1- to 2-inch-long almost-shiny leaves with some light-yellow fall color. Hardy in all Texas zones; **native.**
Chinese Parasol Tree *Firmiana simplex*	Deciduous	35 by 15 feet	Large leaves and a smooth, green trunk make this tree distinctive; appropriate for use fairly close to buildings and patios; unusual seedpods; prone to white scale. Tropical looking tree.
Chinese Pistachio *Pistacia chinensis*	Deciduous	25 to 40 by 20 by 35 feet	Brilliant orange-red to gold fall color; excellent shade tree; leafs out relatively late—early to mid-April; a different species from the one that produces edible nuts. Great tree for Texas landscapes.
Deodar Cedar *Cedrus deodara*	Evergreen	40 to 60 by 20 to 30 feet	Looks like it belongs up North, but does very well in Texas in zones 8 and 9; silvery-green needles; branches form graceful tiers; pyramidal shape more irregular with age.
Flowering Crab Apple *Malus* spp.	Deciduous	10 to 25 by 15 to 30 feet	Bright to dark-green or red to red-purple leaves during growing season. Showy white, pink, red, or blends of these colors; blooms in early spring. Fruits are deep red or red-orange. Hardy in all Texas zones.
Flowering Dogwood *Cornus florida*	Deciduous	20 to 30 by 25 feet	Beautiful spring flowers before the foliage in shades of white, pink, or rose; prefers some shade; best used where there is excellent drainage and acid soils; prone to several pests; **native.**

Trees for Texas

Name	Type	Height × Width	Comments
Flowering Pear *Pyrus calleryana*	Deciduous	30 to 50 by 20 to 40 feet	Narrow upright growth when young becomes broader as trees age; white flowers in spring and brilliant fall foliage not as prominent in warmer portions of the state; older trees prone to branch splitting; 'Aristocrat', 'Bradford', 'Capital', and other cultivars are available.
Fringe Tree *Chionanthus virginicus*	Deciduous	20 to 25 by 15 to 20 feet	Also called grancy graybeard; greenish-white fringe-like flowers in spring as foliage emerges; excellent small ornamental tree; native. The Chinese fringe tree (**C. retusa**) is also recommended; the white flowers are more showy. Use in eastern third of Texas.
Ginkgo *Ginkgo biloba*	Deciduous	50 to 70 by 20 to 50 feet	Attractive fan-shaped foliage reliably turns a beautiful yellow in fall; plant grafted males to avoid undesirable fruit; very slow rate of growth; tough tree with no problems.
Golden Rain Tree *Koelreuteria paniculata*	Deciduous	20 to 40 by 20 to 35 feet	Medium-green to blue-green foliage during the growing season with yellow fall colors. Also has golden-yellow blooms during the growing season. Hardy in all Texas zones.
Green Ash *Fraxinus pennsylvanica*	Deciduous	40 to 70 by 30 to 50 feet	Excellent fast-growing shade tree; yellow fall color in north Texas. A much better tree than Arizona ash.
Japanese Maple *Acer palmatum*	Deciduous	2 to 20 by 3 to 20 feet	Graceful, tiered growth habit; many, many cultivars with various leaf shapes and colors (yellow-green, green, bronze, burgundy); excellent specimen tree; small and relatively slow growing; prefers some afternoon shade. Needs deep moist soils. Not drought tolerant. Hardy in all Texas zones.
Lacebark Elm *Ulmus parvifolia*	Deciduous to semi-evergreen	40 to 60 by 30 to 50 feet	Very fast-growing shade tree; vase to umbrella shaped; attractive trunk with peeling bark; reliable and relatively pest-free; leafless for a short time in late winter. 'Drake' is a super variety.
Leyland Cypress × *Cupressocyparis leylandii*	Evergreen	20 to 40 by 15 to 30 feet	Pyramidal or conical with dark-green foliage. Hardy in all Texas zones.
Live Oak *Quercus virginiana*	Evergreen	40 to 80 by 60 to 100 feet	An outstandingly beautiful but very large tree; popular, but often planted where a smaller species would be more appropriate; destructive roots; best adapted to south Texas; salt tolerant; **native.**

Trees for Texas

Name	Type	Height × Width	Comments
Mimosa *Albizia julibrissin*	Deciduous	30 to 40 by 30 to 40 feet	Light-green, feathery compound leaves during the growing season; non-showy fall color. Old favorite with pink to rose-pink blooms. Hardy in all Texas zones.
Parsley Hawthorn *Crataegus marshallii*	Deciduous	15 to 30 by 15 to 20 feet	Clusters of white-pink spring flowers and red fruit in the fall are outstanding features of this small flowering tree; thorny when young; birds eat the fruit; plant in small areas; **native.** Cedar apple rust could be a problem in poor-air-movement locations.
Pecan *Carya illinoiensis*	Deciduous	60 to 125 by 40 to 100 feet	Edible nuts; 'Choctaw', 'Desirable', 'Cheyenne', and 'Caddo' are good varieties; large trees need a lot of room; brittle wood very prone to breakage; prone to webworms; **native.**
Pines *Pinus* spp.	Evergreen	20 to 125 by 15 to 70 feet	Various species including short leaf pine, loblolly pine, slash pine; tall trees that are best planted in areas with sandy, acid soils; Southern pine borer and pine bark beetles can be problems; **native** and **non native.**
Purple Leaf Plum *Prunus cerasifera*	Deciduous	15 to 25 by 10 to 20 feet	Soft red-purple to purple leaves during the growing season; non-showy fall color. Small ornamental red-purple to purple fruits follow a show of white early-spring flowers. Very hardy in all Texas zones.
Redbud *Cercis canadensis*	Deciduous	15 to 30 by 15 to 25 feet	Small pinkish-purple flowers in great profusion in spring before the foliage emerges; attractive heart-shaped leaves turn yellow before dropping; needs excellent drainage; **native.** The 'Oklahoma' variety is super.
Saucer Magnolia *Magnolia ×* *soulangiana*	Deciduous	20 to 25 by 20 to 30 feet	Large, fragrant pinkish-purple to white flowers in late winter to very early spring before the foliage; often grown multitrunked; numerous cultivars available; scale an occasional problem. In zone, 7 late freezes may occasionally damage.
Shumard Oak *Quercus shumardii*	Deciduous	80 to 100 by 50 to 60 feet	Relatively fast growth, especially if fertilized when young; shiny, dark-green foliage turns red in fall; excellent large shade tree; strong wood resists wind damage; **native.**
Silver Bell *Halesia diptera*	Deciduous	25 by 20 feet	Bell-shaped, white flowers in spring just as the foliage emerges; adaptable and easy; often used as a substitute where dogwoods do not thrive; good for small areas in east Texas. Is not drought resistant.

Trees for Texas

Name	Type	Height × Width	Comments
Southern Magnolia *Magnolia grandiflora*	Evergreen	50 to 100 by 30 to 50 feet	Beautiful tree with dark-green shiny foliage; fragrant, white flowers in May and June; considered messy because of leaf drop; numerous pests; scale is possible; difficult to grow plants underneath due to heavy shade; destructive roots; **native.**
Swamp Red Maple *Acer rubrum* 'Drummondii'	Deciduous	50 to 80 by 40 to 60 feet	Excellent fast-growing shade tree; tolerant of poor drainage; females produce attractive burgundy flowers and fruit in February; better adapted to Texas than northern red maples; **native.** Plant in moist areas. Best used in far east Texas.
Sweet Bay Magnolia *Magnolia virginiana*	Semi-evergreen	20 to 40 by 15 to 25 feet	Generally does not lose all leaves in winter; striking silvery backed foliage; fragrant flowers resemble Southern magnolia but smaller; upright form; tolerates poor drainage; **native.**
Sweet Gum *Liquidambar styraciflua*	Deciduous	45 to 50 by 40 to 60 feet	Upright pyramidal shape when young, broader with age; star-shaped leaves very reliably turn purple, orange, burgundy, or yellow in fall; prickly fruit can be a nuisance; **native.** Some may reach 100 feet tall in Texas. Plant in deep soils only.
Texas Ash *Fraxinus texensis*	Deciduous	35 to 50 by 25 to 35 feet	Long dark-green leaves changing to yellow, copper, rose, tangerine, and lime in the fall; hardy in all Texas zones. **Native;** best ash tree for Texas.
Vitex, Chaste Tree *Vitex agnus-castus*	Deciduous	9 to 15 by 10 to 15 feet	Spikes of lavender-purple, white, or pink in early summer, reblooming in late summer; attractive star-shaped foliage drops early; excellent fast-growing, small ornamental tree. Tough and hardy statewide. Good drought tolerance; **native.**
Weeping Willow *Salix babylonica*	Deciduous	40 to 60 by 30 to 40 feet	Narrow medium-green leaves turning yellow in early fall. Very hardy in all Texas zones. Many varieties available. Relatively short-lived accent trees.
Willow Oak *Quercus phellos*	Deciduous	80 to 100 by 40 to 60 feet	Excellent, fast-growing upright oak with narrow leaves; deserves more use; good for urban sites; leafless for brief period in late winter. Grow in acidic soils only; **native.**
Windmill Palm *Trachycarpus fortunei*	Evergreen	20 by 6 feet	Beautiful palm with a hairy trunk; good in small areas; reliably hardy in south Texas in zones 8b and 9. A palm for the Texas coast and Rio Grande Valley.

Planning

Determining the selection and placement of trees in your landscape are some of the most important decisions you will make. No other plant material is as long-lived or will have as profound an effect on its surroundings. No other plant materials can create the major problems that poorly selected or improperly placed trees will. The most common mistakes are:

- Planting too many trees

- Planting trees that grow too large for their site

- Planting trees not well adapted to Texas

- Planting trees too close to the house

Remember that the trees you plant will grow much larger than the saplings you purchase and bring home from the nursery. It is tempting to plant more trees than you really need, and common to realize years later that you may have made a mistake. Cutting down a tree is never an easy decision, so it is better not to put yourself (or whoever owns the property later) in that situation. Don't forget to enter your plans, notes, decisions, and weather condition in your Texas gardening journal weekly if not daily.

Planting and Transplanting

January is an excellent month to plant trees. Deciduous trees are leaf-less at this time of the year, so when you go to the nursery to make your selection, expect to see bare branches. Don't be afraid to purchase and plant these trees. Their dormancy makes this a great time to get them into the ground, especially balled-and-burlapped specimens. Evergreen species will, of course, have foliage.

Select the right location for the tree in your landscape. To get a feel for how well the tree will fit in the spot you have selected, try this exercise:

- Place the tree where you intend to plant it.

- Look up the expected spread of the branches (use the tree chart on pages 202–205 or another reference such as *Dale Groom's Texas Gardening Guide* (Cool Springs Press, 1997).

- Divide the expected spread by two, and cut a piece of twine or string that many feet long.

If, for instance, the expected spread is 40 feet, cut a piece of string 20 feet long.

- Tie one end of the string to the tree trunk, stretch out the string to its full length, and walk in a circle around the tree.

This is an effective way for you to really see how much space the tree will occupy.

Care for Your Trees

Trees require little care in the middle of the winter while they are dormant. Winter storms may damage trees by breaking branches. Ice storms in north Texas sometimes create heavy ice buildup on branches, causing them to break. Either *prune off* ragged stubs yourself or have a professional tree surgeon do it.

Watering

Water-in newly planted trees thoroughly. Newly planted deciduous trees generally will not need to be watered again this time of the year. Newly planted evergreen trees should be watered as needed if the weather is mild and dry. Established trees will normally not need to be watered this month.

Fertilizing

Newly planted trees normally do not need to be fertilized. Established trees in their first five to ten years after planting can be encouraged to grow faster with annual moderate fertilization. For older trees in good health with good color and growth rate, fertilization is optional. Fertilization is recommended for older trees that show nutrient-deficiency symptoms, are in stress, or have been damaged.

Using a granular fertilizer with a 3:1:2 ratio such as 15-5-10 works well. The amount of fertilizer to use is determined by the size of the tree. In the past, the amount to use was always based on the diameter of the trunk—one pound of 15-5-10 was applied for each inch of trunk diameter—and this method is still often used. Newer recommendations are based on the square footage of the root system.

To determine the square footage of the root system of a tree, measure the distance from the trunk to the outer tips of the branches (called the "dripline"). Multiply that number by two (since roots reach out about twice as far as the branches). Multiply that number by itself, and then by 3.14 to determine the square footage. *Apply* 20 pounds of 15-5-10 per thousand feet of root area.

Example: It is 10 feet from the trunk to the dripline.

$$10 \times 2 = 20$$
$$20 \times 20 = 400$$
$$400 \times 3.14 = 1256 \text{ square feet}$$

So, at 20 pounds of 15-5-10 per 1000 square feet, about 25 pounds of fertilizer would be applied to the tree.

One method of application is as follows: *Apply the fertilizer* in holes 1 to 2 inches wide and about 12 inches deep, spaced 2 to 3 feet apart (use a piece of pipe to make the holes). Make the holes in a dough-nut-shaped area centered on the dripline, and fill each hole with fertilizer to within about 2 inches of the top. If some of the area cannot be fertilized because of concrete surfaces or buildings, reduce the amount of fertilizer applied.

There are other fertilizer methods available, including broadcasting. Tree fertilizers may be purchased in compressed spikes that are driven into the ground. Follow the manufacturer's recommendations on the number to use. There are devices available at nurseries that hook up to a garden hose and inject a fertilizer solution through a metal probe inserted in the soil. Tree-care companies will fertilize your trees for a fee. They frequently use a system that injects a fertilizer solution into the soil.

Pruning

Shade trees may be pruned just about any time. January is an appropriate month to prune most fruit trees such as **apples, pears, peaches,** and **plums.** Pruning fruit trees is rather specific. For more detailed information, contact your local office of the Texas Cooperative Extension Service for free copies of brochures that have information on these activities.

Do not prune spring-flowering trees now. Some of the earliest-flowering trees, such as **oriental magnolia,** will often begin to bloom in late January, especially in south Texas.

Helpful Hints

In Texas, Arbor Day is celebrated on the third Friday in January. Take some time to appreciate the many benefits trees provide, and teach a child how to plant a tree.

Planning

We are approaching the end of the ideal planting season for trees in south Texas, especially those that are balled and burlapped. However, properly "cured" balled-and-burlapped and container-grown trees may be successfully planted year-round. Finalize your decisions on tree planting soon. Trees are often planted for shade. If your patio is too hot and sunny to use during the summer, consider planting a small to medium-sized tree to the south or southwest of the patio to provide cooling shade. Select a deciduous tree that will drop its leaves in the wintertime and allow sunlight to reach the patio when its warmth is welcome. Since the tree will be close to an outdoor living area, consider other features such as flowers, fragrance, and interesting bark. If the tree will overhang the patio surface, remember that flowers or fruit dropping can be messy.

Planting and Transplanting

Finish transplanting trees this month. Gardeners rarely transplant trees. By the time you realize a mistake has been made, a tree is generally too large to move. On occasion, trees will grow from seeds that fall in flower beds or along fences. If you recognize the tree as a type you would like to grow in your yard, and you have a suitable location for it, dig it up and transplant it now while it is dormant. This is generally most successful with young saplings that have trunk diameters of one inch or less.

Continue to plant container-grown or balled-and-burlapped shade trees, flowering trees, and fruit trees while they are still dormant and the weather is cool.

Care for Your Trees

Stake newly planted trees if they seem unstable once planted. Drive three 2×2-inch wooden stakes or metal pipes firmly into the ground beyond the rootball of the tree. Tie cloth strips, strips of old nylon stockings, or wire (covered with a piece of garden hose where it touches the trunk) to the stakes, and then to the trunk of the tree. There should be a little slack in the lines connecting the tree to the stakes. This will allow the trunk to sway slightly and help make it strong. Leave the support in place no more than 9 to 12 months.

Watering

Other than newly planted trees, watering is not necessary this month.

Fertilizing

Finish fertilizing most trees in late February in zones 8 and 9. It is important for the nutrients to be available to a tree as it begins spring growth. See January for directions on tree fertilization. In north Texas, fertilize through March. To help trees grow vigorously, reapply your selected fertilizer in 6 to 8 weeks and again in early fall.

Pest Control

Disease: Some pest problems are better dealt with before they occur. Some **oaks,** especially **water oaks** (*Quercus nigra*), are susceptible to a fungus disease called oak leaf blister. Symptoms of this disease (light-green blistered areas on leaves that eventually turn brown and cause leaf drop) show up in early summer, but by then it is too late to do anything.

If your oaks have had heavy infections of oak leaf blister in the past, spray them with a disease-control aid (or have a tree-care company do it if the tree is large) just as the dormant buds swell and begin to grow. Although the infected leaves are unattractive and leaf drop during the summer is a nuisance, the disease is not life-threatening.

Insects and larvae: Magnolias may become infested with oyster scale, which looks like small white bumps on the foliage. Light infestations are not a problem, but high populations should be controlled.

Trees may be treated with an oil spray now.

Spraying for most fruit trees begins this month. Never use insect-control aids on fruit trees when they are in bloom. Most are pollinated by insects, and the use of these aids may interfere with pollination. Fruit trees are sprayed according to specific schedules depending on the type of tree. Refer to page 291 for a summary listing your disease- and pest-control aids.

Contact your County Extension Service office to obtain spray schedules for all of the most commonly grown fruit trees.

Pruning

If you haven't pruned your fruit trees, do so immediately. It is important to know how to properly prune the type of fruit trees you are growing. Pruning fruit trees is generally done according to strict guidelines, beginning about a year after planting and continuing through the life of the tree. Check references on growing fruit trees for specific recommendations and/or your County Agent's office for fruit tree pruning fact/tip sheets.

Continue to do needed pruning on trees in your landscape. Now is the best time to prune summer-flowering trees.

Helpful Hints

Although considered evergreen, **live oaks** drop some, most, or all of their leaves in late February and early March. Almost immediately, new growth, often with a reddish tint, appears to replace the lost leaves. The amount of leaf drop can vary from year to year but is no cause for alarm. Rake up the leaves and use them as mulch, put them in your compost pile, or store them in plastic bags for later use.

Planning

Spring-flowering trees usually bloom from late January through mid-April. Bloom dates vary, depending upon varieties planted, zones, and the weather. Their beauty makes many gardeners want to include them in their landscapes, and the relatively small size of most spring-flowering trees makes it fairly easy to find room for them. If you can't resist, study your landscape carefully for appropriate locations. Make sure the spot you choose to plant a spring-flowering tree fits into the existing landscape in an attractive and appropriate way. Will the color of the tree's flowers blend with the flowers of other plants in the area that bloom at the same time? Make your decisions and get the tree planted as soon as possible. If you really don't have room to plant one, enjoy the ones you see in other yards. Enter notes on your observations and visits to nurseries, botanic gardens, etc., in your Texas gardening journal along with notes on any planting and pruning you complete this month.

Planting and Transplanting

This is the last month of the ideal planting season, and the last month when balled-and-burlapped trees should be purchased and planted. Spring fever is spreading with warmer weather, and many gardeners are finally getting to the nurseries to purchase trees for their landscapes.

Plant trees properly, following these steps:

1 ***Dig the hole*** at least twice the diameter of the rootball, and no deeper than the height of the rootball.

2 ***Remove*** a container-grown tree from its container. If the rootball is tightly packed with thick encircling roots, try to unwrap, open up, or even cut some of the roots to encourage them to spread into the surrounding soil. Place the rootball in the hole.

3 Place a balled-and-burlapped tree into the planting hole, ***remove*** any nails, nylon twine, or wire basket, and fold down the burlap from the top half of the rootball. The top of the rootball should be level with or slightly above the surrounding soil. It is critical that you do not plant trees too deep.

4 Thoroughly pulverize the soil dug out from the hole and use this soil, without any additions, to backfill around the tree. Add soil around the tree until the hole is half full, then firm the soil to eliminate air pockets—but do not pack it tight. Finish filling the hole, firm again, and ***water*** the tree thoroughly to settle it in.

5 It is not recommended that you add fertilizer to the planting hole, although you may apply some slow-release fertilizer in the upper few inches. The use of a root-stimulator solution is optional. Read and follow label directions on any aid you decide to utilize, including fertilizers and root stimulators.

6 ***Stake*** the tree if it is tall enough to be unstable—otherwise, it's not necessary. Three stakes should be firmly driven into the ground just beyond the rootball. Use strips of cloth or old nylon stockings or wire (covered with a piece of garden hose where it touches the trunk) tied to the stakes and then to the trunk of the tree. Leave the support in place no more than 9 to 12 months.

Care for Your Trees

Keep the area one to two feet out from the trunk of a newly planted tree mulched and free from weeds and grass. This will encourage the tree to establish faster by eliminating competition from grass roots. It also prevents lawn mowers and string trimmers from damaging the bark at the base of the tree, which can cause stunting or death. The mulch should be about 4 inches deep.

People are often tempted to plant a small flower bed around a newly planted tree—but just leave the area mulched. The young tree will not appreciate your digging around it every few months to replant bedding plants.

Watering

There is no need to water established trees. If the weather is mild and dry, water newly planted trees thoroughly as needed.

Fertilizing

Fertilize trees as soon as possible if you didn't last month in south Texas. Now is a good time to fertilize in north Texas. Reapply in approximately 6 to 8 weeks according to label directions. Fertilizer stakes or granular products may be used. Trees that leaf out late, such as **pecans** and **Chinese pistachios,** can be fertilized this month. Trees that are likely candidates for fertilization include those in their first five years after planting (if accelerated growth is desired), those that are suffering from nutrient deficiencies, those that have sustained damage, and those that are in low vigor. For established trees that seem healthy and vigorous and have good color and growth, fertilization is optional.

Pest Control

Continue to spray trees such as **magnolias, Chinese parasol tree,** and **hollies** if they are infested with scale. Use lightweight horticultural oil sprays, making two or three applications spaced ten days apart.

Follow spray schedules for fruit trees faithfully. It is too late to do anything when your ripe peaches have worms in them. Fruit trees are sprayed to *prevent* problems.

Aphids may show up on the new growth of various trees.

Evergreen trees such as **hollies, Southern magnolia,** and others will yellow and drop numerous leaves in spring. This is just the older foliage being shed; it's natural and no cause for alarm. The actual process is called *natural pruning* or *natural shedding.*

Pruning

Do not prune newly planted trees unless it is to remove dead or broken branches. Young trees need all of their foliage to create the food required to establish a strong root system. Identify problems such as poorly placed branches or low forks, and make plans to correct those by pruning some time next winter.

Trees planted a year or more generally need some pruning. As the trees grow, gradually *prune off* the lowest branches on the trunk. Based on the height of the tree, about half the height should be bare trunk and half the height foliage. As the tree grows taller, continue to *remove* the lowest branches until the canopy is the desired height from the ground.

Do not prune **pines** in March or April, as they tend to bleed more this time of the year.

Planning

Keeping simple records about your trees can be very helpful. Record such information as when trees are planted, their names, where they were purchased, what kind of pest problems occur (including when they occur and what treatments are used), and other information you think will be helpful. Keep notes in your Texas gardening journal for use next year.

Planting and Transplanting

Container-grown trees can, technically, be planted throughout the year. But planting trees when the weather is hot may put them at risk for problems. If you still need to plant trees, it would be better to do so now.

Care for Your Trees

When building on a lot with existing trees, plan carefully for how to preserve the trees during construction. Consult with an arborist to identify healthy trees worth saving. Work with the architect to create a design that will preserve desirable trees. Decide which trees can be saved. *Generally, you will need to remove any trees that will be within five feet of the new house.* Communicate effectively with the contractor, and make it clear how important protecting trees on the site is to you.

- Create barriers around selected trees with bright-orange temporary fencing material.

  The barriers should be placed well beyond the reach of the branches. This area should be strictly OFF LIMITS to construction activity.

- Roots can be damaged by filling.

  Most trees will not tolerate more than two inches of filling over part of their root system.

- Roots can be damaged by trenching for underground utilities.

  Move trenches away from trees, or tunnel under roots.

- Roots can be damaged by soil compaction.

  Route heavy-equipment traffic away from tree roots.

- Avoid scrapes on the trunk and broken branches—the barrier will help. Do not allow equipment to be cleaned or chemicals to be dumped under trees.

Continue to emphasize to the architect, contractor, crew foremen, and anyone else concerned that protecting the trees is not optional, it is a critical part of the process.

Watering

The weather is still relatively mild, but sunny warm days and dry weather can mean you need to water. An effective way to water a newly planted tree is to run a hose out to it, lay the end a few inches from the trunk, turn it on trickle, and leave it there for 30 to 45 minutes or longer if needed. Do this for each newly planted tree about once a week if needed. A water bubbler on the end of a garden hose works well in this watering application.

Fertilizing

You can still apply fertilizer. Always apply according to label directions.

Iron deficiencies can show up on certain trees growing in alkaline soils. Several types of **oaks** and **pines** are often affected. Symptoms include yellowing of the foliage, especially the newer leaves. Generally, you will see a pattern of green veins on a yellow-green background. *Treat* the tree with chelated or other forms of iron now if symptoms are noticed. *Apply* sulfur or copperas iron sulfate to the area where the roots are located to help acidify the soil. The best route to avoid these problems is to not plant trees in alkaline soils which require acidic growing conditions.

Pest Control

The tiny, gall-forming insect *pecan phylloxera* causes green, round swellings (galls) to form on leaves.

Spray pecans with various selective insect pest-control aids as buds begin to swell and grow. When you see the galls later in the summer, it's too late to do anything. Refer to page 291 for a summary listing your options. Visit your local retailer for a wide selection of aids and assistance in selecting them. Always apply any gardening aid according to label directions. The Texas Agricultural Extension Service through your County Agent's office has specific pecan and fruit tree spray schedules available.

Animals: Small birds called sapsuckers peck holes in neat rows. The holes just penetrate the bark and cause sap to bleed from them. Later, the sapsuckers return to feed on the sugary sap and any insects that may have been attracted to it. The damage is generally minor, but tightly spaced holes in several rows completely encircling a branch may girdle the branch and, on rare occasions, kill it.

Control is generally not necessary, but when damage begins you can wrap the trunk and lower branches with black plastic, aluminum foil, or burlap for a few weeks while the sapsuckers migrate through your area. An alternative to the wrapping method of discouragement is spraying the holes with a pruning paint.

Pruning

Prune spring-flowering trees this month and next month if needed. Have a definite purpose in mind before pruning. Does the tree need shaping, or lower branches removed? Does it have branches that are poorly placed or blocking a view or a walkway? Are there any dead limbs?

Prune off any freeze damage that may have occurred to tender trees such as **citrus.** It is best to wait until new growth has begun and you can clearly see what is dead and what is still alive. Their susceptibility to cold damage must be taken into consideration before deciding to include tender trees in your landscape. Remember, most Texans should not plant citrus trees unless they are doing it just for fun. If you expect long-term growth and survival from your trees and expect to make use of their fruit, you should not plant citrus unless you live in the Rio Grande Valley. Even in this location, freezes have been known to hit them hard.

Continue to study all your trees for problems that can be corrected by pruning such as low branches, branches over the roof of the house, dead or rotten branches, branches obstructing views, and branches blocking paths or sidewalks or interfering with vehicular traffic. *Prune as needed.* Use the proper tool for each pruning job, keep the tools sharp, and be careful. Tree limbs can be very heavy and cause injury and/or damage if they fall in the wrong or unexpected places.

Planning

Take time to note important information in your Texas gardening journal about the spring season. What pest problems occurred on which trees, and what was done to control them? Should anything be done differently next year? When did spring-flowering trees bloom, and how well did they combine with other plants blooming around them?

Now is a good time to make plans for summer tree care. Newly planted trees should receive water as needed throughout the summer. Identify pruning that needs to be done, and decide what you can do yourself and what needs to be taken care of professionally. Remember pest problems that you had last summer, and make plans to spray this year if necessary.

Planting and Transplanting

You may continue to plant container-grown trees this month, but they are at a great disadvantage to trees planted earlier. Do not disturb the roots of container-grown trees planted this late, even if they are rootbound. Pay careful attention to watering late-planted trees.

If you live along our coast, in the Rio Grande Valley, or are otherwise located in zone 9, plant palm trees now. The best planting season for palms runs from May to August. **Palms** are tropical and do best planted during the summer. Like traditional trees, **palms** are also sold container grown or balled and burlapped. Larger sizes are generally sold balled and burlapped. Plant them following the recommendations given for planting trees in March (page 210). Should you decide to plant **palm** trees in zone 8b, you may or may not be successful over the long term. Other planting zones should actually be viewed as temporary for palm trees. Plant if you wish, but be aware the **palms** may terminate due to freezes during any year.

Care for Your Trees

Promptly *remove* any branches that begin to hang too low over public sidewalks or streets. Individuals may be tempted to pull and break branches over sidewalks, and vehicles can break or rip away branches as they drive by. In either case, the tree could be damaged with ragged stubs or bark stripped off the trunk. *Prune* these branches properly to get them out of harm's way and prevent damage to the tree.

Note: When securing professional tree services, make sure they are insured, qualified, and have a long favorable history in their industry.

Watering

As the weather heats up, it will become increasingly important for you to water newly planted trees if sufficient rain should not fall. Whenever a good rain (1 to $1\frac{1}{2}$ inches) does not fall for a week, run a hose out to the newly planted tree, lay the end with a water bubbler on it a few inches from the base of the tree, and turn the water on trickle. Let the water run for 30 to 45 minutes or longer if needed to thoroughly soak the rootball. Do this as needed until a good rain occurs.

Magnolias are one of the most drought-susceptible trees we commonly grow. As they come into bloom in May, they may appear wilted (the leaves will hang down somewhat) if the weather is dry. In addition, **magnolias** shed their oldest leaves in late spring and early summer, so numerous yellow dropping leaves may also be observed. Put out a sprinkler and water the tree thoroughly if the soil is dry. Don't worry about the yellow, dropping leaves.

Fertilizing

Fertilizers will still be beneficial if applied this month. If you needed to fertilize a tree earlier and didn't, you may now. How vigorous was the growth of trees in your landscape? If more than 6 inches of new growth is apparent, fertilization is optional or not needed. If the growth is between 2 to 6 inches, consider fertilization. If only 2 inches or less of new growth occurred, the tree should be fertilized. Follow directions given in the month of January. Make a note in your Texas gardening journal on which trees should be fertilized next year.

Pest Control

When they are building nests, squirrels chew off small branches to use in the construction. The trouble is that they don't use all of the branches they chew off—lots of them get dropped to the ground. If you find a lot of small branches (about the size of your finger) with green leaves under your shade tree, don't be alarmed. The damage squirrels cause is generally minor.

Pruning

If you need to cut branches from your trees you must do it correctly, especially if they are over 1 inch in diameter. Use a pruning saw especially made for pruning plants. These saws have narrow blades for maneuverability and special teeth for efficient cutting. Make three cuts to remove a branch:

1 The first cut is made about 6 to 8 inches out from the trunk. Position the saw under the branch and *cut upward* about one-quarter of the way through the branch.

2 With the saw positioned on top of the branch a few inches out from the first cut, make a downward cut until the branch falls away.

3 The final cut to remove the stub is very important and should be made properly. Locate the ridge of bark that runs at an angle from where the branch joins the trunk. Position your pruning saw just to the outside of the bark ridge and *saw downward* from it. As you near the end of the cut, slow down, and support the stub with your other hand. It is important to prevent the bark from pulling away from the trunk as you finish your cut.

This method of cutting preserves a layer of protective chemicals located at the base of the branch, which helps prevent fungal infections and decay. *Applying pruning paint to the fresh cut is optional*. However, if oak wilt is present, it is recommended that pruning cuts on oak trees be sealed with a pruning paint.

1.   2.   3.

Limb Removal

JUNE

Planning

June marks the beginning of hurricane season. Trees, in particular, are at risk from the high winds that accompany these massive storms. If you live in the southern part of the state, plan now to take care of your trees in order to minimize possible problems. Do not wait until storms begin to threaten.

Trees that have large dead branches or are totally dead should be dealt with as soon as possible. Dead branches should be pruned off and dead trees completely removed.

Look at the overall condition of your trees. A tree that is sickly, low in vigor, and shows significant signs of decayed areas or termites in the trunk may need to be removed if it poses a threat to buildings.

Trees that are very one-sided or leaning significantly may also need attention. Selective pruning can relieve the weight on the heavier side, balancing out the weight distribution of the canopy. After the prolonged rain associated with hurricanes, the soil is often so soft that trees may topple if their weight is not properly proportioned.

Thinning–After

Thinning the canopy reduces the wind resistance of the tree, and reduces the chances of the tree blowing over or branches breaking.

Look for branches that hang over the house near the roof. Although the branches may not be touching the roof under normal conditions, the high winds of hurricanes can cause trees to bend a little and branches to flail around considerably. These branches can cause extensive damage to the roof and should generally be removed.

Remember, now is the time to do these activities. Enter your thoughts, observations, and actions in your Texas gardening journal.

Planting and Transplanting

Due to extreme heat, the next several months will be particularly bad for planting trees in your landscape, even from containers. But all types of shade trees can be successfully planted during June; this is especially true of container-grown selections. Make sure they receive the water needed to survive and establish themselves. And remember, October is a great tree-planting month in Texas.

Because of their tropical nature, **palms** are best planted in summer, between May and August.

Care for Your Trees

Bald cypress is a popular yard tree. It rarely produces knees in home landscapes, but occasionally does. If they are a problem, use a saw to cut the knees off just below the soil surface. This will not injure the tree.

Watering

If it has not rained for several weeks, use lawn sprinklers to apply 1 inch of water to your established trees. The root system of these trees extends out well beyond the reach of the branches. It's most important to apply water at the dripline (the area under the ends of the branches) at the edge of the canopy.

Recently planted trees should be thoroughly watered anytime rain does not occur for five to seven days—continue this practice for the rest of the summer.

 Fertilizing

Trees often send out a second flush of growth in mid- to late summer. Older established trees do not need to be fertilized again if you fertilized last spring. But young trees you are trying to encourage to grow or trees in stress or low vigor often benefit from additional fertilizer applications this time of year. Use half the rate that was applied in January or February. For complete directions on fertilizing trees, see January.

Pest Control

Watch for signs of pest problems on your trees. Identify the problem and use the appropriate pest-control aid if necessary. Fortunately, gardeners can go for years without seeing a major outbreak of pests on their trees. If you need help identifying a problem, contact your local County Agent, talk to local nursery staff, or use a reference.

In areas of the state where there are a lot of **pine trees,** watch for signs of southern pine beetles. These beetles bore into the trunk of pine trees and feed under the bark. A heavy infestation can quickly kill a tree. Look for holes in the trunk, often with sap coming out of them. Needles may rapidly turn brown. Once a tree is infested, little can be done for it. Trees not infested can be protected by spraying their trunks with insect-control aids. Refer to page 291 for a summary listing your options.

For preventative treatment, spray in early spring or when threat of attack exists. Have infested trees cut down promptly and removed.

Pruning

The type of pruning that may be necessary to correct problems before hurricanes is often best handled by professional arborists.

Arborists (individuals trained in the care of trees) and tree removal services that can do this work are listed in the Yellow Pages under "Trees." Get several estimates for the work. Talk to company representatives thoroughly about the work you see needs to be done and work they see needs to be done. Come to a clear agreement on what the job will entail. A written contract is always best.

Make sure the company you choose is fully insured (ask to see a copy of their proof of insurance). Check with the Better Business Bureau before you make your final decision. It is always a good idea to be present when tree pruning is being done.

Planning

Although not extremely demanding, trees do need occasional attention. Regular, timely care is the best way to handle them. Observe your trees regularly and make plans to take care of problems at appropriate times. (If you see *pecan phylloxera* now, for instance, it may be too late for any control. Mark your calendar, make an entry in your Texas gardening journal, and plan on spraying the tree next April if you want to control this pest.) This is a great month to walk around your landscape and see where additional shade is needed.

After "cruising" your property, enter your observations, thoughts and decisions in your Texas gardening journal. Enter information concerning tree growth, when you watered, the weather, insect pests present, weeds, and any diseases.

Planting and Transplanting

The intense heat of the next few months makes this a stressful time to plant trees in the landscape. It will be easier on you and the trees if you can wait for the weather to cool this fall before you plant—but they may be planted if you want to plant now. **Palm trees** *should* be planted between May and August.

Do not dig up and transplant trees now. The chances of their surviving are poor.

Care for Your Trees

If you have a low place you want to correct, trees will tolerate some fill placed over their root systems, but generally no more than 2 inches a year is considered safe. If you cover only part of the root system, the tree *may* tolerate more fill. Remember, tree roots spread out as much as 2 times the reach of the branches. Leaving a small area around the trunk without fill will do no good whatsoever.

The roots that absorb water and minerals for the tree are located primarily in the upper 18 inches of soil. They need oxygen and grow close to the surface where oxygen is readily available. When excessive amounts of fill are placed over these roots, they suffocate and die. With its roots dead or badly damaged, the tree will die or go into decline. Don't risk a valuable tree. Consult with an arborist or County Agent before extensive filling.

Watering

If it has not rained for several weeks, *apply* 1 inch of water to the roots of trees once every two weeks until it rains. Use lawn sprinklers to water your established trees. The most important area to apply water is the dripline (the area under the ends of the branches) at the edge of the canopy.

For the rest of the summer, recently planted trees should be thoroughly watered anytime rain does not occur for five to seven days (or water as needed). Lay the end of a hose within a few inches of the trunk and let it trickle for half an hour or longer if needed.

Fertilizing

Older established trees do not need to be fertilized again if you fertilized last spring. But young trees, trees in stress, or trees in low vigor may benefit from a second fertilizer application this month. Trees often send out a second flush of growth in mid- to late summer. Use half the rate that was applied in January or February. For complete directions on fertilizing trees, see January.

Pest Control

Large established trees are rarely badly damaged by insects or disease. Young trees, however, do not have as many leaves to lose to insects or fungal infections. Caterpillars can easily eat half the leaves off a young tree in just a few days. Pay more attention to pest control on trees the first five years after planting.

Webworms attack a wide variety of trees but seem especially fond of **pecans.** These caterpillars create large nests of silk at the ends of branches. Their feeding inside the nest causes the leaves enclosed to turn brown.

Although it looks terrible, the damage webworms cause is generally not significant. There may be multiple generations through the summer, so it would require repeated spraying from midsummer to fall to control these pests. If the nest is low enough, prune it off.

Hot, dry weather is just what spider mites love. Conifers such as the **cedar** and **bald cypress** are particularly vulnerable, although spider mites could attack a wide variety of other trees, including oaks. Look for needles or leaves in the interior of the tree to fade and turn brown, gradually extending toward the ends of the branches.

Trees under stress are more susceptible, so keep trees well watered, especially recently planted ones.

To prevent peach tree borers, spray the trunks of **peaches, nectarines,** and **plums** with approved aids. If you see gelatinous sap oozing from spots on the trunk, you know they have attacked.

Following label directions, make one application each month through October.

Pruning

Suckers are vigorous, fast-growing shoots that originate low on the trunk or at soil level. Some trees, such as **flowering pear,** are worse about suckering than others. *Remove* suckers promptly as they appear. *Prune* them off flush with the trunk or at their point of origin (even if it's belowground). If you leave a stub, it will resprout.

Helpful Hint

During the first several years after planting a young tree, keep an area at least one foot out from the trunk mulched. Young trees do not have well-developed bark, and the base of the trunk is easily damaged by mowers and string trimmers. Weed-control aids may be used occasionally if weeds or grass start to grow through the mulch, or pull them by hand. Refer to page 291 for a summary listing your options. Young trees grow faster when grass is not allowed to grow close to them.

Planning

Now is an excellent time to evaluate your landscape and determine where additional shade is needed. Energy bills soar right along with the temperatures, but shade trees in your landscape can help you keep cooler and lower your utility bills.

Trees that shade the house during the summer can lower air-conditioning bills by blocking the sun from the windows, exterior walls, and roof. Research reports show that shade trees can reduce heat gains by 40 to 80 percent, depending on their placement and density. Deciduous trees are generally the best choice. They let the sun shine on the house in the winter when the sun's added warmth is welcome, and provide shade during the summer when it is needed.

Trees should be planted on the southwestern and western side of a house to be most effective. Planting trees to the south and east will also help shade the house.

Plant trees the proper distance from the house and away from concrete-surfaced areas such as sidewalks and driveways. The recommended distances generally depend on the mature size of the tree. Larger trees, such as **oaks,** should be planted at least 15 feet away from sidewalks, driveways, and the house.

Decide on other areas where shade is necessary or desirable. Outdoor living areas such as patios are unusable here in the summer without some sort of shade. Choose small-growing trees for planting close to patios, as they are more in scale and are less likely to damage surfacing materials.

This month is the time to make decisions on where shade is needed and where to plant shade trees, but the ideal tree-planting season is October through March.

Be sure to enter your observations and decisions in your Texas gardening journal. Also visit some local nurseries this month to see for yourself what trees are available and what their sizes and prices are.

Planting and Transplanting

Finish planting **palms** this month. They will need the remaining warm weather to become established before winter. If the **palm** tree is tall, it will generally need to be staked. The supports should be strong to hold the weight of the palm.

The weather is still too hot for this to be a good time to plant other types of trees in the landscape. However, if you want to plant during August, it can be done. Make sure the tree's watering needs are maintained.

Care for Your Trees

Even with good care and regular watering, recently planted trees may look stressed at this time of the year. The foliage may be pale, leaf edges may appear brown and scorched, and little growth may have occurred during the summer. This is not unusual, and you should not be overly alarmed. Keep up good care. Until these trees establish a good root system, they may continue to show late-summer stress for the next several years.

Watering

Whenever a good rain (at least $1/2$ to 1 inch) does not fall for five to seven days, run a hose out to the newly planted tree, lay the end a few inches from the base of the tree, and turn the water on trickle. Let the water run for 30 to 45 minutes or longer to thoroughly soak the rootball. Do this once or twice a week until it rains.

Older, well-established trees rarely need to be watered. Watch the lawn. Whenever the lawn looks drought-stressed, it's time to water shade trees as well. Using a lawn sprinkler, *apply* about an inch of water over the area of the tree's root system. Water deeply and thoroughly when irrigating trees.

Fertilizing

Fertilizer containing quick-release nitrogen should not be applied to trees for the rest of the year. These types of fertilizers may stimulate late growth during the mild to warm fall season—this could reduce the hardiness of a tree and promote winter injury. They may be fertilized with premium-quality long-lasting slow-release fertilizers according to label directions—3:1:2 and 4:1:2 ratio fertilizers work well when fertilizing trees in Texas.

Iron deficiencies can show up on certain trees growing in alkaline soils. Several types of **oaks** and **pines** are often affected. Symptoms include yellow foliage, especially the newer leaves. Generally, you will see a pattern of green veins on a yellow-green background. *Treat* the tree with chelated or other forms of iron now since it will not stimulate growth. *Apply* sulfur or copperas iron sulphate to the area where the roots are located to help acidify the soil. These deficiencies can be completely avoided if acid loving trees are not planted in alkaline soils.

Pest Control

By this late in the year it is questionable whether spraying a pest is worth it. Use your best judgment, but be aware that leaves of deciduous trees often begin a slow decline this month anyway, and they generally start to fall in November.

Pruning

Trim faded flower heads off **vitex** to stimulate another flush of flowers. Spring-flowering trees have set their flowerbuds for next year and should not be pruned. Promptly *prune* any broken branches or damage caused by high winds. Always prune with the proper tools and keep them sharp. Be careful when pruning trees. Tree limbs are often heavy and can cause damage and/or injury if they fall in locations other than where we expect them to.

Planning

Trees often live longer than we do, but age will eventually take its toll on trees as it does with every other living organism. Different trees have various life expectancies. Short-lived trees, such as **flowering crab apple,** will typically live for 15 to 20 years. Many trees will live for 50 to 80 years, and the longest-lived trees, like **live oaks,** will live well over 100 years.

As trees age, they may lose vigor. Decay could develop in the trunk and major branches as a tree's natural resistance weakens. Large dead branches, weaker growth, and overall decline are signs an old tree is reaching the end of its life. Before they actually die, they become a hazard and will need to be removed. Large, dead branches can drop, or the entire tree can blow over (September is generally our most active hurricane month). If you are fortunate enough to have old, mature trees in your landscape, appreciate them. But plan to watch them carefully over the years for signs of decline.

Planting and Transplanting

If possible, hold off on planting trees until the weather begins to cool down next month. However, trees may be and often are planted during September in Texas landscapes. The most important maintenance item for newly planted trees during this month is maintaining a *moist* soil at the root zone area.

Care for Your Trees

Summer thunderstorms can damage trees with high, gusty winds and lightning. Storm-damaged trees often need pruning. This should include sawing off damaged limbs immediately after damage occurs. See page 215 for the proper way to cut the branch. Cuts should not be made flush with the trunk, as this removes the tree's natural defenses against decay. Pruning paints are not necessary.

Lightning strikes are not unusual. As soon as they occur, take pictures and contact your homeowner's insurance company. Trees damaged by acts of nature are usually covered by insurance policies. Lightning can kill a tree, damage it severely, or cause minor damage. If the tree is going to die as a result of the lightning strike, it will generally do so in a matter of a few weeks. Wait at least four weeks after the strike to have any repair work done. Repair work usually means trimming off loose bark and broken branches. Make a note to fertilize the tree next January. Enter your notes in your Texas gardening journal.

Watering

Although temperatures may become milder, September weather can also be sweltering and dry. If your new tree plantings are still alive, you've probably been doing an excellent job of watering. *Keep up the good work.* If pruning is needed and you will be doing the activity yourself, be careful—use the proper tools and keep them sharp.

Fertilizing

This is the last month to fertilize in north Texas for the year. South Texas gardeners may fertilize through October. Apply your choice of fertilizer aids according to label directions. Fertilizer spikes and granular 3:1:2 or 4:1:2 ratio products are known to work well for fertilizing trees in Texas.

Pest Control

Watch over newly planted trees. It is unlikely that pest control will be necessary this late in the year, but young trees need as much foliage for as long as possible to get established. *Control* pest problems promptly. Contact your county office of the Texas Cooperative Extension Service for help with the diagnosis of any problems and for fact/tip sheets on insect, disease, and weed identification and controls.

Pruning

As trees in the landscape mature and grow large, the shade they create will quite often not allow grass to grow well. If you are trying to deal with this sort of situation, here are some things you can do:

- The amount of sunlight reaching the turf can be increased by selective pruning. The lower branches and some of the inner branches may be pruned to allow more light to reach the lawn below.

- Raising and thinning the canopy on older, mature trees is best done by a professional arborist who can determine which branches can be removed without affecting the tree adversely.

After this is done, the existing grass should do better, or if the grass has died out in the area, you can lay new sod and see if it will take. Remember, this is a temporary solution, as the trees will continue to grow over the years and shade will once again become a problem.

If after these efforts you still can't get grass to grow under your tree, it's time to accept the situation (as we gardeners often must do), and stop utilizing your effort and money trying to make grass grow where the shade of the tree simply won't allow it. Unless cutting down the tree is an option, your next step is to look at the area as an outstanding opportunity to plant a shade-tolerant ground cover or create a new garden with shade-loving plants.

The most important thing to remember when creating landscaped areas under a tree is to respect the root system of the tree itself. *Avoid severing any roots larger than 1 inch in diameter.* Use a gardening fork to turn the soil under the tree rather than a shovel or spade, since the fork will damage fewer roots. Normally just the addition of 4 to 6 inches of organic matter and carefully blending it with the native soil is all that's necessary to prepare excellent planting beds. If you intend to fill over an area that will cover a large part of the tree's root system (which extends out well beyond the reach of the branches), do not apply more than 2 inches of soil.

Planning

The fall planting season gets started this month. You may have already made your decisions on the types of trees you would like to plant. If you haven't done this yet, now is the time to begin. Take your time and select just the right tree for each situation. Enter your decisions in your Texas gardening journal. The ideal planting season runs from this month through April.

Visit local nurseries and look at what is available. Ask what other types of trees they will get in later, what sizes will be available, and the prices. If you are planning on purchasing a large tree, you should check on delivery and installation prices since it may be too big for you to handle. *Shop around.*

Planting and Transplanting

It is still too early to transplant trees, but if you have identified a tree you want to move, root pruning it now is a good idea. By cutting some of the long roots this month, new fibrous ones are formed closer to the trunk within the area of the soil to be moved with the plant.

Push a sharp-bladed shovel straight down, then pull straight out of the soil, forming a circle of connected cuts around the tree. The circle should be cut within the size of the rootball you intend to dig up when transplanting the tree later. If you plan to dig a rootball 1 foot out from the trunk, for instance, make your root-pruning cut 8 to 10 inches out from the trunk. The size of the rootball a tree should be moved with is determined by adding 9 inches to the rootball for every inch of diameter of the tree's trunk. (Measure the tree 12 inches above the soil line to determinte the diameter.) Using this rule, a tree with a trunk diameter of 2 inches would need an 18-inch-diameter rootball. *Dig and transplant* a root-pruned tree in early to mid-December.

This month you can begin fall planting of trees into the landscape.

Care for Your Trees

Trees in areas that have a lot of foot traffic or those trees that cars are allowed to park under may eventually begin to suffer root damage due to soil compaction. You will notice low vigor, dieback, and an unusual number of dead branches in the tree. Talk to a professional arborist about injecting water under high pressure into the soil of the root zone to loosen it and improve air content (in the spring a fertilizer solution should be used). Do not allow cars to park on the ground under trees. To alleviate a problem with foot traffic, *apply* a thick layer (4 to 6 inches) of shredded bark or composted wood chips under the tree—as far out as the branches reach, if possible.

Watering

Cooler weather means less stress on trees. Established trees should not need supplemental water for the rest of the year, even if the weather is dry. Continue to *water* trees planted within the past year as needed. This should be the last month you have to worry about watering them.

Fertilizing

Trees should not be fertilized this month with any fertilizer containing quick-release nitrogen.

Pest Control

Spray trees that have scale infestations with a lightweight oil spray. As we move into the fall, do not be concerned about the declining health of deciduous tree foliage. You will begin to see various leaf spot, scorched edges, and other symptoms. The trees are getting ready to shed their leaves, and the spots and blemishes are just part of the process.

Use your landscape diagram to help you in your planning if you want to move a tree or plant a new one.

Pruning

Continue to take care of any pruning that needs to be done on trees in your landscape. Avoid heading-back cuts (see The Importance of Pruning, page 18) that might stimulate late growth. Remember that spring-flowering trees have already set their flowerbuds for next year. Always make sure your tools are sharp and they are the correct ones for the activity. Prune for specific purposes and be careful.

Planning

When you are looking at the young trees offered by nurseries, you may realize it's hard to know what a tree will look like as it matures. When deciding on which trees to plant in your landscape, try to find specimens of mature trees to observe. Local public gardens, botanical gardens, or arboretums are useful to visit, as the plants are often labeled with their names. Ask friends, neighbors, and relatives what kinds of trees they have in their yards, and take a look at them.

Enter your visits in your Texas gardening journal. Photos of your visits secured inside your journal will provide additional help in deciding which trees to plant.

Planting and Transplanting

November and early December are, perhaps, the best times to plant trees in Texas. The soil is still warm from summer, which encourages vigorous root growth. At the same time the weather is cool, and the trees are going dormant, which reduces stress. Generous rainfall during the winter makes constant attention to watering unnecessary. Planting at this time is especially beneficial for balled-and-burlapped trees because they lose so much of their root system when they are dug.

Plant trees properly according to these steps:

1 ***Dig the hole*** at least twice the diameter of the rootball, and no deeper than the height of the rootball.

2 ***Remove*** a container-grown tree from the container. If the rootball is tightly packed with thick encircling roots, try to unwrap, open up, or even cut some of the roots to encourage them to spread into the surrounding soil. Place the rootball in the hole.

3 Place balled-and-burlapped trees into the planting hole, remove any nails, nylon twine, or wire basket that have been used to secure the burlap, and fold down the burlap from the top half of the rootball. The top of the rootball should be level with or slightly above the surrounding soil. It is critical that you do not plant trees too deep.

4 Thoroughly pulverize the soil dug out from the hole and use this soil, without any additions, to backfill around the tree. Add soil around the tree until the hole is half full, then firm the soil to eliminate air pockets—but do not pack it tight. Finish filling the hole, firm again, and then water the tree thoroughly to settle it in.

5 Generally, don't add fertilizer to the planting hole, although some premium-quality long-lasting slow-release fertilizer could be added in the upper few inches. The use of a root-stimulator solution is optional. Always read and follow label directions when applying any gardening aid, including fertilizers and root stimulators.

6 ***Stake*** the tree if it is tall enough to be unstable—otherwise, it's not necessary. Three stakes should be firmly driven into the ground just beyond the rootball. Use strips of cloth or old nylon stockings or use wire (covered with a piece of garden hose where it touches the trunk) tied to the stakes and then to the trunk of the tree. Leave the support in place no more than 9 to 12 months.

Care for Your Trees

Have you thanked your trees lately? Trees provide welcome shade, make our houses cooler and outdoor living areas usable during the summer, and help our environment in many ways. Trees help purify the air. They reduce smog and air pollution problems. They provide shelter and food for wildlife. Where dust is a problem, trees can be placed to serve as filters. Their roots stabilize the soil and reduce erosion. Tree plantings can be effective windbreaks during the winter. Noise pollution can be absorbed by tree plantings by as much as 50 percent. And trees tend to increase the value and sales appeal of property. We may be thinking about how we have to care for our trees, but it's good to think of how they care for us as well.

Watering

Water-in newly planted trees thoroughly, but you should have to do little supplemental watering over the winter. Established trees will not need to be watered this month.

Fertilizing

No fertilizer needs to be applied to trees this month.

Pest Control

Insects: Other than scale, few pest problems require treatment now. Deciduous trees drop their leaves this month and into December. *Check* them and evergreen trees such as **holly** for signs of scale.

Spray with lightweight horticultural oil or other pest-control aid if needed. Refer to page 291 for a summary listing your options.

Live oaks are one of our favorite trees and are widely planted around the state. They often drop a lot of leaves in November. Look at the leaves and you will see that most of them have a golden-tan fluffy growth on the back. This is called wooly oak gall, and is caused by a tiny insect.

Although the leaf drop is a nuisance, the condition is harmless and nothing to worry about. The leaves make excellent mulch or can be placed in your compost pile.

In mid- to late November, trees begin to show off their fall colors. Although not as spectacular as the fall color up North, there is still enough to appreciate. The following trees are some of the most reliable for fall color (those marked with a plus sign [+] will show good fall color even in the warmest parts of the state): **red oak, willow oak, Shumard oak[+], flowering dogwood, Japanese persimmon, ginkgo[+], sourwood, sassafras, flowering pear, Chinese pistachio[+], tallow tree[+],** and **sweetgum[+].**

Disease: Avoid scraping or damaging the bark at the base of a tree, and do not pile soil several inches thick around it. This can lead to fungal organisms penetrating the wood causing decay.

Once decay has started in the trunk of a tree, there is often nothing that can be done to stop it if the tree's own defenses fail.

Pruning

Identify pruning needs and take care of the pruning.

Planning

Plan on getting out and enjoying the fall color on trees in the area. If fall color is something you want to include in your landscape, note which trees put on the best display in your area and plant them.

Spend some time catching up on your Texas gardening journal entries. Record unusual weather, new tree plantings, and anything else you think might be useful later on.

Planting and Transplanting

1 *Dig a hole* for the tree in its new location before you dig it up. It's important to replant the tree as quickly as possible. *Dig the hole* as deep and twice as wide as the rootball you intend to dig with the tree.

2 *Dig the tree.* Get as much of the root system as you can. On average, dig a rootball about 9 inches across for every inch of diameter of the trunk at 12 inches above the soil line (a tree with a 2-inch-diameter trunk needs an 18-inch rootball).

3 Do not let the roots dry out before you plant the tree. *Wrap* them if necessary.

4 Place the tree in the hole at the same depth it was growing. Thoroughly break up the soil removed to make the hole, and use it to fill in around the tree's roots.

5 *Water* the tree in thoroughly.

6 Apply a root stimulator according to label directions.

7 Most trees home gardeners would transplant are small enough not to need staking. If the tree seems unstable, *stake it.*

Early December is an ideal time to plant trees in your landscape.

Care for Your Trees

Any recently planted tree whose stakes have been in place for 9 to 12 months should have the support removed. If you have newly planted trees that will remain staked, check where the ties come into contact with the trunk and make sure they are not causing damage.

Watering

Water-in trees as they are planted, and if weather is mild and dry, water as needed. Established trees will not need to be watered this time of year.

Fertilizing

No fertilizer should be applied to trees this time of year.

Pest Control

Any trees with scale infestations can be sprayed with a lightweight horticultural oil during the winter for control. Make several applications about 10 days apart for effective control. Do not spray immediately before temperatures below freezing are predicted.

Pruning

Winter is an ideal time to prune trees. Deciduous trees are leafless. This allows you to more clearly see the structure of your trees, and you don't have the weight of the foliage to deal with. Evergreen trees may be pruned this time of the year as well.

Vegetables and Herbs

There is something satisfying about putting fresh homegrown vegetables on the table—food that you actually grew yourself. Some believe gardening was originally done in response to needs for food, seasonings, and medicines.

People decide to grow vegetables for various reasons. For many, it is a way to have the freshest possible produce. Other gardeners crave types of vegetables or varieties that are not available at the local supermarket. And, although economy is usually not the main reason these days, the harvest from the home garden can save money.

Thanks to the relatively mild winters of our region, gardeners can harvest something from their vegetable and herb gardens almost 365 days of the year. All that is needed is some planning, along with awareness of the many different types of vegetables and herbs we can grow throughout the year. Naturally, gardeners in south Texas have more harvesting days than their counterparts in north Texas.

Vegetable and herb gardening seasons can be divided roughly into the spring season and fall season, but the intensely hot summer presents its own challenges. Most vegetables grow, produce, and die within their particular season. There are several herbs that live for one season and finish, but there are also many perennial herbs. There are a few perennial vegetables that are year-round residents of the garden, including **asparagus** and **horseradish.**

Vegetable gardeners must be attuned to the seasons and observe the proper planting times for vegetables. Planting times depend on a variety of factors, temperature being a major one. Cool/cold-season vegetables are grown from August to May. They need cooler temperatures to perform their best and are able to tolerate the below-freezing temperatures of the winter season.

Warm-season vegetables cannot experience frost without significant injury or death. They are grown from a period that covers March through November, divided up into the spring planting season, the summer planting season, and the fall planting season. Often only certain heat-tolerant vegetable varieties such as **okra, Southern peas, hot pepper,** and **eggplant** remain productive in the extremely hot months of June, July, and August. Most spring-planted vegetables can be planted again in August and September for fall production. **Tomatoes** are often planted in late June to early July.

Planting dates can vary by two to four weeks from north Texas to south Texas. When reading the vegetable charts on pages 234–235, you will notice that specific planting dates are not given. Instead, an appropriate planting period indicates when a vegetable is best planted. If you don't know the average spring and fall freeze dates, contact local nurseries and/or your Extension Service Agent for the information. You'll want to know the last average killing freeze date for spring and the first average killing freeze/frost date in the fall for your area. North Texas gardeners will generally want to avoid the earliest dates given for spring planting and plant earlier than the latest dates given for fall planting. South Texas gardeners would plant earlier in the spring and later in the fall.

Although herb gardens also have their seasons, planting times are not as critical as they are for vegetables. Herbs are a far more diverse group that includes trees, shrubs, herbaceous perennials, bulbs, and warm-season and cool-season annuals. Several that are easily grown, reliable perennials in the northern United States have difficulty with

Vegetables and Herbs

our hot, humid, and sometimes relatively wet summers along our coastal areas. Included in this group are **sage, thyme, French tarragon,** and the **lavenders.**

Planning the Vegetable Garden

Choose a sunny, well-drained spot. Most vegetables, particularly those grown for their fruit or seeds (**tomato, corn, cucumber, beans**) need at least eight hours of direct sun for best production. Vegetables grown for their roots (**carrot, turnip, radish**) can do well with about six hours of direct sun. Most leafy crops (**mustard, lettuce, chard, cabbage**) can be productive with as little as four hours of direct sun.

Convenience in relation to the house is nice, but a nearby source of water is a more important consideration, since irrigation will be necessary. Vegetable gardens can be beautiful at certain times, but the appearance is variable with the seasons and harvesting. Some gardeners may be reluctant to harvest vegetables because they do not want to ruin the appearance of the garden! For that reason, these gardens are generally not located in a prominent spot in the landscape, if such is possible.

Think carefully about the size of the garden. If you are new to vegetable gardening, start off small and gradu-ally enlarge the garden as you become more familiar with the amount of time and effort involved. Consider the size of your family and the space you have available, too. Whether to plant in traditional raised rows or raised beds is another decision to be made. In high-rainfall or relatively poorly drained areas, raised beds are advised.

Next, decide on the vegetables you want to grow. Make a list of your favorites. The size of the garden is also a factor. Some large-growing vegetables such as **pumpkins**, **brussels sprouts, corn** and **okra** occupy a lot of room and would not be as suitable for smaller gardens—unless you really want to grow them!

Choose vegetable varieties recommended for growing in Texas. Check with your local county office of the Texas Cooperative Extension Service, a branch of the Texas A&M State University Agricultural System. Free copies of vegetable variety sheets are available. They list current variety recommendations based on trials done in Texas. There are many varieties not on the lists which may do very well here but have never been tested. Be as adventurous as you like, but rely on tested varieties for your main plantings.

At this point it helps to draw up a diagram of the garden you're planning. Use graph paper and draw to scale if possible. Make several photocopies of the original and

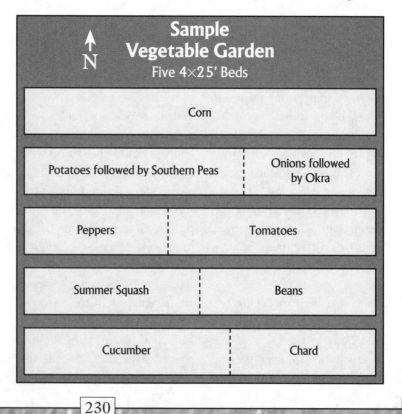

Sample Vegetable Garden
Five 4×25' Beds

Corn

Potatoes followed by Southern Peas	Onions followed by Okra

Peppers	Tomatoes

Summer Squash	Beans

Cucumber	Chard

Vegetables and Herbs

use them to draw in the vegetables you intend to grow—where they will be located in the garden, and how much space will be devoted to each crop.

Soil Preparation

Soil preparation is critical to successful vegetable gardening. Remove any existing unwanted vegetation. This includes any weeds that may have grown up between crops, or lawn grass in a new bed. The plants may be physically removed by pulling or digging them out. Make sure you get the roots. You may also use weed-control aids to eliminate the weeds or lawn grass, and remove or turn under the dead weeds. Refer to page 291 for a summary listing your options. Do not turn under living lawn grass.

Use a shovel, garden fork, or tiller to turn the soil 8 to 10 inches deep. Rear-tined tillers work well for this, especially in heavy clay soils.

Spread a layer of organic matter such as compost, rotted leaves, manure, or Canadian spaghnum peat moss 4 to 6 inches thick over the bed. If a soil test indicates the need for lime or sulphur, sprinkle the appropriate amount over the organic matter.

Thoroughly incorporate the amendments into the upper 8 to 10 inches of soil. Rake the bed smooth and you are ready to shape the raised rows.

Using a hoe or shovel, push soil out of the walkways and up onto the area where the vegetables will be grown. Form a raised row about 3 feet across and 8 to 12 inches high. This is especially important in heavy soils and high-rainfall areas of Texas. Raised beds are often not needed in rapidly draining sandy soils.

Vegetables can also be grown in raised beds. Form the bed's edges with pressure-treated 1-by-8-inch or 1-by-12-inch boards, landscape timbers, molded plastic, cinder blocks, railroad ties, or any other material you feel is suitable. Turn over the soil in the bottom, fill with a high-quality garden soil mix, and then plant.

Planting

Vegetables are generally planted using transplants, or by direct-seeding into the garden. Transplants are used for those vegetables that are not easily direct-seeded, for those that need to be started early in a protected environment before planting later into the garden, or when only a few plants of specific vegetable types or varieties are desired. Most vegetable gardeners purchase their transplants from local nurseries, but you can start your own. Transplants should be planted into the garden according to their recommended spacing.

In direct-seeding vegetables, seeds are planted two to three times thicker

than necessary for the number of plants needed. This ensures a good stand of seedlings. Once the seedlings are up and growing, the extras are pinched off with the thumb and forefinger, leaving behind seedlings at the proper spacing. This process is called thinning.

Pest Control

Pest control is necessary when it comes to vegetable gardening, especially during the late spring, summer, and fall growing seasons in order to have a successful crop.

Before using any pest-control aid, make sure you have properly identified the pest (insect, mite, fungus, bacteria). Refer to page 291 for a summary listing your options. Help is also available from your local nursery and county office of the Texas Extension Service.

Weeds

The best defense against weeds is to take care of any problems promptly and keep your beds mulched 3 to 4 inches deep.

Weed-control aids may be used to eliminate weeds in a bed prior to planting and are particularly useful in controlling perennial weeds such as Bermudagrass, Johnsongrass, nutgrass, and oxalis. These aids are not labeled for use in beds where vegetables are growing.

Pre-emergent weed-prevention aids are applied to weed-free soil for suppressing the growth of weed seeds. Some are labeled for use around vegetables and can be helpful in weed control. Read labels carefully before use, and remember that most cannot be used in an area that is to be or has been direct-seeded. Refer to page 291 for a summary listing your options

Keep beds mulched with 3 to 4 inches of bark, leaves, dry grass clippings, or pine straw. Commercial weed blocking rolled aids/products and other materials are also useful in weed prevention. Promptly pull or hoe any weeds that appear. Get them while they are small. **Note:** Weeds pull best when the soil is moist.

Insects

There are lots of bugs that would just love to eat your vegetables before you get a chance to harvest them. The judicious use of pest-control aids, along with cultural techniques (such as planting early in the season and handpicking), will generally prevent major outbreaks. When choosing to use pest-control aids, always read the label carefully and follow directions exactly.

Major categories of insect pests include **caterpillars, aphids, stink-bugs, whiteflies** and **beetles.**

Although **spider mites** are not technically insects, they are generally grouped with them for pest-control purposes. Control is the same as for aphids, with the addition of mite-control aids.

Visit your local retail nursery for assistance in selecting pest-control aids. Refer to page 291 for a summary listing your options. Make sure you understand the label directions before purchasing your selected aids. Some aids may be retired by manufacturers, and new ones come to the market. Progressive local retailers can provide you with information and help you make informed decisions based on your needs and goals. Another good source of information on insect-control aids is your Extension Service Agent.

Other Pests

Control **nematodes** by rotating crops, adding organic matter whenever beds are being prepared, and planting nematode-resistant vegetable cultivars when available.

Snails and **slugs** chew holes in the leaves of many vegetables, especially leafy crops grown during the cool season. Baits labeled for use around food crops, various traps, and barriers can also be helpful to control these nighttime visitors.

Diseases

Fungi cause the majority of vegetable diseases, although viruses and bacteria can also be problems in the vegetable garden. Rotate crops as much as possible, plant at the appropriate times, space plants properly for air circulation, and keep beds mulched to keep soil-borne diseases from splashing up onto vegetables. Plant the best locally recommended disease-resistant varieties. Fertilize and water as needed.

Garden aids called broad-spectrum fungicides used in the vegetable garden include: chlorothalonil, sulfur, maneb, mancozeb, and copper compounds. Controlling diseases is different from controlling insects. To be effective, disease-control aids must be used earlier, before much damage occurs, and then regularly after this first use. Always use according to label directions.

There is no cure for viral infections. Since most are spread by insects, insect control can help. Weeds may serve as alternate hosts, so keep surrounding areas weed free. Pull up and dispose of infected plants promptly to prevent spread to healthy plants. Visit your local retail garden center or contact the County Agent's office for current information and assistance in selecting disease-control aids. Refer to page 291 for a summary listing your options.

Vegetables and Herbs

Planning the Herb Garden

Unlike vegetables, which require relatively large plantings in order to produce sufficient harvest, a single herb plant will often provide enough for a gardener's needs. Herbs may be grown in the vegetable garden, in their own area, or even among landscape plantings. Since few plants are needed, herbs are also excellent when grown in containers.

Most herbs require direct sun at least four to six hours a day (six to eight hours is best) and excellent drainage. Use raised beds or containers if drainage in your yard is questionable. Locate your herb-growing area as close to the kitchen as possible so the herbs are convenient to use while you are cooking. Those you choose to grow may initially be those you are familiar with and like to use in cooking.

Planting

Prepare the planting area as for vegetables. Containers are also excellent for growing herbs. Because relatively few plants are needed, most herb gardeners buy herb transplants. You may also plant seeds or raise your own transplants.

Cool-season annuals should be seeded or transplanted between September and February and include **borage, celery, chervil, cilantro/coriander, dill, fennel,** and **parsley.**

Warm-season annuals should be seeded or transplanted in March through August and include **sweet basil, perilla, sesame,** and **summer savory.** Actual planting dates will vary depending upon which zone you live in. Your local retail nursery can provide specific planting dates in your area.

Perennial herbs that grow well include **bay, lemongrass, scented geraniums** (grow these in containers and protect during winter in north Texas), **beebalm, burnet, catnip, chives, garlic chives, horseradish, lemon balm, Mexican tarragon, mints, oregano, pennyroyal, rosemary, sage, sorrel, marjoram, thyme,** and **winter savory. Thyme, sage, catnip,** and **scented geraniums** require excellent drainage and are often more successful when grown in containers. Even then, they may succumb to root and stem rots in the hot, wet late-summer season. Several perennial herbs cannot tolerate our normal hot summers at all, including **French tarragon, feverfew, lavender,** and **chamomile.** They are generally grown as cool-season annuals, planted in fall, and harvested in spring and early summer, although a few gardeners have some success with lavenders planted in the warm season. They are usually difficult at best to grow.

Harvesting Herbs

Harvest herbs frequently and regularly, being careful not to deplete all the plant's foliage. Generally, take no more than one-third of the total foliage at any one time. Herbs are more attractive and compact in size when harvested regularly.

Pest Control

Although they have a reputation for being resistant to attack from insects, herbs are occasionally damaged by various bugs. Diseases can be a problem during the hot summer months, especially during rainy periods.

Few pest-control aids have been labeled for use on herbs. Refer to page 291 for a summary listing your options. Visit your local retail nursery for assistance in selecting aids. Remember, herbs are generally chopped and added to dishes before cooking. No one will know if there were a few holes in the leaves. For disease control, make sure herbs are planted in well-drained beds, and space them properly for good air circulation. Plant herbs according to the proper season and choose those that grow well in Texas. A mulch of light pebbles or marble chips seems to help herbs such as **rosemary, thyme, sage, oregano,** and **catnip** avoid stem and crown rots.

Vegetable Planting Chart

Vegetables	Seed or Plants per 100 feet (pl. = plants)	Depth of Seed Planting in Inches	Inches of Distance Between		Average Height of Crop in Feet	Spring Planting in Regard to Average Frost-Free Date (FFD)
			Rows	Plants		
Asparagus	66 pl., 1 oz.	6–8, 1–1½	36–48	18	5	4 to 6 wks. before FFD
Beans, snap bush	½ lb.	1–1½	30–36	3–4	1½	on FFD to 4 wks. after
Beans, snap pole	½ lb.	1–1½	36–48	4–6	6	on FFD to 4 wks. after
Beans, Lima bush	½ lb.	1–1½	30–36	3–4	1½	on FFD to 4 wks. after
Beans, Lima pole	¼ lb.	1–1½	36–48	12–18	6	on FFD to 4 wks. after
Beets	1 oz.	1	14–24	2	1½	4 to 6 wks. before FFD
Broccoli	¼ oz.	½	24–36	14–24	3	4 to 6 wks. before FFD
Brussels sprouts	¼ oz.	½	24–36	14–24	2	4 to 6 wks. before FFD
Cabbage	¼ oz.	½	24–36	14–24	1½	4 to 6 wks. before FFD
Cabbage, Chinese	¼ oz.	½	18–30	8–12	1½	4 to 6 wks. before FFD
Carrot	½ oz.	½	14–24	2	1	4 to 6 wks. before FFD
Cauliflower	¼ oz.	½	24–36	14–24	3	not recommended
Chard, Swiss	2 oz.	1	18–30	6	1½	2 to 6 wks. before FFD
Collard (Kale)	¼ oz.	½	18–36	6–12	2	2 to 6 wks. before FFD
Corn, sweet	3–4 oz.	1–2	24–36	9–12	6	on FFD to 6 wks. after
Cucumber	½ oz.	½	48–72	8–12	1	on FFD to 6 wks. after
Eggplant	⅛ oz.	½	30–36	18–24	3	2 to 6 wks. after FFD
Garlic	1 lb.	1–2	14–24	2–4	1	not recommended
Kohlrabi	¼ oz.	½	14–24	4–6	1½	2 to 6 wks. before FFD
Lettuce	¼ oz.	½	18–24	2–3	1	6 wks. before FFD to 2 wks. after
Muskmelon (Cantaloupe)	½ oz.	1	60–96	24–36	1	on FFD to 6 wks. after
Mustard	¼ oz.	½	14–24	6–12	1½	on FFD to 6 wks. after
Okra	2 oz.	1	36–42	12–24	6	2 to 6 wks. after FFD
Onion (plants)	400–600 pl.	1–2	14–24	2–3	1½	4 to 10 wks. before FFD
Onion (seed)	1 oz.	½	14–24	2–3	1½	6 to 8 wks. before FFD
Parsley	¼ oz.	⅛	14–24	2–4	½	on to 6 wks. before FFD
Peas, English	1 lb.	2–3	18–36	1	2	2 to 8 wks. before FFD
Peas, Southern	½ lb.	2–3	24–36	4–6	2½	2 to 10 wks. after FFD
Pepper	⅛ oz.	½	30–36	18–24	3	1 to 8 wks. after FFD
Potato, Irish	6–10 lb.	4	30–36	10–15	2	4 to 6 wks. before FFD
Potato, sweet	75–100 pl.	3–5	36–48	12–16	1	2 to 8 wks. after FFD
Pumpkin	½ oz.	1–2	60–96	36–48	1	1 to 4 wks. after FFD
Radish	1 oz.	½	14–24	1	½	6 wks. before FFD to 4wks. after
Spinach	1 oz.	½	14–24	3–4	1	1 to 8 wks. before FFD
Squash, summer	1 oz.	1–2	36–60	18–36	3	1 to 4 wks. after FFD
Squash, winter	½ oz.	1–2	60–96	24–48	1	1 to 4 wks. after FFD
Tomato	50 pl., ⅛ oz.	4–6, ½	36–48	36–48	3	on to 8 wks. after FFD
Turnip, greens	½ oz.	½	14–24	2–3	1½	2 to 6 wks. before FFD
Turnip, roots	½ oz.	½	14–24	2–3	1½	2 to 6 wks. before FFD
Watermelon	1 oz.	1–2	72–96	36–72	1	on FFD to 6 wks. after

Vegetable Planting Chart

Fall Planting in Regard to Average Autumn Freeze Date (AFD)	No. Days Ready For Use	Average Length of Harvest Season (Days)	Average Crop Expected Per 100 Feet	Approx. Planting per Person	
				Fresh (pl. = plants)	(Storage) Canning or Freezing
not recommended	730	60	30 lb.	10–15 pl.	10–15 pl.
8 to 10 wks. before AFD	45–60	14	120 lb.	15–16 ft.	15–20 ft.
14 to 16 wks. before AFD	60–70	30	150 lb.	5–6 ft.	8–10 ft.
8 to 10 wks. before AFD	65–80	14	25 lb. shelled	10–15 ft.	15–20 ft.
14 to 16 wks. before AFD	75–85	40	50 lb. shelled	5–6 ft.	8–10 ft.
8 to 10 wks. before AFD	50–60	30	150 lb.	5–10 ft.	10–20 ft.
10 to 16 wks. before AFD	60–80	40	100 lb.	3–5 pl.	5–6 pl.
10 to 14 wks. before AFD	90–100	21	75 lb.	2–5 pl.	5–8 pl.
10 to 16 wks. before AFD	60–90	40	150 lb.	3–4 pl.	5–10 pl.
12 to 14 wks. before AFD	65–70	21	80 heads	3–10 ft.	—
12 to 14 wks. before AFD	70–80	21	100 lb.	5–10 ft.	10–15 ft.
10 to 16 wks. before AFD	70–90	14	100 lb.	3–5 pl.	8–12 pl.
12 to 16 wks. before AFD	45–55	40	75 lb.	3–5 pl.	8–12 pl.
8 to 12 wks. before AFD	50–80	60	100 lb.	5–10 ft.	5–10 ft.
12 to 14 wks. before AFD	70–90	10	10 doz.	10–15 ft.	30–50 ft.
10 to 12 wks. before AFD	50–70	30	120 lb.	1–2 hls.	3–5 hls.
12 to 16 wks. before AFD	80–90	90	100 lb.	2–3 pl.	2–3 pl.
4 to 6 wks. before AFD	140–150	—	40 lb.	—	1–5 ft.
12 to 16 wks. before AFD	55–75	14	75 lb.	3–5 ft.	5–10 ft.
10 to 14 wks. before AFD	40–80	21	50 lb.	5–15 ft.	—
14 to 16 wks. before AFD	85–100	30	100 fruits	3–5 hls.	—
10 to 16 wks. before AFD	30–40	30	100 lb.	5–10 ft.	10–15 ft.
12 to 16 wks. before AFD	55–65	90	100 lb.	4–6 ft.	6–10 ft.
not recommended	80–120	40	100 lb.	3–5 ft.	30–50 ft.
8 to 10 wks. before AFD	90–120	40	100 lb.	3–5 ft.	30–50 ft.
6 to 16 wks. before AFD	70–90	90	30 lb.	1–3 ft.	1–3 ft.
2 to 12 wks. before AFD	55–90	7	20 lb.	15–20 ft.	40–60 ft.
10 to 12 wks. before AFD	60–70	30	40 lb.	10–15 ft.	20–50 ft.
12 to 16 wks. before AFD	60–90	90	60 lb.	3–5 pl.	3–5 pl.
14 to 16 wks. before AFD	75–100	—	100 lb.	50–100 ft.	—
not recommended	100–130	—	100 lb.	5–10 pl.	10–20 pl.
12 to 14 wks. before AFD	75–100	—	100 lb.	1–2 hls.	1–2 hls.
on to 8 wks. before AFD	25–40	7	100 bunches	3–5 ft.	—
2 to 16 wks. before AFD	40–60	40	3 bu.	5–10 ft.	10–15 ft.
12 to 15 wks. before AFD	50–60	40	150 lb.	2–3 hls.	2–3 hls.
12 to 14 wks. before AFD	85–100	—	100 lb.	1–3 hls.	1–3 hls.
12 to 14 wks. before AFD	70–90	40	100 lb.	3–5 pl.	5–10 pl.
2 to 12 wks. before AFD	30	40	50–100 lb.	5–10 ft.	—
2 to 12 wks. before AFD	30–60	30	50–100 lb.	5–10 ft.	5–10 ft.
14 to 16 wks. before AFD	80–100	30	40 fruits	2–4 hls.	—

Source: Texas Agricultural Extension Service

Herb Planting Chart

Annuals

Common Name Scientific Name	Height	Spacing Row	Plants	Cultural Hints	Uses
Anise *Pimpinella anisum*	24 in.	18 in.	10 in.	Grow from seed. Plant after frost. Sun.	Leaves for seasoning, garnish; use dried seed as spice.
Basil, Sweet *Ocimum basilicum*	20–24 in.	18 in.	12 in.	Grow from seed. Plant after frost. Sun.	Season soups, stews, salad, omelets.
Borage *Borago officinalis*	24 in.	18 in.	12 in.	Grow from seed, self-sowing. Best in dry, sunny areas.	Young leaves in salads and cool drinks.
Caraway * *Carum carvi*	12–24 in.	18 in.	10 in.	Grow from seed. Biennial seed-bearer. Sun.	Flavoring, especially bakery items.
Chervil *Anthriscus cerefolium*	10 in.	15 in.	3–6 in.	Sow in early spring. Partial shade.	Aromatic leaves used in soups and salads.
Coriander *Coriandrum sativum*	24 in.	24 in.	18 in.	Grow from seed. Sow in spring, in sun or partial shade.	Seed used in confections. Leaves in salad.
Dill *Anethum graveolens*	24–36 in.	24 in.	12 in.	Grow from seed sown in early spring. Sun or partial shade.	Leaves and seeds used for flavoring and pickling.
Fennel (Florence Fennel) *Foeniculum vulgare*	60 in.	18 in.	18 in.	Grow from seed sown in early spring. Sun, partial shade.	Has anise-like flavor for salad. Stalk eaten raw or braised.
Parsley * *Petroselinum crispum*	5 in.	18 in.	6 in.	Grow from seed started in early spring. Slow to germinate. Sun.	Brings out flavor of other herbs. Fine base and seasoning.
Summer Savory *Satureja hortensis*	18 in.	18 in.	18 in.	Grow in well-worked loam. Sow seed in spring. Sun.	Use leaves fresh or dry for salads, dressings, stews.

Perennials

Common Name Scientific Name	Height	Spacing Row	Plants	Cultural Hints	Uses
Catnip *Nepeta cataria*	3–4 in.	24 in.	18 in.	Hardy. Sun or shade. Grow from seed or by division.	Leaves for tea and seasoning.
Chives *Allium shoenosprasum*	12 in.	12 in.	12 in.	Little care. Divide when overcrowded. Grow from seed or by division.	Favorite of chefs. Snip tops finely. Good indoor pot plant.
Horehound *Marrobium vulgare*	24 in.	18 in.	15 in.	Grow in light soil, full sun, intense heat. Protect in cold climates in winter. Grow from seed, cuttings, or division.	Leaves used in candy or as a seasoning.

* Biennial

Herb Planting Chart

Perennials

Common Name Scientific Name	Height	Spacing Row	Plants	Cultural Hints	Uses
Hyssop *Hyssopus officinalis*	24 in.	18 in.	15 in.	Grows in poor soil, from seed. Hardy. Sun.	A mint with highly aromatic, pungent leaves.
Lavender *Lavandula* spp.	24 in.	18 in.	18 in.	Grows in dry, rocky, sunny locations with plenty of lime in soil.	Fresh in salads, or flowers dried for sachets, potpourri.
Lovage *Levisticum officinale*	3–4 ft.	30 in.	30 in.	Rich, moist soil. From seed planted in late summer. Sun or partial shade.	Of the carrot family; cultivated in European gardens as a domestic remedy.
Oregano *Origanum vulgare*	24 in.	18 in.	9 in.	Grows in poor soil from seed or division. Sun.	Flavoring for tomato dishes, pasta.
Peppermint *Mentha piperita*	36 in.	24 in.	18 in.	Can start from seed, but cuttings recommended. Sun or shade. Cut before it goes to seed. Sun.	Aromatic; used as flavoring oil used in products such as chewing gum, liqueurs, toilet water, soap, candy.
Rosemary *Rosmarinus officinalis*	3–6 ft.	18 in.	12 in.	Grows in well-drained non-acid soil. From cuttings or seed. Sun.	Leaves flavor sauces, meats, and soups.
Sage *Salvia officinalis*	18 in.	24 in.	12 in.	From seed or cuttings. Full sun. Grows slow from seed. Renew bed every 3–4 years.	Seasoning for meats, herb teas; used either fresh or dried.
Spearmint *Mentha spicata*	18 in.	24 in.	18 in.	Grows in most soils. Hardy. From cuttings, division. Sun.	Aromatic, for flavoring, condiments, teas.
Sweet Marjoram *Marjorana hortensis Origanum marjorana*	12 in.	18 ft.	12 in.	From seed or cuttings, as annual, or overwinter as pot plant. Sun.	Seasoning, fresh or dried.
Sweet Woodruff *Asperula odorata* (mild winters)	8 in.	18 in.	12 in.	Keep indoors or in cold frame over winter. Semi-shade.	Flavoring in drinks.
Tarragon *Artemisia dracunculus*	24 in.	24 in.	24 in.	Does best in semi-shade. By division or root cuttings. Protect during cold winters.	European herb of aster family; aromatic seasoning.
Thyme *Thymus vulgaris*	8–12 in.	18 in.	12 in.	Grows in light, well-drained soil. Renew plants every few years. By cuttings, seed, division. Sun.	Aromatic foliage for seasoning meats, soups, and dressings.
Winter Savory *Satureja montana*	24 in.	15 in.	18 in.	Grow in light, sandy soil. Trim out dead wood. From cuttings or seed. Sun.	Seasoning for stuffing, eggs, sausage; accents strong flavors.

Planning

Dreaming about juicy vine-ripened tomatoes? Transplants will not become available in local nurseries until March. But if you want to grow your own transplants, plan on getting seeds planted this month. Visit local nurseries and look through seed catalogs and you will see a huge number of **tomato** varieties available. Try a few new types, but plan on using tried-and-true varieties such as 'Celebrity', 'Jackpot', 'Carnival', 'Better Boy', 'Porter', and 'Sweet 100' for your main crop.

While visiting local nurseries or looking through the seed catalogs, think about other vegetables you want to plant in the late-winter and spring garden. Secure seeds for such cool-season vegetables as **radish, lettuce, beets, broccoli, cabbage, spinach,** and others. There is still time to get them in for planting. It's good to buy seeds at local stores. It is not too early to plan the spring garden. Review records in your Texas gardening journal of last year's garden, choose the vegetables and varieties you want to grow this year, and secure your seeds. Your local office of the Texas Cooperative Extension Service can provide you with a list of recommended varieties.

In zones 8 and 9, some vegetables to plant in January: **beets, broccoli, cabbage, carrots, cauliflower,**

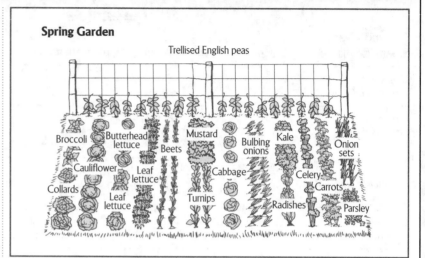

Spring Garden

Trellised English peas

Broccoli, Butterhead lettuce, Beets, Mustard, Bulbing onions, Kale, Onion sets, Cauliflower, Leaf lettuce, Cabbage, Celery, Collards, Leaf lettuce, Turnips, Carrots, Radishes, Parsley

celery[+], **Chinese cabbage, collards, eggplant**[++], **English** and **snow peas, Irish potatoes**[+++], **kale, kohlrabi, leeks**[+], **lettuce, mustard, onions**[+], **peppers**[++], **radish, rutabaga, snow peas, shallots**[+], **spinach, Swiss chard, tomatoes**[++], and **turnips.** Plant **onions** and **English/sweet peas** in zone 7 during January. Plant other listed vegetables during February or follow suggested dates as indicated in the planting chart on page 234–235.

[+]Use sets, or transplants.
[++]Plant seeds in hotbeds or greenhouses.
[+++]Plant seed pieces.

Planting

Some vegetables can be direct-seeded in the garden this month. January weather is frequently rainy. Do not work vegetable beds when the soil is wet, as it will destroy the structure of the soil. Remember to incorporate generous amounts of organic matter into beds before planting. Use transplants of **celery,** as it is too late to seed this long-growing crop. Transplants of **bulbing onions, bunching onions,** and **shallots** may still be planted. **Irish potatoes** are planted from tubers cut into egg-sized pieces, each containing at least one "eye." These are allowed to air-dry for a few days after cutting but before planting, and are known as "seed pieces." Plant in late January in zones 8 and 9 and mid-February in zone 7.

Producing your own transplants of **tomatoes, peppers,** and **eggplants** is a bit tricky, so it's good to know that nurseries will have them available in spring. If you want to grow your own, providing sufficient bright light is the biggest challenge. Indoor light setups have been known to work when producing transplants.

1 Suspend a 48-inch fluorescent light fixture by adjustable chains on hooks over a table in an area where temperatures can be maintained above 55 degrees Fahrenheit.

2 *Sow* seeds in peat pots filled with a damp soilless mix.

3 When the seeds begin to germinate, adjust the light fixture so that the tubes are about 2 inches over the seedlings. As the seedlings grow, gradually raise the light fixture so that it remains at 2 inches above the tops of the seedlings.

4 *Water* as needed to maintain moist but not wet soil.

5 Using a high-middle-number water-soluble fertilizer at half the recommended strength once a week often works well. *In about six to eight weeks the transplants will be ready for your garden.*

Care for Your Vegetables and Herbs

Cool-season vegetables and herbs must be able to tolerate freezing temperatures in order to grow at this time of year. Still, newly emerged seedlings and some vegetables can be susceptible to cold. Place a sheet or tarp over young and newly germinated vegetable seedlings if temperatures lower than the upper 20s are predicted. Harvest any **broccoli, cauliflower, snow peas,** and **lettuce** that are ready if temperatures in the mid-20s are predicted.

Watering

Dry weather is possible but unlikely this time of the year. Keep beds mulched as plants increase in height. Add mulch to a depth of 3 to 4 inches. Other than watering newly planted transplants and seeded beds, additional irrigation is not necessary.

Fertilizing

Depending on when you last fertilized garden vegetables, you may need to sidedress some of them. Many of the cool-season crops such as **broccoli, cabbage, cauliflower, collards,** and other greens are heavy feeders and need a constant supply of nutrients to do their best. Sidedressing means fertilizing vegetables while they are growing.

Sidedress large vegetables like **cabbage** and **broccoli** with a teaspoon of complete fertilizer placed a couple of inches from the base of each plant. Rows of vegetables can be fertilized with about a cup per 10 feet of planting row, and those in beds with about a cup per 30 square feet. Check the package for specific amounts. The analysis 15:5:10 works well for most vegetables grown in Texas. To fine-tune fertilizing needs, have your soil tested. Contact your County Agent's office or the testing lab at Stephen F. Austin State University in Nacogdoches.

Pest Control

Caterpillars, aphids, snails, and slugs may be active if the weather is mild. Control pests when needed with label-approved aids. Refer to page 291 for a summary listing your options. Winter weeds will grow on warm, sunny days. Pull them up promptly and keep gardens well mulched. Pests are usually more active as the temperatures warm. So, this month they are more active in zones 8 and 9 than in zones 6 or 7.

Planning

Springtime planting is upon us, and it's time to decide what to grow, how much to plant, and where everything will go. Remember last year? Did you have so many **cucumbers** you couldn't give them away? Plant fewer this year. Unless your memory is a lot better than most folks', it's important to keep at least a few simple notes each season to refer back to in your Texas gardening journal.

When deciding on the quantity and location of cool-season vegetables, don't forget that lots of warm-season vegetables will be going in next month in zones 8 and 9, and in zones 6 and 7 during April. Some of the cool-season vegetables such as **carrots, cabbage,** and **Irish potatoes** will not mature until late April or May. Keep this in mind, and don't use up too many beds or you will have little or no room to plant next month. Review pages 234–235 for average days of maturity.

Vegetables to plant in February include **beets, broccoli+, cabbage+, carrots, cauliflower+, collards, corn++, Swiss chard, eggplant+++, Irish potatoes+, kohlrabi, lettuce, mustard, peppers+++, radish, rutabagas, snap beans++, shallots, tomatoes+++,** and **turnips.**

+Plant transplants or seed pieces.
++Plant in late February in south Texas in zone 9.
+++Sow seeds in hotbeds or greenhouses.

Planting

February can be intensely cold or remarkably mild. This month separates the gamblers from the more conservative gardeners. In south Texas, usually in zones 8b and 9, a few brave souls will set out early **tomato** transplants in late February, preparing to protect them should a frost threaten.

Early planting of vegetables has more benefits than just beating out everybody else on the block with the first harvest. Early plantings often have fewer insect and disease problems. **Corn** planted in late February and early March will have very few earworms. In zones 8b and 9, plant around the third week of March. Plant through April in zones 6, 7, and 8a.

Finish planting most cool-season vegetables this month, especially in zones 8 and 9. A few gardeners may choose to plant fast-maturing vegetables such as **radish** or **lettuce** into early March. When it comes to planting lettuces, leaf and semi-heading varieties are much more reliable that head types. Some varieties are less likely to turn bitter as the weather heats up. Try romaine types: 'Paris Island Cos', 'Romaine', and 'Valmaine', to name a few.

Care for Your Vegetables and Herbs

Clumps of **shallots** and **bunching onions** planted in fall can be dug up and divided for harvest this month. Lift out the entire clump and divide it in half. Replant one half, and keep the other for harvest. The replanted part will grow until June when it will be lifted and dried, and the small bulbs will be stored for planting next fall.

When **cauliflower** heads are about the size of a silver dollar, pull the leaves over the center of the plant and fasten them together with a clothespin. This process is called *blanching.* Shading the head from light will cause it to come out creamy white. Check every few days to see if it is ready to harvest. Several of the newer cultivars are self-blanching and do not require the use of this technique. Two good cauliflower varieties for Texas gardens are 'Snow Crown' and 'Snowball'.

Watering

Don't forget that newly seeded beds may need watering just about every day until the seeds come up. It is easy to forget that cool weather can be dry. Newly planted transplants need some extra coddling the first couple of weeks after planting. It is generally a good idea to water them in initially with a water-soluble fertilizer or root stimulator. Use a watering can for individual plants or a hose-end applicator for larger areas. Most cool-season vegetables need an even supply of moisture for best production. Make sure they do not become drought stressed between rains, and apply water as needed. Don't irrigate on any preset schedule.

Harvesting Herbs and Vegetables

Many herbs produce in winter in zones 8 and 9 and some in zone 7. Harvest individual lower leaves from **parsley, cilantro, arugula, chervil,** and **dill.** Herbs such as **bay, rosemary, thyme, sage, oregano,** and various **mints** can also be harvested, especially if the winter has been mild.

When just the lower leaves of leafy vegetables are regularly harvested, this is called "cropping." The method allows regular harvest while allowing the plant to continue to produce. Cropping works great on **collards, Swiss chard, leaf lettuce, mustard, turnip greens,** non-heading **Chinese cabbage, spinach,** and **kale.** Harvest **snow peas** frequently, while the pods are still flat and the seeds have not yet developed; mid-February is your last chance to plant them in zones 8 and 9 and March 1 in zone 7. Try planting some edible podded peas such as 'Sugar Snap', 'Sugar Ann', and 'Sugar Bon' as well.

Enter notes in your Texas gardening journal on which dates you fertilized, how much was applied, the fertilizer analysis, and where it was purchased.

Fertilizing

Tender, succulent foliage is what we want from greens such as **mustard, Chinese cabbage, kale, collards, turnips,** and **spinach.** Applications of fertilizers containing nitrogen will encourage lush, tender growth that is best for eating. Fertilizers with a 15:5:10 or other 3:1:2 ratio work well in our vegetable gardens. Apply according to label directions.

Pest Control

Holes in vegetable leaves may mean caterpillar or snail and slug activity. If you see small dark-green or black pellets on the foliage, the culprits are likely to be caterpillars. Silvery trails on the leaves indicate snails or slugs have been there. If in doubt, one discovery method is to put out a beer trap. Place a plastic bowl in the soil up to its rim near the plants and fill half full with beer. Snails and slugs will crawl into the beer and not be able to crawl out. They are not after the alcohol—it is the smell of the yeast that attracts them. If you catch a lot of snails and slugs in the trap, you have a problem with these pests—continue to put out traps, or apply bait to the area. If you don't catch any or catch just a few, your problem is probably caterpillars. Caterpillars may be controlled by handpicking them or using various control aids available at local retailers. Refer to page 291 for a summary listing your options.

Planning

The time for procrastination is over—decisions need to be made for your spring vegetable garden. Over the next six weeks all of the many vegetables that we rely on for early- to midsummer production should be planted either by direct-seeding or transplanting into the garden. If you have been meaning to purchase this year's All-America Selections winners or some unusual or delicious new variety, do so immediately. Remember, it is too late to start seeds for **tomatoes** and **bell peppers** for spring planting. Check at local nurseries to see what transplants they are carrying. Feed-and-seed stores often sell vegetable seeds in bulk. The price is lower than purchasing seeds in packets, which is especially good for larger gardens. The varieties carried are generally based on best locally recommended varieties.

Live oaks around the state drop lots of leaves in February and March. Gather them up, store in bags or bins, and use them to mulch the garden.

Vegetables to plant in March for zones 8 and 9 include **collards, kohlrabi**[+]**, lima beans, mustard, radish, snap beans,** and **Swiss chard.** Plant **cantaloupe, corn, cucumbers, eggplant**[+]**, peppers**[+]**, pumpkin, Southern peas, summer squash, tomatoes**[+]**, water-**melons, and **winter squash** in late March to early April in zone 7, and mid-April in zone 6.

[+]Plant transplants.

This is an excellent month to make entries in your Texas gardening journal. It's a very active month for gardening in Texas.

Planting

There are three ways to plant seeds directly into the garden (this is called "direct-seeding").

Drilling: Seeds are planted in straight lines at the proper depth, but two to three times closer than the plants will ultimately be spaced. If more than one row will be planted in a bed, space the rows at least twice as far apart as the recommended spacing (if the vegetables will be spaced 12 inches apart in the rows, the rows should be at least 24 inches apart). When the seeds come up, thin (pinch off at ground level or roll out) the extras, leaving behind seedlings at the proper spacing. This technique is good if you don't know what the seedlings of the vegetable you are planting look like. The vegetables are in the rows—the weeds are in between.

Broadcasting: Seeds are scattered evenly over a bed area and covered to the proper depth. Two to three times as many seeds are planted as actual plants that will be needed. When the seedlings come up, the extras are thinned out so that the remaining plants are at the proper spacing. This technique is popular with smaller-growing vegetables such as **carrots, radishes,** and **beets,** and greens such as **lettuce** and **mustard.**

Hills: A few vegetables are sometimes planted in hills—raised mounds planted with several seeds per hill. **Watermelons, cucumbers, pumpkins,** and **squash** are some of the vegetables gardeners may plant in hills. **Note:** Learn to recognize the difference between vegetable seedlings and weeds coming up in your plantings.

Care for Your Vegetables and Herbs

If you plant super-sweet **corn** varieties (noted on the seed package or in the vegetable description), they must be isolated from any regular sweet corn you plant. Cross-pollination will reduce the quality of the super-sweet variety. **Corn** is wind-pollinated. To improve pollination, plant corn seeds in several side-by-side short rows rather than one long row.

Transplants purchased in nurseries have been grown in greenhouses and have led a very sheltered, pampered life. Planting them into the real world of the vegetable garden can be a bit traumatic. Hardening off transplants prior to planting helps them deal with the change. It takes about a week. Place the transplants in a partial-sun location for a few days. Allow them to wilt very slightly before watering. Move into full sun for a few days and continue to water as needed, then plant into the garden.

Here's an alternative: When planting transplants, you may prune off a leafy twig from a nearby tree or shrub, and stick it into the ground on the south side of the transplant in order to shade it. The twig should be slightly larger than the transplant. Over the next few days, the leaves on the twig would gradually wilt and wither away, slowly exposing the transplant to more sun. Try to plant transplants on a cloudy day when rain is predicted.

Watering

Newly seeded beds and planted transplants need attention to watering if the weather is sunny and dry. Seedbeds should be watered lightly perhaps every day. Established vegetables need thorough, deep watering as needed during dry weather. Mulch around vegetable plants to conserve moisture in the soil. Remember, warmer temperatures usually mean more watering. However, water only if needed.

Fertilizing

Blend fertilizer into garden beds, along with organic matter, when preparing them for planting. Applying long-lasting slow-release granular fertilizers with each transplant supplies nutrition for the entire season. Water-in newly planted transplants with a fertilizer solution mixed at half strength with water or a root stimulator according to label directions. Sidedress established vegetables to keep them growing vigorously.

Pest Control

As the weather warms up, so does the activity of various pests. Newly-set transplants may be cut off at ground level by a caterpillar called (appropriately enough) the cutworm. Place a 2- to 3-inch piece of cardboard tubing from a paper towel or bathroom tissue roll around the base of the transplant to prevent damage. You may elect to treat **onions, garlic, shallots,** and **leeks** with pest-control aids for thrips if they become a problem. Refer to page 291 for a summary listing your options.

Harvesting Root Crops

Harvest root crops before the roots become too large and tough. Harvest the following vegetables when the top of the root is the appropriate diameter: **radish–1"; carrot–1"; turnip–2"; beet–3"; rutabaga–3"** to **4"**. Brush away the soil on top of the root if necessary to see the size. Harvest **broccoli** when the largest flower buds in the head are the size of the head of a kitchen match. Crop leafy vegetables regularly. Harvest the lower leaves first.

Planning

Even the best-laid plans leave room for spontaneity and change. All of the warm-season vegetables can continue to be planted this month. Cool-season vegetables still growing in the garden should be finished in April, or at least by May in zone 6. Make plans now for which warm-season vegetables you will plant in those areas.

Vegetables to plant statewide in April include **cantaloupe, collards, corn, cucumber, cushaw, eggplant+, honeydew, lima beans, luffa, Malabar spinach, okra, peppers+, pumpkin, snap beans, Southern peas, squashes, sweet potato** (rooted cuttings known as "slips"), **Swiss chard, tomato+,** and **watermelon.**

+Plant transplants.

Don't forget to make entries in your Texas gardening journal. Be sure to include information on temperatures, rainfall, wind, insects and diseases, as well as information on what was harvested, planted, fertilized, and watered.

Planting

Nurseries sell transplants of **cucumbers** and **squash** in cell-packs. The plants are often rootbound by the time you purchase and plant them, resulting in stunted, unproductive plants. It is easier and more productive to direct-seed these plants into the garden. Grow **cucumbers** on sturdy trellises that are at least 4 feet tall for increased production, better-quality fruit, and saved space in the garden.

Do not delay planting many of the warm-season vegetables beyond this month. **Tomatoes, snap beans, lima beans,** and **bell peppers** all set fruit poorly when temperatures are hot. **Squashes** and **corn** are both far more likely to have major insect and disease problems when planted later. Herbs to plant include **basil, perilla, sesame, lemon balm, mints,** and **rosemary** as day- and nighttime temperatures reach into the 70s or more.

Care for Your Vegetables and Herbs

Tomatoes are staked or caged to keep the plants from sprawling on the ground, where the fruit would be more likely to rot. When staking, wait for the first cluster of flowers to appear, and place the stake on the opposite side of the plant's stem. All the flower clusters will grow from the same side of the stem, and this will keep developing fruit from getting caught between the stake and the stem. Train **tomatoes** to one or two main shoots by pinching off the side shoots or "suckers" that appear where leaves join the stem. Do not desucker bush-type tomatoes such as 'Patio', 'Celebrity', and 'Better Bush'.

As mentioned, **tomatoes** may also be grown in cages. The plants can grow quite large (5 to 6 feet is not unusual), and unfortunately the small commercially available tomato cages are usually inadequate. Here's a better solution:

- Purchase concrete reinforcing wire available at building supply stores—you'll need about 5 feet for each tomato plant.

- *Cut* into sections about 5 feet long, using heavy wire cutters.

- *Form* the pieces into cylinders and *fasten* their cut ends together.

- Place the cages over the tomato plants, pushing them into the ground.

- This activity results in cages which are 5 ft. tall and approximately 18 in. across. They are ideal for growing tomatoes and the fruit is easy to harvest.

Tomatoes grown in cages are generally not desuckered.

Watering

Vegetable and herb gardeners who grow plants in containers need to pay careful attention to proper watering. Containers dry out faster than you may realize, and the results of even one severe wilting can be disastrous. The need to check daily is not unusual, especially as the season progresses, when temperatures are higher and plant roots fill the container. They may also need watering daily, but check before watering.

Watering plants in containers by hand is common and effective, but for plants growing in the ground, this is largely ineffective during very dry weather. When watering by hand, water is applied rapidly over a short period of time—the result is shallow water penetration and shallow roots. It's better to water thoroughly and deeply using soaker hoses or sprinklers, which apply water slowly over a relatively long period of time. Vegetable gardens need about 1 to 2 inches of water per week. If there's not enough water from rain, it's up to us to supply it.

Fertilizing

Vegetables planted last month and this month have a good supply of nutrients from the fertil-izer incorporated into the bed during preparation, or from individual applications at planting time with granular slow-release types. Sidedress cool-season vegetables about six weeks after transplanting, and every six weeks thereafter if slow-release fertilizers aren't used. Generally, a high-nitrogen fertilizer such as 15-5-10 works well in Texas gardens.

Harvesting Cool-Season Herbs and Leafy Vegetables

Cool-season herbs and those that thrive during mild weather (such as **parsley, dill, tarragon, thyme, sage, cilantro, borage, lavender, chamomile, chervil,** and **arugula**) are at their peak this month for zones 8 and 9 and will be in May for zones 6 and 7. They will begin to decline toward late May and finish in early June. Harvest them generously over the next six to eight weeks. Any extra can be dried or frozen for use during the summer.

Pest Control

Mild winters in Texas do little to curb the populations of insect pests. Inspect vegetables regularly for signs of damage, and monitor population levels carefully. For those of you trying to minimize the use of pest-control aids, it's generally not necessary to apply them at the first sign of damage. If populations begin to rapidly increase, however, or if the damage reaches unacceptable levels, prompt action may be necessary.

It is important to identify the insect causing the damage. Gardeners sometimes spray their plants after seeing insects only to discover later that these were beneficial predators and there wasn't any need to spray at all.

If you have had disease problems in the past, you may choose to spray some vegetables once a week with a disease-control aid to prevent devastating outbreaks. **Squash, cucumbers, tomatoes,** and **beans** are susceptible to a wide variety of fungal diseases. Visits to local retail nurseries will help you become familiar with the many types of disease-control aids available. Refer to page 291 for a summary listing your options. Always apply according to label directions. Rotating crops and planting only disease-resistant varieties also greatly helps to prevent problems.

Keep vegetable beds weeded and mulched. The mulch should be at least 3 to 4 inches thick.

Planning

Most of the cool-season vegetables still lingering in the garden will be cleared out this month. If you haven't thought about what you want to plant in their place, now is the time to decide. Focus on planting those vegetables that will thrive and produce in the intense heat of June, July, and August. Plant only heat-tolerant/resistant varieties.

May is one of the most productive months in the Texas vegetable garden. If you haven't started keeping records, make it a point to start a Texas gardening journal and jot down some observations. It may be an interesting challenge to get into the habit of keeping records, but you will be glad you did later on.

Vegetables to plant in May include **collards, eggplant, peppers, luffa, okra, peanut, pumpkin, Southern peas, squash, sweet potato** (use slips), heat-tolerant **tomatoes** (seed for transplants), **cantaloupe,** and **watermelon.** Due to heat and pest problems, **corn, cucumber, lima bean, snap bean,** and **Swiss chard** are generally not as productive when planted this late except in zone 6.

Planting

As cool-season crops go out of production and are removed, rework beds and plant heat-tolerant vegetables for production during the summer.

Luffa is an edible gourd that is highly recommended for home gardeners. Some of us first encounter it under the name **"climbing okra,"** and it does require a trellis to climb on. It is related to **cucumbers** and **squash,** but the fruit, when sliced, breaded, and fried, tastes remarkably like fried okra. The vine stays healthy all summer with no spraying, and produces quantities of large, attractive yellow flowers. The fruit should be harvested for eating when about 1 inch in diameter and about 8 inches long. Leave some of the gourds on the vines until they turn brown and rattle when shaken. When the outer skin is pulled off, the inner fibrous "sponge" is revealed. Beautiful flowers, edible fruit, and useful luffa sponges—what more could you ask from a vine that may be grown statewide in Texas?

Watering

Dry, hot weather is not unusual in May. Drought-stressed vegetables may drop flowers and young fruit, and are more susceptible to pest damage. Vegetable gardens need 1 to 2 inches of water per week, and when rain is insufficient, you must make up the difference. To calculate the time it takes your sprinkler to apply an inch of water, place several cans in open areas of the garden. Check the time and turn on the sprinkler. When an inch of water has accumulated in the cans, check the time again. That's how long it takes your sprinkler to apply an inch of water. Make notes of this in your Texas gardening journal.

"Sweating" types of soaker hoses are excellent to use because they keep water off the foliage. This is helpful both in preventing diseases and in slowing their spread. Leave the soaker hose on long enough for it to water the bed thoroughly. After it has been on for 30 minutes, dig into the area several inches out from the hose and see how far the water has penetrated. Continue to apply water until the soil is moist down to 6 to 8 inches.

Fertilizing

If you used standard types of granular fertilizer, it is time to sidedress vegetables planted in March if you haven't already done so. If you used slow-release granular fertilizer, no additional fertilizer is needed. As a rule of thumb, **tomatoes, peppers, eggplant,** and **squash** are sidedressed when they set their first fruit. **Cucumbers, watermelons, cantaloupes,** and **winter squash** are sidedressed when they begin to run. **Beans, peas,** and other legumes are not commonly sidedressed. Choose a fertilizer rich in nitrogen such as 15-5-10 or a 3:2:1 ratio fertilizer, and follow package directions.

Pest Control

Pest problems become worse this month. When using any pest-control aid, read and follow label directions carefully.

Look for beetles such as bean beetles, cucumber beetles, and flea beetles. All of them chew the leaves of a wide variety of vegetables.

Caterpillars will feed on both the foliage and fruit of vegetables. The tomato fruitworm eats holes in fruit. Birds peck holes in **tomatoes** just when they become ripe enough

Harvest Your Vegetables

Harvest **bell peppers** when they reach full size but are still green. You may leave them on the plant until they turn red, but this runs the risk of fruit rot. Harvest **tomatoes** anytime after they begin to turn pink to get them out of harm's way. Ripen at room temperature. They do not need light to ripen, so there is no need to put them in a window. Harvest **snap beans** when pods are the diameter of a pencil. Pick frequently. **Squash** and **cucumber** produce prolifically and need to be harvested almost daily. Their fruit is harvested immature, so don't let them get too big before you pick them. To see if **sweet corn** is ready to harvest, pull back the shuck partway. Puncture a kernel with your thumbnail. If the juice is clear, leave it for a few more days; if the juice is milky, it's time to harvest; and if there is no juice, it is too old. Dig up **Irish potatoes** in late May through June when the tops have turned mostly yellow. Save the smallest potatoes to use in planting a fall crop.

to harvest. If birds are a problem, cover your plants with bird netting, or harvest the fruit in the pink stage and ripen them inside.

Another caterpillar, the squash vine borer, is very destructive to **squash** and **pumpkins** planted in the summer.

Stinkbugs damage **tomatoes** and **okra,** causing spotted tomatoes and curled okra pods. Controlling these green or brown shovel-blade-shaped insects is difficult. Visit local retail nurseries for assistance in selecting an insect-control aid which will help you obtain your goal.

Diseases really take off, especially when weather is rainy. Prompt and regular (every five to seven days) use of fungus-control aids available at local retail nurseries will help control common diseases such as powdery mildew on **squash** and **cucumbers,** rust on **beans,** fruit rot on **tomatoes, eggplant,** and **squash,** and the many leaf diseases that attack tomatoes. Refer to page 291 for a summary listing your pest- and disease-control aids. Apply according to label directions.

Planning

Vegetables such as **snap beans, corn, cucumbers,** *and* **squash** *that were planted back in March through April will finish up this month.* Plan on planting heat-tolerant vegetables to take their place. If you don't need the space right away, or prefer to reduce the size of the garden in the summer heat, mulch empty beds heavily with 6 inches of leaves, grass clippings, pine straw, or other available materials.

Vegetables to plant in June include **cantaloupe, collards, eggplant, luffa, okra, peanuts, peppers, pumpkin, Southern peas, sweet potato** (slips), **Swiss chard,** and **watermelons.** Although **squash** and **cucumbers** can be planted in June and July, production is difficult in midsummer due to pest problems. In late June you can plant transplants of **tomatoes, bell peppers,** and **eggplant** for producing a fall garden.

Continue to keep records and make notes on the performance of your vegetables in your Texas gardening journal. This is a good month to evaluate whether or not early-summer crops lived up to your expectations. Note which varieties did best, which pests were a problem, and what you did to correct the situation. It is also a good idea to add comments on how your relatives', friends', or neighbors' gardens did. They might have grown a vegetable or variety that you want to try next year.

Planting

Transplants of **eggplants, peppers,** and **tomatoes** may be planted this month. Oriental-type **eggplants,** which produce a long, narrow fruit, are often more productive during high temperatures. Many gardeners consider green-fruited **eggplants** less bitter during mid- to late-summer heat. Though **bell peppers** may be less productive due to high temperatures, some small-fruited **sweet peppers** such as 'Banana' or 'Gypsy' are quite productive now. **Hot peppers** are often productive as well as ornamental in the garden and landscape.

You can also plant seeds for fall transplants in late June. It may be easier to raise your own transplants for fall planting because the transplants can be grown outside. Spring transplants must be started early in the year inside a protected location such as a greenhouse or hotbed, or indoors under lights. Plant seeds in cell-packs, peat pots, or any small container, using a soilless mix. Keep evenly moist until the seeds come up; then make sure the seedlings receive sun for most of the day (some afternoon shade is beneficial). Transplants will be ready to go into the garden about six weeks after seeds are planted. We often set out **tomatoes, pepper,** and **eggplants** in late June to early July. So when starting these from seed, allow six weeks minimum to produce transplants. Some seed should then be started sometime in May.

Care for Your Vegetables and Herbs

Mulches are especially important in midsummer. They shade the soil and keep it cooler, in addition to controlling weeds and conserving moisture. A cooler soil is healthier for vegetable roots.

By now most **tomatoes** have already set their main crop. High temperatures interfere with pollination, so don't be surprised if most of the flowers fall off without setting fruit—it's just that time of year. This is why we want to plant heat-tolerant varieties such as 'Porter' so production will continue.

Herbs that do not like the heat are suffering now. Do your best, but there is not much you can do to moderate the effects of heat. Herbs in containers can be moved into slightly shadier locations. Keep herbs somewhat on the dry side to minimize root rot. Regularly harvest herbs such as **basil, perilla, sesame, rosemary, lemon balm, bay, lemongrass, Mexican tarragon, Mexican oregano, garlic chives,** and **mints,** along with others that stay productive during the summer.

Watering

Continue to monitor rainfall amounts. Summer weather patterns in June, July, and August often bring frequent afternoon rains in coastal areas. In the remainder of Texas we are often warm to hot and dry. Water in the early morning if possible. Do not be fooled by quick light showers that do little to thoroughly water the garden. On the other hand, several inches of rain can fall in a day or two. That's when the wisdom of growing vegetables on raised beds or raised rows becomes clear.

Fertilizing

It often does little good to fertilize vegetables toward the end of their productive season. Side-dress only vigorously growing vegetables that will continue to produce for a long period of time.

Vegetables and herbs growing heartily in containers should be fertilized according to label directions with a water-soluble fertilizer. You can choose a slow-release product instead, and apply it once at the beginning of the growing season.

Pest Control

Populations of leaf miners may have gotten to high levels by this time. These tiny insect larvae feed inside vegetable leaves, leaving behind white meandering lines. A few lines in a leaf are not too damaging, but when most of the leaves have numerous lines, the damage can affect the harvest. Control is difficult since the pest dwells inside the leaf. Regular applications of insect pest-control aids will help control the adult stage and reduce the number of larvae in the leaves. Refer to page 291 for a summary listing your options.

Aphids may be a particular problem on **Southern peas** and may also attack **eggplants, tomatoes, peppers,** and other vegetables. Insect-control aids are available at local nurseries and other retailers. Watch for and welcome ladybugs, one of our best predators of aphids. Keeping plants healthy and growing vigorously will help them overcome damage from insect pests and fend off diseases.

Helpful Hints

Try to do most of your vegetable gardening in the early morning or late afternoon to avoid the worst of the heat. Since vegetable gardens must be located in a sunny area, there will be no shade to help. Don't forget–**you** need generous amounts of water in the heat, just like your vegetables.

Hurricane season runs from June to the end of October. Should a hurricane head your way, harvest all the vegetables that are even close to the right stage and get them out of harm's way. Floodwaters could contaminate any vegetables left in the garden, or high winds may blow them away. Put away anything that might blow around in high winds, such as tomato cages, tools, and other loose items. They become deadly projectiles when winds reach 70 to 100 miles per hour. This is especially true of our coastal areas. Take similar action prior to any severe storm if time permits. Think **safety first.**

Planning

"Dreaming" might be a better term for this month than planning. We are all dreaming of cooler weather, but it's still a long way off. In the meantime, our thoughts should be on fall gardens and, believe it or not, cool-season vegetables, too. Seeds for cole crops such as **cabbage, broccoli,** and **cauliflower** can be planted this month to produce transplants. Check over the garden and decide if there will be room to plant them in late August through September when they are ready. If not, decide when space will become available and plan on growing transplants for planting at that time. There will be about six weeks between planting seeds and finished transplants.

Start visiting your local retailers and looking through seed catalogs to make decisions about what to grow in the fall garden. Try some new varieties of **lettuce.** Purchase seed locally or get your orders off this month and in August so you will have seeds in plenty of time for the fall planting season.

Vegetables to plant in July are **broccoli**[+], **brussels sprouts**[+], **cabbage**[+], **cantaloupe, Chinese cabbage**[+], **cauliflower**[+], **collards, cucumbers, luffa, okra, peppers, pumpkins, Southern peas, shallots, squash, tomatoes,** and **watermelons.**

[+]Plant seeds for transplants.

Don't forget to note in your Texas gardening journal which plants/varieties did well and which were poor. Also note temperatures, rainfall, storms, and insect and disease problems as well as planting dates.

Planting

Most Texas gardeners don't plant much in the vegetable garden in July. It's hard enough to get out in the heat to take care of and harvest what we already have. If you can brave the heat, however, there is always something that can be planted.

Plant **pumpkin** seeds this month for Halloween jack-o-lanterns. (The squash vine borer can be very destructive to **pumpkins** and **squash** planted at this time of the year. The borer is a grublike caterpillar that burrows into the stem and hollows it out, causing the plant to wilt and die. If you have had major problems with these insects in the past, treat plants regularly with label-approved insect-control aids.) Refer to page 291 for a summary listing your options.

This is the last month to plant such heat-loving vegetables as **okra, peanuts, luffa,** and, in south Texas, **sweet potato** slips. They should all be planted within the first week of the month.

Shallot and **bunching onion** sets may also be planted. South Texas gardeners tend to call similar plants **shallots,** even **bunching onions** and **green onions** (more properly called **scallions**). **Shallots** are actually a different plant altogether, but in the green stage they all pretty much look and taste the same. Plant "sets" that you saved from your spring crop. You may be able to harvest some as early as October, and then continue to harvest regularly through the winter.

Plant seeds to produce transplants of fall **broccoli, cauliflower,** and additional cole crops, plus others in cell-packs, peat pots, or any small container, using a soilless mix. Keep evenly moist until the seeds germinate, and provide the seedlings with direct sun about six hours a day. Fertilize once a week with an all-purpose soluble fertilizer, high in the middle number, mixed at half strength. These vegetables may also be direct-seeded into the garden, but transplants tend to be more reliable. If you don't want to deal with growing transplants yourself, local nurseries should have transplants of these vegetables available in August through September.

Care for Your Vegetables and Herbs

Continue to harvest vegetables in the garden frequently and regularly. Hot weather causes vegetables to mature rapidly, and it's not unusual to find a giant **zucchini** lurking under the foliage. Remove and discard overly large vegetables to keep the plants productive. **Okra** should be checked every day as pods rapidly become overmature and tough.

Never leave rotten or diseased vegetables in the vegetable garden. They can serve as a continuing source of disease infection.

Watering

Provide at least 1 inch of water for the garden each week if rainfall is scarce. A 3- to 4-inch layer of mulch will reduce the wide variations in moisture content that may occur. Drought-stressed vegetables are more susceptible to such pests as spider mites and whiteflies. When water is applied, do so deeply and thoroughly. Check container-grown vegetables daily and water as needed.

Fertilizing

Tomatoes, peppers, and **eggplants** planted in early summer will often revive and produce well in the fall if kept in vigorous growth. Sidedress them every six weeks and you will be amazed at how productive they can be in September, October, and early November. Always apply fertilizers according to label directions. Slow-release granular fertilizers often are applied only one time per growing season. 15-5-10 or other 3:1:2 ratio fertilizers often work well when growing vegetable in Texas.

If you haven't had your soil tested in two years (or have never had it tested), consider contacting your county office of the Texas Cooperative Extension Service or the soil-testing lab at Stephen F. Austin State University. You can get a soil test done by both for a modest fee.

Pest Control

Keep up with weeds. Weeding in 95-degree-Fahrenheit weather is no fun, so keep beds mulched 3 to 4 inches deep to minimize problems. Maintaining weed-free beds is one of the greatest labor demands of the vegetable garden, and it is not uncommon to see weedy, overgrown gardens this time of year. This is the main reason for not creating a vegetable garden larger than you can practically handle. Next March, when you are contemplating enlarging the garden during the delightfully cool weather, remember what it was like weeding the garden in July, August, and September. Note weed problems in your Texas gardening journal. This information may be used next year to prevent weeds from becoming a problem during our "blast furnace" heat of July, August, and often into September each year.

The hope is that your vegetables escaped any disastrous pest outbreaks this season. Know that sooner or later almost every gardener has gardening disappointments. Don't let them get you down—there is always the next season. And in July, we still have time to successfully produce crops this season.

Maintain regular surveillance of your garden for signs of insect or disease problems. Get help diagnosing problems from knowledgeable gardening friends, references, local County Agents, Master Gardeners, and your local nurseries with the Extension Service, or the staff at local public gardens. Whenever a pest-control aid is recommended, ask if a control you have on hand will achieve your goal. We shouldn't buy more needlessly. Remember, always read and follow label directions when using any pest-control aid. Refer to page 291 for a summary listing your options.

Planning

Even though it continues to be hot, we need to make plans for the fall garden when weather will, at last, be cooler. Some cool-season vegetables can begin to be planted into gardens. Visit area nurseries to find out what vegetable transplants they have or will have. Check out available seeds while you're at it. Send off orders from seed catalogs, if local retailers don't have what you want, so the shipment will arrive in plenty of time for the right planting date. Cool-season planting begins in earnest next month.

The days are becoming noticeably shorter, and the fewer hours of sun relieve a little of the stress on plants in the garden. Take time to jot down some observations in your Texas gardening journal on how your garden did during the summer. Gardening is a learning experience, and the more you remember and learn from past efforts, the more successful you will be in the future. Your gardening journal notes and entries will be valuable for planning next season's garden and will help ensure planting success.

Vegetables to plant in August include **broccoli, brussels sprouts, bunching onions**[++], **cabbage, cauliflower, Swiss chard, Chinese cabbage, collards, cucumbers**[*], **lima beans**[*], **mustard, snap beans**[*], **Southern peas**[*], **peppers**[*+], **Irish potatoes**[+++], **rutabagas, shallots**[++], **squashes**[*], **tomatoes**[*+], and **turnips.**

[+]Plant transplants.
[++]Plant sets.
[+++]Plant small, whole potatoes saved from the spring crop.
[*]Production from harvests may be limited in zones 6 and 7 due to earlier frosts than in zones 8 and 9. These vegetables do better when planted in July.

Planting

Irish potatoes can be planted using small, whole potatoes saved from the spring crop. Warm soils in late summer are full of active fungi, and cut seed pieces are likely to rot if used. Some gardeners have success direct-seeding cole crops such as **broccoli, brussels sprouts, cabbage,** and **cauliflower.** Many gardeners either raise their own transplants or purchase them, finding this method is more reliable than direct-seeding.

Choose bush varieties of **snap beans** ('Provider', 'Top Crop', 'Derby') and **lima beans** ('Henderson Bush', 'Jackson Wonder', 'Baby Fordhook'), as they tend to be more productive in the fall garden. **Snap beans** are so easy and productive that every gardener should plant a few rows if you enjoy these vegetables.

Transplant **tomatoes** and **peppers** by mid-August in zones 8b and 9. In zones 6, 7, and 8a, they should be planted the last week of June or by July 4. **Tomatoes, peppers,** and **eggplants** from the spring planting can be left for fall production if they are healthy. Most **tomatoes** are not worth keeping, but **peppers** and **eggplants** can stay remarkably productive. Heat-resistant **tomatoes** such as 'Porter' continue to produce all summer and through fall until the first killing freeze/frost arrives.

Care for Your Vegetables and Herbs

When a crop is finished, pull it up promptly and throw it in your compost pile. If you don't have anything to plant in the area, mulch with 4 to 6 inches of leaves, grass clippings, pine straw, or other materials you have on hand. Old crops left in place look untidy, allow weeds to grow, and may harbor insects or diseases since they tend to be ignored. **Note:** If your **tomatoes** have southern blight, *do not* compost the dead plants.

Don't forget to harvest your herbs regularly. If you get too high a yield, you can easily dry the extras for later use. Here's how:

- Harvest so that stems are long enough to tie together easily.

- *Rinse* the herbs and *blot* them dry.

- Make small bundles of three to five stems, held together with rubber bands, and insert an unbent paper clip or S-shaped piece of wire for a hook.

- *Hang* the bundles in a cool, dry location indoors with good air circulation.

  In about two weeks, when the leaves are crispy-dry, crumble the herbs and store them in a tightly sealed, labeled container.

Watering

Will it rain today? Gardeners often delay watering if there is a chance it will rain. Days can go by with no rain, and significant damage can occur while the garden waits. If plants need water, don't wait for possible rain. If you water and it rains later, no harm is done, other than using some water and effort. Continue to water regularly as needed.

Water newly planted seeds and transplants more frequently than you do established vegetable plants. Do not water on preset schedules. Do water thoroughly when needed.

Fertilizing

You may incorporate fertilizer when preparing beds for new plantings. Use about one cup of a general-purpose fertilizer like 15-5-10 per 30 square feet of planting area if desired. Continue to side-dress vegetables that have been growing in the garden longer than six to eight weeks when using standard granular fertilizers.

Use premium-quality long-lasting slow-release fertilizer at the time of planting. This method is usually great for gardeners who want to fertilize only one time per season.

Pest Control

Insects have had all summer to build up their populations and can be especially damaging in the late-summer and early-fall garden. Many gardeners put vegetable gardens on a regular weekly spray schedule at this time of the year instead of spraying as needed. Use your best judgment, based on past experience and ongoing new information. Stinkbugs, leaf miners, caterpillars, aphids, whiteflies, beetles, and spider mites are all active. Broad-spectrum insect-control aids will usually handle most of these, although stinkbugs, leaf miners, and whiteflies can be difficult to deal with. Refer to page 291 for a summary listing your options. The key is to not let these pests get completely out of hand before you implement control. Visit local nurseries this time of year and talk to their knowledgeable personnel about pest problems, including insects, diseases, and weeds.

Planning

Cool fronts may begin to make their way into the state, bringing welcome relief from the heat toward the second half of this month. Still, daytime highs regularly reach the 90s well into October. During this transition period, warm- and cool-season vegetables rub elbows in the garden. Most of the warm-season vegetables such as **snap beans, okra, cucumbers, tomatoes, peppers,** and **eggplants** will finish up in November or early December, depending upon your zone around the state as weather becomes colder. It is not too soon, however, to plan the cool-season vegetables that will take their place. This advance planning will allow you to purchase seeds that you will need to have on hand for growing your own transplants timed to be ready to go into the garden as the warm-season vegetables finish.

Vegetables to plant in September include **beets, broccoli[+], cabbage, carrots[**], cauliflower[+], Chinese cabbage[*], collards[*], English and snow peas, Irish potatoes[+++], kale, leek, lettuce, mustard[**], onion, radish, rutabagas, shallots[++], snap beans,** and **Swiss chard[*].**

[+]Plant seeds early; use transplants only in north Texas.
[++]Plant sets.
[+++]Plant small, whole potatoes saved from the spring crop (in zones 8b and 9).
[*]September 1.
[**]First week of September.

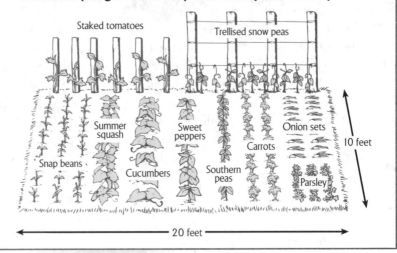

Fall Garden (Fall gardens actually start in late June in Texas.)

Staked tomatoes • Trellised snow peas • Summer squash • Sweet peppers • Onion sets • Snap beans • Cucumbers • Southern peas • Carrots • Parsley • 10 feet • 20 feet

Planting

As we move into the cool season, root crops such as **carrot, radish,** and **turnip** become a prominent part of the garden. Root crops are always direct-seeded—never transplanted. A tiny root first produced by the seed eventually develops into the edible root. It is easily damaged when the seedling is young, and this damage can cause a deformed final product of poor quality. When thinning root crops, do not be tempted to transplant extra seedlings to other spots. You will be disappointed with the results.

Plant **bush snap beans** early in the month in zones 8b and 9. September 1 is the cutoff date in zones 7 and 8a so they will have time to produce a good crop before cold weather. Bush varieties produce faster and concentrate their harvest in a shorter period of time than do **pole beans,** making them preferred for fall planting.

Plant seeds of **bulbing onions, bunching onions,** and **leeks** this month. Sets of bunching onions may also be planted this month, but do not plant sets of **bulbing onions** until December in zones 8b and 9. Plant in late January for zones 7 and 8a. Onion seeds are slow to germinate and need a constant supply of water during the process. The seedlings grow slowly at first, so be patient. **Onions, shallots, leeks,** and **garlic** (planted next month) are long-term residents of the cool-season vegetable garden. **Bulbing onions, shallot bulbs, leeks,** and **garlic** will not be ready to harvest until late May or early June of next year.

Care for Your Vegetables and Herbs

Regularly remove the flower spikes of **basil** to encourage plants to continue producing leaves. Ultimately, the plants will begin to lose steam. Basil transplants should be planted into the garden no later than early September for a late crop. If herbs such as **sage, lavender, thyme,** and **catnip** managed to make it through the summer, they should begin to revive as the weather gets cooler. Remove any dead parts, and fertilize lightly to encourage new growth. Many herbs will have grown vigorously during the summer if not regularly harvested. Cut them back about halfway to get them into shape. Dry or freeze the extra harvest, or share it with friends. Here's how to freeze herbs:

- *Harvest, rinse*, and *blot dry.*

- Remove leaves from woody stems and *chop* finely.

- Place the chopped herbs in a freezer bag, spreading them out in a 1/2-inch layer.

  This makes it easier to break off usable pieces later on when the herbs are frozen solid.

- Force out as much air as possible, seal and freeze.

  Label the bag with the name of the herb, since chopped and frozen herbs tend to look the same.

Watering

This month can be hot and dry, and with new plantings going in, you should pay careful attention to the water needs of the garden. Newly planted transplants and seedbeds are especially vulnerable to drought conditions and may need frequent irrigation. As seeds come up and transplants become established, water deeply and less frequently to encourage a deep root system. Always water on an "as-needed" basis. Do not water on a preset schedule.

Fertilizing

Add fertilizer when installing new plantings. If appropriate, sidedress vegetables that have been growing long enough to need it. Texas gardens usually do well with 15-5-10 or similar 3:1:2 ratio granular fertilizers. Sidedress transplants of cole crops such as **cabbage, broccoli,** and **cauliflower** four to six weeks after they are planted into the garden, and every four to six weeks until harvest if long-lasting slow-release fertilizers aren't used.

Fertilize transplants you are growing yourself once a week with a water-soluble fertilizer mixed at half-strength.

Pest Control

Population levels of insects are high, so be vigilant and treat problems promptly. If a crop is about to finish producing, such as **okra,** you should generally not be as concerned about controlling pests on it as on a vegetable crop that has been planted more recently.

Caterpillars can be particularly troublesome in the fall garden. Control aids which will keep their damage down to a minimum are available.

When turning the soil to plant crops you may encounter white, C-shaped beetle larvae called grubs. They are very common and feed on the roots of vegetables. Simply picking them out and disposing of them is generally all the control that is necessary. Granular grub-control aids can be used to deal with especially heavy infestations. Refer to page 291 for a summary listing your pest-control options.

Planning

October is often one of the nicest months of the year. Working and planting in the garden is a joy when temperatures and humidity are lower. Fall is an excellent time to plant many hardy perennial herbs in the garden. Plan the location of the herbs and think of how many you would like to plant. A few herb plants provide a lot of harvest, so don't plant more than you can use.

Many shade trees drop their leaves in November. Now is a good time to plan on saving them for use in the vegetable garden. Leaves may be stored in plastic bags in an out-of-the-way location for use later on as mulch. Decide now if you have a suitable location. Leaves are also an important source of organic material for our compost piles. If you are not yet composting, get started this year. You are missing out on creating an outstanding free source of the organic matter that is so critical to proper bed preparation. Excellent free information on home composting is available from your local office of the Texas Cooperative Extension Service, often called the County Agent's office by us Texas gardeners.

As warm-season plantings such as **okra, sweet potatoes, watermelons, cantaloupes, Southern peas,** and **pumpkins** are removed, decide on the cool-season vegetables that can be planted in their place.

Vegetables to plant in October include **beets*, broccoli*+, cabbage*, carrots*, cauliflower*+, Chinese cabbage*, collards*, garlic++, kale**, kohlrabi*, lettuce***+, mustard*, onions**, radishes, shallots**,** and **Swiss chard*.**

+Plant transplants by mid-month.
++Plant individual cloves.
+++Leaf and semi-heading varieties are more reliable than heading types.
*In zones 8b and 9 only.
**By October 1.

Planting

Beds you do not intend to plant with vegetables may be planted with a cool-season "green manure" crop. These are seeded into the beds, allowed to grow for a few months, and then turned under to provide organic matter to the soil. Good choices are **elbon rye, vetch, crimson clover,** and **oats.** Do not allow cover crops to set seed. They should be turned under when they begin to bloom, if not before.

Intercropping is a way of maximizing production from vegetable beds. Vegetables that are spaced relatively far apart such as **broccoli, cauliflower, cabbage,** and **brussels sprouts** do not fully occupy the bed early in their season. Use the space between the plants to grow a quick-maturing crop such as **radishes** or **lettuce.** If planted at

the same time, they will be harvested and gone by the time larger plants begin to cover those spaces.

With winter on the way, new gardeners sometimes wonder if now is the time to plant **winter squash.** The answer is *No.* **Winter squash,** such as **acorn, hubbard,** and **butternut,** is grown during the warm season along with **summer squash,** so it should have been planted long before now. The difference is that the fruit of **winter squash** is harvested when the rind is hard, so they are kept in the garden much longer than **summer squash,** which is harvested while still tender. **Winter squash** stores well and may be kept and used during the winter. Hence the name.

Plant **garlic** by separating bulbs into individual cloves and pressing the cloves big end down into well-prepared beds. The tip of the clove should be about $1/4$ inch below the soil surface. Space the cloves 4 to 6 inches apart.

Care for Your Vegetables and Herbs

Fall is an excellent time to have soil tests done. Many soils around the state require lime to raise the pH and provide calcium. A soil test will indicate if you need to apply lime, sulfur, iron, or other pH-adjusting aid, and how much is recommended. If you do not intend to grow a winter vegetable garden, these amendments applied in the fall will have plenty of time to do their work before the spring planting season.

If you notice large knobs, knots, and bumps on the roots of vegetables (such as **okra**), it is a sign that your soil is infested with root knot nematodes. These microscopic roundworms attack and damage the roots of a wide variety of vegetables. You can have your soil evaluated for the presence of nematodes through your county office of the Texas Cooperative Extension Service. Contact them for the proper method to take samples, and send in for analysis.

Mulch heavily any beds that will stay empty for the winter. Winter weeds will grow vigorously in unmulched beds, creating problems when the beds are planted next spring.

Watering

October is typically relatively dry. Water established vegetables thoroughly and deeply as needed. Newly planted seeds and transplants will usually need more-frequent irrigation.

Fertilizing

Add some 15-5-10 or similar 3:1:2 ratio fertilizer to all of those leaves going into your compost pile to make them decompose faster. Sidedress vegetables such as **broccoli, cabbage, peppers, tomatoes, cauliflower,** and **collards** to keep them growing vigorously. Legume crops, which include **English peas, snow peas,** and edible **podded peas,** are usually not sidedressed.

Pest Control

With cooler weather, pest problems don't seem as bad. Diseases are much less common in the cool-season garden as well.

Watch for aphids and control with appropriate insect-control aids. Follow label directions carefully.

Caterpillars may continue to damage vegetables. When they infest leafy greens such as **collard, kale, turnips, mustard,** and **lettuce,** they can eat your produce in no time. Control them with applications of aids you select at local retailers.

Snail and slug populations may be high, and they eat foliage just as caterpillars do. They especially love **cabbage, turnip, mustard,** and **lettuce.** Control with traps, barriers, and baits or other aids before the damage gets out of hand.

Refer to page 291 for a summary listing your pest-control options.

Planning

Freezing temperatures are a possibility in north Texas later this month. As things slow down a little, take the time to record in your Texas gardening journal how well fall plantings of warm-season vegetables did for you. In particular, note the varieties that seemed to do best, along with any pest problems. Also note temperatures and rainfall.

If you still haven't decided whether or not to plant a cool-season vegetable garden, there is still a little time in zones 8b and 9. At least put in a few easy crops such as **shallot** sets, **mustard greens,** and **lettuce** if you live in these zones. Many of the most delicious and nutritious vegetables can be grown here only during the cool season.

Some additional plantings of cool-season vegetables can continue into late winter and early spring. Continue to look through arriving seed catalogs and order vegetable seeds for planting then. Vegetables to plant in November if you live in zone 9 include **beet, cabbage, carrot, collard, garlic, kale, kohlrabi, leek, lettuce, mustard, onion, radish, rutabaga, shallot, spinach, Swiss chard,** and **turnip.** Spring vegetable gardening usually begins for zone 8 in January while it starts in February for Texas gardeners in zone 7.

Planting

Direct-seed root crops such as **beets, carrots, radishes,** and **turnips.** Transplants of **broccoli** and **cauliflower** may still be available at local nurseries, but the possibility of freezing temperatures damaging the heads makes planting them risky, even in south Texas. Transplants of **cabbage, celery, kale, kohlrabi, lettuce, spinach,** and **Swiss chard** can all be purchased and planted this month, or you can plant seeds in the garden in zone 9 now, in January in zone 8, and in February in zone 7.

Care for Your Vegetables and Herbs

When planted early so they will have time to establish and grow, **lettuces,** especially the leaf and semi-heading varieties, are very productive in the cool-season garden. Fall is the best time to plant **lettuces,** as they mature during progressively cooler temperatures. Problems with bitterness that often affect spring-grown **lettuce** do not occur in the fall. Keep **lettuce** growing vigorously with watering as needed and occasional sidedressing with a nitrogen-containing fertilizer such as 15-5-10. There are so many different colors and leaf shapes available now; **lettuce** patches can rival ornamental plantings.

Don't overlook the ornamental qualities of many of the cool-season vegetables and herbs. **Curly parsley** makes a great edging plant for flower beds. **Curly leaf mustard** and **red leaf mustard** are outstanding when mixed with cool-season bedding plants. **Bronze fennel** is used as often in flower beds and perennial borders as it is in the herb and vegetable garden. Watch your use of pest-control aids on vegetables in ornamental beds. The pest-control aids used on ornamentals may not be labeled for use on food crops, which means you should not harvest and eat vegetables sprayed with them. As always, read and follow label directions when using any gardening aid. And it's best to read the label before purchasing to make sure a specific aid is what you want.

Watering

Cooler temperatures and more-frequent rains make watering the vegetable and herb gardens necessary less often during the winter growing season. Watch rainfall amounts and water when necessary. Record your observations in your Texas gardening journal.

Fertilizing

Even though many plants are going dormant for the winter, cool-season vegetables and herbs remain in active growth. Fertilize as needed to help keep them healthy and productive.

Helpful Hint

Take time this month to look for holiday season gifts for relatives, friends, neighbors, or others who enjoy some form of gardening in Texas. Tools, sprinklers, sprayers, power equipment, and books are all welcome gifts by fellow gardeners. When looking for books, let us suggest the following:

- Copies of this book.

- *My Texas Garden: A Gardener's Journal* (Cool Springs Press, 2000)

- *Dale Groom's Texas Gardening Guide* (Cool Springs Press, 1997)

All these publications should be available at local bookstores and garden centers.

Planning

As seed catalogs begin to arrive, you'll most likely find a moment to look at new offerings of vegetables and herbs. There is plenty of time to make decisions and purchase locally or order warm-season vegetable seeds (except **tomatoes, peppers,** and **eggplants,** which should be started from seed six weeks prior to transplanting them), but you should purchase locally or order cool-season vegetable seeds this month or in January.

Take time to make plans in your Texas gardening journal this month for the new year. Purchase holiday gifts for your gardening friends, neighbors or relatives.

December is a good month to have the soil in your vegetable garden tested.

Planting

Some planting may continue in zone 9. Although exceptionally cold severe weather can cause problems, winter weather is mostly mild. Watch the weather and avoid setting out transplants when a major freeze is predicted. In zones 6, 7, and 8, refrain from planting until March, February, and January respectively.

Care for Your Vegetables and Herbs

Any vegetable started in winter will be subject to freeze damage while young. The following lists are quick guides to the ability of some vegetables to endure freezes. Factors such as the age of the plant, prior weather conditions, and the location of the garden will also influence the amount of freeze damage.

Less Hardy (protect if temperatures are to go below 28 degrees): **broccoli** (heads); **cauliflower** (heads); **lettuce; English, snow,** and edible podded **pea** (flowers)

Moderately Hardy (will tolerate temperatures down to mid- to low 20s with little or no damage): **Swiss chard; Chinese cabbage; kohlrabi; mustard greens; radish** (will resprout from roots); **turnip** (will resprout from roots); **spinach**

Very Hardy (will survive temperatures in low 20s and teens): **beets; brussels sprouts; carrots; celery; collards; garlic; kale; onions; leeks; shallots**

Watering and Fertilizing

Monitor the needs of your vegetables, and water and fertilize as appropriate. Winter is usually relatively rainy, and irrigation will seldom be necessary. Long stretches of cold weather will slow the growth of vegetables and reduce the need for additional fertilizer. On the other hand, an unusually mild winter may encourage vigorous growth, requiring additional fertilizer. Watch the weather and use your best judgment.

Pest Control

One positive benefit of cool-season gardening (other than the mild temperatures) is reduced problems with insects and diseases. Diseases are a minor problem, if they occur at all.

Aphids and caterpillars will be active, depending on the weather. During mild periods, watch carefully for their appearance and control if necessary.

Snails and slugs may show up, especially early in the month. Beer traps, baits, and other controls approved for use around food crops will help keep their numbers down.

Do not slack off on weed control. Maintain mulches and deal with any growing weeds promptly. Mulches can also be useful in protecting vegetables during freezes.

Vines, Ground Covers, and Ornamental Grasses

Vines

No other plants can do what vines can do in the landscape. They are indispensable for growing up a pillar, covering an unattractive fence, softening architectural features, or creating screens. A vine-covered arbor provides a shady retreat.

Vines are a remarkably diverse group of plants. They include annuals and perennials and can be woody or herbaceous, evergreen or deciduous. Perennial vines are the most important group, as they become a permanent part of the landscape. Before you use them (and you really should), there are a couple of things you should understand about vines.

First, they're lazy. Rather than putting the considerable effort it takes into growing a strong stem, they use another plant or structure to provide support. Where does all that unused energy go? Into the fastest-growing plants in your landscape! You must be prepared for the extraordinary rate of growth of which vines are capable, and be willing to control them when necessary.

Second, vines climb in two distinct ways: by twining and by clinging. Twining vines climb by wrapping their stems, leaves, or tendrils around a support. They must have string, wire, latticework, trellises, poles, or other support structures they can twist around. Clinging vines can grow on flat surfaces by using roots along their stems or holdfasts. They are useful for covering the sides of buildings or walls without having to build a support. It is very important to know how a vine you want to use climbs.

Vines are grown for their attractive foliage and colorful flowers. Some provide ornamental or edible fruit, and several produce fragrant flowers. When you determine a vine is needed in your landscape, the selection process is the same as for any plant. Decide on the characteristics you would like the vine to have, determine the growing conditions in the area where it will be planted, and choose the vine that most closely fits.

Caring for vines involves controlling and training them more than anything else, as well as watering, fertilizing, and pest control on occasion.

Ground Covers

The term ground cover generally refers to low-growing plants, other than turfgrasses, used to cover areas of the landscape. Perennial, evergreen plants having a running, sprawling, or spreading habit are generally used. Many have variegated foliage or produce colorful flowers while others are more subdued. Ground covers establish an effect in the landscape that provides variation in height, texture, and color that enriches their surroundings. Yet they require far less maintenance than flower beds.

In addition to the beauty they provide, ground covers have practical uses as well. Some ground covers are effective in erosion control while others, because they don't have to be mowed, reduce maintenance in problem areas such as on steep slopes or under low-branched trees and shrubs. Where the roots of large trees protrude, ground covers hide the roots and prevent mowing problems. They provide barriers to foot traffic (most people won't walk through them) and can guide traffic movement through a site. Ground covers are probably used most commonly in confined areas where lawn mowing is difficult or in shade where grass will not grow.

Vines, Ground Covers, and Ornamental Grasses

When selecting ground covers, it is important to carefully consider the characteristics you would like the ground cover to have (height, texture, color, etc.) as well as the growing conditions where it will be planted, such as sunny or shady, dry or moist, and sandy or clay soil.

You should also look at the size of the area to be planted. Only the most reliable, fast-spreading, and reasonably priced ground covers should be considered for large areas. **Mondo grass** (*Ophiopogon japonicus*) and **monkey grass** (*Liriope muscari*) are good choices for shade to part sun. **Asiatic jasmine** (*Trachelospermum asiaticum*) is excellent for sun to part shade.

Whatever type of ground cover you choose, proper preparation of the planting area will help ensure good establishment and faster growth. Maintaining ground covers involves some weeding, trimming back, watering, and fertilizing, but most ground covers are not too demanding.

Ornamental Grasses

Ornamental grasses are an often-overlooked group of herbaceous perennials that thrive in Texas gardens, and they will grow beautifully with minimal effort. The term ornamental grass is applied to grasses and grasslike plants that are used chiefly for their beauty. They are a large and complex group of plants with a wide range of growth habits and culture. This versatile group of plants is becoming increasing popular all across the United States, but still deserve to be more widely utilized in Texas landscapes.

Some of our worst garden weeds are grasses. Crabgrass and Johnson grass are persistent, difficult-to-control pests that many of us are all too familiar with. As a result, many gardeners are reluctant to deliberately plant grasses into flower beds or borders in their landscape.

Ornamental grasses, however, are truly attractive and not rampantly aggressive. Like their weedy cousins, they are tough and susceptible to virtually no insect or disease problems. Ornamental grasses are an excellent choice for gardeners trying to create a landscape that is more self-reliant, requiring less spraying, fertilization, and maintenance.

The strong vertical or fountaining form of many ornamental grasses combined with their feathery flower heads makes a unique contribution to the landscape. Grass foliage moves in breezes and catches the light like few other plants. It adds fine texture and colors such as metallic blues, burgundy, white, creamy yellow, and every shade of green imaginable. Grasses also offer an impressive array of flower plumes and seedheads for added interest at various times.

Most ornamental grasses grow best in full to part sun, but they are tolerant of a wide range of growing conditions. If you are planting them into an existing bed, little improvement will be needed. Turn the soil and then incorporate a 2-inch layer of organic matter in the area to be planted. *Water* them thoroughly as needed until they are established, then just sit back and relax.

Some ornamental grasses are evergreen, but most go dormant for the winter. At some point before the end of February, cut the plants back to within a few inches of the ground. Other than that, occasional watering and fertilizing is all they need.

Vines for Texas

Name	Size/Type	Light	Flowers and Comments
Carolina Yellow Jessamine *Gelsemium sempervirens*	to 20 feet; Evergreen, twining	Full sun to part shade	Yellow, fragrant flowers in late winter to early spring; one of the best vines; vigorous; prune regularly to control; **native;** hardy in all Texas zones except zone 6.
Chinese Wisteria *Wisteria sinensis*	to 50 feet; Deciduous, twining	Full to part sun	Dangling clusters of fragrant lilac-purple flowers in March–April; vigorous, rampant vine that must be carefully controlled; keep away from trees and houses.
Confederate Jasmine *Trachelospermum jasminoides*	to 20 to 60 feet; Evergreen, twining	Full sun to part shade	Very fragrant clusters of white flowers in early summer; may be severely damaged or killed by temperatures in the mid- to low teens; usually hardy in zones 8b and 9.
Coral Honeysuckle *Lonicera sempervirens*	15 to 20 feet; Evergreen, twining	Full to part sun	Clusters of tubular coral red flowers in spring to early summer and scattered through the year; attractive blue-green foliage; easy to control; **native.**
Crossvine *Bignonia capreolata*	to 50 feet; Semi-evergreen, twining	Part sun to part shade	Showy clusters of large tubular yellow and red flowers; large vine not suitable for a small trellis; **native.**
English Ivy *Hedera helix*	to 60 feet; Evergreen, clinging	Part sun to shade	Excellent clinging vine; flowers insignificant; many cultivars with different leaf shapes, sizes, and variegations. Root rot can be a problem in poorly drained locations.
Passion Vine *Passiflora incarnata*	to 20 feet; Deciduous, twining	Full morning to part sun	Dark-green 3 to 5-point leaves; exotic look; intricate blooms, pale to pinkish lavender with 3-inch-diameter fruits; **native.**
Texas Wisteria *Wisteria macrostachya*	to 20 feet; Deciduous, vigorous, robust	Full sun to shade	Sweet fragrance from grapelike clusters of lilac to bluish purple blooms; hardy statewide; **native.**
Virginia Creeper *Parthenocissus quinquefolia*	40 to 50 feet; deciduous, climber	Full sun to shade	Large five-part dark-green leaves changing to brilliant red in early fall; hardy statewide; **native.**

Ground Covers for Texas

Name	Height	Light	Comments
Asian Jasmine *Trachelospermum asiaticum*	12 to 16 inches	Full sun to part shade	Excellent fast-growing vine for covering large areas; shear back to 4 to 6 inches annually; edge sides of bed as needed; evergreen–semi-evergreen.
Aspidistra, Cast Iron Plant *Aspidistra elatior*	2 feet	Shade to full shade	Tall ground cover for deep shade; sword-shaped dark-green leaves; evergreen.
Autumn Fern *Dryopteris erythrosora*	12 to 18 inches	Shade to full shade	Attractive new growth has a coppery-red tint; tough, reliable evergreen fern.
Creeping Juniper *Juniperus horizontalis*	18 inches	Full sun	Needs excellent drainage and air circulation; good for hot, dry, sunny areas; watch for spider mites.
English Ivy *Hedera helix*	8-inch-deep mat	Shade to part sun	Useful for covering large areas and slopes; may be damaged by root rot; use vigorous, fast-growing cultivars as ground cover; evergreen.
Holly Fern *Cyrtomium falcatum*	12 to 20 inches	Shade to part sun	Bold, coarse texture almost shrublike; tolerates drier soil than most ferns; evergreen–semi-evergreen.
Japanese Ardisia *Ardisia japonica*	10 inches	Shade to part shade	Bright red berries in winter, but few in number; choose plain green cultivars for ground cover planting; evergreen.
Lily Turf *Liriope spicata*	8 to 10 inches	Shade to part shade	Grasslike foliage; reliable for large areas, better than *L. muscari* as a ground cover since it spreads faster; evergreen.
Mondo or Monkey Grass *Ophiopogon japonicus*	8 to 10 inches	Shade to part sun	Grassy appearance; thin dark-green leaves; one of best for planting large areas; evergreen.
Sedum *Sedum* spp.	4 to 18 inches tall, depending on variety	Full sun to part shade	Evergreen–deciduous. Fleshy relatively light green leaves; yellow, red, pink, pink-purple, and bronzy-pink blooms; hardy statewide; needs well-drained locations.
Strawberry Geranium *Saxifraga stolonifera*	4 inches	Shade to part shade	Delightful plant for small detail planting; round dark-green leaves with silver veins; stalks of small white flowers in spring; evergreen.

Ornamental Grasses fo

Name	Size	Light	Comm
Acorus *Acorus gramineus*	6 to 12 inches	Part shade to shade	Small wet a detai
Blue Fescue *Festuca ovina*	10 to 12 inches	Full sun	Bur in h loc
Fountain Grass *Pennisetum alopecuroides*	10 inches to 3 feet, depending on variety.	Full to part sun	Fine-textured grass, not too large, cultivars such as 'Hamelin' are only 18 inches; attractive plumes in midsummer; hardy in zones 8 and 9 to statewide, depending on variety.
Giant Reed Grass *Arundo donax*	10 to 15 feet	Full to part sun	Large, coarse-textured upright grass suitable for accent or screen; cut back if damaged by winter freezes; produces 2-foot tan plumes in late summer.
Lindheimer's Muhly *Muhlenbergia lindheimeri*	3 to 4 feet	Full to part sun	Very attractive dome of fine-textured leaves are bluish-gray-green in color; flower plumes appear in fall.
Pampas Grass *Cortaderia selloana*	8 to 10 feet	Full to part sun	Large, mounding fine-textured grass suitable for accent or screen; cut back if damaged by winter freezes; produces attractive creamy white to silvery plumes in late summer; hardy in zones 7, 8, and 9.
Variegated Japanese Silver Grass *Miscanthus sinensis* 'Variegata'	5 to 6 feet	Full sun to part shade	Mounding fine-textured grass with creamy white variegated foliage; outstanding specimen or accent; pinkish-tan plumes in midsummer; there are many outstanding cultivars of this grass species; hardy statewide.
Zebra Grass *Miscanthus sinensis* 'Zebrinus'	5 to 6 feet	Full sun to part shade	Upright to mounding medium-textured grass; blades are striped horizontally with pale yellow bands; attractive plumes in late summer; cut back in February; hardy statewide.

...nning

...s rather catchall chapter ...es three very useful and ...esting groups of plants. There ...e spots and situations in virtually every landscape where vines, ground covers, or ornamental grasses would provide just the right touch. Many ground covers and vines are quiet, unassuming plants that play a supporting role in the landscape, but they can be flashy focal points as well. Ornamental grasses almost always stand out, but their soft, fine-textured foliage rarely dominates a garden bed.

The plant lists at the beginning of this chapter would barely scratch the surface of a complete list of the members of these three remarkable plant groups. Plan on curling up by the fire this winter with a good reference on plant materials for our state.

Planting and Transplanting

Virtually all the hardy perennial vines, ground covers, and ornamental grasses can be planted or transplanted this month.

If needed, now is a good time to transplant or divide your ornamental grasses. *Cut back* the brown foliage, lift the clump, divide it into two to four pieces, and replant them into your landscape or share with friends.

Some ground covers may also be divided and/or transplanted now. This is a good way to create new areas of ground cover without having to buy any plants. **Liriope, lily turf, strawberry geranium, ajuga, Japanese ardisia, aspidistra,** and **ferns** can all be divided now, especially in zones 8b and 9. February is also a good division month. Late February through March are good spring division months for zones 7a, 7b, and 8a. March is a good spring month for divisions in zones 6a and 6b.

Care for Your Plants

Do not allow your ground cover to stay covered by fallen leaves. Rake out, vacuum or mow leaves and use them for mulch or put them in your compost pile. Vining ground covers, such as **Asian jasmine** and **English ivy,** catch at the tines of garden rakes and can make raking difficult. Try using a leaf blower to blow out the leaves; many models can also be used to vacuum up the leaves. Consider planting **monkey grass** or **creeping lily turf** in areas under trees where you will need to rake out leaves.

Pest Control

Insects: Scale is sometimes a problem on plants like **Japanese ardisia** and **aspidistra.** Look over your plants carefully for small white or tan bumps that detach easily when pushed with your thumbnail.

Control with dormant horticultural oil or another insect pest-control aid of your choosing. Refer to page 291 for a summary listing your options. Do not spray if sub-freezing temperatures are predicted within 24 hours. Remember, always read and follow label directions when applying any gardening aid.

Pruning

Some ornamental grasses are evergreen, but most go dormant for the winter. At some point before the end of February or during early spring, *cut back* the plants to within a few inches of the ground. When you cut them back depends on whether you like the appearance of the dead foliage or not. Cutting back should, however, be done before the fresh, new growth comes up in spring.

Do not prune spring-blooming vines now or you will reduce or eliminate their flowers.

Planning

Are there areas where it is difficult to mow or where grass will not grow due to shade? These are ideal locations for ground covers.

Planting and Transplanting

1 *Remove* all existing unwanted vegetation such as lawngrass or weeds from the area. This can be done physically or by using weed-control aids. Do a good job or grasses such as **Bermuda** may present long-term problems.

2 *Till the soil* to loosen it. When working under a tree, use a turning fork to minimize damage to the tree's roots, and avoid severing roots larger than an inch in diameter.

3 Spread 3 to 4 inches of organic matter (compost, peat moss, or rotted manure) over the area, and work it in to the native soil.

4 Remove your ground cover selections from their containers and plant as deep as their soil-balls are tall. After planting is complete, water thoroughly, apply a root stimulator according to label directions, and mulch 3 to 4 inches deep.

Continue to *plant and transplant* hardy perennial vines and ornamental grasses.

Care for Your Plants

Combined with a few of the perennials you find relatively care-free, ornamental grasses will create a bed that is interesting and attractive and normally requires less maintenance than perennial beds.

Watering

Water newly planted, transplanted, or divided vines, ground covers, and ornamental grasses thoroughly when they go in the ground. Thoroughly irrigate existing plantings throughout the month as needed.

Fertilizing

It is usually best to fertilize existing plantings in March. Small amounts of premium-quality long-lasting slow-release granular fertilizers may be applied in each planting hole at planting time. Read and follow label directions.

Pest Control

Insects: Keep an eye out for scale insects on various vines and ground covers. *Spray with a dormant or lightweight horticultural oil or other scale-control aid.*

Weeds: Cool-season weeds will be growing in ground covers now. *Weed beds as needed.* Refer to page 291 for a summary listing your pest- and weed-control options.

Pruning

Virtually all the plants we use as ground covers are evergreen. As time goes by, unattractive old foliage will often accumulate among the healthy leaves, and the planting will need a good shearing back to rejuvenate it. Use hedge shearers, string trimmers, or even your lawnmower adjusted to its highest setting (make sure the blades are sharp, and push the mower through the planting slowly). Clipping every two to three years is generally adequate. For several popular ground covers, it is important that this be done before new growth begins next month. Ground covers that are candidates for trimming now include **lily turf, English ivy, liriope, Asian jasmine,** and **Japanese ardisia.** Use handpruners to selectively prune unattractive leaves from plants such as **aspidistra, autumn fern,** and **holly fern.**

Planning

There are wonderful vines, ground cover plants, and ornamental grasses available at local nurseries. By far the best place to purchase plants is your local retailer. We can look at each plant "in person" before purchasing and choose individual plants if desired. Visit several retailers in your area to help determine who has the plants you like best. This is usually a good month statewide to find a large assortment of locally available landscape plants.

Planting and Transplanting

Finish up ground cover plantings this month so they will have some time to become established before the fierce heat of summer arrives.

1 *Plant* the ground cover into well-prepared beds at the proper spacing. Proper spacing varies with the type chosen, so check with the staff at the nursery or consult references. Planting at the closest recommended spacing will provide quicker coverage, but it will mean a higher initial investment.

2 After the area is planted, *mulch* with 3 to 4 inches of leaves, pine bark, cypress mulch, or shredded pine straw. Until the ground cover fills in, weed control is very important. Your best defense is a good layer of mulch. Handweed as necessary to maintain good weed control. In addition, most ground covers spread faster when mulched.

3 *Water* the area thoroughly to settle things in, and you are done.

Plant vines this month. Prepare the spots by removing any unwanted plants (weeds or turfgrass), and *turn over the soil.* Add about 4 to 6 inches of organic matter, and thoroughly *dig it in.* When you plant the vine, make sure the top of the rootball is even with the soil level, firm the soil around it, and *water it in.* Apply a premium-quality long-lasting slow-release granular fertilizer, and *mulch* 3 to 4 inches deep around the plant to control weeds and conserve moisture.

Apply premium-quality long-lasting slow-release granular fertilizer.

Care for Your Plants

When deciding on how far apart to space new ground cover plantings, look at your budget. Planting an area with ground cover is an investment. Decide on how much you are prepared to invest in the project, purchase as many plants as your budget will allow, and space them evenly throughout the area. You may discover they end up farther apart than recommended—but most of us do not have an unlimited gardening budget. You can wait for those plants to fill in, or when more funds are available, purchase more plants and *install* them evenly among the originals. Over time, you will fill up the bed while staying within your budget.

A second approach would be to plant a smaller area according to recommendations and expand the area as time and funds become available.

Watering

Warmer temperatures and active growth make watering increasingly important if regular rainfall does not occur. Newly planted ground covers, vines, and ornamental grasses need the most attention. They are vulnerable to drying out until they have a chance to grow a strong root system into the surrounding soil. *Water* new plantings as needed to maintain a moist soil, especially those in full sun.

Fertilizing

Fertilize established ground covers, vines, and ornamental grasses this month. Choose a long-lasting slow-release premium-quality granular fertilizer appropriate to your area, and apply it according to package directions. Fertilizers with 4:1:2 or 3:1:2 ratios, including 15-5-10, 16-4-8, 18-6-12, 19-5-9, and 21-7-14 are known to work well in Texas soils. When fertilizer is sprinkled over ground cover plantings, *water* immediately afterwards to wash the fertilizer granules off the foliage and on to the soil. It is particularly important to fertilize ground covers that were cut back. *Fertilize* vines moderately and only if you need to stimulate extra growth. If your ornamental grasses have not yet begun to grow, wait until next month to fertilize.

Pest Control

Mild weather is perfect for using lightweight horticultural oils. These excellent pest-control aids will control scale, aphids, spider mites, and various other pests.

Treat now if you see scale on any of your vines or ground covers.

Caterpillars are an occasional pest for some vines. Look for chewed leaves or holes in the foliage. If the damage is minor, just keep an eye on it.

Sprinkle premium-quality long-lasting slow-release fertilizer over your plantings (then be sure to water immediately).

If the damage warrants spraying the plant, treat with approved pest-control aids available at your local retailers. Refer to page 291 for a summary listing your options.

Pruning

Carolina yellow jessamine should be finished blooming by now. *Trim it back* if necessary.

If you have not cut back brown ornamental grass foliage and plan to do it, do so as soon as possible. Don't wait until you see the new growth. If new growth has already started, make your pruning cuts just above it. There's not much you will need to do to ornamental grasses after this for the rest of the growing season.

Helpful Hint

After you cut back your ornamental grass, lay the clippings on the lawn and run your mower (with a bag attached) over them. The chopped grass blades make great mulch, or they can be added to your compost pile.

Planning

Look around your land-scape for places where a container would make a nice addition, such as patios, porches, or decks. Vines will need some sort of support. Some ornamental grasses also work well as container plantings. Give vines and/or ornamental grasses a try this season as container plantings.

Planting and Transplanting

Ground covers and vines need to be planted as soon as possible. Grasses are so tough they can be planted throughout the summer, but if you want to transplant or divide some that are already growing in your landscape, do it now.

Care for Your Plants

Vines tend to grow strongly upwards. If you use a vine to cover a fence or trellis and want it to be full at the bottom, this can be a problem. When you plant the vines, *weave* the long stems horizontally along the lower portion of the fence or trellis. As the vine grows upwards, continue to weave it back and forth through the support. When a vine reaches the top of its support, don't just cut it off. Take the ends of the vine and *weave* them back downward. This takes some effort, but the result will be much more attractive and the vine will be fuller from top to bottom.

Watering

Use a sprinkler to apply $1/2$ to 1 inch or more of water as needed when the weather is dry. Tree roots will compete with the ground cover plants for water. Make sure there is enough water for both.

Fertilizing

Fertilize this month if you did not do so in March. Apply fertilizer to ground cover plantings in particular, especially those that are still growing to fill an area. Use a premium-quality long-lasting slow-release granular fertilizer appropriate to your area such as a 3:1:2 ratio fertilizer like 15-5-10. W*ater* immediately to wash the fertilizer off the ground cover foliage and down to the soil.

Fertilizing vines is optional, and not recommended if they have a history of growing vigorously. Fertilize to stimulate growth, or if in low vigor or have poor foliage color.

Ornamental grasses are often planted among annuals, perennials, and shrubs, and will benefit from the fertilizer scattered throughout the bed for everything else. (Overly generous fertilization of ornamental grasses can produce tall, weak-stemmed plants prone to lying over.)

Pest Control

Stay on top of weed control by using mulches wherever possible, and *handweed* where needed. A good, thick stand of ground cover generally prevents many weeds from growing, but some will still occur.

Weeds in ground covers can be controlled with several selective weed-control aids available at local retailers. Refer to page 291 for a summary listing your options. Make sure the ornamental plants in the bed are listed on the label as tolerant of the selected aid.

Pruning

Prune spring-flowering vines such as **Carolina yellow jessamine** and **wisteria** after they finish flowering. Instead of pruning off long strands, weave them back into the supporting structure to thicken up the vine.

Planning

Walk through your landscape as often as you can. Carry a shoulder bag with snips, hand-pruners, a spray bottle of premixed weed-control aid, and a 12-by-2-inch piece of cardboard or rigid plastic. Stop and lightly prune vines and ground covers and pull a few weeds or spray them with your mixed weed control. Check out insect and disease problems.

Planting and Transplanting

Planting ground covers and vines this late means you will have to put extra effort into getting them established in the heat. This primarily means paying careful attention to watering. Ornamental grasses are tougher, and can be planted throughout the summer.

Care for Your Plants

Some ground covers will require occasional pruning. Make a point of looking at your vines every week, and tend to the training, weaving, snipping, and pruning it takes to keep them where they belong. Keep an eye out for insects and diseases.

Watering

Established vines and ornamental grasses are often included in beds or plantings with other plant materials. If you water the area enough to keep the other plants happy, the vines and grasses will be happy too.

Established beds of ground cover will need water only when it is unusually hot and dry. Newly planted ground cover will need more attention. *Water* as needed, thoroughly, whenever a week or so goes by without a good rain. Irrigate when needed to maintain a *moist* soil.

Fertilizing

To provide the greatest benefit, fertilizer should have been applied last month. If you haven't fertilized ground cover areas, particularly those that are still filling in, do so as soon as possible. Evenly *sprinkle* a general-purpose, premium-quality long-lasting slow-release granular fertilizer over the area following package recommendations, and *water-in.*

Vines and ornamental grasses don't usually need much fertilizer, but if you are trying to stimulate growth, they can be fertilized as well.

Pest Control

Watch for insect and disease problems on vines and ground covers. Aphids may show up on the new growth of many kinds of vines.

If present, caterpillars are only a minor problem.

Low-growing ground covers with succulent leaves such as **ajuga, strawberry geranium,** and **hosta** may be attacked by snails and slugs. *Treat these areas with snail and slug-control aids, or set out homemade traps.* Control aids for all types of pests are available at local retailers. Refer to page 291 for a summary listing your options.

Pruning

The best time to do extensive or radical pruning is immediately after flowering. Continue light pruning and training through the summer. Selectively *prune off* unsightly leaves from **aspidistra** and **ferns** to keep them looking neat and attractive.

Vines that we use as ground covers (such as **Asian jasmine** and **English ivy**) don't have the good sense to stop at the edge of their beds, and will grow out onto sidewalks or other areas where they are not wanted. *Prune back* the edges of those plantings occasionally.

Planning

Your lawngrass is growing vigorously now. This is a good time to identify areas where the grass is not thriving or has disappeared entirely. The most frequent cause of poor growth is too much shade. Plant a shade-loving ground cover in the location, and quit dealing with turfgrass.

Our most shade-tolerant grass, **St. Augustine,** requires 4 hours of full sun or 8 hours of 50 percent sun and 50 percent shade in order to grow over the long term. Enter your observations in your Texas gardening journal.

Planting and Transplanting

Shady areas are less stressful during summer heat. If you don't want to wait until this fall to plant a bare shady area, decide what kind of ground cover you would like and *plant* it now. Just make sure you keep it well watered and mulched. Tough, easy ground covers, such as **monkey grass, creeping lily turf,** and **Asian jasmine,** should do okay if planted this late as long as they are kept well watered.

When working under a tree, use a turning fork to minimize damage to the tree's roots, and avoid severing roots larger than an inch in diameter whenever possible. Four or more inches of organic matter may be blended with your native soil to develop beds suitable for ground cover plantings. Follow the bed preparation steps recommended in February.

Care for Your Plants

Evaluate how well vines are growing on the support provided for them. Whether the vine is trained on an arch, fence, pole, trellis, or latticework—is it turning out as you intended? Decide if:

- *The vine is too large and rampant* and has overwhelmed the support.

- *The support is not strong enough* to hold up the weight of the vine.

- *All of the growth is at the top,* and the bottom and middle of the vine is bare.

- *The vine does not like the growing conditions* and is not doing well.

If there are problems, decide on a solution:

- *Replace the vine* this fall with one that would be more suitable.

- *Replace the support,* if practical, with one that is stronger or larger.

- *Prune the vine* regularly to keep it the size and shape desired.

- *Prune the vine* so that the structure it is growing on, such as an arch, column, or building, is not completely covered.

Watering

Daytime highs in the mid-90s Fahrenheit and nights in the upper 70s will place tremendous stress on plants in our landscapes over the next three or four months. Plants use water much faster when it is hot. If it has not rained for more than ten days, *water* established ground cover plantings. Use a sprinkler to apply about an inch of water to the area. Remember, trees' roots will also absorb some of the water. Monitor plantings under trees closely. New plantings should be deeply watered when rain has not occurred for seven to ten days.

Irrigate infrequently, but when water *is* applied, do a thorough job and water deeply. Your goal is to maintain a *moist* soil in your ground cover's root zone.

Ornamental grasses rarely need to be watered once established. Recently planted grasses should be watered as needed if the weather is dry.

If you are growing any specimens of vines, ornamental grasses, or ground covers as container plants, they may need to be watered every day. *Check them often and water as needed.*

Fertilizing

Fertilizers applied in spring or early summer are sufficient, and none needs to be applied now.

However, if you did not fertilize during early spring, you may do so this month. Premium-quality long-lasting slow-release 3:1:2 and 4:1:2 ratio fertilizers work well in Texas soils. These include 21-7-14, 19-5-9, 18-6-12, 16-4-8, and 15-5-10. Always read and follow label directions.

One tool of application which works well is a rotary or broadcast fertilizer spreader. Set according to the labels on fertilizer containers, then apply them evenly and accurately. They may be pushed through most ground cover beds while distributing the fertilizer of your choice.

Pest Control

Hot, muggy weather and lots of rain make diseases worse this time of the year. Leaf spot diseases caused by various fungal organisms can attack **ardisia, Confederate jasmine,** and **liriope.** *Trim off*  any badly damaged foliage and *spray* with your selected pest-control aid according to label directions.

Weeds in ground cover plantings can be quite a nuisance. Nutsedge or nutgrass is a difficult weed with very thin yellow-green leaves and a nutlike bulb. A specialized weed-control aid is available and labeled for use on several types of ground covers, and it will do an excellent job of selectively eliminating the nutsedge. **Bermudagrass** and other grassy weeds also cause problems. Weed-control aids will do a good job controlling these weeds and can be used over the top of several commonly used ground covers. Refer to page 291 for a summary listing your disease- and weed-control options. *Read the labels of these products carefully and use them strictly according to directions.*

Pruning

Other than regular maintenance work on vines, little pruning needs to be done now. Keep beds of **Asian jasmine** edged as needed so they will look neat.

Planning

Record information on the performance of plants in your landscape in your Texas gardening journal. It is the best way to avoid repeating mistakes and helps you do a better job of caring for your plants. Take some time, while you escape the heat indoors, to make some notes on your ground covers, vines, and ornamental grasses. Important information includes blooming times, when and where various plants were planted, where you got them, when pest problems occurred, if any, and what was done to control them. Photographs or videotapes are also excellent for recording how things look and change from season to season.

Planting and Transplanting

It's hot—"blast furnace" hot. Planting of almost all plant materials is difficult this time of the year. If you have to get out and plant in this heat, disturb the roots of the plants as little as possible and keep them well watered. The sturdier ground covers such as **lily turf** and **monkey grass** will tough it out if planted now, and ornamental grasses can be successfully planted as well. Regular watering will be the key to success when planting this time of year.

Care for Your Plants

Keep ground cover beds well mulched, especially those that have not yet filled in. Don't expect recently planted ground covers to fill an area in a single growing season. There is an old saying about the growth of ground covers: "The first year they sleep, the second year they creep, and the third year they leap." If your ground cover is not growing as fast as you expected, perhaps your expectations were too high. Let it get established this year, and anticipate more growth next year.

Many ornamental grasses begin to bloom in July. Notice how attractive the plumes are waving above the foliage in different shades of silver, cream, and tan with tints of bronze, burgundy, or gold.

Watering

Water is especially critical this time of the year. Most established plantings can get by with an occasional deep watering when the weather is dry. Recent plantings, especially of ground covers, should be watered thoroughly whenever a week passes without rain. Do not be tempted to water every day—you will encourage fungal diseases. It is much better to water deeply and occasionally than lightly every day.

When irrigating, be sure to apply sufficient quantities to thoroughly water your plantings. Water when needed, not on any preset schedule.

Fertilizing

Ground cover areas fertilized this spring can be fertilized again this month. *Sprinkle* a long-lasting premium-quality slow-release granular fertilizer evenly over the area and *water it in.* One-half cup of 15-5-10 will cover 30 square feet and encourage vigorous growth. This is most important for ground cover plantings that have not yet covered the entire bed. Well-established ground covers that have densely covered their beds do not necessarily need fertilizer beyond the spring application.

Pest Control

Ajuga is susceptible to crown rot—plants will suddenly wilt and die even though the soil is moist. The disease can spread rapidly through a planting, wiping out years of growth. Because of this disease, a gardener should really think twice before planting **ajuga** over large areas.

At the first sign of trouble, drench the bed with a disease-control aid. Repeat the application every two to four weeks until the weather cools down in October.

Aspidistra is virtually indestructible (hence the common name **cast-iron plant).** It does sometimes become infested with a white scale which occurs primarily on the leaf stems and lower portions of the foliage. *Spray with a scale-control aid during the cooler early-morning hours for control.* Leaf spot may also attack **aspidistra.** *Prune out infected leaves. If the problem is serious, spray with disease-control aids.*

Visit your local retailer and decide which garden aids you wish to use in your gardening activities. Aids include fertilizers as well as those that control insect pests, weeds, and diseases. Refer to page 291 for a summary listing your options.

Spot-treat with weed-control aids to control tough weeds. Do not get these on desirable plants. Keep beds well mulched. Pull weeds promptly when they appear. Grassy weeds can be controlled with selective weed-control aids, and so can some broadleaf weeds and sedges. These aids will not hurt ornamental plants listed on the label as tolerant of them.

Pruning

Some vines, such as **coral honeysuckle,** bloom sporadically throughout the summer. The more you snip on these, the fewer flowers you will have. Rather than trimming off long shoots, try weaving them back into the main part of the vine or the support.

Planning

August is a popular month for family vacations. If you are going to be gone for more than a few days, ask a friend or neighbor to water outside containers for you. Ground covers planted in the ground this spring or early summer will also need to be watered if it doesn't rain. Before you leave for your vacation:

- *Water* everything thoroughly.

- Make sure beds are weeded and mulched.

- *Edge* ground cover plantings that need it.

- *Trim* vines.

- *Remove* spent flowers from vines and ground covers.

Planting and Transplanting

Cooler weather is just a couple of months away so wait until then to plant, thus avoiding this extreme heat. Containers of ornamental grasses may be available at local nurseries. You can plant them now to fill in gaps in perennial borders, but be prepared to *water as needed to maintain a moist soil in your plant's root zones.*

Care for Your Plants

Last month it was mentioned how ground covers grow slowly the first year after planting, and then speed up as they become better established. Vines can be the same way. If you watch the trellis disappear under a mound of green foliage and tendrils are reaching for you as you walk by, it's time to do some serious pruning.

Watering

Proper watering is critical during this time of the year. Do not think that watering beds by hand is adequate. As relaxing and therapeutic as it is for the gardener, it may not be good for your plants. Use soaker hoses or sprinklers, and leave them on long enough for the water to moisten the soil down about 4 to 6 inches. Morning is the best time to water so that plants will be well supplied with water going into the hottest time of the day. Late-afternoon or early-evening watering with sprinklers is less desirable.

Fertilizing

Spring and midsummer fertilizer applications are all that ground covers need. If you did not fertilize last month, *fertilize* ground cover plantings now. This second fertilizer application is particularly recommended for plantings that have not yet grown to fully cover their area. Apply your selected fertilizer according to label directions.

Pest Control

Spider mites thrive in the hot, dry weather of August. **Juniper ground covers** are especially susceptible to spider mites, which cause browning of the needles. Control (according to label directions) with the aids you have decided to use. Refer to page 291 for a summary listing your options.

Hostas are often badly damaged by snails and slugs and need attention.

Continue to use baits and/or traps to control snails and slugs.

Pruning

Finish up major pruning jobs this month. Vines that bloom in the spring, such as **wisteria** and **Carolina jessamine,** need time to grow and set flowerbuds before winter. Trim back ground covers that have gotten overgrown. Avoid much pruning after this.

Planning

Now that the summer season is coming to a close, take some time to walk around and evaluate the plantings in your landscape. You will probably see successes and a few failures as well. What worked and what didn't work?

We tend to live with the landscape problems we create (or those that previous owners of the property created for us). If you see a problem, decide on a solution and take action. Note your decisions in your Texas gardening journal for future reference. This is also a good time to visit local nurseries and become aware of which plants are available, their sizes, and their prices. Enter this information in your Texas gardening journal as well.

Planting and Transplanting

It's been a long, hot summer. It is still too hot to transplant anything. It's still too hot to do much planting either. Rest up and save your energy for the planting season that is right around the corner.

Care for Your Plants

Strong, gusty winds can blow down stalks in clumps of ornamental grasses. The stalks often straighten themselves back up, but sometimes they need a little help. Push the stalks that are lying down back up, and use green twine in a loop all the way around the plant to hold the stalks in place. If it seems a better solution, *cut back* the stalks that lay over.

Watering

September can be hot and dry, so continue to *water when necessary.* When watering, do a thorough job. *Water* deeply and occasionally rather than lightly every day.

Fertilizing

This is the last month that general fertilizing of landscape plants is done in Texas. If applying fertilizer this month, apply your selected products according to label directions, and water thoroughly.

Pest Control

Pests have had all summer to build up population levels. Inspect plants frequently. To minimize the impact on beneficial insects, spray only infested plants, if at all.

Rain that occurs soon after they are applied may wash off and reduce the effectiveness of many pest-control aids. Refer to page 291 for a summary listing your options. *Repeat applications* as needed.

Pruning

Minimize pruning now to limit flushes of new growth. *Remove* excessively long shoots from vines, but do not shear back the whole plant. *Trim* the edges of ground covers if needed.

Helpful Hints

Flower plumes or seedheads of ornamental grasses can be cut and used in arrangements. Spray with a little clear shellac to keep them from shattering.

Planning

With careful planning and selection of plants, there can always be something wonderful going on in your landscape. Ornamental grasses are all decked out with feathery plumes in shades of beige, silver, creamy white, and tan with tints with highlights of bronze, gold, and burgundy. The plumes in combination with the grasses' handsome foliage offer a striking effect.

Enter information concerning your plans, decisions, and actions during October in your Texas gardening journal.

Planting and Transplanting

October begins the fall planting season, especially for ground covers and hardy perennial vines. When planting ground covers, proper preparation of the planting area will help ensure good establishment and faster growth:

1 First *remove* all existing unwanted vegetation such as lawngrass or weeds from the area. This could be done physically, or you can use weed-control aids. Refer to page 291 for a summary listing your options. Just make sure the activity is done thoroughly now before planting, because weed control in existing plantings may be difficult.

2 Next, *till the soil* to loosen it. When working under a tree, use a turning fork to minimize damage to the tree's roots, and avoid severing roots larger than an inch in diameter whenever possible.

3 *Spread* 4 to 6 inches of organic matter (compost, peat moss, or rotted manure) over the area, and *work it in.*

Care for Your Plants

Mulches in your beds have probably decayed and thinned over the summer, but this is not a bad thing. Organic mulches add organic matter to the soil as they decay. Mulches do, however, lose their effectiveness in controlling weeds when they become too thin. If needed, *add new mulch* over the old to create a mulch depth of at least 3 inches.

Watering

You can generally relax as the weather cools. October may be dry and mild to hot some years, so watch the weather and *water* if needed.

Pest Control

Pre-emergents, also called weed preventers, may be applied to ground cover beds to suppress the growth of cool-season weeds. Apply before weed seeds germinate and according to label directions. Refer to page 291 for a summary listing your options.

Pruning

Pruning should be kept to a minimum. Any pruning done now to spring-flowering vines will reduce the number of flowers next spring.

Most ground covers should not be pruned. If needed, edge beds of **Asian jasmine** as well as other ground covers to keep them neat.

Planning

November weather can run from delightful to downright chilly. Deciduous vines like **wisteria** will begin to look tired, and the foliage will begin to die before it drops. We use very few deciduous ground covers, but **hostas** have become fairly popular. They generally go dormant this month. Mark the location of the plants to avoid damaging them later if you dig in the bed.

Make plans to conduct one or more shopping trips this month for the gardeners or want-to-be gardeners on your holiday gift list.

Planting and Transplanting

Continue to *plant* hardy perennial vines and ground covers. They will not grow over the winter, but they will send out new roots and get existing roots established. As a result, they will outgrow plants that are planted next spring and not have to be tended so much next summer.

You can also dig, divide, and transplant ground covers this month.

Care for Your Plants

If you planted one of the more tender tropical vines such as **mandevilla, allamanda,** or **bougainvillea,** you now have three choices. The first is to let winter do what it will. These vines grow rapidly and can be treated as annuals after an entire summer of flowers. *Plant* new plants next spring if they don't make it through the winter. The second is to *mulch* them thickly over their roots and lower stem to a depth of about 10 inches. If the tops freeze, the roots have a chance of surviving, especially in zones 8b and 9. For more information, see the section on winter protection in the introduction (pages 20–22). The third option is to dig the vines up, pot them in appropriate containers for their root systems using "professional" potting soil, and bring them inside for the winter.

Watering

Cool to cold moist weather generally makes watering this month unnecessary. *Water* newly planted or transplanted plants as needed if the weather turns mild and dry.

Fertilizing

Fertilizer is not needed at this time.

Pest Control

Few, if any, pests bother these plants this time of the year.

Weeds: Handweed gardens as needed and maintain a 3- to 4-inch-deep layer of mulch to keep weeds under control.

Insects: If the weather is still mild, some caterpillar damage may occur. *Treat as needed if desired.*

Check vines and ground covers for the presence of scale insects. They will look like white or tan bumps on leaves or stems that detach easily when pushed with your thumbnail. *Refer to page 291 for a summary listing insect-control aids. Follow label directions.*

Pruning

Pruning should be kept to a minimum. Growth has generally slowed considerably or stopped. If you have kept up with maintaining control during the main growing season, things should be looking just fine now.

Planning

Gardening does not stop in Texas during the winter, but it does slow down. This is a good time to go over all of your gardening tools. How many were broken or lost last summer? In what condition are the rest? What needs to be replaced? What needs to be repaired? Are there tools you need that you don't have? With gift-giving season right around the corner, this is a good time to pick out some new tools. Don't forget the gardeners and want-to-be folks on your holiday gift-giving list. Visit nurseries, garden centers, hardware stores, and bookstores to see what's available.

Planting and Transplanting

You can plant ground covers and hardy perennial vines throughout the winter, but early December is an especially good time. The weather is generally still mild, and the soil is warm from summer. If planted now, plants will make strong root growth and be ready to grow vigorously next spring and summer. The weather conditions over the next several months mean you can just about water them in and walk away.

Nearly all ground covers can be dug, divided, and transplanted this month. This is a good time to transplant vines as well in zones 8 and 9. If you live in zones 6a, 6b, 7a, or 7b, wait until February to transplant most vines and ground covers.

Care for Your Plants

Cut back the dead growth of vines after freezes kill them back. Put some mulch over the roots to protect them from the cold.

Watering

Water-in newly planted or transplanted ground covers and vines. Cool weather and regular rainfall make the need for additional irrigation unlikely. Water if needed to maintain a *moist* soil. Do not apply water on any preset schedule.

Fertilizing

No fertilizer is required by these plants until next spring.

Pest Control

Take a rest. Few pest problems are likely to show up on these plants during the winter. Scales are an exception.

If you see scales on vines or ground covers, spray with a dormant oil or other scale-control aid of your choices, according to label directions. Refer to page 291 for a summary listing your options.

Pruning

To keep things looking neat, selectively *prune out* damaged, brown, or diseased leaves from plants such as **aspidistra** and **ferns.** Otherwise, little or no pruning should be done to ground covers or vines this month.

When cold weather browns the foliage of ornamental grasses, you can cut them back immediately or wait. Some gardeners admire the way ornamental grasses look when they are dormant—others just think they look like dead grass.

Texas Cooperative Extension Service

Fax and Telephone Numbers by County

County	Fax	Telephone
Anderson	(903) 723-2810	(903) 723-3735
Andrews	(915) 524-1473	(915) 524-1421
		(915) 524-1422
Angelina	(409) 634-6427	(409) 632-8239
Aransas	(361) 729-3937	(361) 790-0103
Archer	(940) 574-2833	(940) 574-4914
Armstrong	(806) 226-2189	(806) 226-3021
Atascosa	(830) 769-2330	(830) 769-3066
Austin	(409) 865-8786	(409) 865-5911
Bailey		(806) 272-4583
		(806) 272-4584
Bandera	(830) 796-8121	(830) 796-7755
Bastrop	(512) 332-7287	(512) 332-7286
		(512) 518-7186
Baylor	(940) 888-2258	(940) 888-5581
Bee	(361) 362-3283	(361) 362-3280
		(361) 362-3281
Bell	(254) 933-5312	(254) 933-5305
		(254) 933-5306
Bexar	(210) 930-1753	(210) 467-6575
		(210) 467-6578
		(210) 732-9300
Blanco	(830) 868-2348	(830) 868-7167
Borden		(806) 756-4336
Bosque	(254) 435-6231	(254) 435-2331
		(254) 435-2332
Bowie	(903) 628-6719	(903) 628-6702
Brazoria	(409) 864-1566	(409) 849-5711
Brazos	(409) 775-3768	(409) 823-0129
Brewster	(915) 837-7393	(915) 837-2265
Briscoe	(806) 823-2359	(806) 823-2131
Brooks	(361) 325-9048	(361) 325-4402
Brown		(915) 646-0386
		(915) 646-7410
Burleson	(409) 567-2370	(409) 567-2308
Burnet		(512) 756-5420
Caldwell	(512) 398-3867	(512) 398-3122
Calhoun	(361) 552-6727	(361) 552-9747
		(361) 552-9748
Callahan		(915) 854-1518
Cameron	(956) 361-0034	(956) 399-7757
		(956) 440-7220
Camp	(903) 856-3078	(903) 856-5005
		(903) 856-5060
Carson	(806) 537-3724	(806) 537-3882
Cass	(903) 756-8923	(903) 756-5391
		(903) 756-5483
Castro	(806) 647-3218	(806) 647-4115
		(806) 647-4116
Chambers	(409) 267-3962	(409) 267-8347
Cherokee	(903) 683-1827	(903) 683-5416
Childress	(940) 937-3479	(940) 937-2351
Clay	(940) 538-5052	(940) 538-5042
Cochran		(806) 266-5215
Coke		(915) 453-2461
Coleman		(915) 625-4519
Collin	(972) 548-4694	(972) 548-4233
		(Metro) 424-1460
Collingsworth	(806) 447-5418	(806) 447-2313
Colorado	(409) 732-6694	(409) 732-2082
		(409) 732-2530
Comal	(830) 620-3446	(830) 620-3440
Comanche	(915) 356-3710	(915) 356-2539
Concho	(915) 732-4429	(915) 732-4304
Cooke	(940) 668-5402	(940) 668-5413
		(940) 668-5415
		(940) 668-5416
Coryell	(254) 865-7404	(254) 865-2414
Cottle	(806) 492-3107	(806) 492-3151
Crane		(915) 558-1139
		(915) 558-3522
Crockett		(915) 392-2721
		(915) 392-2722
Crosby	(806) 675-2348	(806) 675-2347
		(806) 675-2426
Culberson		(915) 283-8440
Dallam	(806) 244-2252	(806) 244-4434
Dallas	(214) 904-3080	(214) 688-0903
		(214) 904-3050
		(214) 904-3051
		(214) 904-3053
Dawson	(806) 872-5606	(806) 872-3444
		(806) 872-5978
		(806) 872-7539
Deaf Smith	(806) 363-7007	(806) 364-3573
Delta	(903) 395-4417*	(903) 395-4417
Denton	(940) 565-5621	(972) 434-2052
		(940) 565-5535
		(940) 565-5536
		(940) 565-5537
		(940) 565-5538
Dewitt	(361) 275-3512	(361) 275-5132
		(361) 275-5731
Dickens	(806) 623-5553	(806) 623-5552
Dimmit	(830) 876-2957	(830) 876-5271

*Call first before faxing.

Texas Cooperative Extension Service

County	Fax	Telephone
Donley	(806) 874-3054	(806) 874-2141
Duval		(361) 256-3651
Eastland	(254) 629-2080	(254) 629-1093
		(254) 629-2222
Ector		(915) 498-4071
Edwards		(830) 683-4310
Ellis	(972) 923-5184	(972) 923-5175
		(972) 923-5186
El Paso	(915) 860-0331	(915) 859-7725
		(915) 859-7856
		(915) 859-7973
		(915) 772-0475
Erath	(254) 965-1472	(254) 965-1460
Falls	(254) 883-1415	(254) 883-1410
		(254) 883-1413
Fannin	(903) 583-1092	(903) 583-7453
Fayette	(409) 968-5295	(409) 968-5831
Fisher		(915) 776-2171
Floyd	(806) 983-4909	(806) 983-4912
Foard	(940) 684-1947	(940) 684-1919
Fort Bend	(281) 342-8658	(281) 342-3034
Fort Bliss	(915) 860-0331	(915) 568-1343
		(915) 568-4878
Fort Hood	(254) 865-7404	(254) 286-5338
		(254) 286-6684
		(254) 286-6780
		(254) 287-2437
		(254) 287-2943
		(254) 287-6774
		(254) 287-9048
		(254) 288-2862
		(254) 288-5156
		(254) 618-7443
		(254) 618-7444
Franklin		(903) 537-4017
Freestone	(903) 389-7858	(903) 389-3436
Frio	(830) 334-2752	(830) 334-0099
Gaines	(915) 758-4031	(915) 758-2977
		(915) 758-4006
		(915) 758-4040
Galveston	(281) 534-4053	(281) 534-3413
Garza	(806) 495-4444	(806) 495-4400
Gillespie	(830) 997-6378	(830) 997-3157
		(830) 997-3452
		(830) 997-7047
Glasscock		(915) 354-2381
		(915) 354-2477
Goliad	(361) 645-2427	(361) 645-8204
		(361) 645-8205
Gonzales		(830) 672-8531

County	Fax	Telephone
Gray	(806) 669-8029	(806) 669-8033
Grayson	(903) 893-5207	(903) 813-4201
		(903) 813-4202
		(903) 813-4203
		(903) 813-4204
		(903) 813-4206
Gregg	(903) 758-3345	(903) 236-8428
		(903) 236-8429
Grimes	(409) 825-1803	(409) 825-3495
Guadalupe	(830) 372-3940	(830) 379-1972
		(830) 379-2153
Hale	(806) 291-5266	(806) 291-5267
		(806) 291-5271
		(806) 291-5274
Hall	(806) 259-5078	(806) 259-3015
Hamilton	(254) 386-8727	(254) 386-3919
Hansford	(806) 659-2025	(806) 659-4131
		(806) 659-4132
Hardeman	(940) 663-6302	(940) 663-6301
Hardin		(409) 246-5128
Harris	(281) 855-5638	(281) 855-5600
		(713) 349-0880
		(713) 440-4900
Harrison	(903) 935-4875	(903) 935-4830
	(903) 935-4837	(903) 935-4831
		(903) 935-4835
		(903) 935-4836
Hartley	(806) 235-2316	(806) 235-3122
Haskell	(940) 864-2546*	(940) 864-2546
		(940) 864-2658
Hays	(512) 393-2136	(512) 393-2120
Hemphill	(806) 323-8392	(806) 323-9114
Henderson	(903) 677-7222	(903) 675-6130
Hidalgo	(956) 383-1735	(956) 383-1026
		(956) 383-5721
Hill	(254) 582-4021	(254) 582-3551
		(254) 582-4022
Hockley	(806) 897-3104	(806) 894-2406
		(806) 894-3159
Hood	(817) 579-0396	(817) 579-3280
Hopkins	(903) 439-4909*	(903) 885-3443
		(903) 885-3726
Houston	(409) 544-8053	(409) 544-3255
Howard	(915) 264-2239	(915) 264-2236
		(915) 264-2237
Hudspeth		(915) 369-2291
Hunt	(903) 408-4281	(903) 408-4101
		(903) 886-5363
Hutchinson	(806) 878-4021	(806) 878-4026
Irion		(915) 835-2711

*Call first before faxing.

Texas Cooperative Extension Service

County	Fax	Telephone
Jack.........	(940) 567-3021	(940) 567-2132
Jackson.......	(361) 782-3351	(361) 782-3312
Jasper	(490) 384-8226	(409) 384-3721
		(409) 384-4481
Jeff Davis..............		See Brewster County
Jefferson	(409) 839-2310	(409) 835-8461
Johnson.......	(817) 556-6375	(817) 556-6370
Jim Hogg		See Duval County
Jim Wells.....	(361) 668-2802	(361) 668-5705
Jones.........	(915) 823-4241	(915) 823-2432
		(915) 823-4242
Karnes.......	(830) 780-4530	(830) 780-3906
		(830) 780-3907
Kaufman.....	(972) 563-0558	(972) 563-0233
		(972) 563-0960
Kendall................		(830) 249-9343
Kenedy	See Kleberg or Nueces County	
Kent........	(806) 237-3115	(806) 237-3345
		(806) 237-3751
Kerr	(830) 257-6573	(830) 257-6568
Kimble...............		(915) 446-2620
King........	(806) 596-4664	(806) 596-4451
Kinney...............		(830) 563-2442
Kleberg......	(361) 592-7741	(361) 595-8566
Knox........	(940) 454-2002	(940) 454-2651
Lamar.......	(903) 737-2446	(903) 737-2443
Lamb	(806) 385-6485	(806) 385-4222
Lampasas		(512) 556-8271
La Salle......	(830) 879-3267	(830) 879-2213
Lavaca.......	(361) 798-2162	(361) 798-2162
		(361) 798-2221
Lee.........	(409) 542-2362	(409) 542-1728
		(409) 542-2753
Leon.......	(903) 536-3804	(903) 536-2531
Liberty	(409) 336-4565	(409) 336-4558
Limestone.....	(254) 729-2540	(254) 729-5314
		(254) 729-8229
Lipscomb	(806) 862-2603	(806) 862-4601
Live Oak.....	(361) 449-3068	(361) 449-2733
Llano	(915) 247-2449	(915) 247-4849
		(915) 247-5159
Loving	See Reeves or Pecos County	
Lubbock	(806) 762-4178	(806) 747-2625
		(806) 767-1190
Lynn........	(806) 998-4562	(806) 998-4562
Madison	(409) 348-9685	(409) 348-2234
Marion.......	(903) 665-3132	(903) 665-2272
		(903) 665-2421
Martin.................		(915) 756-2251
		(915) 756-3316

County	Fax	Telephone
Mason		(915) 347-6459
Matagorda.....	(409) 245-5661	(409) 245-4100
Maverick......	(830) 773-6450	(830) 773-5064
McCulloch		(915) 597-1295
McLennan.....	(254) 756-3549	(254) 757-5180
McMullen	(361) 274-3618	(361) 274-3323
Medina......	(830) 741-6182	(830) 741-6180
Menard..............		(915) 396-4787
Midland		(915) 687-1351
Milam.......	(254) 697-4635	(254) 697-3382
Mills	(915) 648-2806	(915) 648-2650
Mitchell.......	(915) 728-8319	(915) 728-3111
Montague	(940) 894-2001	(940) 894-2831
Montgomery ...	(409) 788-8394	(409) 539-7822
		(409) 539-7823
		(409) 539-7824
		(409) 539-7825
Moore.......	(806) 934-9765	(806) 935-2593
....		(806) 935-2594
Morris		(903) 645-2222
Motley.....	(806) 347-2220	(806) 347-2733
Nacogdoches ...	(409) 560-7894	(409) 560-7711
Navarro.....	(903) 654-3026	(903) 654-3075
Newton.....	(409) 379-4060	(409) 379-4831
Nolan.................		(915) 235-3184
		(915) 236-6912
		(915) 236-9011
Nueces	(361) 767-5248	(361) 387-7101
		(361) 767-5216
		(361) 767-5217
		(361) 767-5220
		(361) 767-5223
		(361) 854-4112
Ochiltree	(806) 435-2081	(806) 435-3831
Oldham......	(806) 267-2362	(806) 267-2692
Orange	(409) 882-7087	(409) 882-7010
Palo Pinto	(940) 659-2655	(940) 659-1228
Panola	(903) 694-2909	(903) 693-0380
Parker......	(817) 598-6159	(817) 599-6591
Parmer.	(806) 481-3610	(806) 481-3300
		(806) 481-3619
Pecos.......	(915) 336-6107	(915) 336-2541
		(915) 336-3163
		(915) 336-3959
Polk.......	(409) 327-6897	(409) 327-6828
Potter......	(806) 373-7946	(806) 372-3829
		(806) 373-0713
Presidio.................		(915) 729-4746
Rains.....	(903) 473-4298	(903) 473-2412
Randall......	(806) 655-6320	(806) 655-6325

*Call first before faxing.

Texas Cooperative Extension Service

County	Fax	Telephone
Reagan		(915) 884-2335
Real		(830) 232-6673
Red River	(903) 427-5510	(903) 427-3867
		(903) 427-3868
Reeves		(915) 447-9041
Refugio	(361) 526-2825	(361) 526-2825
		(361) 526-4340
Roberts	(806) 868-3381	(806) 868-3191
Robertson	(409) 828-1112	(409) 828-4270
Rockwall	(972) 882-0374	(972) 882-0375
Runnels	(915) 365-5932	(915) 365-2219
		(915) 365-5042
		(915) 365-5212
Rusk	(903) 655-8856	(903) 657-0376
Sabine	(409) 787-4753	(409) 787-2194
		(409) 787-3752
San Augustine	(409) 275-9447	(409) 275-3644
San Jacinto		(409) 653-2396
San Patricio	(361) 364-6237	(361) 364-6234
San Saba	(915) 372-5425	(915) 374-5416
Schleicher		(915) 853-2132
Scurry		(915) 573-5423
Shackelford		(915) 762-2233
Shelby	(409) 591-0151	(409) 598-3223
		(409) 598-7744
Sherman	(806) 396-5670	(806) 366-2081
		(806) 366-2122
Smith	(903) 535-0884	(903) 535-0885
Somervell	(254) 897-9323	(254) 897-2289
		(254) 897-2809
Starr	(956) 716-8197	(956) 487-2306
Stephens	(254) 559-2362	(254) 559-2313
Sterling		(915) 378-3181
Stonewall	(940) 989-3566	(940) 989-3510
Sutton	(915) 387-5537	(915) 387-3101
		(915) 387-3604
Swisher		(806) 995-3721
		(806) 995-3726
Tarrant	(817) 884-1941	(817) 451-2877
		(817) 884-1291
		(817) 884-1294
		(817) 884-1553
		(817) 884-1942
		(817) 884-1944
		(817) 884-1945
		(817) 884-1946

County	Fax	Telephone
Taylor	(915) 672-9148	(915) 672-6048
Terrell		(915) 345-2291
Terry	(806) 637-2588	(806) 637-4060
		(806) 637-8792
Throckmorton	(940) 849-3220	(940) 552-9941
		(940) 849-3321
Titus	(903) 577-1779	(903) 572-0261
		(903) 572-5201
Tom Green		(915) 659-6524
		(915) 659-6525
		(915) 659-6527
		(915) 659-6528
Travis	(512) 473-9611	(512) 385-0990
		(512) 473-9600
Trinity	(409) 642-2040	(409) 642-1421
Tyler	(409) 283-8285	(409) 283-8284
Upshur	(903) 843-5492	(903) 843-4019
Upton		(915) 693-2281
		(915) 693-2313
Uvalde	(830) 278-2072	(830) 278-6661
Val Verde		(830) 774-7591
Van Zandt	(903) 567-4699	(903) 567-4149
Victoria	(361) 572-0798	(361) 575-4581
Walker	(409) 435-2429	(409) 435-2426
Waller	(409) 826-7654	(409) 826-7651
Ward	(915) 943-3138	(915) 943-2682
		(915) 943-4112
Washington	(409) 277-6223	(409) 277-6200
Webb	(956) 721-2230	(956) 721-2626
Wharton	(409) 532-8863	(409) 532-3310
		(409) 532-3371
		(409) 532-8040
Wheeler	(806) 826-3282	(806) 826-5243
Wichita	(940) 716-5589	(940) 716-5580
Wilbarger	(940) 553-4422	(940) 552-5474
Willacy	(956) 689-2031	(956) 689-2412
Williamson	(512) 930-4407	(512) 930-4400
Wilson	(830) 393-7319	(830) 393-7357
Winkler		(915) 586-2593
Wise	(940) 627-8070	(940) 627-3341
Wood	(903) 763-2092	(903) 763-2924
Yoakum		(806) 456-2263
Young	(940) 549-8140	(940) 549-0737
Zapata	(956) 765-9748	(956) 765-4663
Zavala	(830) 374-3351	(830) 374-2883

Note: Area codes and actual phone numbers may change. We have made an attempt to publish the most current area codes and actual phone numbers available.

*Call first before faxing.

Glossary

Acclimate: to become accustomed to a different environment.

Aeration: to expose to the circulation of air to improve health (often refers to lawns). This is normally accomplished by punching holes into the soil by machine or hand.

Alkaline soil: soil with a pH greater than 7.0. It lacks acidity, often because it is high in calcium—most often true of clay soils.

All-purpose fertilizer: powdered, liquid, or granular fertilizer that contains the three key nutrients—nitrogen (N), potassium (P), and phosphorus (K). It is suitable for maintenance nutrition for most plants and may also called general-purpose fertilizer.

Annual: a plant that lives its entire life in one season. It is genetically determined to germinate, grow, flower, set seed, and die the same year.

Anti-transpirant: any product, compound, or aid used to reduce the loss of water vapor through a plant's leaves (transpiration).

Arborist: an individual trained in the care of trees.

Balled and burlapped: a tree or shrub grown in the field whose soilball was wrapped with protective burlap and twine when the plant was dug up to be sold or transplanted.

Bare root: a plant that has been packaged without any soil around its roots. (Often roses, young shrubs, and trees purchased through the mail arrive with their exposed roots covered with moist peat or sphagnum moss, sawdust, or similar material, and wrapped in plastic.)

Berm: (1) a narrow raised ring of soil around a tree, used to hold water so it will be directed to the root zone. (2) a designed raised planting area, often in front of a home.

Biennial: a plant that is grown for two growing seasons, then dies after flowering and setting seed.

Bolting: the sending up of a flower stalk by a leafy vegetable. It generally signals a decrease in quality and the end of the productive season.

Bract: a modified petal-like leaf structure on a plant stem near its flower. Often it is more colorful and visible than the actual flower, as in dogwood.

Broadcasting: a type of direct seeding. Seeds are scattered evenly over a bed area and covered to the proper depth. Two to three times as many seeds are planted as the number of actual plants that will be needed. When the seed comes up, the extras are thinned out so that the remaining plants are at the proper spacing.

Bromeliads: popular, easy-care houseplants that slowly lose vigor and die after blooming but can be regrown from side shoots, or pups.

Budding: a form of grafting in which vegetative buds are attached to root stock.

Bud union: the place where the top of a plant was grafted to the rootstock; usually refers to roses.

Canopy: the overhead branching area of a tree, including foliage.

Chelated iron: iron in a form immediately available to plants, often in a fertilizer used to treat iron chlorosis.

Climber: a plant grown upright by twining, aerial roots, tendrils, or holdfasts.

Clinging: a way vines grow and attach to flat surfaces by using roots along their stems or holdfasts. They can cover the sides of buildings or walls without requiring a support.

Cold hardiness: the ability of a plant to survive the winter cold in a particular area.

Compost: organic matter that has undergone progressive decomposition by microbial and macrobial activity until it is reduced to a spongy, fluffy texture. Added to soil of any type, it improves the soil's ability to hold air, nutrients, and water and to drain well.

Corm: the swollen energy-storing structure, analogous to a bulb, under the soil at the base of the stem of a plant such as crocus and gladiolus.

County Agent/Extension Agent: employee of a state's university who provides information and assistance to farmers and homeowners about agriculture, horticulture, agronomy, soil analysis, and pest controls. Extension agents are usually officed in each county seat of the state.

Cormels: small buds that can develop around the base of a corm.

Cropping: a harvesting practice. Only the lower leaves of leafy vegetables are regularly harvested, so the plant will continue to produce.

Crown: (1) a rosette of leaves on a short stem. (2) the base of a plant at, or just beneath, the surface of the soil where the roots meet the stems.

Crust: a relatively dense/heavy soil surface which reduces emergence of seeds.

Cultivar: a CULTIvated VARiety. It is a form of a plant that has been identified as special or superior and is purposely selected for propagation and production.

Damping-off: a disease that lives in the soil and causes seedlings to die soon after they emerge.

Deadheading: a pruning technique that removes faded flower heads from plants to improve their appearance, prevent seed production, and stimulate further flowering.

Deciduous: a tree or shrub that, unlike an evergreen, loses all its leaves in the fall.

Desiccation: drying out of foliage tissues, usually due to drought or wind.

Desucker: to remove side shoots, or suckers.

Diatomaceous earth: a dust-like material (composed of the spiny shells of one-celled algae) that can be placed in a ring around a plant. Snails and slugs do not like to crawl across the tiny sharp particles, and they tend to leave those plants alone.

Direct seeding: planting seeds directly into the garden.

Division: the practice of splitting apart perennial plants to create several smaller-rooted segments. The practice is useful for controlling a plant's size and for acquiring more plants; it is also essential to the health and continued flowering of certain plants.

Dormancy: the period, usually the winter, when perennial plants rest, temporarily ceasing active growth. "Go dormant" is a verb form, as used in this sentence: *Some plants, like spring-blooming bulbs, go dormant in the summer.*

Drilling: a type of direct seeding. Seeds are planted in straight lines at the proper depth, but two to three times closer than the plants ultimately will be spaced. When the seeds come up, the extras are thinned, leaving behind seedlings at the proper spacing. This technique is good if you don't know what the seedlings of the vegetable or flower you are planting look like. The desirable seedlings are in the drills—the weeds are in between.

Glossary

Drip irrigation: method utilized to place small amounts of water directly to the root zone of plants. This is very effective and saves 50% or more on water usage.

Dripline: the distance from a tree's trunk to the outer tips of the branches.

Dry soil conditions: achieved when the soil is allowed to dry (pencil or chopstick inserted two-thirds into pot is dry) before watering.

Epiphytic: a plant that grows on another plant, depending on it for mechanical support but not for nutrients or water.

Established: a newly planted tree, shrub, or flower that has begun to produce new growth (either foliage or stems). This is an indication that the roots have recovered from transplant shock and have begun to grow and spread.

Evergreen: a perennial plant that does not lose its foliage annually with the onset of winter. Needled or broadleaf foliage persists and continues to function on a plant through one or more winters, aging and dropping unobtrusively in cycles of three or four years or more.

Fertilizer: a substance added to a soil's environment that provides one or more essential nutrients.

Filling: building up the level of low-lying land with material such as soil.

Floret: a tiny flower, usually one of many forming a cluster.

Flower scape: a leafless flower stalk that grows directly from the soil, such as a tulip.

Foliar: of or about foliage—usually refers to the practice of spraying foliage, as in fertilizing or treating with insect-control aids; leaf tissues absorb liquid directly for fast results, and the soil is not affected.

Fungicide: any compound, product, or other gardening aid used to prevent, control, eradicate, or eliminate plant diseases caused by fungi.

Gardening aid: any substance, product, material, insect, barrier, compound, or control utilized by gardeners to achieve their goals. This includes fertilizers, beneficial insects, insect controls, weed controls, disease controls, baits, and traps.

Genus specie: a plant's scientific name. Genus is the classification of a plant, and specie refers to a distinct kind of plant within the classification. An example is *Quercus* (the oak genus) *shumardi* (specie) commonly called Shumard Red Oak.

Germinate: to sprout. Germination is a fertile seed's first stage of development.

Grafting: a method of propagation in which part one plant is united with a section including limbs and the root system of a second plant.

Graft union: the point on the stem of a woody plant with sturdier roots where a stem from a highly ornamental plant is inserted so that it will join with it. Roses and fruit trees are commonly grafted.

Habitat: the native/natural environment of a plant.

Harden-off: the process of gradually acclimating plants from an indoor environment to an outdoor environment.

Hardscape: the permanent, structural, nonplant part of a landscape, such as walls, sheds, pools, patios, arbors, and walkways.

Herbaceous perennials: plants that live from year to year without producing woody stems.

Herbaceous: a plant having fleshy or soft stems that die back with frost; the opposite of woody.

Glossary

Herbicide: any compound, product, or other gardening aid used to control, abate, or kill unwanted plants.

High light: for houseplants, east or west window, south window in winter, 500 to 1000 foot-candles. High light for houseplants outdoors means 4 to 6 hours of direct sun, preferably morning.

Hills: raised mounds formed in a type of direct seeding. They are planted with several seeds per hill.

Hybrid: a plant that is the result of intentional or natural cross-pollination between different varieties, cultivars, species, or, rarely, genera.

Impeller: the part of a water pump that moves the water.

Insecticide: any product, compound, or other gardening aid used to kill, control, or eliminate insects.

Intercropping: a way of maximizing production from vegetable beds. Vegetables that are spaced relatively far apart such as broccoli, cauliflower, cabbage, and brussels sprouts do not fully occupy the bed early in their season. The bed space between the plants can be used to grow a quick-maturing crop such as radishes or lettuce which will be harvested and gone by the time larger plants begin to cover those spaces.

Iron chlorosis: an iron deficiency most common in acid-loving plants. Leaves turn a yellow-green color, while the veins of the leaves stay dark green.

Irrigation: the process of applying water to a plant.

Lime: ground limestone used to add calcium to the soil and to raise its pH level or make it more alkaline. Dolomite lime adds both calcium and magnesium.

Low light: for houseplants, north window, 75 to 200 foot-candles. Low light for houseplants outdoors means no direct sun.

Medium light: for houseplants, south window in summer, 200 to 500 foot-candles. Medium light for houseplants outdoors means minimal direct sun (in the early morning).

Melting out: a condition in which herbaceous plants suddenly collapse, wither up, and die. Sometimes the dead tissue is slimy to the touch.

Moist soil conditions: achieved when the soil is allowed to dry slightly (feels dry when finger inserted about 1 inch) before watering.

Mulch: a layer or blanket of material over bare soil to protect it from erosion and compaction by rain, and to discourage weeds. It may be inorganic (gravel, fabric) or organic (wood chips, bark, pine needles, chopped leaves).

Naturalize: (1) to plant seeds, bulbs, or plants in a random, informal pattern as they would appear in their natural habitat; (2) to adapt to and spread throughout adopted habitats (a tendency of some nonnative plants).

Nectar: the sweet fluid produced by glands on flowers that attract pollinators such as hummingbirds or honeybees, for whom it is a source of energy.

Organic material, organic matter: any material or debris that is derived from plants. It is carbon-based material capable of undergoing decomposition and decay.

Peat moss: organic matter from peat sedges (United States) or sphagnum mosses (Canada), often used to improve soil texture. The acidity of sphagnum peat moss makes it ideal for boosting or maintaining soil acidity while improving its drainage.

Perennials: plants that live for three years or longer. Unlike annuals and biennials, perennials do not die after flowering and setting seed. Technically, trees, shrubs, lawngrasses, and bulbs are all perennials, but gardeners use the term "perennial" as an abbreviation for "hardy, herbaceous perennial"—a group of nonwoody, hardy plants grown for their attractive flowers or foliage. Some herbaceous perennials are evergreen and never go completely dormant, while others go dormant, lose their leaves, and essentially disappear at certain times of the year, usually winter.

Pesticide: any compound, product, or aid used to eliminate, abate, control, kill, or reduce unwanted pests including insects, diseases, and weeds.

pH: a measurement used to indicate the acidity or alkalinity of water or soil. A pH of 7 is neutral, numbers below 7 indicate an acid condition, and numbers above 7 indicate an alkaline condition.

Photosynthesis: a process plants use to create sugar from carbon dioxide and water. The energy source is light (usually sunlight).

Pinch: to remove tender stems' tips by pressing them between thumb and forefinger. This pruning technique encourages branching, compactness, and flowering in plants, or it removes aphids clustered at growing tips.

Pollen: the yellow, powdery grains in the center of a flower. A plant's male sex cells are transferred to the female plant parts by means of wind or animal pollinators to fertilize them and create seeds.

Pre-emergent: a weed-control substance applied to beds before weed seeds sprout. It will suppress the growth of weeds and is sometimes called a "weed preventer."

Pups: the side shoots on a bromeliad. They can be used for propagating the plant.

Rhizome: a swollen energy-storing stem structure, similar to a bulb, that lies horizontally in the soil. Its roots emerge from its lower surface, and growth shoots from a growing point at or near its tip (as in bearded iris).

Root flare: the transition at the base of a tree trunk where the bark tissue begins to differentiate and roots begin to form just before entering the soil. This area should not be covered with soil when planting a tree.

Rootbound (or potbound): the condition of a plant that has been confined in a container too long. Its roots are forced to wrap around themselves and even swell out of the container. Successful transplanting or repotting requires untangling and trimming away of some of the matted roots.

Scion: the upper portion of a grafted plant that produces the foliage, attractive flowers, or high-quality fruit or nuts.

Self-seeding: the tendency of some plants to sow their seeds freely around the yard. This creates many seedlings the following season that may or may not be welcome.

Semi-evergreen: a plant that tends to be evergreen in a mild climate but deciduous in a cool/cold one.

Shearing: the pruning technique whereby plant stems and branches are cut uniformly with long-bladed pruning shears (hedge shears) or powered hedge trimmers. It is used when creating and maintaining hedges and topiary.

Glossary

Slow-release fertilizer: long-lasting fertilizer that is water insoluble and therefore releases its nutrients gradually as a function of soil temperature, moisture, and related microbial activity. Typically granular, it may be organic or synthetic.

Soil testing laboratories: facilities that can analyze soil for its nutrient content and pH. Private labs are available as well as the Stephen F. Austin State University Soil Testing Lab and the Texas Agricultural Extension Service Soil Testing Lab. Consult the Yellow Pages and/or contact SFASU Soil Testing Lab or your County Extension Agent to learn about these services.

Sooty mold: a black fungal deposit on foliage. It indicates the presence of sucking insects.

Stock: the part of a grafted plant that provides the roots but should never be allowed to sprout and grow.

Subsidence: the sinking or settling of soil to a lower level.

Succulent growth: the sometimes undesirable production of fleshy tender leaves or stems that results from overfertilization.

Sucker: a vigorous, fast-growing shoot, often undesirable. Underground plant roots produce suckers to form new stems and spread by means of these roots to form large plantings, or colonies. Some plants produce root suckers or branch suckers as a result of pruning or wounding.

Sulfur: an element or nutrient usually added to the soil to reduce its pH level or make it more acidic. Often added in combination with iron. Also used as an insecticide and fungicide.

Thinning: the process of eliminating or removing small seedlings for the remaining plants to have room to grow to full maturity.

True bulb: consists of a compressed stem and a growing point or flower bud enclosed with thick, fleshy, modified leaves.

Tuber: a type of underground storage structure in a plant stem, analogous to a bulb. It generates roots below and stems above ground (example: dahlia).

Twining: a way vines climb by wrapping their stems, leaves, or tendrils around a support.

Variegated: having various colors or color patterns. The term usually refers to plant foliage that is streaked, edged, blotched, or mottled with a contrasting color, often green with yellow, cream, or white.

Weed-blocking aid: any product that effectively blocks weeds from emerging when utilized according to label directions. This product is available at retailers, usually on rolls, and may be utilized in all types of gardening.

Summary of Pest Control Options

According to the dictionary, a pest is defined as, "A person or thing that causes trouble, annoyance, discomfort, etc.; nuisance; specifically, any destructive or troublesome insect, small animal, weed, etc.". Additionally, the suffix *cide* is defined as, "killer, killing." Put the two together, and we have pesticide or any aid used to kill, eliminate, control, or prevent pests. Pests encountered by Texas gardeners include insects, mites, diseases, weeds, plus, at times, small animals such as gophers and moles. For some, our hot, dry summers are a pest.

While we can't control the weather, we can help ourselves and our gardening goals by planting the best locally-adapted plants and their varieties plus provide proper care for them as suggested in this book. Remember, healthy well-adapted plants have fewer problems with any pest.

The aids/controls/products listed in this section are some that are available to the gardener in today's marketplace. These products can be found at local nurseries, garden centers, farm stores, hardware stores, and mass merchandisers. The market is constantly changing, and because of this, some products, brand names, active ingredients, and uses also change. Utilize local retailers, as they can be an invaluable information source when deciding which aids, if any, will be used. Not all products, active ingredients, packaging, and forms are available at every retailer.

Review the following information on Insect Pests, Disease Pests, and Weed Pests, and use it as a guide when visiting local retailers.

Insect Pests and Some Controls

Aids/controls/products are listed alphabetically and not in order of preference or recommendation by the authors. This following list is compiled from available information and is believed to be accurate and correct. But it is not an absolute list. Common and/or trade names of aids/controls/products listed are capitalized and active ingredients are in lower case letters. Insect-control aids/products are constantly changing. Texas gardeners may utilize any of the various aids/controls/products listed if available at local or area retailers.

Remember, not all insects are pests. Only use insect aids/controls/products when and if needed to help you achieve your personal gardening goals. Always read and follow label directions/instructions when utilizing any insect pest-control aid. Insecticides derived from naturally occurring components and compound ingredients are also pesticides.

Summary of Pest Control Options

Insects

Name	Controls	Plants Affected	When Pest Active
Ants	acephate, Amdro, borax, carbaryl, diazinon, malathion, permethrin and pyrethrum	Few if any plants are affected; nuisance to people	Year-round, especially in warm seasons
Aphids	acephate, carbaryl, diazinon, insecticidal soap, neem, permethrin, and pyrethrum	Any plant with tender new growth	Year-round when plants are actively growing
Armyworms	Conserve, diazinon, Oftanol, Orthene, Proxol, Sevin, and Talstar	Texas lawn grasses	Usually summer; may occur spring and fall
Bagworms	(BT), diazinon, malathion, Orthene, and Sevin	Cedar, juniper, and arborvitae	Usually in active growing season; remain year-round if not physically removed
Beetles	diazinon, malathion, and Sevin	Vegetables, some trees, and flowers	Usually in warm seasons
Billbugs	diazinon, Merit, Oftanol, and Talstar	Plants with tender shallow root systems, usually annuals	Year-round; most active in warm, moist times
Borers, Woody Plants	diazinon and thiodan	Trees and old large shrubs	Most active in spring and summer
Caterpillars	(BT), diazinon, malathion, and Sevin	Many plants with tender growth, vegetables, and annuals	Most active in spring; also active through fall
Chiggers	diazinon and sulfur	None; nuisance to people	Warm seasons
Chinch bugs	Astro, diazinon, Mocap, Orthene, Sevin, Talstar, Tempo, and Turcam	Texas lawn grasses	Hot, dry summers
Crickets (common and mole)	diazinon, Oftanol, pyrethrums, resmethrins and Sevin	Mole: any plants they cut the roots of; Common: nuisance to people	Warm and especially moist seasons
Cutworms	diazinon and Sevin	Vegetable transplants most affected	Most active in spring
Earwigs	Baygon, diazinon, malathion, metaldehyde, pyrethrums, resmethrins, and Sevin	Plants not normally affected; nuisance to people	Year-round; most active in warm seasons

Summary of Pest Control Options

Insects

Name	Controls	Plants Affected	When Pest Active
Fire ants	Amdro, diazinon, Orthene, and pyrethrums	Any plants under which they build nests; major nuisance to people	Year-round, especially in warm, moist seasons
Fleas	Baygon, (DE), Demize, diazinon, malathion, Petcor, pyrethrums, and Sevin	None; nuisance to people and pets	Year-round; most active in warm seasons
Flies, house	baits, diazinon, Dipterex, fly strips, and fly papers	None; nuisance to people	Warm seasons
Fungus gnats	diazinon, insecticidal soaps, malathion, pyrethrums, and resmethrins	Usually non harmful to plants; most often found in houseplants; may be a nuisance to people	Year-round; most active in growing season
Grasshoppers	No Lo Bait, Orthene, pyrethrums, and Sevin XLR	Almost any plant	Summer, especially when hot and dry
Grubs	diazinon, Dylox, Mach 2, Merit, Mocap, Oftanol, Proxol, Sevin, and Turcam	Texas lawn grasses	May be active year-round; most damage in cool seasons
Lacebugs	Cygon, malathion, Orthene, and Sevin	Ornamental shrubs, such as azaleas and pyracanthas	Summer
Leaf cutter bees	Baygon, malathion, pyrethrums, resmethrins, and Sevin	Any plant in the landscape with relatively tender leaves	Warm seasons
Leaf hoppers	diazinon, Orthene, Sevin, Talstar, and Turcam	Vegetables and ornamentals, including roses	Warm active growing season
Leaf miners	Cygon, diazinon, malathion, and Orthene	Trees to vegetables	Active growing season
Leaf rollers	malathion, methoxychlor, Orthene, and Sevin	Various plants in the garden, including cannas	Active growing season
Mealybugs	diazinon, lightweight horticultural oils, malathion, and Orthene	Any tender plant; houseplants	Year-round indoors; active growing season outdoors
Millipedes and centipedes	diazinon, pyrethrums, resmethrins, Sevin, and Talstar	None; nuisance to people	Year-round; most active in warm, moist seasons

Summary of Pest Control Options

Insects

Name	Controls	Plants Affected	When Pest Active
Pecan nut casebarer	(BT), diazinon, malathion, and Sevin	Pecans and hickory	Active growing season
Phylloxera	dormant oils and malathion	Pecans and fruits	Active growing season
Plant bugs	dimethoate, insecticidal soaps, pyrethrums, resmethrins, rotone, and Sevin	Vegetables	Active growing season
Scales	dormant and light-weight horticultural oils, lime-sulfur, and Orthene	From trees to houseplants	Year-round; most active in growing season
Scorpions	Baygon, diazinon, malathion, Prelude, pyrethrums, Suscent, and Tempo	None; nuisance to people	Warm, moist seasons
Slugs and snails	metalhyde, Sevin, and traps	Young tender shallow-rooted foliage plants, including hosta	Warm growing season
Sod webworms	Astro, Conserve, diazinon, Mach 2, Mocap, Oftanol, Sevin, Talstar, and Turcam	Texas lawn grasses	Summer heat
Sowbugs/pillbugs	diazinon, Sevin, Talstar, and Turcam	Annuals and vegetables	Warm, moist seasons
Spider mites	diazinon, Kelthane, lightweight horticultural oils, pyrethrums, and sulfur	From trees to houseplants	Year-round indoors; hot, dry times outdoors
Spiders	No control is normally needed; diazinon, pyrethrums, resmethrins, and tetramethrins	None; nuisance to people	Year-round indoors; most active in growing season
Springtails	Often, no control is needed; diazinon, Dycarb, and Turcam	Primarily houseplants	Year-round
Squash bug	insecticidal soaps, methoxychlor, nicotine sulfate, pyrethrums, rotone, and Sevin	All types of squash	Warm growing season

Summary of Pest Control Options

Insects

Name	Controls	Plants Affected	When Pest Active
Squash vine borer	Sevin and thiodan	All types of squash	Warm growing season
Stinkbugs	insecticidal soaps, malathion, pyrethrums, rotone, sabadilla, and Sevin	Primarily vegetables, including squash	Warm growing season
Thrips	diazinon, malathion, Orthene, pyrethrums, resmethrins, rotenone, and Sevin	Roses are main plants affected	Active growing season
Ticks	Baygon, diazinon, pyrethrums, resmethrins, and Sevin	None; nuisance to people and pets	Year-round; primarily in warm seasons
Wasps, hornets and yellow jackets	premerhrin, pyrethrums, resmethrins, Sevin, and Wasp Freeze	None; nuisance to people	Warm seasons
Webworms, fall and tent caterpillars	(BT), insecticidal soaps, malathion, Orthene, and Sevin	Trees and shrubs sometimes; Texas lawn grasses	Warm seasons
Whiteflies	diazinon, insecticidal soaps, malathion, pyrethrums, and rotone	Primarily ornamentals, including gardenia and lantana	Warm growing season
Woolly oak galls	No control is normally used or needed; diazinon, malathion, and Orthene can be used	Oak trees	Year-round

Insect Pest Bio-Control Options

Bacillus Thuringiensis (BT): a specific control for several larvae/caterpillars/worms.

Green lacewings: their larvae feed on numerous insect pests.

Ladybugs/beetles: they prefer certain sucking insect pests, including aphids, mealybugs, and spider mites.

Natural insecticides: diatomaceous earth (DE), neem, nicotine, pyrethrum, rotone, and sabadilla are used to control insect pests.

Nosema Locustae: a protozoan spore specifically utilized for grasshopper control.

Praying mantis: prefers grasshopers, crickets, bees, wasps, and flies as their food sources.

Trichogramma wasp: a miniature wasp that attacks the eggs of 200+ insect pests.

Disease Pests and Some Controls

Aids/controls/products are listed alphabetically and not in order of preference of recommendation by the authors. This list is compiled from available information and believed to be accurate and correct. But it is not an absolute list. Common and/or trade names of aids/controls/products listed are capitalized and active ingredients are in lowercase letters. Disease-control aids/products are constantly changing. All aids/controls/ products listed may or may not be available at your local or area retailers.

To prevent plant diseases, plant disease-resistant varieties when possible. Maintaining the health of plants also helps to prevent plant diseases. Remember, it is better to prevent plant diseases than to cure them. Always read and follow label directions when applying any disease-control aid.

Before treating for plant diseases it is wise to identify the specific pests. If you are unable to identify the problem(s) take samples to local retailers. They can correctly identify the problem(s) and recommend specific treatments to control the disease pest(s) if controls are needed.

Should you wish to confirm a retailer's identification or simply wish to handle the problem without consulting local retailers there is a third method to identify plant diseases. Contact your County Extension Agent's office and ask for the following: 'Texas Plant Disease Diagnostic Laboratory' form number D-1178. A sample is reprinted here.

Complete the form as accurately as possible. Follow all the instructions for collecting plant specimens as well as packaging and mailing. When you receive the diagnosis, it is your decision to follow their suggestion/recommendations or decline. This has proven to be a very accurate method of identifying plant disease pests in Texas. See page 281–284 for a list of Texas Agricultural Extension Agent (county agent) phone numbers.

Summary of Pest Control Options

Diseases

Name	Controls	Plants Affected	When Pest Active
Algae	Bordeaux Mixture, Daconil, Dithane, dry conditions, Fore, Mancozeb DG, Minicure 6 F, and Thalonil 4L	Almost any plant in warm, moist, high humidity locations	Warm, moist seasons/conditions
Anthracnose	Bordeaux Mixture, Daconil, and Manab	Trees, vegetables, lawn grasses, and berries	Spring
Bacteria	Agrimycin, Bordeaux Mixture, and Kocide 101	Pears, pyracanthas, and apples	Spring and summer
Blackspot	Bayleton, Daconil, Fung Away, Funginex, and Daconil	Roses	Active growing season
Brown patch	Bayleton, Daconil, Defend, Fung Away, Manab, Penstar, Rubigan, and Terraclor	Texas lawn grasses	Usually spring and/or fall
Cotton root rot	No controls available; plant resistant varieties	Trees, especially dogwood; shrubs, especially wax ligustrum	Year-round; most active in warm seasons
Crown Rot	Daconil, good soil drainage, and Terraclor	Any plant especially those rosette form, especially African violets	Year-round; most likely in warm, moist seasons
Downy mildew	Bordeaux Mixture, captan Folpet, Manab, Manzate, sulfur, and Zineb	Vegetables	Active growing season
Fruit rot	benomyl, Bordeaux Mixture, captan, Daconil, Funginex, Maneb, and sulphur	Stone fruits	Throughout fruiting seasons
Gray mold (Botrytis)	Banner Maxx, Daconil 2787, Thiram, and Zineb	Annuals and perennials, especially amaryllis, carnations and geraniums	Active growing season
Gray leafspot	Bayleton, Daconil, and Fung Away	Texas lawn grasses	Warm, moist seasons
Leaf spots	Bordeaux Mixture, Daconil 2787, Funginex, Heritage, Terraclor, and Thalonil	Flowers, especially roses; shrubs, especially red tips; trees, especially redbud	Warm growing season

Summary of Pest Control Options

Diseases

Name	Controls	Plants Affected	When Pest Active
Oak leaf blister	Copper Sulfate	Oak trees	Active growing season
Phytophora	No controls; practice good cultural techniques; rotate crops	Annual vinca, petunias, and other annuals	Warm growing season
Powdery mildew	Banner Maxx, Bayleton, Daconil 2787, Funginex, Rubigan A. S., and sulfur	Roses, crape myrtles, and vegetables	Warm growing season, especially with humid conditions
Pythium blight	Alliette, Banol, Heritage, Mancozeb, Koban, Prodigy, and Subdue	Texas lawn grasses	Warm growing season
Root rot	Daconil 2787, Terraclor, and well-drained growing conditions	Any plant	Year-round; most likely in cool/cold seasons
Rusts	Daconil 2787, Hlorothalonil, Maneb, Myclobutanil, Terraclor, Zineb	Vegetables, roses, and Texas lawn grasses	Warm growing season
Rhizoctonia	Bayleton, Daconil 2787, Defend, Fore, Penstar, and Terraclor	Vegetables	Active growing season
Scab	Benlate, Benomyl, captan, Daconil, sulfur, and Topsin M	Pecans and hickory apples	Spring, summer, and fall
Soil-borne diseases (living in the soil)	Daconil and Terraclor	See rhizoctonia and phytophora	See rhizoctonia and phytophora (both are soil-borne diseases)
Stem canker	No controls available; remove infected small plants and dead parts of large plants	Roses and trees	Year-round
Stem rot	Good cultural practices; Terraclor, and Zineb	Plants with herbaceous stems	Warm growing season
Take-all patch	Banner Maxx, Heritage, Patchwork, Rubigan, and Rubigan A. S.	Texas lawn grasses	Fall and winter
Viruses	No controls available; plant resistant varieties	All plant groups	Year-round; most active in warm growing season

See the following pages for more information concerning disease pests.

Texas Plant Disease Diagnostic Laboratory
Texas Agricultural Extension Service
Room 101, L.F. Peterson Building
College Station, Texas 77843-2132

Accurate and complete diagnosis depends on submission of an appropriate specimen with thorough background information. Complete this form and submit with the specimen. Diagnostic charge is $15 per specimen. Refer to the back of this form for sampling and mailing instructions.

Name _____ Date _____ County _____

Company _____ Phone _____

Address _____ Plant _____

City _____ Zip _____ Variety _____ Acreage _____ Plants affected % _____

Damage symptoms: _____ Wilted _____ Yellowed _____ Dead plants _____ Leaf spots

_____ Other

When was problem first noticed? _____

Pattern of damage: _____ Occasional _____ Small groups of plants _____ Large areas _____ Entire field

Crop grown previous year? _____ Any obvious disease problems? _____

Age of tree, shrub or plant? _____ Date planted _____ Soil pH _____ Neighboring crops _____

Has soil been checked for: _____ Nematodes _____ Fertility

Enter appropriate information on plant care chemicals used recently:

Type _____ Application date/other information

Fertilizer _____

Fungicide _____

Insecticide _____

Nematicide _____

Herbicide _____

Irrigation or watering program _____ Date of last rain _____

Where is damage occuring: _____ Next to building _____ Pavement _____ Road _____ Fence row

_____ Low spot in field _____ Other

Would prefer to receive diagnosis by: _____ Letter _____ Telephone _____ Fax No.

Use additional sheet of paper for additional information that might be helpful in diagnosis.

COST OF TESTING IS $15 PER SAMPLE

Enclosed is $ _____ in the form of _____ personal check, _____ cash or _____ money order to cover the cost of processing _____ (number) samples covered by this form. **Please make checks or money orders payable to the Texas Agricultural Extension Service.**

Instructions for Collecting, Packaging and Submitting Plant Specimens

Proper collection, packaging and shipment of plant specimens are extremely important to successful diagnosis of plant disease problems. Inappropriate specimens, specimens arriving desiccated or in advanced stages of decay or specimens damaged in shipment are of little or no use in attempting to diagnose plant disease problems. The most rapid and accurate diagnosis results from proper specimen collection and shipment together with submission of complete background information concerning the problem. *IT IS ESSENTIAL THT THE DIAGNOSTIC FORM BE FILLED OUT AS COMPLETELY AS POSSIBLE.*

The following procedures are suggested to insure that the specimen arrives at the laboratory in the best possible condition:

COLLECTION OF PLANT SPECIMENS

1. Submit only freshly collected specimens. If possible, send several specimens showing a progression of symptoms. Keep specimens refrigerated until shipment.

2. Where specific plant parts are affected (leaf spots, root rots, stem rots, fruit rots, flower blights, stem cankers), submit the affected part in as many stages of the disease as are showing. If practical, submit the whole plant. Enclose specimen in a plastic bag. Do not add additional moisture.

3. For plants showing wilting, yellowing, stunting or general decline, send the entire plant including the root system. Dig the plant carefully so as to disturb the root system as little as possible. Shake away excess soil. Do not wash soil from the root system. Enclose the root system in a plastic bag and seal it at the base of the plant stem to prevent soil spillage. Then enclose the entire plant in another plastic bag and seal. Do not add additional moisture.

4. For leaf spots, submit leaves showing various stages of infection. If possible, send twigs or branches with leaves still attached. Enclose leaves in a plastic bag. Do not add additional moisture. Package bagged specimen in a cardboard box to prevent crushing during shipment.

5. For lawn and turf disease, submit a 3- to 4-inch diameter plug taken where the healthy and diseased areas meet so the sample will contain both diseased and healthy turf. Take the plug 2 to 3 inches deep and include the adhering soil material. Enclose the plugs in a plastic bag. Do not add additional moisture.

PACKAGING AND MAILING

1. Package all specimens securely to prevent damage during transit.
2. Cardboard boxes usually help prevent crushing.
3. Add packing material such as crumpled newspaper to prevent specimen damage during shipment.
4. Mail specimen early in the week to avoid specimen deterioration at the post office during the weekend.
5. For each plant specimen submitted for diagnosis there is a $15 charge. MAKE REMITTANCE PAYABLE TO: The Texas Agricultural Extension Service. Place remittance and completed information form in an envelope and attach this envelope to the package containing the specimen. The attached envelope must also have standard letter postage.

Mail to:

Texas Plant Disease Diagnostic Laboratory
Texas Agricultural Extension Service
Room 101, L.F. Peterson Building
College Station, TX 77843-2132

Educational programs conducted by the Texas Agricultural Extension Service serve people of all ages regardless of socioeconomic level, race, color, sex, religion, handicap or national origin.

Issued in furtherance of Cooperative Extension Work in Agriculture and Home Economics, Acts of Congress of May 8, 1914, as amended, and June 30, 1914, in cooperation with the United States Department of Agriculture, Zerle L. Carpenter, Director, Texas Agricultural Extension Service, The Texas A&M University System.

Reprinted by Permission.

Weed Pests and Some Controls

Aids/products are listed alphabetically and not in order of preference or recommendation by the authors. This list is compiled from available information and is believed to be accurate and correct. But it is not an absolute list. Common and/or brand names are capitalized and active ingredients are in lowercase letters. Texas gardeners may utilize any of the various names listed if available at local or area retailers. Always read labels before purchasing and follow application instruction during application instructions when using any weed-control aid.

Generally, there are far more varieties or types of broadleaf weed pests than grassy ones in Texas landscapes and/or gardens. To be effective, a pre-emergent should be applied before weed seeds emerge or germinate. A post-emergent is utilized after weed pests have emerged and are actively growing.

Weeds

Broadleaf Weed Pests	Pre-Emergent Controls	Post-Emergent Controls
Bur clover, chickweed, dandelion, dock, field bindweed (wild morning glory), henbit, wood sorrel, plantain, purslane, and wild onion	Betasan, Dacthal, and Gallery	Banvel 4S, Confront 3L, and 2, 4-D, glyphospate, Prompt 5L, Sencor, and Trimec

Grassy Weed Pests	Pre-Emergent Controls	Post-Emergent Controls
Bahiagrass, crabgrass, dallisgrass, goosegrass, Johnsongrass, nutgrass (nutsedge), poa annua (annual bluegrass), quackgrass, and sandbur or grassbur	Balan, Barricade, Betasan, Dacthal, Dimension, Surflan 4AS, and Team	Acclaim Extra, betazon, DSMA, Fusilade II, glyphospate, illoxan, Image, and MSMA

Bibliography

Adams, William D. and Thomas LeRoy, *Common Sense Vegetable Gardening for the South*, Taylor Publishing Company, 1995.

Beales, Peter, *Classic Roses*, Henry Holt and Company, 1997.

Bender, Steve, editor, *The Southern Living Garden Book*, Oxmoor House, 1998.

Bender, Steve, editor, *Southern Living Garden Problem Solver*, Oxmoor House, 1999.

Brickell, Christopher, editor, *The American Horticultural Society Encyclopedia of Garden Plants*, Macmillan Publishing Company, NY, 1993.

Cotner, Sam, Ph.D., *The Vegetable Book . . . A Texan's Guide to Gardening*, Texas Gardener Press, 1996.

Courtier, Jane and Graham Clarke, *Reader's Digest Indoor Plants*, Reader's Digest, 1997.

Druitt, Liz, *The Organic Rose Garden*, Taylor Publishing Company, 1996.

Gill, Dan and Joe White, *Louisiana Gardener's Guide*, Cool Springs Press, 1997.

Greenlee, John, *The Encyclopedia of Ornamental Grasses*, Rodale Press, 1992.

Groom, Dale, The Plant Groom™, *Dale Groom's Texas Gardening Guide*, Cool Springs Press, 1997.

Hill, Madalene and Gwyn Barclay, *Southern Herb Growing*, Shearer Publishing, 1987.

McDonald, Elvin, *The New Houseplant*, Macmillan Publishing Company, 1993.

Odenwald, Neil and James Turner, *Identification, Selection and Use of Southern Plants for Landscape Design*, Claitor's Publishing Division, 1987.

Ogden, Scott, *Garden Bulbs for the South*, Taylor Publishing Company, 1994.

River Oaks Garden Club, *A Garden Book for Houston and the Gulf Coast*, Pacesetter Press, 1979.

Seidenberg, Charlotte, *The New Orleans Garden: Gardening in the Gulf South*, University Press of Mississippi, 1993.

Wasowski, Sally, *Gardening with Native Plants of the South*, Taylor Publishing Company, 1994.

Welch, William, *Perennial Garden Color*, Taylor Publishing Company, 1989.

Whitcomb, Carl E., Ph.D., *Know It & Grow It*, Lacebark Publications, 1985.

Index

Index

Index

Index

Index

Index

About the Authors

Dale Groom, The Plant Groom™, again shares his valuable experience and more than 30 years of knowledge with Texas readers. A horticulturist and native Texan, Dale is nationally known as an accomplished author, radio/television host, speaker, consultant and columnist whose column, *Ask The Plant Groom*™, is syndicated. Dale also produces and hosts *The Plant Groom*™ television series which airs nationwide and he hosts *The Plant Groom*™, a live radio call-in show. The author is a member of the Garden Writers Association of America. Groom is also a certified professional nurseryman and is a plant and flower show judge.

A native of Brownwood, Texas, Groom descends from several generations of farmers and gardeners. He received his Bachelor of Science degree in agriculture from Stephen F. Austin State University, and a Master of Science degree in horticulture from East Texas State University. The author also established the Ornamental Horticultural program at Tyler Junior College.

Dale and his wife of 31 years, Judy, live on their farm in northeast Texas, where they garden and enjoy rural Texas life.

Dale Groom

Dan Gill is an Extension horticulturist with the Louisiana State University Agricultural Center, a position he has held since 1980. Gill teaches, gives lectures and demonstrations and writes articles on gardening. Known to New Orleans area listeners as the popular radio host of the *WSMB Garden Show*, Gill is featured weekly in gardening segments on the local CBS affiliate station. The author also writes the "Weekend Gardener," a weekly column for *The Times-Picayune,* and his Southeast Louisiana Zone Report appears monthly in the *Louisiana Gardener Magazine*.

The author received his bachelor and master's degrees in horticulture from Louisiana State University. In addition, Gill is a member of many groups including the Louisiana Horticulture Society, the Metro Area Horticulture Foundation, the Louisiana Nursery and Landscape Association, the Louisiana County Agricultural Agents Association and the New Orleans Horticultural Society.

Gill lives and gardens in the historic New Orleans neighborhood of Algiers Point.

Dan Gill